DRIFTWOOD VALLEY

DRIFTWOOD VALLEY

By Theodora C. Stanwell-Fletcher

Animal Sketches by John F. Stanwell-Fletcher

AN ATLANTIC MONTHLY PRESS BOOK

LITTLE, BROWN AND COMPANY · BOSTON

1946

Published August 1946
Reprinted August 1946 (twice)
Reprinted September 1946
Reprinted October 1946
Reprinted November 1946

ATLANTIC—LITTLE, BROWN BOOKS
ARE PUBLISHED BY
LITTLE, BROWN AND COMPANY
IN ASSOCIATION WITH
THE ATLANTIC MONTHLY PRESS

PRINTED IN THE UNITED STATES OF AMERICA

TO

MOTHER and DAD

Preface

J. and I had dreamed, separately before we ever knew each other, together after we did, of living "somewhere in the wilds of British Columbia." We lived in the Driftwood Valley of north central British Columbia during the period of 1937–1941. After our first year and a half there we went back to Pennsylvania, where I remained for two years for the birth of our daughter, whom we planned to have at that time. During this interval J. went back to the Driftwood region and worked there alone through a spring and summer. We then both returned to British Columbia for another nine months.

J.'s background was one of old English public schools; seven years with the British Army in India as physical-training instructor, riding master, and a teacher of history and mathematics of his regiment; nine years in Arctic and Subarctic Canada, first as a member of the Royal Canadian Mounted Police, later as an independent trapper and explorer, with stretches in between in great cities of the world. My background included American schools and college, graduate work in a big university, and stretches in between spent in New Zealand, the Dutch East Indies, Asia, the British Isles, and Subarctic Canada. J. and I had both acquired a taste for the loneliness and realism of out-of-the-way places and peoples. And we both had always possessed an unquenchable love for, and curiosity about, wild animals.

We had, therefore, a certain congeniality of outlook and a similarity of feeling about fundamentals, so that being in love and having a mutual desire to live in and study the wilderness of British Columbia were not just coincidence or fate, but the logical conclusion reached by two persons who, despite the fact

that they had lived in different parts of the earth and under-
gone different experiences, possessed minds which had all along
traveled the same grooves.

The chapters that follow, which are made of my diary, are the
story of a wilderness and our relationship with it; a tale of those
still vast solitudes of northern British Columbia, so hard and
inaccessible that much of them has not yet been lived in, or
even penetrated by mankind. The province of British Columbia is larger by almost 40,000 square miles than the combined
states of Washington, Oregon, and California; or about equal
in size to the combined areas of the United Kingdom, France,
Belgium, Holland, and Denmark. It is a land of infinite variety,
possessed of mighty mountain ranges with lofty snow-clad peaks
— many still unnamed and unsurveyed — vast virgin forests,
great lakes and rivers, and a wealth of minerals, furs, and other
natural products. Its climate varies from the cold of subarctic
winter to the heat of temperate summer. There are cold barren valleys, warm fertile ones. Except for portions of Alaska
and the Northwest Territories the flora and fauna in the extensive uninhabited stretches must approximate more truly than
elsewhere on the North American continent an undisturbed
condition.

We wanted to make detailed and accurate observations on
the life of the Driftwood region; to understand the lives and
problems of the wild things about us as they passed through all
four seasons of the year, particularly during the long winter of a
far-northern forest, a season in which comparatively few scientific studies have been made of wildlife. First it was necessary
to identify species accurately; to find out names of the animate
and inanimate things which made up our environment. We
therefore collected flora and fauna for the British Columbia
Provincial Museum at Victoria. The Museum provided us with
much helpful equipment, permits, and valuable information.
The very few white men who live in a world primarily given
over to wildlife and the native Indian trapper and hunter are
either fur traders or prospectors. If not included in these cate-
gories they are, in the minds of the native inhabitants, prob-

ably up to no good. Working for a museum, we found, gave us a certain standing; though how anyone, especially a white woman, could want to live "away off up there," without at least the lure of a search for gold or fur, was incomprehensible.

Indian names for places, as yet unexplored and unmapped, we have spelled phonetically. The white inhabitants of that country who have known Indians all their lives would probably feel that we, after a mere three years there, could have comparatively little accurate knowledge of these people. Yet the fact that we lived in the wilderness just as the Indians did, subsisted on it almost entirely, used the same modes of traveling and camping in all seasons, perhaps afforded us a rather. different type of insight into their characters as a whole. Several of them in their special type of pidgin English sometimes tried to tell us this: —

"You live like us, see? All time you do same like we do. You know. Other white man he not live like us. He not know, see?"

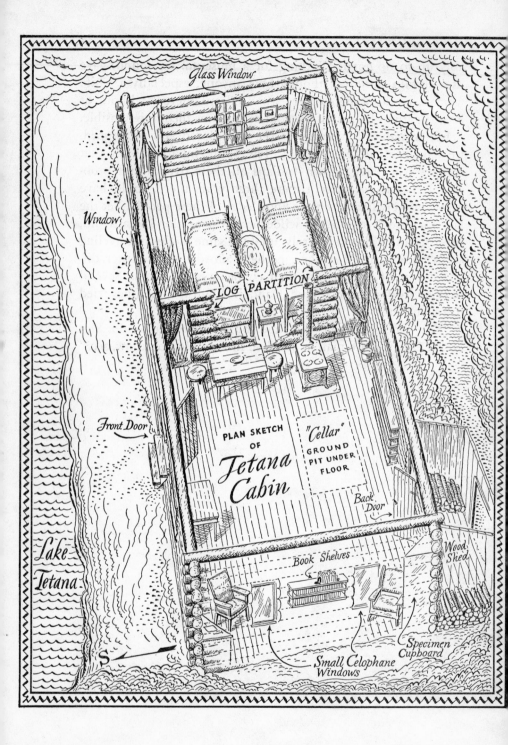

Glass Window

Window

LOG PARTITION

Front Door

PLAN SKETCH
OF
*Tetana
Cabin*

"*Cellar*"
GROUND
PIT UNDER
FLOOR

Back
Door

Wood
Shed

Lake
Tetana

S

Book Shelves

Specimen
Cupboard

Small Celophane
Windows

The Cabin in Moonlight

Lake Tetana, as Seen from the Cabin

Contents

Contents

Illustrations

Part One

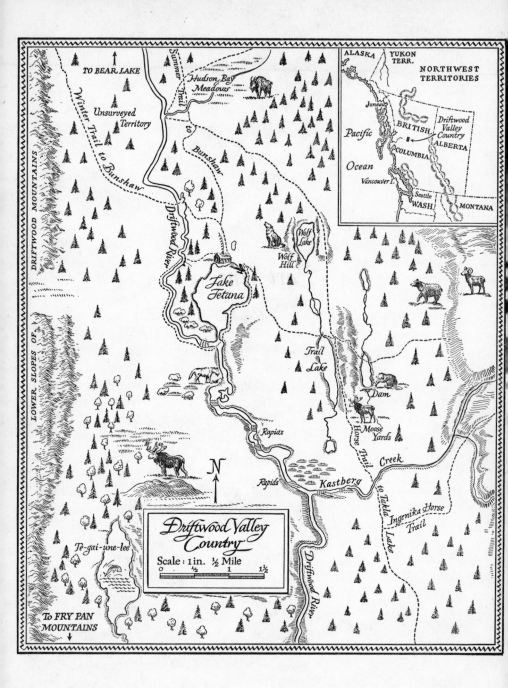

TO BEAR LAKE

Unsurveyed
Territory

DRIFTWOOD MOUNTAINS

Winter Trail to Bunshaw

Summer Trail

to

Hudson Bay
Meadows

Bunshaw

Driftwood River

Wolf
Lake

Wolf
Hill

Lake
Tetana

Trail
Lake

LOWER SLOPES OF

Rapids

N

Rapids

Te-gai-une-lee

Kastberg

Dam

Moose
Yards

Horse Trail

Creek

to Takla Lake

Ingenika Horse
Trail

Driftwood River

To FRY PAN
MOUNTAINS

Driftwood Valley Country

Scale : 1 in. ½ Mile

0   ½   1   1½

ALASKA YUKON
TERR.

NORTHWEST
TERRITORIES

Juneau

Pacific

Ocean

Vancouver I.

BRITISH

COLUMBIA

Driftwood
Valley
Country

ALBERTA

Seattle
WASH.

MONTANA

CHAPTER I

We Find Tetana

Hazelton, B. C.   *August 26, 1937*

We've traveled by rail as far as we can into northern British Columbia. We left the train at this small town which, on the maps, seems nearest as the crow flies to the country we hope to penetrate. Hazelton, once a distribution center for the Cassiar and Omineca gold fields and an important gateway into the North, is now just a peaceful little place. Its frame houses and stores, its Hudson's Bay post, and its Catholic and Anglican churches sprawl along broad, muddy roads full of leisurely pedestrians and playing children (chiefly little Indians in rubber boots). It is typical of most northern frontier towns except that it has an unusually lovely setting. It lies on a fertile flat at the junction of the Skeena and Bulkley Rivers, with the jagged mountain pile of Rocher Deboulé towering above it. In every direction wooded slopes and ridges rise in the distance to higher ridges and mist-covered ranges. Huge weather-beaten totem poles along the river streets show the relationship of its Indians to the Alaskan and Pacific Coast tribes.

The Hazelton Hotel, its front looking across a small, old Chinese laundry to the great mountain topped with clouds and glimpses of snow, is set at the very edge of the rushing Skeena. When we first arrived, early the other morning, there seemed to be no one in the hotel at all, but a man strolling by along the road was very hospitable.

He said, "Just go in and pick yourselves a room. Any room'll do!"

So we explored and upstairs came to a small empty bedroom filled with a soft roar of running water. One window looks to the mountains, the other is just over the river, and it is equipped, as are all the bedrooms, wonderfully enough, with real hot and cold running water. As no one appeared, J. signed our names in the registry book on a counter, and we made ourselves at home. Two days later a large and easy-going individual turned up who appeared to be a sort of temporary host. Since the hotel has no restaurant, we eat in a rooming house some distance away, or at a tiny Chinese place. There never is a northern frontier town, no matter how insignificant, without a Chinese laundry and restaurant.

While J. has scouted the town for information about the country ahead of us, I've attended to the packing, a complicated process, which consists of storing civilized apparel in trunks and suitcases to be left here, and stuffing all manner of duffel bags and canvas pack sacks with wilderness equipment — tents, bedding, rough clothes for all seasons, materials for plant and animal collecting, and medical supplies. Since our room is too small to hold anything but a bed, bureau, and washstand, all packing has to be done in a storeroom downstairs. The only way to reach this is to pass through the bar, seemingly always full of silent men seated at tables covered with glasses and beer bottles. At least whenever I encounter them they are all rather oppressively quiet and polite. If they are edified by the sight of a young lady tramping back and forth, arms bulging and shoulders hung with every sort of thing from huge, mud-covered boots to pink rayon underwear, they've never betrayed it. The downward slant of their noses implies either that this is a scene with which they are familiar and consequently indifferent to, or that my struggling figure and red cheeks don't even come within range of their vision.

The results of J.'s efforts to secure concrete information about the country where we're going and how to get there are not exactly encouraging. Over a year ago we picked as a possible region for our future home the Driftwood Valley, situated at about 56° north latitude. This valley, north of the big lakes of Takla and Babine, must lie about two hundred miles northeast of the southern tip of Alaska and, by roundabout horse trail, appears to be two hundred miles north northeast of

Hazelton. According to the few uncompleted, and apparently inaccurate, maps (there is considerable variation in spelling and location of the same natural landmarks for example) , it possesses a desirable variety of mountains, lakes, and forests. As far as we can discover, few white people have been there and little, if anything, is known of the plants and animals. Apparently no one has ever made studies of its wildlife, though we understand that Mr. E. A. Preble of the U. S. Biological Survey passed through in 1913. One of the most attractive points about the Driftwood Valley is the large adjacent territory marked "unexplored" and "unsurveyed."

Most of the inhabitants of Hazelton know little or nothing about the region. Official or unofficial, the comments about our going there are all alike. *It is no country for a white woman!* J. is a fool if he thinks he can take one there to live. In vain I protest that I want to live in the wilds as much as J. does. The men eye my rather slight figure in skeptical silence or with pitying smiles. Obviously they think that I have no idea of what I'm getting into. Well, maybe I don't! I'll soon see.

We're well armed with permits and papers of recognition from the Provincial Museum. We also have permits from the British Columbia Game Commission to take large mammals, and permission from the Department of Mines and Resources, National Parks Bureau, Ottawa, to collect migratory birds. And we have permits to carry pistols from the Chief of Police, and miners' licenses in case we strike gold, and heaven knows what others. We have taken pains to show all these to the authorities here — the Game Warden, the Mounted Police, the Provincial Police, and the Indian Agent who has jurisdiction over these parts; also to explain to everyone our special type of work and our attitude toward the Indians and their country. There appear to be no laws about property or objections to one's building a home in the far-off land to which we are going. How could there be when, unless something very terrible happens, no representatives of the law apparently ever penetrate it?

We have been told that the few Indians who live in the Driftwood area will resent white people coming in to explore

and live on their land and game. Anyone thought to be inter-
fering with their trap lines — and they will assuredly believe
we are doing this very thing — is likely to be driven out of the
country or shot. More than one famous character, outlawed for
a shooting affair, has hidden out in the Driftwood region or
adjacent territory. Such characters may be at large, right now,
anywhere in those parts. The climate is terrible. Means of communication with the outside world are nil. If we go there neither
police nor game authorities — no one in fact — can be responsible
for our safety. Why not pick a place near Hazelton to study animals? There are plenty around here — too many. It would be
cheaper and safer. How to get to the Driftwood Valley? There
is no way to get there. Oh yes, we could try flying. No, better
board a train again, go back to a town farther east, take a two-
hundred-mile boat trip to Takla Lake, and then hike thirty —
no, a hundred — miles up to the Driftwood. No, better go by
pack horse across country. There is a passable trail to Lake
Babine and another from Babine to Takla. That trail? Why
there isn't any trail at all in places. A strong man couldn't get
over it, let alone a woman. The bushes are so thick you can't
cut your way through with an axe, and no horse or human
could cross the mud flats and rivers. The trail goes through
the worst grizzly country (grizzlies are apparently the species of animal most universally feared and respected). Why,
grizzly bears drop off ledges on people passing below. "Once
my father — ," and so on.

However, despite their discouraging opinions of our undertaking, we've enjoyed our contacts with the inhabitants of
Hazelton. The other day J. went to telephone a local authority
about certain extra licenses we needed — the number of these
appears to be unlimited. When he asked the man if he'd be "in"
if we called next day, the voice that replied, before the receiver
went down with a bang, shouted: —

"*In,* wha' da ya mean 'in'? Where else would I be in this
God-damned place?"

One of the very nicest and most helpful of Hazelton's citizens
is Mr. Sargent, who owns the hotel and one of the main stores.

He is going to store our trunks and suitcases in his warehouse. And we are especially grateful to the sergeant of the Mounted Police for helping us to get hold of one Ben Ridsdale, a half-breed Indian, with four good horses, who will take us across country by the aforementioned trail, which he has traveled before, to the Driftwood Valley. After weighing all the facts we can gather, we have decided that traveling by horse appears to be the most reliable means of transportation. We can explore the country as we go, and when we settle on a homesite we shall have horses to haul logs and a man to help put up the cabin. Ben has promised to stay with us long enough to assist with the building.

Ben's help is especially needed in view of the serious accident J. had sledding in the hills of Pennsylvania last winter, when he smashed one kidney and most of his back and abdominal muscles very thoroughly. Although he made a remarkable recovery, thanks to Dr. Molyneaux's skill as doctor and surgeon, plus his own fine physique, he is not yet able to carry his full share of heavy work. Because of this accident we put off our departure for the wilderness from spring to late summer, and our time for getting a home up before winter is dangerously limited.

J. and I hope that the native Indians will work for us. From all accounts the Indians of the region to which we are going are not like the Indians of American reservations, who are more or less on show for tourists. Apparently their only contacts with white civilization have come from business with fur traders, and occasional visits from a missionary priest or game warden. They are living on the wilderness as their forefathers have done before them. We shall be strangers, white people, going into a land that has belonged to them and their families for generations. We want them to see for themselves that we do not wish to change their country or interfere with their lives in any way. If they take us into their world and introduce us to their ways they may possibly feel a certain responsibility for our safety and well-being and a greater interest in our work and viewpoint.

We have been told that probably the Indians' worst quality is their inability to do what they promise, to stick at one job and carry it through. When we were asked how long we would expect an Indian to work for us, and we said a month or two, there was dubious headshaking.

"You might get a couple of weeks' work out of a few of 'em," said a reliable informant, "but I reckon a month's too long, even for a good Indian. And," he added, "I ought to know; I've worked with 'em twenty years."

However, we have hopes of Ben, who is highly recommended on all sides and is, moreover, not all Indian.

                                   Hudson's Bay Co. Post
                        Lake Babine   *September 3*

On August 28th we said good-bye to those last definite indications of so-called modern civilization — railroads, car roads, and telegraph poles — and set off northeastward into the unknown depths of a wild and mountainous land. Ben with the two pack horses, Bessie and Bill, each carrying two-hundred-pound packs, went ahead. J. and I, riding Jessie and Danny, brought up the rear. Ben said he always prefers walking in this country, because if he rides he's too tired at the end of the day to do his work. One of my strongest memories of the eighty-mile trip across to Babine will be of Ben's tall lean figure striding with easy slowness along the primitive trail. His pace never seemed to change or tire and he easily outstripped the horses. The horses have all behaved well so far, which is a blessing! What with fallen trees to negotiate constantly, bushes so thick you can hardly squeeze through them, mountain torrents, and mudholes which are more like sinkholes, the going has been very tough. In places the trail completely petered out and we had to make our own, but Ben appears to be familiar with the country and the proper directions.

During most of the first two days it poured rain. In spite of oilskin trousers and parkas we were soaked to the skin. Riding through drenched masses of undergrowth that grew far above our heads was just about like riding under water, and we hardly saw the country around us. On the second evening it cleared, though bushes still showered us as we passed through.

J. was so pleased to be really off that not even floods dampened his spirits. He always looks rather nice when it rains, because his black hair — what there is of it — curls all over his head. His bright blue eyes sparkled with the zest of new adventure, which is always in his blood and which comes to him straight from generations of adventuring British forebears. And though he is still pale from his long hospital experience, his body looked almost as broad and big as ever.

Danny is primarily a saddle horse and has been fairly well-mannered, but he has a habit, which scares me stiff, of leaping straight into the air when something startles him. J.'s horse, Jessie, who has not been ridden much, is rather skittish, but J. controls all her antics, big and little, so easily with those strong hands of his — so hard and muscular, and yet with the finely shaped fingers which no amount of rough work can spoil and which proclaim the artist and romanticist. I never could have married a man whose hands I didn't like!

The second day I began to feel dead-tired and was disgusted at myself for being so out of condition. I had a slight sore throat acquired at Hazelton where there was something of an epidemic, but I decided on a plunge when, at our second night's camp, we saw a pool in a roaring stream near by. The water felt very, very cold when I put my hand in, but I reminded myself sternly that I had never been sorry for an icy swim yet or failed to be revived by it. I undressed on a small sandy spit where my footprints mingled with the very fresh prints of a bear; they looked exactly like those of some gigantic human being. I devoutly hoped that the bears, especially grizzlies, wouldn't choose to come and catch fish, or bathe, or whatever they did here, at that particular moment. The late afternoon sun shone across the sand, black masses of spruce lined the shore beyond the foaming stream, mountains closed in the valley. But even after my lightning dip I felt, for once in my life, too miserable to be thrilled by wild beauty.

Later, I could hardly clean up the supper things and crawl

into bed. In spite of quantities of aspirin I shook with waves of chills. I was horrified to find my pulse a hundred and forty so that I probably had several degrees of fever. At first I didn't tell J.; it was just unthinkable that I should be sick as I was starting on about the greatest adventure of all. I couldn't be! We were two long days of traveling beyond Hazelton and several days away from the small Indian settlement of Babine on ahead. Besides we had only food enough to last the few days until we reached Babine. But by midnight my pride went to the winds and I woke J. by squeezing down into his sleeping bag and imploring him, meekly, to warm me up.

He must have been worried because he was extremely cross. He promptly gave me a Frosst pill and poured brandy down me, though I said that this would probably kill me on top of all the aspirin. By early morning I was drugged into sleep and woke a few hours later with the chills gone. But I was so weak and dizzy it was all I could do to get up on Danny.

The scrub and burnt-over forest prevalent near Hazelton had given way to tall virgin trees of spruce, hemlock, and cedar. Through lacy, dark green branches we caught glimpses of bare jagged ranges and rushing waters. The shrubs were mostly a species of elderberry, and there were many willows and red-osier dogwoods. Yellow-shafted flickers, juncos, red-breasted nut-hatches, and Canada jays were common, though it was too late in the season for many birds. But I could scarcely see, much less really enjoy, anything and could only cling to the saddle and let Danny go his own way. As he seemed to know quite as much as I did about how to pick a path, we got along fairly well.

By early afternoon we reached Ben's tiny trap-line cabin, set in grassy meadows in a deep valley. Ben's maternal grandfather was an Indian; as a boy Ben trapped and hunted and learned his best wild lore from his grandfather on this very land. If I were too ill to go on, he and J. thought this was the place to stop since there was sufficient grass for the horses. There was also a possibility of getting wild game for food, as Ben was familiar with all the likely spots.

I climbed off my horse and lay down in the warm grass. The next thing I knew J. was carrying me to bed. He dosed me again with his strong pills, and Ben went off to hunt food. Probably I never appreciated a camp more. The tent, open at both ends, was pitched in grass on the bank of a big creek; alternate waves of hot scented air from sunlit fields and cold spicy whiffs from bare mountain peaks drifted through it. Almost instantly I was sound asleep. When I woke, it was dark. J. was bending over a fire by the tent door, and Ben, riding Danny across the field, was shouting: —

"I got some meat!"

Only those who have been hungry in a wild land, and dependent on game for food, can know how those words sounded. Ben had had the good fortune to see a young moose in one of the "likely spots" up along a mountain range, had killed it with one shot from J.'s big. .348 rifle, and was riding home, in triumph, with the meat across his saddlebow. We were well supplied for days now no matter what happened; if our other food gave out, we should still have that most important thing of all — fresh meat. Soon the smell of the young moose heart covered with onion and lard that J. was cooking made me hungry. After I had eaten a little, I felt stronger and astonishingly better. The next day, except for weakness, I was almost cured and we were off on the trail again.

We loved the country around Ben's hunting and trapping ground and when he suggested generously that we build our cabin right there, we were honestly tempted. It would have been so much easier to stop and make a home while there was still a month or two of open weather. But the region was not quite beautiful enough; there were no snow-covered mountains and big lakes; it was not quite the untouched wilderness which has been in our minds and hearts for years. Studies had already been made of the wildlife around Hazelton and along the Skeena River. We wanted virgin territory. So we went on.

Sometimes, in the denser undergrowth, there was a horrid smell like rotten cabbage. I supposed it came from food the

horses had eaten. The horses shied and trembled, often refusing point-blank to pass through thick bushes, and we had
endless trouble with them. It dawned on me finally that the
nasty cabbage smell was bears — possibly grizzlies — that might
be observing us as we passed. Ben, well acquainted with grizzlies, which have a peculiar odor of their own, confirmed this;
and he and J. traveled steadily with loaded rifles over their
arms.

Around our evening campfires Ben regaled us with hunting
tales, stories of marten and fisher and lynx, of encounters with
cougars, which are not uncommon in the Hazelton country,
stories of trapping and hunting. But most of all he talked about
grizzlies. Once, he said, way back in the days when steamboats
first began to penetrate this country, an old Indian sitting on
the bank of the Skeena near Hazelton heard a great roaring and
puffing. Supposing it to be a giant grizzly, he ran for his gun;
and then he saw a steamboat coming up the river! Another time
Ben's grandfather, right along this very trail, surprised a
grizzly, shot, and wounded it. And it was on top of him before
he could get away or fire again. After a terrific struggle, during
which he half choked it, he finally managed to pull his gun
and kill it before he himself was fatally mangled.

At the end of this narrative Ben shook his head and concluded, "My grandfather, he was some strong man."

We spent five days on the trail between Hazelton and Babine.
At night when the weather was clear, we rolled up in our
sleeping bags on the ground without bothering to put up a
tent. Since we were usually up with the sun around six, off on
the trail at eight, and traveled steadily all day with only half
an hour out for lunch (tea, hardtack, and chocolate), we were
glad to go to bed at sundown. Even when the days were hot,
it grew cold after sunset and we woke in the morning covered
with white frost. Our camps are always made in grassy plots
where there is sufficient feed for four horses, and water for
them and ourselves. The horses crop around us at night, sometimes stepping over our sleeping bodies. Thus far they have
never trod on us! If one wakes in the night and sees a huge

Grizzly Bear

dark form looming above, one has to be extremely cautious about making a sudden movement or noise.

Several times we've scared up coveys of spruce grouse along the trail. The first time this happened I, from a land of closed game seasons and limited bags, was scandalized to see J. and Ben killing every bird in sight. But when I learned how to skin one (there is no need to pluck a grouse), had put it on a green willow stick, roasted it over a fire, and eaten every bit of it except the feet, head, and guts, I was far less scandalized. Ben's moose spoiled in the hot mountain sun and after two days had grown so odorous and worm-eaten that we were hungry for fresh meat again. Tender grouse flesh was a fit food for gods, and one grouse per person was hardly enough for a meal.

Several days beyond Ben's country, climbing down a long ridge of the Babine Mountains, we came once more to fresh signs of fellow human beings. And then after a hair-raising crossing of the small Babine River, which our horses swam, and floundering through mud and quicksands, we arrived at a small Indian settlement on a big lake. This lake, Ben said, was a north arm of the hundred-mile-long Lake Babine. The settlement consisted of huts and cabins of the Babine Indian tribe; on the outskirts were the whitewashed, red-roofed buildings, familiar to every traveler in the North as a post of the "Governor and Company of Adventurers of England trading into Hudson's Bay," commonly known as "Hudson's Bay Company," "the Bay," "H.B.C.," "Here Before Christ," and so on.

We are staying at the small house of the young white man, Mr. Stevens, the apprentice who is in charge of the post while the manager, Mr. Forest, is away. We've been here two days waiting for a bad storm to rain itself out. Mr. Stevens, though he'd never heard of us until we suddenly dismounted at his doorstep late in the afternoon, was most hospitable. The post managers of the H.B.C. may vary as to character and personality, but they always seem to be remarkably capable men and wonderfully hospitable hosts whether you run across them on barren arctic tundras or in vast stretches of forested wilderness.

Judged by looks and manners, Mr. Stevens might have stepped from a Harvard club, but he can cook, really cook, and run a big fur post, and deal with a crooked bunch of trouble-making Indians. He and Mr. Forest must live lonely lives. Except for the settlement's schoolteacher and his wife, they have few contacts with white people.

Yesterday while Mr. Stevens and J. went fishing, I retired upstairs to enjoy the unusual luxury of a nap. I was rudely waked however, by a loud banging on the front door. When I called down to ask who was there, an Indian voice inquired for Mr. Stevens. I replied that he was not in — though I had a distinct feeling that the man knew this as well as I did — but that he would be back any time. The Indian then marched in without invitation (Indians are not supposed to come into the living house except under special conditions), and began an unpleasant string of questions and complaints while I was hurriedly dressing. What was the matter? Poor lady was alone. Was I sick? Why didn't I come downstairs? Could I give him food, clothes, tobacco, money? He was sick, he had nothing, he could not go, I must give him money, money. To all of which I called "No," I had nothing, he had better leave before Mr. Stevens returned. He then started to climb the ladderlike stairs that lead straight to our bedroom, a whine and a more insistent demand with every step.

I was rather scared. Without really thinking, I grabbed my little .25 automatic, buttoned my shirt, and with pounding heart confronted a nasty-looking unkempt individual just as he reached the top. We stared at each other, then I began to draw the pistol from its holster. His eyes moved from my face to my hands, his mouth flew open, and suddenly, without a sound, he backed down the steps two at a time and out the door.

Exceedingly pleased and rather astonished, I retired again. Here was I, a mere snip of a female, who had never shot anything but a .22, and that only for fun, reacting quite in the approved fashion and with the greatest success, with a deadly-looking pistol of which, up to now, I've been terrified!

When J. and Mr. Stevens were on their way home they met

my visitor, who shouted angrily and shook his stick at them. Not knowing what it was all about, they paid no attention to him.

Ben's comment on the affair was a disdainful shrug. "The trouble with these people," said he, "is, they're *too Indian*."

We've made further inquiries here about Indians who might know something of the Driftwood Valley. Through the help of Mr. Stevens, we have located one who is said to have done considerable trapping and hunting there. This is Dominick West, a quaint little man with bright black eyes, who came to see us this morning. He listened impassively to our eager questions. What we wanted, we told him, was a lake surrounded by good forest that has not been burned, where no one else lives, that is in big mountain country, and far enough away so that we shall not be disturbed by visitors. After a long silence, in which he stood with bent head considering perhaps what he could tell us, or perhaps wondering whether he should tell us anything, he began abruptly, in a broken pidgin English, to talk about a lake with a soft musical name which sounded like "Te-tan-a." He likes this lake in the Driftwood Valley so much, he said, that he often travels far out of his way just to look at it. It is so "pletty." The water is different from other lakes. One can see white stones on the bottom. The forest around it is not burned. There are mountains, "beeg" mountains, all over, but one can see out. It is not like a "plison." There are moose, good fur, lots of fish. Nobody lives there. A few Indians trap in the region, have winter or summer camps there, but it is very "lonely."

At the end of all this J. and I glanced at each other and our glances said, "Now we have something to go on. No matter what anyone says we must see this Te-tan-a." We wonder what "Te-tan-a," which we take to be an Indian expression, means. Dominick either did not know or could not explain it to us in our language.

Takla Landing   *September 7*

We found the trail from Babine to Takla Lake better traveled and less rough than the one from Hazelton to Babine. It led across some high plateau-like country which in places had been burnt-over and, somewhat desolate, made us more determined than ever to persevere toward the Driftwood region.

When one speaks of country's being "burnt-over" this does not necessarily imply that it is a much-traveled or inhabited land. Some of the wildest territory of the Northland, that has had only one party in fifty years traversing it, may be badly injured from fire just because that one party was careless with cigarettes or campfires.

On our second day out from Babine, we began to meet small companies of strange Indians. These, Ben explained, after brief conversations with them, were Takla and Bear Lake Indians on their way to Babine for "the Games." Games and "potlatches," apparently a combination of funeral and celebration, are, he says, held every summer at Babine or Takla. Whole families from all the country around come by foot, a hundred miles or more, just to attend these gatherings for a few days. Although Ben speaks what he calls Hazelton Indian, which is somewhat different from the Indian spoken here, he apparently made himself understood very well. There are, we have been told, some seven different Indian dialects used around these parts.

J. and I looked at these Indians with interest. Some of them might be from the Driftwood Valley country. They seemed to be traveling in family groups, stopping now and again at raspberry or blueberry patches along the way. Men and boys, carrying large guns, walked in front, while children, women, and old people came straggling along behind. The women were so hung over with fire-blackened pots and pans and bundles, protruding from every part of their patched clothes, that they looked like traveling tinkers of medieval days. They wore headbands to which ropes from the bundles were attached, so that their heads received part of the weight. Young girls and little boys walked with small, panting pack dogs, which they alternately shoved or hauled off the trail as we rode by.

This was our first meeting with the pack dog, that is to the Indian of this country what the husky dog is to the Eskimo. The pack dog is perhaps even more useful and essential, for he is worked during summer as well as winter. At Babine we learned that sled dogs are used comparatively little because the snow is usually too deep and soft for sleds. The pack dog, from the time he is big enough to travel, accompanies his master on every trip with his burden strapped on his back. When he is too sick or too old to go a step farther, he is left behind in the forest or, if he happens to be near a settlement, he is tied to some tree until he dies of starvation. This is so that he will not stray back to his home and take food from the useful dogs. The Indians do not believe in killing dogs, no matter how sick or injured, and since they apparently feed them only when they are working, the dogs are usually small and in bad condition; a sorry contrast to the big huskies of Eskimo country.

The Indians stared hard at me. Ben said that some of them had perhaps never before seen a young white woman, and that they were interested in my light hair and blue eyes.

The little Indian girls had merry red-brown faces and were rather pretty. At the end of the last family came a small boy and an old man. The boy was sick, Ben said. He kept sitting down along the trail and was urged on by calls and shouts from the girls and women ahead. The man, with white hair and a long white beard — a strange contrast to his dark brown face — seemed very old.

With a certain emphasis, Ben said, "This is old Bear Lake Tom."

Bear Lake Tom. We had seen his name often. "Bear Lake Tom's Hunting Lodge" and "Bear Lake Tom's Trap Line" are shown on all maps of the Driftwood Valley. We wanted to talk to him, hear what he thought of our going into his country, but he could not understand, or speak, much English. Ben, in his own language, tried to tell him a little. When Ben had finished the old man looked at us and said — he sounded neither pleased nor displeased, perhaps just philosophic — "Lots of white man, he come now."

One small group of Indians, traveling by themselves, were quite friendly and talkative. The man told J. that his name was Duncan Tom. J. misunderstood and insisted on calling him "Drunken Tom." This amused Ben vastly. For days afterward, at unexpected times and places all along the trail, he kept breaking forth into hearty and prodigious guffaws.

One of the things we like about Ben, in addition to his cheerfulness and courtesy, is his fondness for the horses and the fact that he takes such unfailing care of them. By this time we know the characters and idiosyncrasies of each of the four horses, just as they must know ours. The two pack horses, traveling the trail ahead, are especially entertaining.

Old Bill is a veteran pack animal, small and neatly made, wise beyond all imagining. No matter how bad the trail, he never gets into trouble. He knows to the fraction of an inch how much space there is between two trees and whether he can get through without scratching his pack. He knows exactly how safe are the logs and bridges which must be crossed, and how deep or dangerous every mudhole is. Before he passes over a bad spot, he smells and feels it with a twitching pink nose, and taps it with a front foot. He is old and tires more easily than the other horses. When we rest on the trail, he finds a smooth spot, eases his body gently to earth, sighs, and shuts his eyes. When we're ready to go, Ben whistles and shouts, "Get up, Bill," and Bill sighs again, rises leisurely, and takes his place on the trail, all without having disturbed his pack in the slightest.

Bessie does not possess the cool head of old Bill. She is fat and good-natured, apt to fly into panics. So far she has never refused to go anywhere and her motto, J. says, is "under, over, or through." She's frequently in difficulties. If there's a tight squeeze between two trees, instead of finding her way round to a larger opening she makes a dash, struggles frantically, and gets her pack caught. Steep banks, which Bill picks his way up by careful zigzags, Bessie takes with a whirl and a rush, and nearly turns a back somersault. The afternoon we reached Babine, the horses were turned loose in a pasture near the H.B. post. As their custom is, they all four rolled over and over to free their backs from the feel of those horrid packs and saddles. Bessie promptly rolled into a shallow ditch and lay kicking gently. J. and I said, "Trust Bessie," and watched with amusement, till Ben suddenly rushed out to pry her loose with fence rails. We hadn't realized that she was wedged in. If she had been left, Ben says, she might have died, since horses who believe they are unable to rise often give up trying. Once on the Babine–Takla trail, we came to a high bridge of loose rotten logs. It looked bad, but before Ben could check him old Bill had started across, smelling the logs at intervals and stepping as lightly and daintily as a cat. He, of course, got safely over, but Bessie started with her usual rush-and-run system and before she was a quarter of the way across, down she crashed through the bridge and, four legs kicking frantically, hung suspended by her pack, with nothing between her and the water thirty feet below.

At first we were all struck dumb. Then Ben and J. began to figure how to get her out. Should they chop through the bridge and let her fall clear through, perhaps breaking a leg or two? Should they try to haul her up with ropes? Would the bridge hold them if they walked out to her? While they were still considering, Bessie gave a sudden vast heave, and somehow, miraculously, hauled herself up onto the bridge again. She turned, made a frantic leap for the bank where we stood, and landed safely with no injury other than a bloody nose and a fat body quaking with terror. Old Bill was the only one who negotiated that bridge successfully; the rest of us climbed down the high bank and forded the stream.

Two nights from Babine, and we came to the west shore of Takla Lake. Through field glasses, we could see signs of a settlement two miles across. Ben and J. built four huge smoke fires to signal the ferryman — one smoke, as the custom is, for each horse, to indicate how big a barge to bring.

We looked eagerly at what we could see of the eighty-mile-long stretch of water. It seemed more beautiful than Babine, and closer to the country which we think may be ours. The same moderately high rolling mountains surrounded it, but away to the north, perhaps forty or fifty miles off, were hazy outlines of great purple peaks, lofty and snow-covered — the kind we had dreamed of. Ben thought these were near the Driftwood Valley and that somewhere in that direction must lie the Lake Te-tan-a. After several hours, a small old motorboat appeared on the horizon. When it reached shore J. and I climbed in beside a completely unhurried, unsurprised, and taciturn boatman, leaving Ben to follow later when they could get a scow across to carry the horses.

We made camp on the east shore of Lake Takla above the Hudson's Bay post which lies at the north end of this two-mile-long, sparsely inhabited little settlement. The Macintoshes, who are in charge of the post, have been most kind and supply us with vegetables fresh from their garden. We are waiting for a shipment of winter food supplies, which was to have come long ago by boat along a chain of lakes and rivers from Fort St. James on Stuart Lake, a hundred and sixty-five miles south.

Apparently people here, like those in Hazelton and Babine, do not know much about the Driftwood region, nor have they heard of Tetana. One white man, a German, who is waiting here for a plane, has a small trading post on Bear Lake north of the Driftwood Valley. He has told us something of a lake which he thinks may be Tetana, though he does not know it by that name. He has traveled back and forth through the Drift-wood Valley, but his descriptions are not so alluring or en-couraging as those of Dominick. Mrs. Aiken, who keeps the post office and store at the south end of the settlement, is the only white person I've seen so far who apparently likes the wilderness and appreciates our viewpoint. All the whites here, like typical northerners, appear to be bridge fiends and are scandalized when I say I don't play. They've never seen any-one with ordinary intelligence who doesn't care about bridge!

Today when I was alone in our tent there came a sudden loud knocking on a tree outside. When I peered out through the tent flaps I saw an old Indian, dressed in a long black coat and black felt hat. He wore gold-rimmed spectacles, and he was tapping decisively on my tree with his walking stick.

In accents weighted with portentous gravity, he announced, "I have come to look at your foot."

And waving aside my open-mouthed astonishment he was down on his knees measuring my foot with a piece of string before I could say a word. When I had recovered enough to make inquiry, it transpired that he, Daniel Tegee, "Chief of Takla Indians," had been ordered by my husband to make me moose-skin moccasins — two pairs. Moccasins made by him and his wife were superior in material and fit to any others. He, Daniel, was a great hunter. The moose he killed had the best skin in the country. His wife could fix the skin and sew it better than any woman in Takla. My husband did well to recognize this. He then took his leave with the same gravity and firm courtesy with which he had appeared.

As soon as J. returned I told him about old Daniel's visit and he confirmed the order for moccasins, adding that two pairs would hardly be enough. Later we should have to get more.

"But what do I want with more than one pair?" I was bewildered, thinking of the fancy beaded affairs one buys at home for bedroom wear; I thought J. was being foolishly extravagant.

He said, however, that if the weather gets very cold, we shall have to abandon shoes entirely just as he did in the Arctic Barrens, and wear soft moccasins to keep our feet warm.

Takla Lake   *September 9*

We've discovered an Indian, one Vincent, a son of old Bear Lake Tom, whose trap line is said — and this is confirmed by the game warden's map we brought from Hazelton — to run as far north as the general location of Tetana. He claims to know Tetana and his descriptions coincide with those of Dominick. People either can't, or won't, tell us much about "Vinson," as they call him, but he is apparently the only person around who can actually guide us to Tetana. If we're to live near his trap line, it seems advisable to take this chance to make his acquaintance and show him what our work is to be so that he can see that it will not interfere with his. And, since we also feel that Vinson may have a better right than anyone else to benefit financially from our coming, we have hired him to take us up the Driftwood and stay long enough to help J. and Ben with the cabin wherever we finally decide to build it.

We've cooled our heels here at Takla waiting for the long overdue freight scow which, so they tell us, may still not appear for weeks. It is getting so late in the season that we have decided to go on without the supplies and have stocked up here with extra food. Johnny French, a Takla Indian who lives at the north end of the lake, has promised to come and tell us when our supplies arrive, so that Ben can return later with the four horses to fetch them. But I wonder if we shall ever really see them — our winter food, household equipment, and, above all, the two small boxes of precious books which we spent weeks selecting.

J.'s attitude lately has worried me. He seems to doubt the wisdom of continuing still farther afield. Even Takla is a hundred and sixty-five miles by waterways from the nearest town, car road, telephone, and doctor. This morning, after agreeing with all my arguments in favor of trying the Driftwood and Tetana Lake, J. remarked darkly that if *I* am not satisfied with Tetana, it will be too late to turn back or go farther. Once we reach it, there we must live, whether we like it or not. And he put a damper on everything with a gloomy, "Well, we're going, but I think we're fools!"

Tetana Lake   *September 14*

We are actually here! We left the Landing on September 10th and traveled by launch twenty-five miles to Bulkley House, the site of an old abandoned trading post at the north end of Takla Lake. There Ben met us with the four horses, having traveled forty-five miles around by shore. From Bulkley House we started up the Driftwood Valley. This time three horses carried packs and J. rode Danny. I was only too pleased to walk, for I was beginning to appreciate Ben's statement that riding makes him more tired than walking. I thought I could hop over mudholes and climb logs with less effort than I could cling to the heaving form of Danny when he negotiated these obstacles. I was a lot more sure how I should behave under a given set of conditions than he would, and I found that I was no more tired after hiking sixteen to twenty miles a day than if I had ridden it.

And with every mile up the Driftwood River J. and I grew happier and more sure that we were not fools after all. *For this was our country.* Here was a land of luxuriant forests fed by many waters. Everywhere it was green and luscious to the eye; with the exception of two old scarred patches along the trail on the second day, there were few signs of old fires. The more southerly tree growth of hemlock and cedar had given way to miles of spruce and balsam and sturdy pines. Along the river were dense willow swamps or big sphagnum bogs.

Above Bulkley House the river was some seventy feet wide, deep and slow and winding. The masses of old logs and floating debris accounted for its name. To the west, thousands of Canada geese which were gathering for their autumn migration rose from the broad marshes in great honking, clamorous clouds. The geese were well beyond range of our guns and I was glad that (this time at least) the wonderful creatures were safe from us. But J. says wait till I have tasted wild goose!

As we proceeded north, the river grew smaller and swifter. The trail, a narrow, sometimes almost indistinguishable, path, led above white cascades or beside gravel bars and grassy banks; then across willow swamps and through deep mudholes, where the horses sank to their bellies and floundered helplessly. We trod on soft needle-carpeted floors of dry pinewoods; then over beds of deep moss, lit by scarlet bunchberry, beneath great dark spruces. At each new opening along the trail were thrilling pictures of the Bait and Frypan (on some maps spelled Firepan) ranges silhouetted against the sky now in the west, now to the north. Some were high, perhaps eleven thousand feet, and bore eternal snows. Others were too starkly precipitous to hold the snow. We could see now and again through

dark green trees the glitter of far-off ice fields and glaciers.
Probably few, if any, of the big peaks have ever been climbed
by man. The sounds and sights and smells of this country were
different; there was a tang in the air which spoke of the true
North. We felt a lifting of the heart with every turn of the trail.

"Even if Tetana isn't what we want," said J., "anywhere in
this valley looks good to me."

I agreed. But still I had to see Tetana before I could be
satisfied.

We spent a night at "Bear Lake Tom's Hunting Lodge." I
was surprised to find that a place so prominent on all the maps
was only a dingy overgrown little clearing, full of rough stumps
and charred logs. I'd forgotten that in the vast uninhabited
stretches of the North, one tree cut by man, or a tiny camping
spot used only once, is important and worthy of notice.

Yesterday at the end of the second day from Bulkley House,
just when I was reaching that all-too-familiar stage of not caring
what happened, Vinson abruptly abandoned the trail and
headed due west. We crossed half a mile of treacherous oozy
bog that lay north of a small lake, and picked our way for
another mile through thick, moss-carpeted, log-strewn woods.
Then suddenly Vinson paused and pointed down at blue-green
water sparkling through the trees.

"Tetana," he remarked indifferently.

The afternoon sun lay across the still surface of a small,
shallow, crystal-clear, vividly colored lake. The water reflected
the fantastic mountains of the Frypans, now far to the south,
and the bare rugged tops of the Driftwood range rising beyond
the western shore. The winding shores were covered with dense
luxuriant sprucewoods. Clumps of poplars, dressed in autumn
gold, were scattered on hills and banks. Small marshes on the
east and west, which hinted darkly of mosquitoes, added touches
of red-brown and yellow. A little "brush wolf," or coyote,
stared at us from a high bank, and vanished. Wild ducks and
muskrats swimming out from shore split in two the mirrored
forests and mountains. At the moment it all looked peaceful
and pleasant rather than spectacularly beautiful.

I don't know whether on my very first view of Tetana I was disappointed, or only vaguely satisfied. J. was charmed with it. All three men, viewing it with practical eyes, were well pleased. They noted at once the lake's clear spring-fed waters, the close proximity of big lodge pole pines that are the perfect material for logs and firewood, the high dry north bank ideal for living purposes, and the open poplar groves that let in air and sunshine.

But it was Ben's comment that encouraged me most for, by this time, he must have known almost as well as we did exactly what we wanted.

"*Well,*" he said, "I never thought you'd find a place as good as this."

CHAPTER 11

Building the Cabin

Lake Tetana — Elevation 2420' According to
Our Aneroid Barometer   *September 18*

When I stuck my head out of my down sleeping bag this
morning, there was frost an inch thick on the cover. J., as usual
already awake (a monotonous habit he has), began our invariable morning conversation: —

"How you can sleep or *breathe* with your head buried — "

"I can't sleep unless my head *is* buried; it's the only way to
keep warm; and I can breathe perfectly; my nose is always
out —"

I dressed under cover as much as possible, fishing for wool
socks in the bottom of my bag. The easiest way to have wet
socks dry by morning is to take them to bed with you. J. was
up, dressed, and starting the fire before I was ready. J. is one of
those annoying mortals who are ready for action the minute
they open an eye. Training and character, he says.

Making a fire in this country is a work of skill. Instead of
paper we use thin chips shaved off with a razor-sharp knife
from exactly the right kind of wood. J. never fails to leave
freshly cut chips ready for the next fire, the last thing at night
when he goes to bed or just before he starts off for the day to
work.

To fill our kettle this morning, we had to hammer ice on the
water buckets and put pieces in to melt. The temperature at
night is now 10 to 20 degrees below freezing. Beyond the waters
of Tetana stretched virgin country — endless miles of densely
forested hills and valleys sharp and clean in the morning light.
The far-off line of jagged, snow-lined Frypans was purple, and
close beside us were the Driftwoods whose tops, now powdered

with fresh snows, have become high and imposing, instead of just a bare and rugged range as they appeared at first. The air was so pure and sparkling I wanted to drink it.

But I never can really take in the scenery until breakfast is out of the way. J. starts off early to work. Winter is coming and we must have the cabin ready soon. Vinson told us that once at his winter camp twenty miles down the river from here his thermometer went to 73 degrees below zero and the snow was over ten feet deep. His horse nearly died because its eyes and nostrils were frozen shut and it could scarcely breathe!

As soon as the breakfast coffee is on, I hurry to beat up bannock, a new dish which J. has taught me. Fresh hot bannock is a most delicious thing. It's a mixture of flour, baking powder, salt, and water stirred to the correct thickness and fried in hot lard in a pan on top of a stove or open fire; or, if mixed with lard, it can be baked in an oven like loaves of bread. Next to meat, it is the northern man's most important food. It takes the place of bread and cake and apparently withstands any sort of weather conditions. J. was taught to make it by Eskimos of northern Hudson Bay, and the Indians here make it in somewhat similar fashion.

Occasionally we've had a speckled trout (Vinson says Dolly Varden) caught in the river a mile away, or grouse with a bit of bacon. Usually we have dried fruit. Sometimes we share a fresh orange, frozen solid, one of our hoard of three dozen carried on horseback from Takla. We supply the two Indians mostly with the same food we eat, but things like oranges are strictly for us. We must stay here all winter, with little chance of getting added stores; every bit of fresh fruit put in our systems now may help in the months to come.

When breakfast things are cleaned up and bedding hung out to air, I refill the flimsy water pails (twice the size of ordinary pails) which once held fancy crackers and struggle up the steep bank with them. I'm beginning to realize what my place here is to be. At first I was so fresh from a world where courteous gentlemen rush to relieve ladies of burdens that I was annoyed and rather amazed that none of the men ever offered to fetch water for me. As for men helping to cook or wash dishes as they do on camping trips at home, that would be the height of absurdity. They have more vital things to do. As a matter of fact, though, J. has often helped with meals. He is teaching me a lot about wilderness dishes and various primitive, but tasty, concoctions made from few materials.

Ben and Vinson no doubt are pitying J. for his foolishness in having such a wife and often say: —

"What a useless woman that white one is! Many things she doesn't know how to cook; she is even too weak to cut trees for firewood."

A woman here performs any job of which she is physically capable, including many of which she may suppose herself incapable. The man's whole time and energy are consumed in performing those deeds which only his strength and skill make possible. Felling huge trees, carrying logs in on his back, building cabins, hunting, killing, and butchering moose or bear, packing dogs and horses, making boats, guiding them down or pushing them up rivers, paddling across lakes in high storms, shoveling out a winter's camp in a ten-foot snow level, cutting a trail for days through unbroken swamps and undergrowth.

I'm gradually beginning to get the feel of a great wilderness, to absorb the astonishing peacefulness of it. There are no human beings in this land but us. Our nearest neighbors must be a few Bear Lake Indian families some thirty or forty miles north, and the few white people and Indians of Takla Landing seventy-five miles south. By J.'s pedometer, Tetana is thirty miles from the north end of Takla, which, in turn, is forty-five from the Landing. So the nearest telephone, railroad, or car road is now some two hundred and forty miles away. Hundreds, perhaps thousands, of miles of land around are uninhabited, unexplored, unmapped. J. and the two Indians are the only people in my world. No family or friends or strangers enter into it; no one writes, telephones, or passes by. There are no daily papers, no radios, no conversations with anyone all day while the men are at work. At night and first thing in the morning we discuss the cabin, food supplies, weather — just the necessary elements of daily life. None of us has had news from the outside world for weeks, nor do we expect to have for as many months to come. There is nothing, therefore, except our own everyday experiences for us to worry about.

At first, the thing which struck me most forcibly was the complete and utter quiet of this world. Occasionally the ring of axes on wood or the call of a bird or squirrel breaks the silence, but much of the time the stillness is absolute. It is a sort of invisible presence which seems to haunt one day and night, and intrudes on all one's most private thoughts and occupations.

I find myself constantly standing still just to listen to nothing, and I never have enough of looking. The Driftwood Mountains change every hour, yet they are always there, constant and strong and serene. They must be six miles away, but they seem to rise just beyond a few wooded ridges. They form a range some forty miles long. In places they are rounded and solid; in others, reaching eight and nine thousand feet to peaks and saw-toothed rims, they become grand and thrilling. Their peaks, outlined with fresh white, are clear red at dawn, harsh and cold when the sun gets high, warmed and softened by a silver haze at noon, violet and gold when the sun sinks behind them, white and black under the glorious stars of these autumn nights. Their valleys and indentations, their invisible hollows, may hold any kind of waterfalls, little lakes, grizzly bears, or mountain goats.

And always, close at my feet, lies Tetana, whose loveliness steadily grows on me. It is a mile long, with a depth of eight to twelve feet and clear as pale green glass. When the sun shines into it, the color is bright green emerald, and where the sky is reflected into it, it is aquamarine. Every foot of the clay bottom is visible. Huge springs gush out in several places under the banks and give the water its wonderful translucent quality. Big patches of some kind of a bright yellow Mimulus, or monkey flower, are in full bloom in the shallow water beside the springs.

Except for the two small patches of grassy and willow-grown marshes on the east and west, the shores curve in graceful sweeps through dark pointed evergreens. The east shore, rising high in a ridge of pine and spruce, is drawn like a half-moon whose farthest horn extends in a rounded point forested with big trees. Beyond the first point a narrow little promontory sticks out sharply toward the very center of the lake. It is overgrown with willows and alders, but one lone fir tree, perfectly shaped and pointed, is set at the outward tip. Beyond this again is the rounded portion of Tetana and the outlet flowing directly into the Driftwood River, which rises somewhere northwest of the Driftwood Mountains. The west shore makes two slow broad curves by the big marsh and along a dark belt of forest, until it too joins the outlet. Beyond the lake rise two high rounded twin hills, and above these are the Frypans painted on the sky in a line of little blocks, spires, and rounded points, colored in white and gray and blue and purple.

The forest, undulating in velvet carpets across hills and valleys, stretches as far as the eye can follow, the yellow-green of pinewoods alternating with blue-green of spruce and balsam. To the east and north are more mountains, shaped like the Driftwoods, or sliced off into flat tops that fall in sharp gray precipices.

This north shore of Tetana has been used as a camping place by Indians. There are bits of charred logs from old fires; in places trees are scarred with ugly marks. An Indian letter is written on a large pine near our tent. A flat area, a foot square, was cut smooth on the trunk and in big childish characters are these words in pencil: "I get hard time here snow very deep no fur no food bad I go now to babine — " The rest, except the signature, is illegible, but the date shows it was written five years ago. In several places between here and Babine, we saw other "letters" written on trees; this is a customary way of leaving messages for family or friends.

By a lucky coincidence, J. and I picked the same spot for the cabin (our arguments over camp sites are apt sometimes to be rather warm). It lies on this north bank with thick forest behind, and an open view in all other directions down the lake and across the valley. Below are the springs bubbling out into the lake. A few large trees of pine, spruce, balsam, and poplar are scattered about; there is no feeling here of being imprisoned by forest and wilderness. If we had planted and grouped the trees and shrubs ourselves, we could never have made a nicer arrangement. Almost daily we remember Dominick and are grateful.

September 21

Several kinds of chickadees are about, and they make me feel almost as though I were at home. They are such dainty, friendly little things. The most common, the northern species, wear warm brown-velvet caps. There are also red-breasted nuthatches, and Canada jays or whisky-jacks. These jays, with their sweet clear whistles and gurgles, are tame and gentle. They come almost up to us and watch with big black eyes everything that we do. Pine grosbeaks and siskins fly by in flocks, and ospreys come over the lake. One morning an osprey flew heavily just above this bank with a huge fish clasped in its claws, and soon a bald eagle followed, flying so low that you could see the white gleaming head and hear the swish of his huge wings.

But the most thrilling of all are the wild ducks that come to the lake around dusk each night. American mergansers, green-winged teal, mallards, and goldeneyes — both the American and Barrow's, which are new species to us. The mergansers, coming with a rush overhead, sound like a storm. When they hit the lake, they aquaplane twenty or thirty yards across water.

Until we can get a skin identified by the Museum, we are not sure whether the grouse, which are common and very tame, are a species of spruce or Franklin's, as the two are closely related and almost alike. We've eaten quite a number of them as well as some wild ducks, for we're badly in need of meat. Twice, when Ben, whistling loudly every step of the way in order not to surprise a moose or a bear, has been taking the horses half a mile north to a small grassy meadow surrounded by willow thickets, he has killed grouse by throwing stones at them.

Small flocks of rusty blackbirds are stopping here on their way south. J. collected one which I made up for the Museum.

The skin doesn't look too bad, but it doesn't look too good either. I foresee endless hours of toil ahead trying to achieve a respectable bird skin. J. can make up mammals, but he has never done birds.

Skinning a bird may be no more difficult than skinning a small mammal; the skin is peeled off the body so that only the skull, wing, and leg bones remain, and then turned right side out again. But arranging the feathers properly after the skin has been turned inside out is an awful job! The feathers of a bird lie in certain tracts along the body, and they and the wings must be arranged exactly right when you wrap up the prepared skin. Once the skin has dried the feathers can't be changed, and if they are set wrong, the result is wretched-looking. To prepare a skin it is powdered inside with a preservative like borax or arsenic, and then stuffed with cotton to take the place of the body. It still takes me an hour to do even a small bird which an expert might do in twenty minutes.

We loathe this collecting business. We've always hated the big scientific expeditions which, with their passionate zeal for specimens, are apt to go through a region and create havoc among all the live things. But in order to get accurate identifications of species here we've vowed to collect, if possible, two specimens of each resident bird and several dozen of each of the small mammals to send the Museum. Skulls only of most of the larger animals will be sufficient because teeth and skull characteristics usually form the most reliable scientific means of determination for mammals. We hope to acquire gradually all sorts of animal skulls and heads from the Indian trappers. But our real joy and chief occupation is to be a study of the behavior of wild things in their native habitat, photographing and sketching when we're lucky enough to see them close at hand. Tetana and the territory immediately surrounding it are to be kept as a kind of sanctuary for observation purposes. Collecting is to be done as much as possible away from it.

A northern species of toad is common along paths and through the woods. We've also seen a few wood frogs with the familiar black mask across the eyes. But reptiles are unknown.

The Indians have never seen a snake or a turtle anywhere in these northern parts. They do know salamanders, though. One day Vinson brought in a big salamander (perhaps the long-toed *Ambystoma macrodactylum*) which he had dug out of the bank below the cabin. It was over four inches long with yellow-green splotches across its back. He and Ben watched its death throes in our jar of formalin with considerable interest and awe. Indians say that a salamander, which they call "long frog," bears gold on its back and that if one kills it he will lose his money and all worldly possessions.

September 23

The east end of this north shore rises abruptly to a high little hill covered with an open grove of poplars. This is my favorite spot. J. calls it Teddy's Hill. As I climb I can see new and grander and ever more enchanting views, framed in silver trunks and yellow leaves, of the Driftwood Valley and the curving lines of Tetana below. The hill extends back into a long series of ridges full of deep hollows and high hummocks. Small blue-green balsams, luxuriant and thick and soft as velvet, whose fragrance is wafted on every wind, grow in the wet depressions. If one follows the ridge north the Bear Lake Mountains come into view, the highest of which, partially snow-covered, is shaped something like an extinct volcanic crater. To the west, between the Driftwoods and the Bear Lake ranges, is one glimpse of glacier-covered peaks. I climb the hill often just to gaze at these, wondering if we shall ever get close to them, and if they're as grand and spectacular as the tantalizing little picture indicates.

No forests have such lovely floors as these northern ones. Scarlet bunchberry is scattered everywhere over deep green moss — moss so thick it feels as though one were walking on pillows. There are masses of oak and lady ferns, Lycopodiums, trailing Linnaea, blueberried Clintonia, and other plants which I do not know. On drier, more open ridges, lodge pole pines and aspen poplars are the chief trees, with an occasional small white birch, and dense thickets of small Shepherdia, or soopolallie, bushes. The thick forests are largely white spruce, although on wet eastern slopes heavy stands of magnificent balsam trees, some a hundred and twenty-five feet high, with an almost jungle-like undergrowth of devil's-club and alder, predominate. Wet hollows and boggy areas contain shaggy black spruce. Swamps, covered with dense willows and alders far above our heads, are scattered for miles all across the valley. Along the river we have found enormous balsam poplars with a DBH (diameter breast high) of over five feet. It is this balsam poplar, so the Indians tell us, which is used for making dugout canoes.

Occasionally we see fresh droppings of bear and moose. Dozens of smooth poplar trunks back of the cabin site have been scarred by bear claws. Some, in series of fours, have probably been made by black bears, but more, in the series of fives which are the sign of the grizzly, indicate that the latter may be particularly common. When the grizzly places his foot in the mud or scratches a tree trunk all five of his claw marks usually show distinctly, while, since the fifth toe and claw of the black bear is comparatively small, only four of his appear. The hugeness and freshness of some of these scratches present an awesome picture of the bear that stood up only a few days, or perhaps hours, ago to claw fiercely and leave his own defiant marks around. The other morning Ben found Bessie running frantically in the meadow with her hind leg torn. He believes that a grizzly was after her.

Along higher ridges are whole groves of aspens, with the bark peeled in long strips eight or ten feet above ground. These tears, made by bull moose when they rub velvet from their new horns in early winter, seem high, since the horning of a large moose is said to occur at six or seven feet. But when one considers that the moose may be standing in some feet of snow (whatever the depth is here at the time) this height does not perhaps seem so stupendous. We also have reason to believe from what the Indians say that the moose here may form an unusually large race.

For three nights in succession I've been disturbed by a moose snorting just back of our tent. Probably it has wanted to reach the lake and is annoyed to find a tent always in the way, because it backs off quickly, and goes into the bushes again. By the time I wake J., the moose has always vanished and it's too late. Just as well, perhaps, for shooting a moose in the dark, especially a bull, does not seem to me a very safe pastime. Autumn is mating time for the moose and no animal, it is said here, is more dangerous than a bull moose in the rutting season. He is full of fight and, out of sheer gusto, may pitch into the first large living thing that he sees.

If I should come on a grizzly standing eight feet tall, or a moose towering to a height of seven, the pistol and big knife which J. insists on my wearing (here a pistol, hunting knife, and matches are just as much part of daily equipment as clothes) wouldn't be much protection. Probably my best bet will be to stand still, then retreat *slowly* and climb a tree — if one is handy. Black bears climb, but moose don't, and grizzlies are not supposed to! But the very best bet will be not to meet a bear or a moose at all. I don't suppose that they are any more anxious than I am for an encounter. J. and I believe (and so far we have never been able to learn anything to prove the contrary) that the average wild animal, except for the rare bad individual who has run amuck, does not, unless it is cornered and wounded or its young interfered with, deliberately attack a human being. At any rate as I tramp about, like Ben, I always whistle or sing to give fair warning, and I've spotted a lot of trees that won't be too thick to climb in case of necessity.

I can't take even a stroll away from camp without being alert for danger. But I think, though I'm always afraid, that I rather like the fear. It is stimulating to realize that it is the keenness of my senses and intelligence and no one else's which will keep me safe. It's a kind of challenge to know that if I relax sight, sound, smell, and instinct, I can, in five minutes, lose all sense of direction, or, in a second, be sucked down a quagmire, slip on a bank and be carried off in a swift current, corner unexpectedly a dangerous animal, or be hopelessly cornered myself — and the chances are that no one else would ever know or be near enough to help. And there is always the thrilling feeling, in a place that shows no signs of man, that perhaps I am the first human ever to have set foot in this particular spot.

I find the red squirrels great company. They are so abundant at this end of Tetana that we wonder if they're congregating here to escape the marten, which is probably their worst enemy. Or is it because, in company with many wild animals who are not harmed by man, they enjoy the novel behavior of human beings? The sound of a human voice seems to frighten them, but if I whisper they keep still and stare at me with bold black eyes. When they're scared they sit up with one paw pressed to a thumping heart. Every squirrel around is occupied with making a huge winter nest in some low thick balsam. Since martens can climb so easily, a low tree is doubtless just as safe for the nest as a tall one. These nests are composed chiefly of the sphagnum moss which forms endless carpets through the woods, and also large bunches of hair from an old moose skin left in the grove back of our tent. Many contain bits of mushrooms and other fungi; these, since certain fungi are favorite squirrel foods, must be used for light lunches when the squirrels are too lazy to get up and go to their winter hoards. One nest is decorated — we suppose it's a decoration — with a fox skull. Countless squirrels are in a state of feverish activity. I have an idea that the same individual has a finger in more than one nest, just for the sake of doing something, because the autumn sting in the air warns him that he ought not to waste a moment of time preparing for winter. They all expend much energy in gathering fresh spruce and balsam cones — luscious-looking pink-green things which take the place of nuts hoarded by squirrels farther south — into huge mounds around tree roots and old logs. Some piles which J. and I measured are fifteen to twenty feet in circumference and four to five feet deep.

Signs like these give rather ominous warnings of winter. At any rate snow levels here must reach seven feet or so; several lines of old axe blazes are eight or nine feet above ground.

For over a week there has been a burst of autumn coloring such as I have never seen, even in the hills of New England with their October scarlets and reds. I had supposed that in the Far North, where there is such a predominance of conifers over hardwoods, there would be little autumn brightness. But here clumps of poplars and willows, scattered through the deep dark of evergreens, have taken on a pure brilliance of gold, orange, and scarlet, so that even on dull gray days the sun seems to be shining; nor does the dark of a black-clouded night completely shut out the colors that light hills and forests across the valley. The heavy early frosts and luxuriant growth must be responsible for such supreme brightness; and there is always the dark of the conifers to relieve and set it off.

Ever since our arrival at Tetana, one serene cloudless day has followed another, each full of the yellow and orange autumn lights. The first hours of the morning are frosty and sparkling. But by noon the sun is as hot as summer. Jackets and wool shirts are thrown off in a heap and I flee to the shade of a big tree. After feeling uncontrollably fresh and strong, I'm simply prostrated with laziness, but when, almost asleep, I sink to the mossy earth, clouds of stinging little black flies, that pest of the north woods, appear from nowhere. By half past three, the tree shadows lengthen suddenly, and before even half my wool things are on again, the cold night is there; I'm piling up the campfire, almost hugging sparks and smoke as I cook supper.

The moon grows fuller every night now and floods down the lake and blackens the mountains. Stars in this northern latitude, even in bright moonlight, flame like fires. Last night we looked down through the white trunks of poplars on the hill to the lake glittering with moon and stars, and over snow-powdered ranges close by and way beyond.

Johnny French and his small son appeared unexpectedly last week. Johnny has never been far up this valley or seen this lake, but by following our several-weeks-old tracks they found us without difficulty, though once a bull moose disputed the trail

with them, and they had to climb a tree. They brought the welcome news that our freight had come and been taken by launch
to the north end of Takla.

So Ben has made three trips down and back and has thus
traveled over the rough, in places nonexistent, trail some hundred and eighty miles in eight days. Everything has been
brought safely, even three glass windows, the twelve-inch looking glass, and a small hand mirror. The looking glass pleases J.
even more than it does me, because he has been obliged, for
weeks, to shave by the tiny mirror on my vanity case. Ordinarily
men in the wilderness, until they are unfortunate enough to
possess a wife, go bearded from one year's end to another.

Every pound that has arrived seems more than worth its
weight in gold. Every book, blanket, article of food, dried or
tinned, every package of nails for the cabin, every case of
matches, bottle of medicine, cake of soap, dish towel, roll of
oilcloth, we've received with gusty sighs; if any of them had
been lost there is no way of replacing them.

Once while Ben was gone, J. and Vinson took a day off to
explore country east of us. I stayed at Tetana and, for the first
time, began really to comprehend what loneliness is. There was
not a sight, sound, or movement of another human being. If
anything happened to J. or the Indians, I should be thrown entirely on my own resources; *no one*, probably for months and
months, would know about my insignificant existence. Our
family and friends, people "outside," don't expect to hear
from us before midwinter. Probably I should not be capable of
going for help; I've not learned yet to travel or exist by myself
in this country.

"Now," I thought, "you've reached an experience you've
wanted all your life. We'll see how you like it, what sort of
character you really have!"

The day itself was not so different from other days except that
it was more than ever profoundly quiet. There was no chopping or hammering, occasional call, or faint smell of tobacco,
all of which are now a customary, taken-for-granted part of this
life. When it grew late in the afternoon there was not a sign

of J. or Vinson, who had expected to be back "well before dark." I began to be more and more scared.

Twilight blanketed the forests. Sunset colors on water and mountains, which I always revel in, I hardly noticed. This time they didn't seem important except that they said, "Night is coming." They were not even beautiful; they were just impersonal, unhelpful.

At last, for the sake of doing something, I started along the path to the Takla trail with a gun and a flashlight. If I got closer by a mile to where J. might be, I could call. If he was in trouble perhaps I could hear him. The danger of surprising a bear or a moose in the dark was nothing compared with the horror of not knowing where he was, of going on being alone.

I walked the mile to Trail Lake, christened recently by us because it lies along the horse trail to Takla, thinking all the while that in the darkness I might not be able to trace the blazes back to Tetana again. But I wanted to get to the open marsh where a call, unmuffled by trees, might travel farther. If no answer came, I would be sensible and find the way back to camp.

I didn't really hope to hear anything, and I was giving up when suddenly, unbelievably, J.'s voice called, "Tedd — ee, where are you? I'm com — ming, I'm com — ming!" And I could hear him starting to sing in his lovely bass. He must still be far away. There was a sort of double burr to the syllables so that what I heard was probably the echo. But, thank God, he *was* all right, and he was on the way home!

Later, when he reached camp, he said that he had called from a ledge two miles east of Tetana looking back across this valley. The air at the moment was so clear and still that his voice had carried perfectly. Knowing that he was a "little" late, thinking that I might be lonely or worried, he had given me a call on the off chance that I might hear. He had not heard me.

September 29

A huge pile of dirty clothes, accumulated from our trip across country and from weeks of camping out, has been hanging heavy on my conscience. I've put them off and put them off, but yesterday I made up my mind that washed they must be if we are not to live in the same clothes all winter.

A wash day here is not a well-ordered affair! There seemed to be endless complications involved. There was no hot water, no tubs or wringers or clotheslines. Even if I had wanted to do my washing in the lake, the water of Tetana is far too benumbing to the hands. Those huge, flimsy cracker pails filled with water had to be carried up the bank to heat over the campfire. Half the time the fire wouldn't burn. The wood was too damp, or too green, or something. I wasted a lot of time scouting around the woods for better logs. Clouds of smoke and blowing ashes blinded me. Once a pail upset just as it was getting hot. There was nothing to do but curse, climb down to the lake, refill the pail, struggle up the bank again, and heat more water. I had exactly two pails — one to wash in, the other for a reservoir of clean water. For rinsing I used two washbasins and the stewpot. Washing in a tub raised to the proper height is, by the way, quite different from bending double over one set on the ground. And of course two pails of water were not nearly enough. I had to wash piecemeal, using up what water I had till it became too black. Then I'd take the pails I'd washed in, climb down for more water, haul it up the bank, find more wood, hang over the pails till they were hot, and start scrubbing and rinsing and wringing all over again.

The garments we wear in this country, moreover, are great heavy woolen things — underwear and socks half an inch thick, heavy shirts, pairs and pairs of huge dirty trousers (including J.'s riding breeches and my jodhpurs), sweaters, dirty mittens, filthy handkerchiefs, towels, and pillowcases. Thank heaven, we don't use bed sheets. I despaired of ever getting them all properly wrung out. When I was only halfway through my back felt broken and my hands had dissolved into red spongy tissue.

After endless hours — the whole day in fact — I did finish. Two hours were left before supper. With groans and moans I was stretching out upon the ground when it occurred to me that, if there was to be a supper to cook, I must prepare the two green-winged teal shot by J. the day before. I was rather new at this game too. It took all of the two hours to pluck, singe, clean, and cut up the tough ducks, with a few precious vegetables, in a stew. I would almost certainly have thrown the bloody, nasty-smelling things into the fire long before they were ready for the pot if I hadn't been so desperately hungry for any sort of meat. Although mergansers are the most common ducks here and easier to obtain than the others, they feed on fish and are, therefore, like most flesh eaters, no good as food for man.

Any sign or smell of blood or animal flesh always brings forth our friend the weasel. His lithe snaky body appears and disappears and reappears like a bad dream. One of us may be gazing at a bush near the tent when suddenly there is a tiny movement, a flash of whiskers and black eyes. "Hi, here's the weasel!" But even as we look, behold there is no weasel. We go to the bank and gaze down on the lake, and there again, almost at our feet, are sparkling eyes, whiskers, a tiny wet black nose, all set on a snake's neck with no body. This time the weasel appears in full view and passes briefly along the bank in a series of flashing, fairy-light, curving leaps.

When we first saw our weasel in early September, he was light brown on top and cream underneath, and he had a black brush on the tip of his long, most expressive tail. Now we're having early snowstorms and he is getting paler every day. His reddish-brown coat is changing to a washed-out tan; he looks the way I imagine a person getting leprosy looks. Today we even saw a pure white spot on his brown head. He has also been getting tamer, if the adjective "tame" can ever be applied to a weasel. That is, he runs freely — far too freely — through our tent and provisions and sometimes across our bodies at night. He is in and out all day long. When he's in a hurry — and he never wastes time — the air is full of arcs made by his little body. He melts from one position into another. On several occasions he's run off with salted grouse skins which I had carefully prepared for the Museum. Once, I caught him dragging under a clump of willows with frantic speed and ferocity a skin three times his size. Another time he pulled all the cotton stuffing out of mice skins which J. had been fixing, thereby destroying days of hard work. We were so angry we would have slain him on the spot if we could have caught him. But when we scold, he stops and looks at us, mischief in every quirk of him, and we can't stay cross for long. And really we are glad to have him around, since a very large part of a weasel's diet consists of mice and rats. He is as good as, or better than, a cat.

Our weasel has wonderful eyes. They are red or green in changing lights and they never lose that bold wickedness. Sometimes he and the least chipmunks (probably the gray-headed) play hide-and-seek around boxes and trees. These chipmunks are about the size of a large mouse. They carry their tails defiantly straight up in air, and they climb trees if the weasel gets too near. Trees may not be common haunts of chipmunks as they are of red or gray squirrels, but chipmunks climb much more than is generally supposed. Often, here at Tetana, I see them high up in tall spruce or pines.

September 30

The big pine logs have now all been cut, peeled, and hauled to the cabin site. Ben has made a creditable set of swivel trees from small poles, and harness and reins from rope and stray bits of leather.

J. and these Indians don't have any of the machinery or paraphernalia I've always seen around a house in the making. They have no tools other than axes, hammers, two saws, and a very few nails. Yet our cabin, which is about thirty feet long by twenty wide, is going up rapidly and properly.

There are all sorts of ingenious ways of doing things when one doesn't have all the gadgets. The foundation logs were leveled off by fastening a bottle full of water on the center of each of them in turn. When the water is perfectly balanced, a little bubble forms on the upper center of the bottle. A string is stretched at the same level from end to end of the log. and the log is lowered or raised accordingly.

Weasel

The great logs were each hauled and lifted slowly and painfully into place. As they were laid one on top of another (two long logs alternating with two shorter ones), the ends were carefully fitted into each other at the four corners. Grooves were cut near the end of each log, so that the log above locks snugly into the one below. Moss was packed in the grooves first so that no cracks will let in cold air.

The gable ends are beginning to go up and soon the roof rafters will be laid. Ben and Vinson spent a day or two hunting a certain kind of huge spruce tree whose branches are far above ground. From these trees the "shakes," twice as long as ordinary shingles, are to be made. Pines and balsams won't do because their branches begin too near the ground. Branches make knotholes in wood, and there must be no holes in the shakes if one wants a weatherproof roof. The Indians found spruce trees that suited them a mile away by the river. First they felled the trees, then cut them into sections of big round stumps; from these Vinson is to make the shakes, while J. and Ben continue work on the cabin. It may take several thousand shakes to cover our roof.

Things aren't going nearly so smoothly as it sounds! The two Indians don't get on well together, for one thing, and they are becoming a constant worry and anxiety. Last night J. remarked, "Well, I expect Ben to be off any day now — "

"Ben?" I was aghast. "Didn't he promise to stay till the cabin was up? I've been expecting Vinson to leave, but I thought Ben — he's *got* to stay till the heaviest things are done. He knows *you* can't do it. How could we live in a tent with the temperature 70 degrees below or whatever it is? What's wrong with Ben anyhow?"

"Says he's got to get home. Afraid of being stuck here. You can't blame him. He's got to get four horses back over nearly two hundred miles of mountain trails before snow blocks them and before the grass — which is their only food, remember — gets covered. Besides, we had quite a set-to over the roof today. I'm sick of this business — they're both of 'em getting too fresh — think they can do anything they damned please — "

"Well," I said, "if only you could make things a little clearer — you say one thing one day and another the next — "

"Clear!" J. yelled. "I'd like to see *you* try to make 'em understand. By golly, *you* give the orders tomorrow — "

For a week Vinson has been threatening to leave. He's always too tired now or too sick to work. And he keeps telling dark tales about the habits and morals of the Bear Lake Indians, who, he claims, poach on other people's trap lines. They'll be down soon, he says, to make trouble for us. Vinson went to his camp down the river not long ago and brought back his wife and a cute brown baby girl. He said Ben wouldn't do any cooking and he had to do it all and clean up, besides. Their tent interior did appear to be a completely indistinguishable mass of bedding, clothes, and food. Though Martha is very efficient and does many of the jobs Vinson is supposed to do, we can't decide whether she makes things more or less difficult. Our winter food stock is dwindling with alarming rapidity, for they didn't bring supplies of their own. These people apparently think that we have a kind of trading store with a year's provisions on hand. We can't turn them away or let them go hungry for then Vinson would leave, too. *Anyone* able-bodied is needed desperately in our race to get a shelter up. There is nothing for it but to try to keep the peace, hold them all as long as we can, and have faith that we may somehow get in more supplies before winter is actually upon us.

Fortunately the Indians appear to respect J. considerably. Though he's not able yet to show what feats of strength he's capable of, he is more than their equal at handling a gun. They don't say much, but they shake their heads at some of his shots with pistol or rifle. Though they must think many of his notions about the cabin crazy, they seem to be impressed with his broad knowledge of practical details. In his dealings with them J. is considerate and generous, but if he gets angry for a just cause, he can be quite terrible. I believe Vinson is afraid of him!

Always two peoples of different languages and ways of living have difficulty understanding one another. That is, I suppose, our greatest trouble with these Indians. Although Ben and Vinson speak English unusually well for this country, it is inevitable that they should not always understand our wishes and orders. (And we can't ever be sure just how much they really want to understand!) There is a sort of mutual caution between us all as to characters and intentions.

Last names and titles in this country are customarily dropped. It's amusing to have a perfect stranger walk up and address you by your first name. So far everyone calls J. "Jack" and, though J. does not object to this, he does — incongruously — object to *my* being called "Teddy." He takes pains to speak of me constantly as Mrs. Fletcher. This puzzled the Indians. They were always asking what my name is. Now they compromise and address me tactfully as "Missus."

We had counted on fresh meat. The lack of it has made serious inroads on other winter staples such as flour and lard and bacon. The men have taken turns hunting moose, but with no success so far. J. has managed to obtain fish, grouse, or wild ducks occasionally. On one of his trips to Bulkley House, Ben, with what must have been a quite remarkable shot from J.'s pistol (which he took along for protection), killed a young mountain goat at a salt lick on the trail above Bear Lake Tom's place. He brought the meat back to camp, though, alas, not the head which we would have given our eyeteeth to obtain for identification. The meat was sweet and juicy and delectable, but one small goat didn't feed us all for long. It is always a question as to how much time we dare take off from building; whether, when it becomes really cold, it will be worse to be without food or without shelter. Although the Indians are certainly not heavy eaters they consume quantities of jam and sugar. When J. demanded that they go easy on these, there was an awful ruction. They all almost left, then and there!

October 6

Six days ago an unexpected diversion came in the midst of our cabin building. During a fall of heavy wet snow, the usual quiet was shattered by the roar of a plane which we could barely

see, though it flew low overhead. It disappeared for a time, returned again, and circled round and round above Tetana. We
all believed that the lake is too short and winding for even a
small plane to make a safe landing. Nevertheless, out of the
whirling snow, a small red plane suddenly descended, landed
on the water, and came within an ace of smashing against this
shore. As the plane hit the surface, the heavy ice and snow on
the wings forced it down and, to save it from going under
water, the pilot "gave it the gun," hard. He came roaring
straight at our bank, turned at right angles in the nick of time,
skimmed off the lake onto the marsh, and embedded the pontoons deep in muck, a few yards short of a large spruce tree.
Two dapper youths in city dress hopped out and brought up
short, amazed apparently at sight of a white woman. This was
their first trip in this country. ("My God, what a country!")
They had been flying a prospector and his outfit to a mine up
north of Bear Lake and when they were coming out got caught
in the storm. Tetana was the only lake right then that showed
signs of human habitation and they had to land somewhere
anyhow. They had to remain with us until they could dig the
plane out of the marsh.

They had no bedding, emergency tools, or food — except for
a paper bag of beans and rice which they turned over to us.
We lent them half our bedding, our one and only shovel, and
fed them as best we could on our already scanty rations. Two
extra mouths made further inroads on our winter store, and J.
spent long and fruitless hours scouting the woods for meat or
game.

After four days of strenuous labor the pontoons were dug
out. The horses and men pulled, pushed, strained, and shouted
mightily — the plane was afloat again at last. Next day, after
emptying out every pound of material that he could, the pilot
took off. With prayers and suspended breath we all watched
until the plane rose and cleared the tallest trees at the end of
the lake. I doubt whether the nervous young pilot was any
happier about it than we were. Here we have traveled thousands
of miles to reach a wilderness undisturbed by man, only to have

a plane crash almost on our doorstep. The prospect of having it stuck indefinitely in our wild lake, with more strangers perhaps coming in to pull it out, has been awful! Even in these few days their visit has cost us much time and energy which ought to have gone into building, not to mention the inroads on our winter's food. Today the mechanic, who was a nice young chap and a fine worker, took Vinson and Ben's two best horses and started to hike out to Takla, carrying with him the plane supplies, and a small bill to his company for food and the service of Vinson and the horses, for all of which we pay a daily good-sized sum.

Just before the plane descended on us, the weather turned so cold that we were obliged to move our fire and all our cooking equipment into the tent. J. boarded up one half of the opening with the lids of wooden packing cases, and put our one-and-a-half-by-one-foot iron stove inside, with the stovepipe sticking out through the boards. We can now fasten one flap of the tent door across, shut ourselves in, and be as cozy as we please. The tent holds our beds, duffel bags, boxes of food, and stove fairly comfortably, though since it is only eleven by seven feet we must be extremely systematic about keeping everything in its place. When the two airmen were added to our ménage and we had to spend long hours inside because of the bad four-day storm, things became definitely too cozy. Our wet clothes had to be dried constantly, and when I was cooking meals over the tiny stove with four of us inside the tent, life was not what it might be. I could never stand upright and had no space even to sit, let alone cook, serve a meal, and wash dishes.

October 12

The long cozy evenings which J. and I now spend in the tent are the nicest part of the day. A tiny lantern, or even one candle, lights up the whole inside. When the fire has died and it gets cold, we go to bed, pour on the box between us two puddles of hot wax in which we anchor two candles, and take turns reading aloud. Barrie's plays or *Winnie-the-Pooh* restores our humor, no matter how exasperating the day has been. I never realized, until I heard J., how much a British accent adds to the charm of these British authors.

Last night and early this morning we heard a real chorus of coyotes. They give shrill barks and yelps, interspersed with howls, which sound eerie and fearsome. We have also heard what Ben said was a wolf, calling off in the distance. It was a weird, rather musical call, quite different from the coyotes. The Indians say that when coyotes begin to howl in companies it means a big change of weather.

One evening last week J. collected the rare pygmy owl right by our tent. Apparently this makes a northern record of this species for British Columbia. Odd that J. should have been the first to collect a pygmy owl as far north as Yakutat, Alaska, several years ago, thereby setting a record for Alaska also. Another pygmy has since been to visit us on several occasions, not only after sunset, but also during the daytime. When we hear it in the distance we can call it right up to us. You can reproduce its notes perfectly if you give a whistle with a "hook" in it. The end of a little series of "hooks" is followed often by a musical trill like the trill of the screech owl. These owls are the cutest, prettiest little things, about the size of a large fat sparrow, with gray-brown feathers soft as down. I made up one for the Museum and, for once, it turned out to be a lovely job.

October 17

Still another human being has penetrated our fastness, a Dane named Aagie Nelson. When Vinson took the plane mechanic down to Takla, we told him to bring back a strong man, any man in fact, even for a week or two, if he possibly could. When Vinson finally returned, we were agreeably surprised to see also a large white man with a pair of snowshoes slung over his shoulder. Aagie was a prospector who was temporarily out of work before he went "outside" after his summer's prospecting, to take over a new job for winter. As we looked at his broad powerful body and rosy face and heard his quiet, slow voice, we felt a sense of ease and relaxation. Here, if we were not mistaken, was the reliable help we needed so desperately, but had never dreamed of getting.

"Brought my snowshoes along," he said. "Thought I might have to hike out in deep snow."

Vinson also brought back half the price of our "bill for services rendered" to the plane men, and a message from the pilot (who, by the way, left us without even a "thank you" for our hospitality, such as it was) to the effect that that was all we'd get and he hadn't had much to eat anyhow!

Each day Aagie works long and regular hours, things are more shipshape, and J. and I begin to feel confident that we shall have a roof over our heads after all. At first the erratic work of the Indians steadied down as they were forced to follow Aagie's example. But Ben has announced suddenly that he must go and we can't urge him to stay longer, though there is still much to be done. Vinson and Martha also are to go in a few days. However, life will undoubtedly be pleasanter after they leave. We've had about all we can stand of all of them as, possibly, they have of us! Aagie, although he will have to snowshoe alone the seventy-five miles to the Landing, will try to stay until the heaviest jobs are completed; the floor laid, doors and windows in place.

Aagie is a grand companion, one of those rare people possessing so much within himself that external things don't affect him. Every evening we all huddle round our tiny stove. Aagie and J. play cribbage with tireless energy and roars of mirth, while I read, write up notes, or look on. Aagie always retires early to his sleeping bag on the floor of the cold little provision tent where he reads Ernest Thompson Seton's *Lives of the Game Animals* by candlelight. He is so fascinated that sometimes he reads far into the night. If this is what studying animals means, he can, he says, understand why J. and I love our work and like to live far off from man.

Every morning since Aagie has been with us we've had big thick pancakes for breakfast, cooked one at a time in a frying pan. Aagie says pancakes are the only breakfast that really "sticks inside" his ribs till lunch.

J. has built a low partition of small poles across the west end of the cabin to form a bedroom, and the doors and windows have all been cut in the logs. There are five windows, and the two doors will each have a window cut into them later. The Indians are amazed and amused because their cabins usually boast of one door, and the white men's cabins which we've seen so far aren't much better. They usually have one or two windows and are dark and stuffy. Our cabin is light and airy with views in every direction. Nor should the windows, carefully chinked, make the inside colder. On the contrary, we believe they will make it sunnier in winter, and cooler through the heats of summer. Each window is on a level with our chairs and beds so that we can see the world as we sit or lie abed almost as well as if we were out in it. The three glass windows were brought from Takla on horseback; the others were made from a roll of flexible cellophane one sixteenth of an inch thick. This material is as clear as glass and may be obtained at northern posts in yard-length, lightweight rolls which can be packed and carried easily. Its only disadvantage is that it can't be washed and scrubbed and must be renewed every year or so.

I spent a week carrying gunnysacks into the woods, filling them with the best quality of sphagnum moss, and dragging them back to the cabin. When I had a pile of moss that must have weighed a quarter of a ton, J. and I set to work on the important task of chinking. Damp moss had to be fitted between all logs, inside and out; under roof rafters, around doors and window frames, in fact in every imaginable crack or cranny. When as much moss was pushed in as every space could hold, it had to be jammed and hammered with a wooden mallet. We cut and peeled small pine poles, fitted them between the logs, and nailed them in place, so that the moss would be held firmly in the cracks in all weathers. Unless enough moss is wedged in and unless it is held firmly in place, it will fall out before the year is half over, for when it is warm the frost in it melts and the moss expands and oozes out.

We moved into the cabin last night, on the very day that the back door was hung. Aagie had been keeping the stove going for several nights in order to dry out the new damp logs and woodwork. Each evening we leaned out of our tent and gloated over what we saw. Pale yellow light streamed from the windows of the cabin, which, thanks to J., is long and low instead of the usual box-shape. Great, pure-white snow mountains rose behind the big black firs against a glittering star-studded sky. It all looked rather like an unbelievably pretty Christmas card.

This morning Aagie put on his pack, consisting of sleeping bag, food, and clothing, and our mail, the last we expect to send out all winter. I stuck our very last cake of chocolate in his pocket and, with his snowshoes under his arm, he was ready to start on the lonely four-day (if he is lucky) hike for Takla.

"Hope we'll be seeing you again some day, Aagie — "

"Not likely," said he matter-of-factly. "In this country you don't see people again, 'less you just happen to run across 'em."

And this is a queer, rather sad, it always seems to me, truism of human relationships in the Northland. People whom one has come to know in a few weeks far more intimately than neighbors who have lived next door for twenty years back in civilization drop wholly out of one's life by moving on to other places. Some of J.'s best comrades in the Arctic, the "finest fellows" he ever knew, he's never heard of again, partly because some of them can't read or write, partly because there are no mails, partly because, inured and toughened to the life of the frontier, they part from old associations with fatalism and philosophy.

Aagie said good-bye as simply as he greeted us a few weeks ago and we, rather sadly because we have liked him so much, watched his big sturdy figure pass slowly out of sight down the bank, along a patch of open lake shore and into the dense pines and spruces.

We are left alone at last to the silence and the northern wilderness.

November 7

Most of our time so far has been spent around home completing odd jobs. J. has had to make all our furniture except the stove. Beds and easy chairs have been fashioned with pine poles for frames and rope and canvas for flexible parts. Shelves and tables are made from pieces of the wooden boxes that carried in our supplies. After they are gone, when we want shelves or anything, J. will have to go out and chop down a tree to get even one small board.

Thanks to the trouble which he has taken over innumerable details, the cabin has become a never-failing source of comfort and pleasure. It is all the perfection of little things that makes a home in this land bearable; for the world must be limited largely to one's cabin when, for nine or ten months of the year, one is forced to spend much of the time inside its four walls.

Two small bookshelves run along the east gable end. One shelf holds our big volume of Kipling, Barrie's plays, Shakespeare, John Buchan, Wodehouse, *Winnie-the-Pooh,* the *Oxford Book of English Verse,* Liberty Hyde Bailey's *Wind and Weather, Great Companions,* Rauschenbusch's *Prayers, The Gypsy Trail,* and detective stories, which we love but which are useless, because they have to be read quickly and then we never want to see them again. The other shelf contains Seton's *Lives of the Game Animals* in four volumes, and various reference books on the flora and fauna, geology and geography, of northwest Canada as well as a large Medical Treatise and Dictionary. On the gable wall above the bookshelves we tacked a Grenfell rug, with wild geese flying north against a gold moon and dark blue sky. The geese flying north will remind us, through all the long winter, of the coming of spring.

The natural satin brown of the log walls needs no adornments. Yellow window curtains, made from cheap dress material which I bought in Hazelton, are a special joy to J. Was there ever a man who didn't love curtains! Every window frames a picture lovelier than any conceived by an artist. When I remember cabins of trappers and traders with their walls plastered with calendars and moving-picture beauties, I sigh with satisfaction as I gaze about our own abode.

The stove is in the center near the partition in order to heat both the "bedroom" and the main room. Shelves and cupboards and small tin flour and sugar barrels are placed along the wall next the stove. The drum oven is a special convenience; I can bake bread and pies and cake and roast meats in it as long as I regulate the fire carefully in the stove below.

A drum oven is an important part of equipment in any northern cabin. It is a small, lightweight, metal barrel, fitted with shelves and a door in the inside portion. The hollow outer portion connects top and bottom with the stovepipe. Lying in a horizontal position the oven is fitted into the pipe three or four feet above the stove, so that heat from the fire coming up the pipe on its way to the outside passes through the hollow and circulates all round the little box inside. A drum oven weighs around ten pounds, is about three by one and a half feet in size, and can be carried easily on a horse, dog sled, or man pack.

Our "medicine cabinet," a box containing two shelves, hangs on the bedroom side of the partition near the stove. We have a fairly comprehensive stock of bandages and drugs and disinfectants; aspirin and Frosst tablets, cathartics, iodine and mercurochrome, S.T. 37, morphine, tetanus antitoxin. The sight of the last two makes me shudder.

The lack of lumber was a tremendous handicap when it came to laying the floor. It has taken eighty-four axe-hewn boards, ten feet long and about eight inches wide, to make the floor, not to mention the numbers that went into roof boards and rafters. Each board, after it was split out of a log, had to be leveled and smoothed off with an axe. The boards are rough and uneven and don't fit together like straight-edged boards cut by ripsaws or machines. The only thing I can do, when I sweep, is to swish dirt and crumbs about so that they fall through huge cracks to the ground below; this gives me the feeling that we shall eventually be living over a garbage heap!

With an adze brought up on the last trip from Takla J. has begun laboriously on hands and knees to plane off every board. It takes hours of time, but by doing a little every day for months he says we'll have a floor to be proud of.

Under the floor we dug a small pit five feet long, three feet wide, and four deep. To reach down into it we lie flat and lift up small sections of the floor boards. This is our "cellar," and very convenient it is to store supplies in. It should also be a safe place for perishables during severe temperatures.

Our greatest trouble is the roof. The rough shakes, which don't fit closely over each other as shingles do, are constantly contracting and expanding under the alternate cold and warmer temperatures. Some have already cracked or split in two, leaving gaps overhead. As long as it is cold enough to keep the snow on the roof from melting we have a dry house, but when the temperatures moderate (as they do, so far, every three or four days) the snow melts and drips through the cracks, so that we're in a constant state of emptying basins and bowls placed at intervals over the floor, and moving our precious books, food, and specimens from one dry spot to another. When we get too fed up with this state of affairs, J., mouth and pockets full of nails, climbs to the roof with a load of extra shakes under one arm and a hammer under the other. I stay inside the cabin and with a long pole tap the roof at the leaking spots. Then, guided by banging and shouting from me below, J crawls from one point to another and inserts a shake under the cracks. This goes on until his hands are numb and my neck so cramped from holding the unwieldy pole and keeping my head inverted that I have to do exercises to straighten out again. The first time, we tried to stop the cracks with moss and scraps of old cloth from flour and sugar bags. These merely acted as sponges, and were much less successful than inserted shakes. Moreover new cracks seem always to be developing.

Our days are so full that we sink into bed right after supper, too exhausted even to read aloud any more. But it's a nice kind of fullness. There is no strain about it. We do what we can and want to do each day and know that nothing really has to be done by such and such a date or hour. I'm beginning to believe that complete independence from other people's ideas and actions is almost the nicest thing in the world. J. says he discovered this in the Arctic long ago!

CHAPTER III

The Coming of the Snow

Tetana   *November 9*

We've had several cold snaps; thermometer down to zero or below. And the usual quiet of Tetana is broken now and again by the noise of ice making on the lake. This comes on the coldest nights just after sundown. The peculiar throbbing silence of the winter dark is shattered horridly by a ripping, zooming noise that passes across the lake from one shore to another. Sometimes it crackles or booms. It always makes my blood tingle and my skin prickle. Then, off in the forest, comes a loud crack like a pistol shot, so sudden that it makes us jump! This is just a tree splitting in the cold. At times, all this fills me with a foreboding of something sinister to come. But when I wake to a bright morning, with light fresh snow sparkling, and the stovepipe pouring forth clouds of white smoke in the cold air, I forget the foreboding and feel nothing but exhilaration and a mighty anticipation.

Today J. called excitedly to "come out quick!" Far in the north was an odd new noise which sounded for all the world like a pack of old, seasoned, baying hounds whose notes are low and musical. And then slowly, from the northwestern sky, came a ragged V of fifty-four big white birds, flying high, and talking to each other in deep soft voices. They were swans, the larger bodies and long outstretched necks differing from the smaller, more compact forms of wild geese.

"Trumpeters! Gosh, they must be trumpeters!"

Neither of us had seen or heard the rare trumpeter swans which are now almost extinct except in a few localities on this continent, but we've often read about their notes, said to be strikingly deep and sonorous compared with the higher, thinner ones of the common whistling swans. And we've been told by the game wardens that there are trumpeters in this country. A number have been collected and their tracheae, which have an additional loop or curve in contrast to those of the whistlers, have been examined for positive identification. Large companies of swans winter somewhere between Takla and Stuart Lakes, where, according to reports, they are sometimes caught by sudden frosts while sleeping and frozen into the thin ice, where they become easy prey for foxes and coyotes. No one seems to know how far north they go to nest in summer.

The appearance of the trumpeters should be a foretaste of spring, since the birds that pass south over a place on their autumnal migration are usually to be seen going north over the same area in early spring. At this season greater numbers of birds seem to be in evidence, probably because of sexual excitement, the more brilliant plumages of the courtship period, and the fact that the spring migration is a more regular and orderly movement. Birds have definitely fixed routes of travel just as human beings do, and a wide valley in a land of mountains is often a bird migration route. Perhaps the Driftwood may prove to be an important bird highway, and if rare things like trumpeter swans pass over it . . . !

While we were still living in the tent another smaller weasel, probably a female, joined our friend, and when we moved to the cabin they moved with us. They haunt the walls and the spaces under the floor. They are now the beautiful ermine of fabulous evening cloaks. Except for enormous bushy black tail tips, they are both a lovely cream-white all over. They frisk around on shelves outside by the back door, like two white kittens, knocking over cans with an awful clatter, stealing bits of meat, hissing and spitting if we disturb them, just as though this were their house and not ours.

In the spruce woods on the east shore, J. caught a weasel by the foot in a small trap. It was not hurt, so he brought it home and put it in a box covered with wire screening. Because of its size and the fact that it was so bold and unabashed, we were almost certain it was our special friend and kept it a few days

before we let it go. In common with most wild animals that
I've had in captivity, it did its best to keep its living quarters
scrupulously clean and neat. It was so fussy that even when it
made water it promptly lapped it up, with no apparent unhealthy results.

November 12

We've had our first real winter snow. A soft powder, fluffy
as flour, has draped over everything a foot and a half deep.
Every one of the billion fir trees and bushes near and far has
turned into a lovely thing. Last night a young moon in blue-
velvet sky etched the white knife-cut mountain rims with silver. Big fir trees and the cabin cast long violet shadows across
snow like mother-of-pearl. Stars, burning and sparkling, were
reflected in the patch of lake not yet frozen. And over everything was the great blanket of spotless white, and a silence so
deep and unbroken that it rang in our ears and in our hearts.

This morning when the sun came up — now long after eight
— the whole world turned to dazzling splendor. The willows
edging the lake below, and the dark spruces above, danced
with brilliant color. Huge flakes of hoarfrost, some an inch
thick, lay all across the snow. It looked exactly as though
myriads of diamonds had been scattered over hill and lake and
tree.

During bad weather, we fix up the cabin, but on good days
we now take tramps away from Tetana to explore the valley.
One of our favorite walks follows an irregular line of indistinct
old blazes leading down the east side of the lake to the outlet
where, after passing through a narrow open channel thirty yards
long, the waters of Tetana shoot out into the swift, still unfrozen little river and form big circles of clear deep green before they are swept off in the gold-brown current. In a small
back eddy we always scare up a few winter ducks feeding in
weeds and grasses that gleam like quicksilver and emerald under the crystal-clear moving water. These form a select little
company composed of two female American goldeneyes with
sleek brown heads, and six male mallards in their gorgeous

violet-green and gray and white. On a high bank a broad opening under old spruces and pines looks out clean across the valley
to the Driftwoods, back up Tetana, north to the Bear Lake
Mountains, and south down the river to the Frypans and Bait
ranges.

The blazes continue intermittently down the east bank of
the Driftwood for miles. Sometimes they swing far inland to
avoid a big impenetrable willow swamp, then they go back
to the river again and wind along high open banks. In sheltered places poplars and willows still hold autumn leaves now
dusted with snow; patches of pale yellow or russet, or the scarlet
berries of a shrub, make splashes of color against high spires
of a clump of snow-laden spruce. Still pools and backwaters
reflect sunlit peaks and snowy willows. Perhaps this is some
Indian trapper's line, used occasionally. We have found faint
traces of old camps — charred ends of logs or tall stumps
marked with axe cuts.

We never miss a chance to explore banks or flat bars for
tracks. Signs of muskrat runways and cut grasses were common
along all backwaters of the river before snow came. Now there
are fox tracks and droppings, signs of mink, otter, and once what
we took to be a fisher trail. At least the footmarks, like a gigantic mink,[1]

were different from anything we've seen.

One of our cherished ambitions is to study the habits of the
fisher, which belongs to the family of minks, weasels, otters,
and the like. The fisher is a close relative of the marten, but
darker and larger (some three feet in length compared to the
marten's two), and very active both in trees and on the ground
of coniferous forests. It feeds on small mammals, rabbits and
squirrels, and also eats water animals such as frogs and fish.
It is strong and fierce, said to be capable of killing a lynx, and
is apparently one of the few animals that prey on the porcupine
by attacking it on the quill-less underside. It is supposed to be

[1] Tracks not drawn to scale.

nocturnal in habit, and the Indians told us that a fisher is seldom, if ever, seen except in traps. Its fur is so rich and beautiful and rare that one small skin sometimes brings a price as high as $120. The fisher is to be found only in wildernesses, and it is said to be more common here in these Caribou, Chilcotin, and Omineca districts of British Columbia than anywhere else in North America. Even so, it looks as though our chances of watching fishers and studying their habits would be slim.

This may hold true of many of the larger mammals. For the protected big game of National Parks, which is often unnaturally tame in its relationship to man, does not exist in a world as yet in such a primitive stage that men must kill the wild creatures, even as they in turn prey on each other, to obtain the necessities of existence.

In one place beaver cuttings, along a bank of poplars, extend for a quarter of a mile. Two huge balsam poplars with a DBH of forty-two and forty-six inches were cut and felled by the beavers. The marks of their strong teeth are clearly discernible all around the big stumps. But the old broken-down beaver dams and lodges are empty and deserted. It looks as though Indians had completely trapped out a large beaver colony.

Learning to read tracks is like learning to read the pages of a book. Every little mark means something; every change of pace, every stop, tells a story. And fresh snow that has hardened just enough to bear impressions without blurring is the ideal kind of page to read. Studying tracks has always been one of my special interests, and J., during his years of traveling and hunting in the Arctic, acquired a store of knowledge about winter signs that is invaluable to us both.

On October 1st we saw the last chipmunks. They apparently have all gone into hibernation for the winter. And there are now no fresh bear signs. According to the Indians, bears by the end of October are permanently holed up for winter in caves on the mountainsides or under stumps and brush piles in the forest. Now since we're able to follow trails through the snow, we find tracks of other animals fairly common. The snow is so light that walking, even when there is a foot or more, is fairly easy. It's odd how after the first snows, one suddenly becomes aware of the fact that a region which up till then has appeared to be quite empty of animal life is after all a well-populated one. Mouse, weasel, squirrel, rabbit, fox, and coyote trails make checkerboard patterns everywhere.

In deep woods the tiny mice tracks like those of white-footed mice at home, run in a series of fours and twos with the tail mark between: —

and some, which must have shorter tails like the shrews, have the tail dragged to one side: —

At the edges of swamps and meadows are the uneven little footprints — the meadow mice and lemming variety: —

Weasels, like a huge mouse, are also easy to distinguish: —

The large rabbit prints must be the snowshoe rabbits: —

Coyote and fox tracks, like big and little dog tracks, tend to follow those of the rabbits, which are, no doubt, one of their chief foods. The red squirrel prints conform to the usual squirrel pattern: —

and there are other tracks evidently made by flying squirrels which the Indians say are quite common. These tracks are much like the reds' except that they're lighter and more uneven, and usually have double lines between the footmarks. These double lines are probably made by the patagium (the furred folds of skin between front and hind legs) dragging in soft snow: —

Flying squirrels are chiefly nocturnal in habit. This morning when we went tracking over toward Trail Lake, a story of the nightly activities of a flying squirrel was written all over the snow under a big spruce. Out of a little hole in the big hollow tree which is its house (J. shinned up a small spruce near by and found a few telltale gray silky hairs sticking to the bark around the hole) had come a little gray, velvet-furred flying squirrel, tail flat and soft in contrast to the rounded brushy tail of the red squirrel, eyes, so much bigger and softer than the beady eyes of the red, gleaming emerald in the dark night. Near the hole, marks of its foot and body were all across a snowed-over branch from which, spreading its patagium, it had floated like a falling leaf and landed gently in the snow some yards beyond the base of the home tree. Then, like a red squirrel, it had jumped lightly to a big pile of spruce cones by a fallen log, and had begun its evening meal. Perhaps this was its own winter hoard, perhaps it was a red squirrel's (there were red squirrel tracks there too), but since the red squirrel was probably asleep the flying squirrel could feed freely, though it must constantly keep nose, ears, and eyes alert for a prowling fox or marten. The footprints of the flying squirrel had blurred over and all but obliterated a mouse track. There was a tiny spot of blood, and some indistinguishable impressions in the snow which might mean it had caught a mouse. Flying squirrels like animal flesh as well as the usual squirrel fare of vegetable matter. Here the whole story ended abruptly for huge blobs of snow had fallen from a branch and covered all tracks completely.

Some well-marked moose trails lead to small "moose yards" where families apparently gather to feed, sleep, and shelter together. We've come on two of these east of Trail Lake. In each,

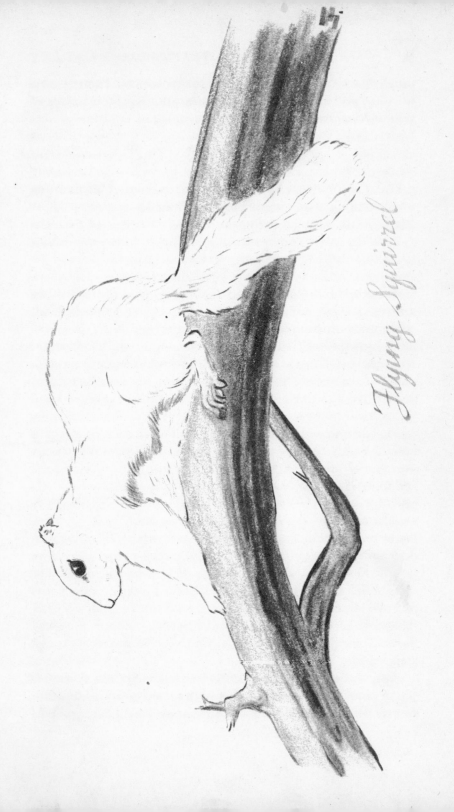

Flying Squirrel

thick patterns of tracks covered several acres and willows had been heavily fed upon. Numbers of hollows contained two or three huge beds or depressions, made by their bodies, and there were copious droppings which were still warm and fresh enough to steam in the cold air. The moose must have left just before we got there, though we had been walking so quietly in the soft snow that we thought our movements soundless. And there seemed to be no wind to carry our scent. The moose are protected from man and wolves, their chief enemies, by their size and the keenness of huge ears and noses.

Several miles east of Tetana is a long, narrow little valley of marshy ponds and swamps containing a beaver dam over three hundred feet long. Last month as J. was watching the beaver house, he heard overhead a slight rustle in a high spruce, and there was a big velvet-footed Canada lynx. Even as he caught a glimpse of the silver fur and heavily tufted ears it melted, without a sound, across a branch and vanished. Here we recently discovered fresh rounded footpads of a lynx leading all across the same snowed-over beaver house. The lynx is extremely fond of beavers as a food.

In the woods back of the cabin and around Tetana, we often follow a marten trail, which also reminds one of the trail of a big mink.

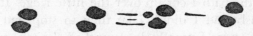

This tan, or dark brown, graceful creature inhabits primarily pine and spruce forests and lives on all kinds of small land animals. One of its chief foods is the red squirrel. It's interesting to note that with the introduction of red squirrel pelts on the fur market, the annual returns of trapped marten from these areas have so far shown a marked decrease. From Ben and Vinson we gathered that martens are trapped so extensively by the Indians that they have become wary of man and avoid the immediate neighborhood of any occupied cabin. Formerly the marten lived in virgin forests throughout northern North America, but now it is found only in less civilized parts of Canada and a few Northeastern and Western states. Here the marten is still one of the most common and valued animals of the trap line. One day, north of the meadow, we tracked one which bounded along lightly for half a mile. Then it climbed a tree and we lost it. Another, very near our cabin, stalked a grouse through a clump of thick balsams, and caught and ate it on the spot; feathers and blood splotches were left to tell the tale. From what we've seen so far, it appears that each marten keeps to a certain area, roughly two square miles in extent. Marten tracks usually wander in circles, or, when they head in a straight line for some distance, turn back in a parallel direction, until they reach their starting point again.

One day J. was lost for about three hours chasing around after a marten. He kept catching enticing glimpses of it (it looked something like a cross between a weasel and a little fox). He made so many crisscross tracks that he couldn't backtrack at all. He thought he was some ten miles from home — nothing looked familiar — when suddenly he was considerably startled to hear me singing. And he found himself in the big poplar grove back of the cabin!

And I was lost one afternoon just coming home over Teddy's Hill and scared myself almost to death. I had been with J., who was chopping wood in the spruce east of Tetana, and instead of following the path I cut up over the little ridge. It was snowing furiously and I didn't take time to stop and look back every so often, as I usually do. I reached the top, expecting to look down directly on Tetana and the cabin, and I simply couldn't believe my eyes, because there was no cabin or lake at all. Through flakes whirling so fast they made me dizzy, I was gazing on a strange stretch of forest. There were no mountains or familiar landmarks anywhere. My heart almost stopped. It was such a shock that I forgot for a few minutes that all I had to do was backtrack. But I had to hurry, because even then my trail was almost covered and it would soon be dark. I retraced a quarter of a mile before I reached a place that I recognized. Instead of keeping along the hill which I thought I knew every step of, I'd turned off almost at right angles, headed north,

and then west, until I'd come out on an entirely new little
ridge.

We've been so busy just working to live that until lately we
haven't been able to do much collecting for the Museum. But
J. has now set out a few small steel traps for medium-sized
mammals like mink and marten, and we've both been able to
put several dozen mouse traps out every few days. Each new
species we get is a thrill. Yesterday we caught one of the lovely
little flying squirrels. The mouse traps have yielded white-
footed and red-backed mice, and a kind of tiny shrew which we
take to be either *Sorex cinereus* or a pygmy. Also, alas, I've
caught two chickadees. The bait of raisins and oatmeal must
have looked so tempting to them in all this waste of snow. The
soft little things were held only by a foot and apparently were
otherwise uninjured, but they were quite dead. One was brown-
headed; the other, which we think is Gambel's or Grinnell's,
was black-headed with a white line just above the eye.

Shrews must be common. We've even seen them inside the
cabin. Their bodies are around three inches in length including
the tails. They have long quivering little snouts, eyes so small
they are almost invisible, and tiny ears hidden in fur. We've
caught several in empty pails and tried to keep them alive by
giving them a continuous food supply — dead flies and raw
meat — and water, and cotton batting and moss to hide in. But
though not hurt at all, they never live more than a few hours.
A shrew must be a most highly sensitive creature. At home in
Pennsylvania on several occasions, seemingly healthy shrews,
a much larger species than we get here, have shuddered and
then died in my hand after a sudden loud noise or shaking. It
looked as though they simply died from shock. Others acquainted with the habits of the shrew have made similar notes
on their remarkable sensitivity.

November 13

I have had so much to write about lately that I haven't even
mentioned the really important visitors we've been having from
Bear Lake. The first was one Michelle Charlie. "Son of Bear

Lake Chief," he told us, otherwise known as Bear Lake Charlie.
It seems customary for young Indians in this country to use
their father's given name as their last name. Chief Charlie's
last name we understand is Haimadam, but his children are
called Michelle Charlie, Maggie Charlie, William Charlie, and
so on. Michelle was a tall well-built fellow with a not especially
pleasant face. He spoke fairly good English and he talked very
big. He impressed us with the fact that his father holds a position of importance and that he, his son, is to be admired and
respected also. His father, Bear Lake Chief, he told us, will
come one day to see us, though he is "very sick man. He spit
blood all the time."

Michelle was impressed with the size of our cabin, and filled
me with apprehension by remarking, "This fine place; Bear
Lake Indians make big dance here mebbe."

To which J. retorted, inhospitably, "Oh no you won't!"

Michelle traps and hunts down this valley, mostly, we gather,
on the other side of the river. He spoke coldly of Vinson and
says he has no right here. He had with him a few laden pack
dogs and a younger brother. They brought several big skins
which he thought we might like for our cabin. Michelle said
politely that any price we wanted to give would be all right.
"Just what you think, Jack." J. seemed to understand what he
really meant, and set to work bargaining.

As soon as they began to examine skins and quote prices, the
faces of both J. and Michelle, which had been wreathed in
polite smiles, suddenly lost every vestige of expression. J.'s was
as dead-pan as the Indian's, and their voices grew low and
elaborately casual. This is what invariably occurs on the instant
that a true Northerner, be he white man or native, sees a piece
of fur.

Michelle and J. took what seemed to me an unnecessarily long
time to arrange for the exchange of skins and a little food and
money, but when it was all satisfactorily concluded, we had two
good black bears and a small thick white mountain goat to
add to our furnishings and give satisfaction not only to our
eyes but to our bodies. Since they have now been thoroughly

aired, and sunned, and frozen out of doors, we use them under our feet and in our easy chairs, and I take two of them to put under my bedclothes every night. For the first time now, I am really almost warm enough at night. A canvas bed without a mattress allows a most unpleasant amount of cold to come up underneath, no matter how many coats and jackets and trousers I use for padding.

At first I was greatly perturbed because our bedroom window wouldn't open wide. I come from a family of fresh-air fiends, and I supposed no one could sleep in health without a good gale blowing through the room. J., impervious to my protests, instead of fixing the window so that it could be thrown open more fully, bored three *holes* — the size of a human eye — in the bottom, and made a panel which could slide across one or all of them. Though I go to bed each night in an indignant state of suffocation from lamp and tobacco fumes, with only three holes to let in fresh air, I must admit I wake each morning more than refreshed — in fact chilled stiff. It seems that even a tiny stream of air, if sufficiently cold, creates enough draft to provide a perfectly healthy amount of oxygen.

We sent a letter by Michelle to the white trader at Bear Lake to ask him for a stove larger than the one we now own. Michelle reported one was for sale. We didn't really expect to see it, but a week later Michelle appeared again with the stove strapped on his back.

He had carried it some thirty or forty miles — we don't yet know the exact distance — from the Bear Lake settlement. It is an iron stove, two and a half feet long by a foot wide, larger and far more useful for both heating and cooking than the tiny one we had. It must weigh some sixty pounds. Because the lake was partly frozen — too much so for a boat, but not hard enough to walk on — Michelle said he hauled the stove most of the way on his own back, while his dogs carried the lids and door and pipe lengths in their packs. J. paid him well but even so we wonder whether it was enough. We've acquired a fair idea ourselves of what traveling in this country means.

We offered Michelle $4.00 a cord if he would cut firewood

for us. On a farm at home this would be a munificent offer. But Michelle shrugged and remarked that at Bear Lake he gets $6.50 a cord. J. was indignant at such a scandalous price in this forested country, and said he'd cut all the wood himself if it killed him, before he'd pay that much to any man for a single cord. But as time goes on we're beginning to understand the Indian's viewpoint. A large part of his life must be composed of cutting wood, even during summer. And he must have to cut an enormous quantity to keep himself and his family warm through these winters. Moreover, J. says if he has been fortunate enough or skilled enough, he may, with one day's labor catch a valuable fur animal like the fisher that will bring him as much for a single skin as he would earn in two weeks cutting wood.

The addition of the larger stove, plus a tin washtub brought up on the last trip from Takla, has made washing clothes a hundred times more simple. Also by melting and heating snow I save carrying endless pails of water. I must have acquired some strength already, for I can do a two weeks' wash (quite a pile, because, in order to be really warm, all your wool things must be kept clean by frequent washings) in three hours without becoming completely exhausted. Rope stretched back and forth from the cabin crossbeams makes an excellent and convenient clothesline.

Our other visitor has been a young Indian named Sapolio (of all things!), also from Bear Lake, who appeared soon after Michelle's first visit. Sapolio is as different from all the other Indians whom we've seen thus far as night is from day. He has a strong, rather dour face with remarkably keen black eyes, and he is as quiet and withdrawn and self-contained as the others have been free and garrulous. He appeared first one morning when we were working on the cabin. Instead of greeting us with loud protestations he looked us over long and silently, and said then: —

"What you do here?"

We explained in detail, for he behaved as though he had the right to ask. He appeared to be neither pleased nor distressed

Canada Lynx

over our coming; his general air implied that he would reserve opinion and wait to see how we turned out. When we told him we had no meat he said he was hunting moose.

"I get meat, come back," said he; "no come back, no meat."

That very afternoon he appeared again with ten pounds for us, having been the first of all the Indians around here this autumn to have hunted successfully. We paid him five cents per pound, which we understand to be the usual price. Fresh moose has a strong, distinct, rather unpleasant smell. It reminds me of disinfectants in a hospital ward and this makes it a bit hard to down at times. J. says I will soon get used to it. If moose is to be our chief diet, I hope so!

J. went with Sapolio the next day on a short exploring trip. About five miles north of here they found a bull moose who must have been vanquished in a great fight with a stronger brother. With glazed eyes it was swaying on its feet, blood flowed freely from many wounds and the antlers were badly broken. When they shot the poor thing, they found its whole body terribly mauled and bruised.

The next time Sapolio visited us was a few days ago, and this time he paid a real visit. He was taking a freshly caught fisher skin to the trading post at Bear Lake. It was the first fisher I'd ever seen. The long, rich, glossy, almost black fur, with slightly grayish head and shoulders, was certainly beautiful. Sapolio grew slightly more easy and friendly as we all drank tea inside the cabin. Instead of warning us about the bad characters of the other Indians, as they have each done, he mentioned them not at all and refused to be drawn on much of any subject, with the exception of wildlife. His impassive, dark face lighted up when we began to question him about the habits and abundance of certain animals.

J. has already sketched various mammals — mice and weasels and rabbits and bears. Although he's had no training in drawing, I think he has the gift of making animals live on paper, especially with regard to eyes and facial expressions. And I've been interested to note that these Indians, so intimately acquainted with wildlife, are struck with this too. Ben and Vinson

and Michelle, and now Sapolio, have all pored over J.'s creatures
and exclaimed: —

"By gosh, just like! He look like that. How you make him
that way?"

It seems that J. knows as much about furs and skins as these
Indians do and that they know he knows — the condition of the
fur, the season, even the month, in which it has been taken,
whether fully prime, whether the animal has been properly
skinned, and so on.

Sapolio did not ask for any food as the others have done, and
he did not apparently want to sell or trade anything. He is
certainly far more the "silent Indian" of fiction and, though
we can't quite make him out, we rather like and respect him.
He seems to have greater strength of character than the others,
and is evidently a lone wolf who asks help from no one. He
traps on his own and has thrown us into further confusion as
to whose trap line is whose, by declaring that his, and not
Vinson's, goes past Tetana and part way down this valley. He
says he always trapped here with his father and, since his father
died, this trap line belongs to him. The game warden told him
so. Our favorite river trail leading south is Sapolio's and the
old camps have been his.

We are inclined to believe Sapolio a bit more than the
others. Perhaps this is because he does not, like Michelle and
Vinson, repeatedly assure us that he never lies! This whole
business of trapping is an ugly blot on wilderness life. I wish
we might be in a region where trapping does not exist. The
agony to the mind and body of the creature in the trap — especially the larger, highly developed mammals — is terrible to
think of. I suppose most trappers do not think of it. They become hardened to it. But, since trapping for fur is a great in-
dustry of the North which furnishes a livelihood for many
thousands of men, I can see that the facts concerning it must be
faced. But of all forms of exploiting the wilderness and its
products, the trapping of the fur animals seems to me the most
cruel.

Hunting is a very different thing. Not many wounded animals

in this country escape to suffer. The hunter has no ammunition to waste. He needs food or clothing desperately. When he shoots, he shoots to kill. I wish that traps might be invented, and used, which would kill the animal as it is caught. But none, so far, have been made which satisfy the trapper. The Indian deadfall, still used here occasionally, where a log is arranged to fall and crush the animal, seems infinitely more humane than the steel trap. But it is, alas, evidently much less effective.

If traps were visited regularly and often, it would be somewhat less terrible. But a man cannot cover a fifty- or a hundred-mile trap line more often than once a month, say. And apparently most of these Indians do not visit their traps with any regularity. They are too shiftless or weather conditions are too severe. They can, if they will, subsist on the country quite well for indefinite periods, without trading fur at all.

November 14

After sunset yesterday (the sun sets now behind the mountains at 3 P.M.), we had come in from our chores outside and were sitting by the roaring stove over our usual cups of tea. J. insists on afternoon tea no matter what or where, and it is a habit that I am rapidly acquiring. I'm learning that afternoon tea means much more than just drinking tea and eating sweets. Here it means warmth to the body and rest to the mind, congenial companionship after a hard or lonely day. To me especially it means security, for after tea we are both safe at home until another day.

As we drank our tea and reveled in the easy chairs, the last daylight faded and the world was locked in the silence and glittering snow and moonlight of the early northern night. Then, suddenly, outside came a burst of rippling notes. *Birds*, singing a clear, sweet song on a bitter night with the temperature at zero and two feet of snow! It couldn't be possible. But the music was still there, now just above the cabin roof, now down over the lake. We rushed out bareheaded and there by the open water patch below our bank were three fat little gray dippers, or water ouzels, with short bobbing tails. A pair were around early this month, but they did not sing. Neither of us had an idea that any bird ever sang at night in the depths of winter, much less a northern one. In vivid moonlight we could see them distinctly dipping and bobbing on rocks in the cold shining water — and singing. Their song echoed back and forth so that all the lake was ringing with it. When we went inside again the birds flew above our roof and poured their music down on us. No European nightingale, singing in a hot, lush summer evening, ever wove the spell of enchantment that the dippers did with those crystal tinkles, which matched so perfectly the icy purity of the winter night.

November 24

The snow is now over three feet deep, and the thermometer drops a little lower each day. On several mornings lately it has been 15 or 20 below. Three pairs of dippers are now with us constantly and we're beginning to believe that they intend to stay all winter. They've become our greatest source of music and gay company. The colder it is the more they seem to like it. They spend most of their time in open patches of water below the cabin or around a near-by point.

For a distance of at least thirty yards from shore where the deep springs gush out under the banks, the lake is still unfrozen. The temperature of the water doesn't seem to be affected by the temperature of the air. The water stays at 38 degrees F. whether the thermometer outside our cabin reads 32 above or 20 below.

Here the dippers swim and dive and hunt for insects along rocks and pebbles of the bottom, or float on the surface like miniature ducks. Sometimes they dive down in one spot, swim far under water, or below an expanse of ice, and come up in an open hole thirty feet away, as dry and merry and sparkling as if they had never been near the water. Their aquatic skill is remarkable, and their powers of flight no less so. When they tire of swimming or feeding, they fly high in the air, over our cabin or above the forest, singing as they go and chasing each other in endless games. And they spiral down from the sky, showering music, like the English skylarks. They sing on and off all through the day and often some hours after dark, as they did when we first heard them. They are quite tame and friendly. When I go to the lake for water, one always flies over, perches on a rock near by to sing, or begins to feed.

On the twentieth J. collected a northern shrike (our second one) feeding on a red-backed mouse which it had just caught; the mouse was still warm. I prepared the shrike for the Museum but, though the mouse skull was still intact, the skin was too badly torn to make up. We're determined to stick to our vow and collect two or more specimens if possible of everything for purposes of correct identification. With the birds, which we love especially, it is easier to collect a new species as soon as we see it before it becomes a real friend to us. Moreover, when a new bird appears it is well to get it at once, for we never can be sure how long it will stay, or whether it will reappear ever again!

The first time we saw them we also collected one of the dippers. Now, when I remember the small plump body which I skinned, I can understand how dippers keep warm and dry in icy waters and bitter weather. The uropygial gland over the tail, which birds may use for oiling their feathers, was unusually large; the feathers themselves seemed exceptionally oily and therefore could not easily become wet. Beneath the skin was an almost continuous layer of dense fat that must be a real protection against cold. The stomach was full of half-digested water insects. The remarkably strong well-knit little wings accounted for the dippers' skill in both flying and swimming, and no doubt make up for the lack of webbed feet possessed by most water birds that swim as continually as they do.

A tame female American goldeneye now spends all day in the open water along with the dippers. She is a sweet thing with her sleek red-brown head, orange-tipped bill, and yellow topaz eyes. She too dives and splashes merrily in ice water when the temperature is far below zero.

J. has begun to snare varying hares, or snowshoe rabbits. He makes a little loop at the end of a piece of wire and hangs it across a rabbit runway. The rabbit runs into it, the branch from which it is hung snaps up, the loop tightens and the rabbit must be choked to death instantly, for there are never any signs of a struggle. Apparently these rabbits are cannibals, for we sometimes find a dead one partially eaten. All around the carcass there are nothing but other rabbit tracks and bloody patches where they've placed a bit of their brother's flesh to feed on. The Indians say that they have frequently noted this same occurrence on their trap lines.

The rabbits are lovely-looking things, their huge cushions of feet covered with the soft pale yellow fur that acts as a snowshoe. The thick fur of their bodies, light brown next the skin but white on the surface, is soft as down and is shot with delicate pencil marks of black, and their big ears are edged in black velvet. Their faces have small tan markings, and their eyes are large and brown. They are far lovelier than the insipid pink-eyed white things sold as pets. I'm beginning to fancy an evening cloak of snowshoe rabbit, with a collar of white, black-velvet-bordered rabbits' ears! J. has sworn that I shall have enough skins to make a short coat, anyhow.

J. is collecting a series of rabbits for the Museum. Supposing they would be a pleasant change from the tough, strong old moose meat, we tried eating several. Their flesh is sweet and tender like dark chicken, but oh, the smell! It reminds us of the most disgustingly odorous type of sewage. When J. has skinned one, and I've cleaned it, we've both been so nauseated that we can scarcely swallow it, even after it is cooked. We shall have to give up eating rabbits unless we are actually starving.

The Indians tell us that rabbits have been scarce, but this year are abundant again. Apparently the rabbit population fluctuates considerably, both seasonally and geographically. For several years while rabbits were scarce or nonexistent in this valley, they were thick in the valley on the west of the Driftwoods some fifteen miles away; and though common this year around us they are, apparently, much scarcer in regions north and south of here.

In summer, snowshoe rabbits are brown, but now they blend so perfectly with the snow that we seldom see one alive, though

Snowshoe
Rabbit

F. Gray-headed Chipmunk

there must be hundreds judging from the tracks which are like those of an ordinary cottontail with very big feet. Once, when I was sitting on a stump, I saw one under a willow against a snowbank. I must have been looking at it for ten minutes and never would have noticed it except for the black edge of one ear.

November 26

J. saw a strange sight this morning: a snowshoe rabbit *swimming* in the lake just beyond our bank. It went in leaps and jerks, with great thrusts of its hind feet, and swam out with apparent ease for about forty feet toward the goldeneye. When it was within eight or ten feet, the duck paddled aloofly away, looking as though she weren't sure what to make of it. By the time J. called me the rabbit had turned and come back to shore. When we went out, floundering in deep snow, we could see its tracks leading down to the water where it had apparently gone in with deliberate intent, coming out later on the bank in the same spot. There were no tracks of any other animal.

November 30

We're out of meat again except for bacon and a few canned things. For a time we managed to get grouse, but they've become very scarce. Moreover their meat is horribly strong because they must now feed exclusively on evergreens since there are no longer buds and leaves of deciduous trees. Instead of grouse flesh we feel as if we were eating spruce bark; their crops are crammed to bursting with spruce needles.

J. is able sometimes with the .22 to shoot small white fish that come into the open water below the bank. Trout seldom run up into this lake — probably it's too shallow and lacks sufficient food — and are confined to the river. But one morning we found a six-pound Dolly Varden, nicely cleaned and decapitated, lying on an icebank by the springs. It had probably been left by an otter, and we appropriated it promptly, with best thanks. It made us three good meals.

Most of all, we long for fat. Nothing here seems greasy

enough, and we pour grease out of a pan on bread or even eat it plain. Our bodies, which use ever-increasing stores of energy, are apparently preparing themselves properly for the mighty cold to come. We have plenty of butter, which keeps indefinitely in sealed tins. But even butter, in addition to bacon grease, is not enough. J. says we must have fat meat, which only a moose can provide. At this season moose are fat, for their bodies too have been storing up for winter.

J. now spends day after day out hunting. He usually goes east beyond the valley of beaver ponds because moose tracks are more common there than elsewhere. He won't let me go with him, for, if he gets on the track of a moose, I can't travel nearly as fast or as far as he can. So I stay at home, trying to occupy myself usefully while he's away. Several times he's been gone until after dark. I find that doing a big baking of yeast bread or washing clothes is the best way to absorb mind and energies, but — I'm scared stiff all the time he is gone! I'm always stopping to look at the weather and listen for shots. We've agreed that two shots fired close together, in a series of two, will be our signal of distress. As the day wears on, I get into a fever of listening and waiting, unable to settle down to anything. This sort of thing, far more than a lack of meat, is wearing me thin.

I wonder if J. has any idea how I feel when I'm left behind. It's not that I mind being alone — though I'm always a bit apprehensive that some tough Indian or white man may appear that I won't be able to handle — it's the dread of J.'s not coming back, of his getting hurt, or lost, or sick from his old injury. He always tells me the general direction he expects to travel but, when one chases a moose, one never has any idea in what direction the moose may finally lead one. He says "don't worry" if he doesn't come back one night, but to wait until well on into the next day before I start to search for him!

CHAPTER IV

Deep Winter

The ever-increasing depth of snow makes the land ever more beautiful, and makes us more and more hard work. There are now five feet on the level, and still the snow comes down every few days. It falls straight, in dense quiet clouds that suffocate us. It's like a giant flour sifter being turned on, and off, and on again. There is never any real wind and almost as soon as it clouds over flakes begin to fall. In five minutes the mountains, the forests, the lake, are blotted out; there is nothing but a white whirlpool beyond the windowpanes and we are living in a world made solely of the space within four walls of the cabin. Every sound is muffled. Our voices seem to come from far away and we're inclined to shout at each other. Sometimes it makes us feel as though we were living under water. Even in the deep sleep of night we can never escape from the sensation that it is snowing. And if we wake, we feel the way one does when, rising too slowly after a long dive in deep water, one struggles for breath. When I was a child I could never have enough snow. Safe in a well-heated house, the more snow, the more I rejoiced, and the more security I felt. But this is something different. The very quietness and persistency of it all is somehow ruthless and frightening.

"The only thing that keeps us from being buried alive," I often say to J., "is the cabin. How can animals live in this? What on earth happens to Indians out on a trap line miles from home?"

Then J. tells me about the terrible blizzards of the arctic tundra where snow, unhindered by hills or trees, is blown by sixty-mile gales over the flat expanse, and no man or beast can live through it unless he can stay under shelter until it has blown itself out. But J. says the deadly stillness and monotony of snowfalls here is far harder on the nerves, though less fraught with danger.

In a world so completely white (even the dark green of woods is now hidden under heaped-up snow) one might suppose there would be a monotonous lack of color. But the snow is always reflecting lovely shades from sky and clouds, red and gold and green of sunrises and sunsets, blue and purple lights and shadows. And the little open water patch of Tetana is a mirror for the sky.

Many of the tallest trees are bowed nearly double under the great weight of snow, but it is surprising how few of them ever really break. Always, after a storm, before the fresh breezes appear to chase the clouds away, a gentle stir comes, only a breath at first, that sways the trees softly, and frees them gradually and carefully of their terrible burden. When one constantly watches the workings of a wilderness one comes to know that things are cared for with a surprising orderliness and steadfastness — it would seem with definite purpose. It gives one a sort of faith, and a deep, abiding comfort.

As soon as the snow stops we open the door, climb into the snowbank outside, and begin to clear out the entrance and caches of wood. We now have another shovel which J. made from a pole and the sides of an old box. The windows have continually to be dug out to let in daylight. And one, or both, of us pull thundering masses of snow off the roof because we're afraid that the weight (so much greater than we ever anticipated) may break the rafters. If snow is allowed to remain on the roof long enough for the heat from the cabin to melt it, it turns to ice and becomes impossible to scrape off.

We can't even step outside our door any more without snowshoes. Snowshoes are as essential a part of walking as one's own two legs. Skis are not used in this country. The snow is too deep and soft, the forest too thick and extensive, and no traveling on the mountains is done until spring. When the snowshoes are not in the cabin being dried off (it's important to keep the webbing dry so that snow won't stick to it and add extra pounds of weight), they are stuck upright in a drift, and, as we go out, we step directly into them. We have three pairs, bought last fall when we came through Takla. They are larger and quite different from the flat snowshoes used in the Eastern United States, or the little round bear paws which are all that are necessary in the Arctic. These have high upturned toes and the webbing, except that directly beneath the feet, is very fine and breaks easily. The turned-up fronts and fine webbing are necessary in this climate, for the snow is so soft that flat pointed toes would trip one and coarse webbing would let one sink far below the surface.

Our snowshoe trails are beginning to radiate in every direction. They're covered constantly by fresh snow, but if they're not neglected too long, we can usually find traces of them. Since there is no wind, the snow seldom drifts and sometimes there is a faint depression to indicate a trail, or we can feel with our snowshoes a certain hard line underneath all the fresh snow as opposed to the softness on either side. We try to reopen the trails after each new storm, and we've marked them by big blazes chopped as high up on trees as we can reach. Walking on a trail that already has some sort of firm foundation is the only way to get about. The snow is so deep and fine that it's an exhausting business to go through it even on snowshoes.

We are completely cut off; for it would be impossible to travel more than a few miles a day on an unbroken trail.

This is a dead world. Even the clear throbbing silence that we knew at first is muffled by the deep snow that blankets the trees. When we walk in the forest, we feel as if our ears were stuffed with cotton. I'm more terrified than ever of being separated from J., for we've discovered that even a loud pistol shot can't be heard a quarter of a mile away, and shouts don't carry for more than twenty yards.

Now there are practically no signs of animal life. When snow in this country is too soft and deep for man to travel it is also too difficult for animals. The squirrels, except for two that haunt our feeding station, seem to have retired permanently to winter quarters. There is not a marten track. Even the moose, with their long legs, have evidently found the snow too deep, for they appear to have left this region entirely. All the little mammals have retired to subterranean passages way below the surface. By setting traps far down under old logs and stumps, we are still able to catch mice and shrews.

But we begin to wonder if our sole contribution on winter habits of animals in forests of the North is to be a statement to the effect that all but the smallest either leave the country or go into a state of hibernation and hole up completely!

December 11

I am fairly proficient at negotiating the steep bank, filling two pails with water, and hauling them up again to our front door where they must be eased *down,* one at a time, through the narrow snow entrance. Digging out a path is pure waste effort since it is filled in a twinkling. Snow is inclined to pile on the bank, and as there is a great drift all across it at least ten feet deep, this daily process of fetching water takes time and strength. Sometimes I trip and the world turns to a tangled mess of arms and legs and snowshoes and water and upset pails. If J. is not near I have to be particularly careful because I can't always manage to pull myself up out of the layers and layers of icy down. J.'s snowshoes are twice the size of mine because he is almost twice as heavy. But he has become adept at hopping about on them while he chops down a tree, lops off the branches, and cuts it into lengths of log which both he and I can carry on our shoulders.

Getting firewood is the worst job of all. We had no time to acquire a proper winter's supply, and this is a handicap in experiencing a northern winter, which no one would ever choose to face. When temperatures drop to 30 or 40 below, a hot fire burning night and day is a necessary part of life. We are doubly handicapped, for we were not only unable to lay in a supply ahead of time, but also J. should not yet do a strong man's full-time job. Nevertheless he must do this and more every single day in order to keep us alive.

First, he tramps about until he finds a dead tree with the wood well-seasoned and light enough to handle and burn well. Then he hits the tree with his axe and jumps back, while hundreds of pounds of snow fall from the branches. He repeats these gymnastics until the tree is nearly free, and he can chop it down without being knocked flat and buried under an avalanche. When the logs are cut they must be carried to the cabin, half a mile or even as far as a mile away. The few Indians that camped at Tetana now and again for years before we came have exhausted most of the good firewood near at hand. We now burn two or three trees (about twelve or fourteen inches in diameter) every twenty-four hours.

I carry the smaller logs. J. taught me how to balance them on my shoulder and hold them with one arm, in order to save strength and muscles as much as possible. It takes time and maneuvering to get the log to balance perfectly and, once loaded, I think a long while before I painfully set the log down, end up in snow, in order to rest. J. has to load me and then I must keep on until I reach the cabin, because I cannot load myself.

At first I thought this logging job would be the end of me. When I follow, sweating and panting, in J.'s tracks, balancing on my shoulder a log half the size and weight of his, my lungs almost burst and my ribs and shoulders feel as though they were being torn from their sockets! Sometimes I struggle along far behind J., tears streaming down my face from sheer physical pain. But I think my muscles *are,* at last, beginning to adapt themselves a little, for now it does not seem quite so hard. Even when the logs are hauled to the back door, the woodcutting labors are by no means finished. For the logs must be sawed into proper lengths to fit our tiny stove, and these in turn must be split before they can be carried in and burned.

But despite all the daily hardships which sometimes seem almost more than our bodies can endure, we are deeply content. I can't think of anyone in the world with whom I'd change places. This must be what is meant by perfect happiness. There is infinite satisfaction in hard physical work well done, and in the completely relaxed, quiet nerves that follow. And there are the diamond sparkling air, the beauty on which we feast our eyes, the nights and days which we share in close companionship, undisturbed by any other human beings.

The very few birds and animals that have stayed around the cabin in the depths of this great winter are becoming our warm friends and comrades. We all share a common bond in the hardships of intense cold and deep snow. The crumbs and scraps of food that we can save from our own meager meals, we put out on the snowbanks. The tiny chickadees, the Canada jays, puffed into soft gray feather balls against the cold, and the two squirrels, now await our every emergence from the cabin door in hopes of food. The birds are so eager that they have begun to fly directly to our hands and shoulders. The dippers, feeding on an apparently inexhaustible supply of water insects, still make lovely music and play in the open water along with the friendly little goldeneye.

During the day the sun stays always in the southern sky; it passes across from southeast to southwest. It doesn't come up till half-past nine in the morning; by half-past two in the afternoon it goes down behind the Driftwoods. Soon after three it's dark, and we come in, light our little coal-oil lamp, pile up the stove, and settle down for tea and games, reading, writing, or skinning specimens. Our eyes, which once grew tired from reading by bright electric lamps, don't ever seem to grow tired here, though we read far longer than we ever did at home. J. is going straight through the rather fine print of Shakespeare's plays.

After supper, when dishes are washed, I wind the clock and cross off the calendar. This is a ritual followed religiously at the same time every night. If one day is neglected, we might never find it again. But we are becoming surprisingly efficient at telling time by the sun without the aid of watch or clock. We are not nearly up to the Indians, however. Even on sunless days they seem able, nearly always, to tell the correct time within half to three quarters of an hour. We have tested them by our watches over and over again. J. fills in a daily weather chart; this serves as a check on the clock and calendar. We sink down then in our chairs, moccasined feet stretched to the stove, with sighs of sheer joy in the certainty that nothing will disturb us. For by twilight in winter every living thing must be holed up safely in order to survive the cruel night.

When the spirit moves us, say about once a week, we take a bath. I mean a real bath in the washtub. J. packs the tub with snow and sets it on the little stove (which it almost obliterates) to melt. A full tub of snow becomes one third of a tub of water, or much less, depending on whether the snow is solidly packed, or dry and light. We keep adding snow until we have the desired amount of water. When the water is hot, we set the tub on the floor and proceed. Since there is some slight feeling over which of us shall have the first bath in pure water and which the second in dirty, we take turns. I am just able, by sitting with knees drawn up to my chest, to squeeze my whole body in the tub. J., at least twice as large as I, must hang his legs out. He feels rather bitter about this. We scrub each other's backs because the slightest turning projects a flood across the cabin. Nothing is softer and sweeter than snow water, and we always use one of the two cakes of lavender soap for these special occasions.

No one need suppose that, because we take tub baths rather rarely, we go dirty! I have never felt cleaner in my life. There is no dirt, anyhow, in this great pure snow world to make one feel unclean.

Dressed in a few, warm, lightweight clothes, I'm always delightfully comfortable, warmer really than I ever was at home in winter. I wear light wool "long-handled" underwear, woolen ski pants, shirt and sweater, and three pairs of wool socks and a sort of light slipper, which we made from pieces of Hudson's Bay blanket, under the moose-skin moccasins. Ever since cold weather set in we have worn moccasins exclusively just as J. predicted. These are as soft and flexible as chamois skin and so light I feel as if I were going around barefoot. As long as they are dry, my feet keep warm all day, even when I'm out in deep

snow. Tight, or stiff, shoes that bind the toes in the slightest
degree are useless. This costume, with the addition of a parka,
wool cap, and two pairs of mittens (woolen ones inside and
moose skin outside) when we go out, seems to be exactly right
even in the coldest temperatures which, so far, have reached 38
below.

Thanks to J.'s instructions I'm learning countless little
wrinkles on how to care for clothes in winter. Every speck of
snow must be brushed off before it has time to melt in the
warmth of a cabin or campfire. Sometimes one spends five or
ten minutes scraping snow off moccasins (above all, moccasins),
trousers, jacket, and cap with a big knife, stick, or mittens.

The fewer the clothes, the more freely and lightly one's
body can move and hence the warmer one is. But one must
have two sufficiently woolly layers and something windproof
for outside. To pile on additional layers, however, is a great mistake, either when dressed for outside or going to bed. Extra
clothing in bed, I find, not only hampers the circulation, but
also prevents the heat of my body from warming the sleeping
bag around me. Going to bed without any nightclothes on, as
the Eskimos do, is really the warmest of all. J., reverting to the
days when he traveled and camped with the huskies, often goes
to bed stark naked. I've tried it and it works well — until morning. Getting out of bed, naked, with the thermometer *inside*
the cabin at zero, or below, is just too rude a shock.

But I am surprised that I don't feel the cold more. At home
10 or 20 below is considered so severe that people hardly dare
venture out. Here we think nothing of it. I sit nonchalantly
around in the woods, watching J. set traps, or chop, and scarcely
remember that it is cold at all.

December 14

The other afternoon, when we supposed that the softness of
the six feet of snow now on the ground would make it impossible for any living thing to be abroad, we were, literally, scared
stiff when a strange voice outside suddenly shouted, "Hey
Jack!" When one has lived for weeks and weeks in a world still

as death, with no sight or thought of other human beings, the
first sound of an unknown voice is terrifying.

The voice belonged to a tall old Indian with iron-gray hair;
even before he told us we knew that this was Chief Bear Lake
Charlie. Later, as he sat in the cabin drinking tea, I was fairly
fascinated by the sight and sound of him. He is big and finely
built like Michelle. Although he had that day snowshoed eight
or ten miles through the great depth of snow, in order to pay
us an hour's visit, he did not seem at all fatigued. He did not
look ill, nor did he show any signs of having to "spit blood" according to the gruesome description of his son. Underneath a
Mounty's old broad-brimmed Stetson, a dark silk handkerchief
was tied round his head; he needed only gold rings in his ears
to look the perfect pirate. He wore a bright red bandana around
his neck, a gray wool shirt, gray flannel trousers with an array
of pink and blue gingham patches, and the usual wet moose-skin
moccasins on his feet. His rifle he carried in a beaded and
fringed moose-skin case, and he was accompanied by the strong
pungent smell of wood smoke which I am beginning always to
associate with these people. He had a funny high squeaky voice
that sounded oddly in his powerful chest, and all the time
that we were listening to his steady flow of polite conversation,
he examined us as carefully as we did him. When he was not
holding his cup, he fingered the large crucifix hung round his
neck. The crucifix was a guarantee as to the truth of all state-
ments, for he reminded us repeatedly that he, "Big Bear Lake
Chief, could not lie."

After tea, when Charlie had accepted some of J.'s tobacco,
and they both were smoking, we all relaxed and the conversation became more general. From Charlie we learned what
seems to be the true Indian meaning of the word "Tetana."
Charlie told us that it is a phrase which means "The lake that
flows into the river."

After we had all extolled Tetana, we talked of the winter,
which Charlie declares to be more severe than usual.

"The moose he go, ebery one to south. Beeg trail he make in
snow, all go same way. Bad winter come now. I don' know what

de matter. I neber see dis before. No good, dis. Bad luck for
Indian and white man. Moose go: no food, no clothes, no
medicine."

We discussed trapping and the proper directions of the
various trap lines that pass through the Driftwood Valley. J.
showed Charlie, as he has shown each Indian who comes here,
the exact number of steel traps he possesses — about ten ranging
from a number 0 to a number 4 — and our official permits, explaining that we are not interested in fur or trading. We want
only one or two skins of each of the medium and large-sized
mammals for the Museum, and all the heads and skulls we can
get. We're especially anxious for the Indians to realize that we
have no desire to acquire fur, or take enough animals to interfere in the slightest degree with their trap lines. I wonder
whether they believe us.

Charlie asked a few tactful and leading questions about the
other Indians who have been here, but we refused to be drawn
into divulging any bits of information that we have gathered
from anyone.

Charlie's trap-line claims agree more or less with Michelle's.
Each Indian, so far, has declared that the others are poaching
on his lines. None of their claims exactly correspond to the
ones marked on our copy of the game warden's map. We seem
to be in the midst of serious controversy, but there is no way of
checking up until we can write to the game warden or Indian
agent and receive a reply; and that may not be until next year.
Charlie hinted darkly concerning the bad qualities of the other
Indians, in particular Vinson, who he says "make trouble all
time."

We tried to tell Charlie of our interest in the wilderness and
what our work is, and he was excessively polite and encouraging. He has always been the white man's friend.

"All white man, he want me work for him all time. I good.
More better than other Indian. I know what white man he do,
see?"

We arranged with Charlie to have his boys come a few days
after Christmas to take us for a visit to the Bear Lake settle-

ment. And we traded flour and sugar which he wanted for some dry old moose meat and a piece of tough, but delicious, frozen grizzly. Anyhow we have a little meat again and can obtain nourishment by boiling it for hours and chewing each mouthful five minutes. We also bought from Charlie a beautiful big robe made out of marmot skins. The hoary marmot looks like a great, soft gray woodchuck and inhabits these mountain ranges above timber line. Its fur is much prized by the Indians for blankets because it is warm and light and quite durable. About twenty marmots make a robe big enough to cover a double bed.

Before he left Charlie requested a tin can, a candle, and a piece of wire. "Night come," said he, "before I get my camp. Eight, ten mile. Mebbe the trail, I lose him. I make the lantern."

And with the big knife hanging to his belt, he cut away one side of the can and made a hole in the bottom. In the hole he wedged the candle, and he fixed a wire handle at the top. With much chuckling he then lit his lantern and showed us how, by keeping the closed side to the front, the flame would be protected and give forth good light.

"Good-bye Jack. Good-bye Missus. I go now."

And he trudged off on his huge snowshoes, a great, slightly bent, bowlegged figure, his gun over one arm, his tiny tin-can lantern dangling from the other.

So far the Bear Lake Indians about whom we were warned don't seem very terrible. We are in fact inclined to be more agreeably impressed with them than with the Takla Indians. They have a finer physique and, on the surface at least, their manners are better. I noticed that Charlie, like each of the Indians whom we've known so far, appears to have a peculiar sensitivity to our unexpressed thoughts and feelings. This is understandable when one realizes how much more these people depend on the keenness of perception and instinct than on printed words and speech.

Christmas Eve   *December 24*

We've had a long spell of warm, melting weather. Until to-day we almost despaired of seeing the sun again. The temperature has been 32 or 34 degrees above, and masses of snow plus warm air created a blanket-like fog and a dampness that seemed to stifle our very breathing. We could have been living on a waterless, treeless, hill-less plain for all the sign we ever saw of lake, forest, or mountain. Walking on snowshoes, which were heavy and sodden with melting snow, was exhausting; getting firewood an ordeal of strength and endurance.

There have, however, been a few partially clear nights when forests and hills and mountains, glittering with white crust, have appeared again for brief intervals. It has been full moon and, for a few hours at a time, the world was almost too lovely for mortal eyes. Shafts of moonlight, coming between clouds, turned the high edges of the Driftwoods to lines of white gold; lower slopes were deep and black. And luminous beams, like a searchlight, shot across the lake and forest. Sometimes one peak alone was all lit up, while others, soft, hazy dreams, were smudged with violet shadow.

Today we are greeted by a cold snap — just in time for Christmas. It is brilliantly clear and the mountains stand out once more — so distinct that they seem almost on top of the cabin. This afternoon the sun went down behind the Driftwoods at two-fifteen and the mercury began to drop and drop. It went from 36 above to 39 below, a drop of 75 degrees in a few hours. I keep wondering how on earth our bodies can possibly adapt themselves to such extreme changes, but we appear to be in perfect health.

And the cabin, piled round with snow, now keeps warm with only a moderate fire in the stove, no matter what the temperatures. Tonight with the thermometer outside at 40 below, the thermometer inside is 59 above. During the few daylight hours when there is bright sunlight, we scarcely need even a small fire, because the sun, shining in all our windows, creates so much heat.

After supper, when stars were flashing above the snow piled to within a foot of the top windowpanes, I went outside to view the world.

"You won't feel cold," remarked J., "*at first,* but watch your lungs."

As I opened the door I wondered what he was talking about. With the first breath, I knew. I choked and gasped and sputtered. In this temperature one's breath freezes as one inhales and less oxygen than usual is taken into the lungs. Except for this, I simply was unconscious of the cold. By taking little short breaths I found that I could breathe sufficiently well. The snow underfoot was so hard that it didn't seem like snow at all. As I stepped on it, it tinkled musically like pieces of metal striking together.

In these very low temperatures, the air is crystal clear. Over the absolute stillness of the icy night, the stars looked as though they had come alive. These were not the serene, peaceful, far-off stars of summer skies; these were flashing and sparkling and burning, fanned by invisible fires to dazzling life. These were more brilliant than I had ever seen them anywhere, in the tropics or on high mountain tops; the light they shed across the earth was as revealing as clear moonlight. The white lake, the white mountains, the white forests, were glittering in their radiance. At the back of the cabin I saw the Great and Little Bears, the Big and Little Dippers, etched brilliantly and enormously on the sky. The Milky Way was not a narrow band of white light, but a broad twinkling path of individual shining stars stretched across the whole zenith. And to the south, most marvelous of all, was the giant Orion, followed by the Dog Star, Sirius, marching above the Driftwood Valley. The blue-white, moving, living fire of Sirius seemed to light the whole of Lake Tetana. Other stars, flashing darts of red and blue and yellow, danced on the highest peaks and white knife-like edges of the mountains. I could *hear* the stars as they pulsed and moved above me.

When I realized suddenly that I was almost too stiff to move, I went in, and J., who has seen before the sky of an arctic

night, smiled in understanding at the expression on my face.
I thought of the verse from Paulus Gerhardt's old hymn: —

> Now all the heav'nly splendor
> Breaks forth in starlight tender
> From myriad worlds unknown;
> And man, the marvel seeing,
> Forgets his selfish being,
> For joy of beauty not his own.

Christmas Day

Last night when we went to bed the windows on the inside
were covered with frost an inch thick; the logs in the walls, and
the shakes in the roof, cracked like gunshots, as they were split
by the cold; and out on the lake the ice kept up an almost steady
booming, interspersed with the horrid ripping and tearing that
always makes my spine tingle. During the night I was waked
repeatedly by such terrific cracks in the logs that I thought the
cabin was coming down on our heads. When the temperature
is falling, we expect a drop of 15 or 25 degrees during the night,
beginning at sunset, but last night it broke all records.

This morning I was the first one out of bed. These days I
can hardly wait to get up. Whether this is because I'm always
hungry, or because the night is so long, I don't know, but it is
refreshing to be able to jeer at J. as he lies lazily in bed with
his morning smoke. Although when we went to bed last night
we piled up the stove with slow-burning green wood, this
morning the fire was practically out. It was still dark outside;
dawn had not yet begun although it was long past eight. The
windows were so densely frosted that it seemed as if daylight,
even if it were there, could never penetrate the cabin. I lit the
lamp, then carefully laid the pile of shavings, as always un-
failingly prepared by J. the evening before, in the front of the
stove and applied a match. After which I delicately laid on
more shavings and then larger and larger sticks. Everything was
ice cold and I was careful not to touch any metal with bare
hands, having learned from bitter experience that skin, especially moist skin, freezes fast and is sometimes peeled right off
at the slightest contact with very cold metal. Still clad in bath-

robe and slippers, I went to scrape away the frost and read the thermometer outside. I realized then that, although I didn't feel chilled, I could hardly move my arms.

"I'll just see what the temperature is *inside* first," I thought, and went to peer at the thermometer hanging above our dining table. It read 25 below. Gosh! That couldn't be right! How could we sleep like that, how could I be wandering around with only a wrapper on? I *must* see what it was outside!

I couldn't even find the mercury. It dawned on me, after a time, that it had gone its limit and jammed at 50 below. My exclamations roused J. and we were so busy arguing over the thermometer that we forgot to say "Merry Christmas." I was convinced that if the mercury could have gone beyond 50 it would have read at least 60 below. J. said it was not much colder than 50; that he could tell from past experience in the Arctic just how many degrees the temperature drops when it gets beyond 45 below. For one thing, if it is 55 or more below, when hot water is poured out of a window, it freezes solid before it reaches the snow level. I could hardly wait until we had hot water to try this experiment. Sure enough — when, later, I poured a stream from the teakettle onto the snow outside, the water steamed and twisted into threads, but did not turn actually solid till it reached the ground. We must put out our unused thermometer whose scale goes to 60 below.

By the time dawn was coming we had scraped two peepholes in the frost on the panes; and we stood quiet to watch the winter sunrise. The radiant peaks of the Driftwoods, cut like white icing into pinnacles and rims against the apple-green sky, were brushed with pink, that, even as we watched, spread down and down and turned to gold. Rays of the rising sun, coming between the pointed firs of the east shore, stretched straight across the white lake, and as they touched it huge crystals, formed by the intense cold, burst into sparkling, scintillating light. The snow-bowed trees of the south and west shores were hung with diamonds; and finally the willows, around our cabin, were decked with jewels as large as robins' eggs that flashed red and green and blue. No Christmas trees decorated by human hands were ever so exquisite as the frosted trees of this northern forest. The sky turned to deep, deep blue, and the white world burst into dazzling, dancing colors as the sun topped the forest. The dippers, undismayed by a cold that froze dumb all other living things, broke into their joyous tinkling melody by the open water patch below the bank. And our first Christmas Day in the wilderness was upon us.

After a breakfast of canned grapefruit which we had been saving especially, and pancakes with the last of our syrup, also preserved scrupulously for Christmas, we did our usual chores. I cleaned the cabin and began a round of baking. In addition to bannock, which I bake daily either in the drum oven or in an open frypan on top of the stove, I made tarts of strawberry jam and a chocolate cake. As these favorite articles of diet make inroads on a meager supply of crisco, jam, and sugar we have them only for very special celebrations.

When I went outside to scatter crumbs for our furred and feathered friends, the jays were almost too stiff to move. Instead of flying down to snatch the food before it left my hand, they sat on the spruce branches, their feathers so fluffed up that I could hardly distinguish head from tail. Sometimes they moved near the smoke from our stovepipe, which was giving forth some warmth. The chickadees, tiny as they are, though also tremendously puffed out, were slightly more active than the jays.

Why are some animals in this country so much better equipped for cold than others? There are the dippers, for example, whose nerves and organs are, seemingly, completely unaffected by an almost arctic temperature. Twice, during this month, we've watched a pair performing the act of coition on a snowbank.

Toward noon the temperature moderated enough for us to enjoy a tramp. That is, it had gone up from 50, or whatever below it was, to 36 below. Our snowshoes tossed up clouds of crystals. Young trees which, in autumn, had reached above our heads had been completely covered with fresh snow, so that they were transformed into great mounds and small hills. Wherever we looked our eyes were dimmed by the twinkling brilliants scattered before us. The azure of the sky above, the unsullied whiteness below, the mountains and the woods, the intense pureness of the air, were exhilarating beyond imagining. And there was not a sound or a motion, anywhere, to distract our senses of sight and feeling.

Soon after noon the temperature began dropping again, fast. Our faces, which we rubbed constantly with wool mitts, began to show a tendency toward frostbite, and J.'s right big toe, once badly frozen in arctic tundras, was starting to pain severely. So we turned homeward.

As daylight faded, the rays of the sinking sun tinted the snow with red and lavender. The mountains grew purple and then came that period which, if I could make a choice of the wonders of all the twenty-four hours of a winter's day, seems the most wonderful of all. It is that moment of white twilight which comes on a particularly clear afternoon, after the last colors of sunset fade and just before the first stars shine out. I don't suppose its like can be seen anywhere except in the snowbound, ice-cold arctic places. Everything in the universe becomes a luminous white. Even the dark trees of the forest, and the sky overhead, are completely colorless. It is the ultimate perfection of purity and peace. But even as one looks and wonders, the white sky takes on a faint pale green, there are the stars, and then the great winter's night is upon one.

We had our Christmas dinner at five: dehydrated potatoes and onions and a bit of moose steak, especially saved and tendered, baked in a pan with stuffing. For dessert there were the jam tarts and chocolate cake. With these vanished the last vestiges of Christmas, the things which made it a little different from our other days.

Have we greatly missed the things that make Christmas Day in civilization? Other loved human beings, Christmas carols, wonderful food? I suppose so, but I think that this lack is more than made up for by the deep contentment of our healthy minds and bodies, by our closeness to and awareness of the earth, and of each other.

CHAPTER V

Siwashing

New Year's Day has come and gone and there has been never a sign of old Chief Charlie's sons who were to have come right after Christmas to guide us to Bear Lake. So tomorrow, we shall start out to find Bear Lake for ourselves.

We're in a bit of a tough situation. There is no letup for J. in the incessant daily tree chopping. He's not strong enough to cut sufficient wood at one time to last several days. No matter how hard I try, I am not able to cut big trees. Now J.'s injured back is beginning to show unmistakable warning symptoms. We've decided that we *must* have help with the wood, and if no one will come to us, we must go and fetch someone. The only inhabited place, short of Takla Landing, is the Indian settlement at Bear Lake.

We know the direction of the lake and with any luck in finding the trail, we may reach the settlement in two or three days. We can then visit the trader whom we met last summer at Takla and, possibly, find some Indian who just may be ambitious enough to return with us and cut wood, especially if we offer him an outrageous sum — by this time, we're willing to pay if necessary $7.00, or more, for a cord! Anyhow we figure the trip is worth trying and better than letting J. continue to run the risk of cracking up seriously.

We've made up our packs with care and only after hours of figuring out absolute necessities: food, sleeping bags, guns, and axe. Since we can't carry the additional weight of a tent, we'll have to siwash under trees. This term appears to mean camping out without shelter, other than what one makes from the natural materials at hand. Indians of the north who camp in this manner are commonly called Siwashes. We have few illusions about traveling in winter, but snowshoeing is easier than it was in December; the deep powdery snow has settled and hardened a little. After the bitter cold of Christmas week the temperatures are mild — around zero and above. It is clear. Now is the time to be off, before a new storm or fresh cold sets in.

We have in our knapsacks one frypan, one pot, two cups, spoons, knives, a can opener, a tiny first-aid kit, and extra socks, moccasins, and mitts. Food supplies for four days in the way of tea, powdered coffee and milk, sugar, salt, baked beans, bacon, raisins, prunes, and chocolate. I made up packets of cocoa, sugar, and powdered milk, each enough for one cup, which will need only the addition of boiling water. J. showed me how to bake a very hard stiff bannock that will keep almost indefinitely. Yeast bread is useless in low temperatures; it simply crumbles to pieces. Strapped on top of our knapsacks are the fur marmot robe, our two lightweight down sleeping bags (they each weigh one and three-quarters pounds), and a piece of canvas that can be used as either cover or windbreak. We each have a pistol, hunting knife, and matches; J. will carry the big game rifle, axe, and whetstone (dull knives or axes in this country are worthless). I carry the .22; we must try to shoot grouse for meat along the way and, if we see some rare winter bird, it will be posible with the .22 to collect it for the Museum.

If only we could forget that we are Scientists, our packs might be reasonably comfortable! In addition to the absolute necessities, we have cameras, field glasses, notebook, and skinning kit. J. carries the heavy movie, I the Leica. The chief weights are the cameras and guns. J.'s rifle alone weighs nine pounds. His whole outfit amounts to almost sixty pounds, about twenty pounds too much for him in his condition. I have thirty, and my pack feels at least ten pounds heavier than it should. But we can't seem to cut the loads down further by even an ounce.

We've examined our snowshoes for any weak spots in webbing or frame. The harness is freshly greased and softened, and tested for a perfect fit on each foot. If snowshoes or harness give way, or feel uncomfortable, traveling becomes difficult or actually impossible. The experienced traveler of the northern wilderness fusses over and tests the condition of his feet and footgear before every trip, even more carefully than the man in civilization checks over his car before he begins a long tour.

I've given the cabin a thorough straightening up; nothing is more depressing than to return to an untidy abode. We've stored perishables, such as the morphine and tetanus antitoxin, and all cans and bottles in the "cellar." After the temperatures of Christmas week one can't tell what may happen.

We start at daybreak and I *hope* my next heading will be "Bear Lake."

Tetana   *January 6*

Safely back again, thank heaven, but alas! We did *not* find Bear Lake!

On January 3rd, just before we started, I was afflicted with one of my dropping spells. I upset a whole pan of beans all across the floor. The beans, our only breakfast food, were to have stood by us all day, not to mention the fact that here you daren't ever waste a single thing, not even one bean. J. eyed me and sniggered audibly. I wasn't sure whether I was more relieved at this attitude or disgusted at his heartlessness. Finally we ate a little stew, one of four precious cans that were to have been saved till spring, and at nine, when it was light enough to see, started off for Bear Lake. Despite the seven-foot snow level we followed the trail without difficulty three miles north to the long narrow stretch of willow flats and open marshy fields, called by the Indians Hudson Bay Meadow. Three jays, who had been gathering up breakfast crumbs and trilling and twittering around as we put on packs and snowshoes, began, as is their invariable custom, to follow us away from the cabin; but the farther away we got, the more harsh and scolding and definitely disapproving their notes grew.

"Well, by golly! the little beggars really know we're going on a long trip this time," said J.

They followed us all the three miles to Hudson Bay Meadow,

Canada Jay

J. '38.

J. '37

Red Squirrel

where, with parting angry chatters, they left us in disgust. The chatters said: —

"If you insist on going off from a perfectly good home at this time of year and, what's more, leaving us without food to depend on, it's your own lookout; don't blame us if you have a bad time and don't get back safely!"

The highly intelligent behavior of these jays is becoming one of our most interesting studies. So far, when we've left the cabin together, the jays have followed us for half a mile or so, their notes, like plaintive question marks, seeming to inquire: —

"Where are you going?"

But when only one of us has left they never appeared to notice. They had not, until the other day when we set out with heavy packs, ever followed us steadily for so long a distance, scolding continuously.

Apparently most birds can't count. If two people go into a bird blind and one walks away the birds evidently suppose that both have gone and soon return to their nest or behave in an otherwise natural manner. Some observers claim, however, that crows can distinguish differences in numbers of people; and nearly all authorities admit that crows, and various members of their family such as the jays, show an exceptional intelligence for the bird world. It looks as though these Canada jays were not only aware of the difference between one and two persons, but, like dogs, were able also to detect changes in the general appearance and wearing apparel of human beings. Since they act as scavengers and hang around the Indians of this country who are always breaking up camps or leaving cabins to go elsewhere for a time, the jays have probably learned to understand this mode of behavior and realize that it means a cessation of one of their best food supplies.

When we reached Hudson Bay Meadow, we had our first rest. With grunts and groans we dropped our packs, and unhung the cameras and field glasses and guns which cramped our arms. J. leaned against a tree to smoke, I sat on the crossed heels of my snowshoes. Though the Driftwood and Bear Lake Mountains were still west and north, their shapes had changed a little and they wore a slightly new aspect. We gazed up the long winding so-called meadow, a half mile wide, now just a flat white expanse under a sheet of snow.

J. waved across a stretch of forest-covered hills and ridges to the end of the Bear Lake range — "The trail leads over there; then we should strike the lake."

"That doesn't look bad," said I; "we might be there before night?"

"Even if we reach the south end of Bear Lake, though, remember it's another long day up to the settlement, if what we've heard about distance is accurate."

Surprisingly enough, the snow was very much deeper on the other side of the meadow. Axe cuts made usually some six or seven feet above ground, to indicate a winter trail, were practically covered; and then suddenly, we couldn't find any blazes at all. The snow was at least eight or nine feet on the level and it was softer than it had been around Tetana. We floundered about helplessly trying to uncover more blazes on the trees, or see any marks left by human beings.

Never in my life have I imagined so much snow. It was terrifying. The whole familiar world was buried, covered, suffocated. There was not a sign of life other than the big trees which were curiously dwarfed against the high level of the white crust and seemed to be almost buried themselves. No birds or animal tracks. Just nothing at all but snow and trees and silence. Finally, after we had wasted a whole hour of precious time, and it seemed hopeless, we discovered an old pitch-covered axe mark again, then a few more, mostly buried, but they were leading in the right direction. By digging around trees at intervals, we slowly and tediously unraveled the trail. Farther on where the snow seemed less high again, we found blazes more easily. We took turns breaking trail, because it is infinitely less tiring to follow in other snowshoe prints which have helped to mash the snow down. When we lost the trail we went back to the last blaze and hunted until we found it again. Twice there were blazes leading in two directions, but each time one set petered out before long and we returned to the other.

As usual we traveled in complete restful silence. To be able to gain thoughts and impressions all one's own, unsullied by vocal observations from companions, exactly as if one were walking by oneself, is sheer pleasure. This gift of quiet is one which inhabitants' of the civilized world don't possess. They don't understand that impressions are often far more impressive if no word is spoken. Besides, when one travels a wilderness, being quiet so that one can really use one's senses of sight and hearing and feeling is a necessary safeguard. Though sometimes I accuse J. of being garrulous in polite society (when I am apt to be rather quiet), the minute he strikes the wilds J. becomes the big silent man! (J. always adapts himself to environment better than I do.)

When we were first married and took guests walking in our Pennsylvania woods, I used to be perturbed because J. refused to take part in the conversations. In fact, he often wandered off by himself, or refused to go along at all. Now I think I comprehend perfectly. After years in wildernesses with comrades who were themselves of the wilderness, J. found it extremely distasteful to walk in wild places with people who chattered. J. told me once how, after traveling all day with an Eskimo across the Barrens, he was unable to elicit any verbal response whatever from his companion. Later, in reply to J.'s comment on this mode of companionship, the Eskimo remarked that as they both had eyes and could see the same things, where was the use of talking?

In the early afternoon we called another halt and sat down to eat bannock and raisins. We longed for hot tea but, since every sort of dry stick or branch was buried in snow, we should have had to chop down a dead tree for even a tiny fire; and we decided not to waste time or energy. We had been traveling steadily through thick timber. The mountains were invisible and there were no means of judging progress. But we had at least been following the trail with some success, and we set blithely off again after lunch. J. was fairly sure that we were heading toward a little lake directly south of Bear, where Charlie has a winter cabin. There were, Charlie had told us, two lakes "right together" and a hill, and on the hill was his cabin. You couldn't miss, he said. Soon the blazes stopped again, and we started the usual side trips scouting in opposite directions. This time we had no success. J. didn't come back and I heard his voice, way in the distance, calling to me to "wait right there." I was in a valley. The sun was getting ominously far off in the southwest. It was too cold to sit down and rest, though I had dumped the pack.

Bang! Bang!

Two muffled shots to the northwest. J.! Something *had* happened. He was lost, hurt, and I must answer. I waited, then pulled the pistol out and pressed the trigger, twice. It almost deafened me. My heart thumped and thumped, and I listened for what seemed to be hours. At last I saw J. swinging across a small open swamp.

When he was near enough, he shouted angrily, "Hey, what's the idea? Do you know what you've done? I was trying to signal old Charlie in case his cabin's anywhere around, then you had to shoot and drown out a reply. Couldn't tell whether he answered or not. Why *can't* you use your head better?"

I was too relieved to see him again, and too appalled at my impulsiveness, to think up a retort. If Charlie had shot in answer, he would not shoot again. No person experienced in the ways of the wilderness uses a single unnecessary shot. Ammunition is precious: it is heavy to carry, and often impossible to obtain in the particular make or quantity needed.

J. had not found the trail but, from a hill, he had seen the Bear Lake Mountains again. We decided to blaze our own way and climb a steep ridge to the northwest. From there we might be able to look over the country — possibly see Bear Lake itself, or the two lakes and a hill where Charlie's cabin was supposed to be. We should camp soon, for we must have sufficient daylight left to find a sheltered spot with dry firewood, and water, or ice, if possible. No northern traveler drinks melted snow unless necessary. Although snow water, which has been boiled and mixed with tea, does not seem unwholesome, melted snow has a singed or burnt taste, and quenching one's thirst on the trail with snow is most unwise, because one is never satisfied and only grows more and more thirsty. Also snow invariably makes one's mouth sore. Since we had no tent and very little bedding, J. must cut wood enough to last all night.

The hill proved to be steeper and higher than it looked. Part of the way we climbed on hands and knees, every movement impeded by packs, cameras, guns, and snowshoes.

J. passed encouraging remarks to me now and again, and when we finally reached the top he said, "Nice work, Teddy. Not many women could have made a climb like that with such a pack on."

I hereupon forgave him for his just anger at my carelessness in shooting back in the valley, and felt cheered. We seemed to be on a narrow ridge and, sure enough, through trees ahead were light sky and a sort of jumping-off place. When we reached the edge, there was a steep drop of five to six hundred feet down to a long, narrow, lonely little lake. Beyond the lake were the unending, deeply forested hills and ridges, beyond them again — *still* beyond and apparently as far away as they had been at Tetana — were the Bear Lake Mountains. No sign of Bear Lake, or "two lakes right together," not a track of man or beast, no curl of smoke, or Indian cabin — just snow and stillness. Perhaps we had climbed a hill never climbed before by man, perhaps we were gazing on a lake not seen yet by any man. The sun was gone behind the Driftwoods.

"We must find a way down," said J. wearily, "and camp in the first likely spot. We've left it too late now."

After we'd climbed, and slid, down a series of long steep banks we reached the lake shore and followed it until we saw a sheltered place on a small point of land which jutted out onto the ice. We made camp without looking further, for there was barely enough daylight left for J. to get firewood.

While he was cutting the nearest dead trees — in this case spruce and much more difficult to handle than pines because they're so thickly branched — I broke off boughs and carried them in armfuls to put on our bed and under our feet. In winter, spruce, though less soft, makes a warmer bed than balsam because it's more wiry. In my haste to get the boughs in before dark I forgot to be cautious about tackling a tree loaded with snow. I started to break the branch of a large spruce, a thunderous avalanche descended, I was knocked flat, and buried, head and all, though not so deeply that I couldn't, after hefty kicking, get up myself. J. had no time to laugh. But I had to waste valuable minutes brushing snow off, so that it wouldn't melt and wet my one change of clothes when I got back to the fire.

The first thing I learned about making camp in winter is that, instead of being able to rest and relax at the end of a hard day's trip, one must force one's tired and exhausted muscles to new effort, to several more hours of even more strenuous work. It becomes a question of making a camp that will keep one alive through the long bitter night. Even when we had done all possible chores before dark and sank stiffly down on the bed of boughs, it was not sufficiently warm for us to relax and rest until the huge fire had burned long enough to throw out great heat. And then there were shifting smoke and sparks to contend with constantly. Snow melted by the fierce heat made our feet wet; the sides of our bodies next the fire scorched, the sides away from it were cold and stiff. As soon as possible I tried to boil water for tea and, at the same time, hold a fry-pan of food over the huge flaming logs without allowing myself or the food to get burned.

The two immediate essentials at the end of a winter's trip are heat, before the body grows dangerously numb and chilled (which it does the instant one stops moving), and food to put inside it, so that it can recover from severe physical strain.

J. made our fire out of five spruce logs, six to eight feet long and around twelve inches thick. First, with his big knife, he cut a pile of paper-thin shavings from chips of dry pitchy wood. Then came small split pieces on top, laid with infinite care (to start a fire in very deep snow is a hundred times more difficult than to build one on open ground and we had no extra matches to waste over it either). Now the flames spread through the shavings, now they struck a blob of snow, sizzled and died, then caught again, and the sticks crackled, while J., kneeling on his snowshoes, patiently and cautiously laid on one big log after another. The fire began to send out a tremendous heat and, at first, it seemed unnecessarily big. But I soon discovered that, though my face almost blistered, there was barely heat enough to keep us warm in the fast-dropping temperature. As the wood burned it melted gradually into the seven-foot snow level on which it rested, and the whole fire of flaming logs sank farther and farther below us. J. had chopped through snow and ice on the lake to get water for tea, a job which *I* must learn to do, for the man should spend all his time cutting and carrying trees while the woman does the easy things — makes camp, cuts ice for water, cooks supper.

To watch the pot and frypan I had to kneel on the snowbank and lean above the fire, receiving directly in the face clouds of sparks and smoke made wherever snow touched the logs.

By the time we were ready to eat, it was pitch-dark. We took turns eating beans and bacon out of the pan. In the flickering flames it was hard to see bannock and cups of tea set out between humps on the bed. The beans and bacon, which had been so hot that they almost burnt, froze hard in the pan before we had eaten more than a few mouthfuls; but they were food, and any kind of nourishment was good. When we finished J. stepped into his snowshoes again. I went with him to hold the flashlight while he cut more trees for wood. We still didn't have enough to last the long night.

"Shall we ever be able to rest?" I thought despairingly. "How long will J.'s back hold out?"

At last we had six big logs laid out by the fire, and we sank down once more on our bed. Now the thing to be done was to dry mittens, moccasins, socks, and anything else that was wet. We hung them on sticks stuck at angles in the snowbank around the fire, and we stood the snowshoes up near by; but they all had to be watched and turned every minute before sparks or flames ruined them. A burned mitten or sock or moccasin may mean a frozen hand or foot the next day, and a frozen extremity may eventually mean death. This is why extra mittens, socks, and moccasins are just as much necessary equipment as food, matches, knife, axe, and firearms. Mittens are soaked from sweat, socks and moccasins are invariably wet from snow melted by sun or campfire.

The night was cloudy. When darkness fell, mountains, forests, and lake were blotted out. There was nothing beyond the little circular room of red firelight. We were too exhausted to talk and, even if I had wanted to, J. was already asleep in his light little bag. It was my turn to watch, feed the fire, and guard the drying clothes.

In all the time I had for reflection, during long hours of inaction, there was nothing but the immediate present. Family and friends, a home and life which had been so much a part of me, scarcely entered my head. I was supremely indifferent about them. Perhaps it was because they were all so far away. Perhaps it was because physical necessities and discomforts and impressions were so prominent and absorbing.

When my two-hour watch was over, I could scarcely hold my head up and I expected to fall asleep instantly. I waked J., took off moccasins and mittens, and rolled my jacket into a pillow. Then I struggled into the little bag which is not ever warm enough in temperatures much below freezing, unless it has additional outside covering. It was warm at first, because J. had kept it inside his while he slept. But though I pulled half the marmot robe over it, and though there were thick layers of boughs between the bed and the snow, the cold rose up, under, over, and through me. Even my bones grew cold. It was impossible to relax enough to sleep. After all, being smoked out or burnt while sitting by the fire was more restful than being chilled to death lying on a bed of snow.

So I spent the rest of that long night awake by the fire. Heat had melted a great circular space; I was in a small hot room surrounded by crystal walls five feet high; where snow had melted completely away just in front of the fire there was a tiny patch of bare ground; green vines and leaves, fresh and unharmed, sparkled in red light. This great, wonderful, terrible mass of white stuff was not just beauty or danger to men of the Northland; it was also protector and guardian to animals and plants which hid beneath it; the mice and squirrels and bears, the tiny flowers of the forest floor, all those live things too small or clumsy to be abroad during winter. When men knew how to use snow and how to guard against its dangers, it was their guardian as well.

Daylight came after eight-thirty, and we started breakfast. Trees and hills began to appear; we were no longer shut in a red room with inky blackness beyond it. Scalding water poured in cups of powdered coffee made a heavenly drink. Eyes, swollen from smoke and flames, felt wide-awake again. I was less tired than I've often been after fitful sleep in a soft bed on a hot summer's night. Bannock and bacon and bits of dried fruit sank pleasantly into a hollow tummy. J. too, although he had had poor sleep (for him!), was rested and ready to be off.

We decided to go on in the direction of the Bear Lake Mountains and if we had still seen no signs of Bear Lake or Charlie's camp by noon, we would turn back, retrace our tracks to the main trail, and start home for Tetana. We had food for about one more day, since we'd seen no grouse or other meat anywhere.

As we left the lake we climbed up long, gentle slopes, partly open and free from forest. On these grew giant firs a hundred feet high and four feet thick, trimmed as smoothly and gracefully as any tree in a well-kept garden. Beneath dense branches were open places almost free of snow. Almost every other tree seemed to be an ideal camping place with a tent of thick branches sweeping to the ground. If we had had sufficient food I would have made another camp right there, for the sheer pleasure of being in an almost perfect tree house. J., however, pointed out that there was no firewood, no small dead trees, no water. If we hadn't known that we were probably walking on top of thick undergrowth — willows and alders and devil's-club, all hidden by seven or eight feet of snow — we might have supposed that this was some beautiful, cultivated park. Beyond the height of land, up which we slowly pushed our way, were great mountains, white against a silver-gray sky. The deep green of trees, dotted here and there over the smooth expanse of snow, relieved the white-gray monotony.

It was all so quiet, so pure, that for a time we forgot the dangers — the fact that the silver sky meant snow, that we had lost all trace of the trail, that we had about one day's food supply, that we were, seemingly, as far as ever from Bear Lake and help with woodcutting.

On ahead J. called, "See what I've found!" There was an axe mark on a tree just at snow level and I, who all my life have longed for places which showed no sign of man, was as thrilled as if he had achieved a gold strike. So some human being, besides ourselves, had been here; perhaps we were not far from the trail and Bear Lake. But after a few more marks, the blazes petered out and we supposed it had been merely some Indian's trap line in years past. We knew we ought to turn back, but each new little hill in the long rise of land looked as though it were the last, and we wanted, desperately, to reach the height and see what lay beyond.

Ominous flakes were drifting down by the time we came unexpectedly out on the shore of a big lake with long winding points and wooded islands. We tramped at least a mile over its surface before we were convinced that we had seen most of it, that it was not Bear Lake. The Bear Lake Mountains, almost hidden by falling snow, were still miles to the northwest, with nothing to indicate that we were any nearer Charlie's cabin. We were dead tired and had a long way to go to get back to the main trail before snow obscured our tracks, so we left without exploring farther. We traveled fast five or six miles back down our trail to the camping place, where we stopped only long enough for a bit of lunch. Then we went on down the valley, for J. wished to avoid the high hill we had climbed the afternoon before, and thought he'd locate an easier short cut. I was very fearful that we might never find the main trail again, but I had some faith in J.'s powers of observation, or whatever it is that gives him his infallible sense of direction. He said that finding his way in a country of hills and mountains was child's play compared with traveling the unmarked flats of the Arctic Barrens.

In the course of the afternoon we found one more new lake, from a hill we saw still another. There seemed to be "two lakes together and a hill" in every direction, but there was never a sign of an Indian trail, camp, or cabin.

At last, after climbing a low ridge, we dropped down into a swamp and there, almost hidden by fresh snow, were our tracks of the day before. We were back on the main trail again. Scarcely a day's trip now between us and the cabin, warmth and food and *safety*.

The woodcutting would work itself out somehow. Perhaps I could learn to chop more. Even the risks of being without wood seemed less than those of tramping over a far northern wilderness, in deep winter, without adequate food or shelter, hunting for places that never materialized.

The snow had almost stopped. We were on a trail doubly well marked, not only by our own tracks, but also by tree blazes. Walking in a trail already trodden down by two sets of snowshoes is so much easier than walking in unbroken snow. Up above the still trees, cloud banks were rolling across from the northwest. The wind had shifted. This meant clear cold weather. We were a day from the cabin, and we had enough food for two meager repasts. Despite hard traveling, lack of sleep, and inadequate food, we were full of health and strength. We felt happy and carefree.

When we'd passed up several possible camping places, I reminded J. that he was being most unusually particular.

"Have you forgotten what day it is?" he asked. "I wanted to make you an especially nice camp."

I remembered then that this was my birthday and our wedding anniversary.

We camped finally in a grove on a bank high above a stream. A circular space around a big pine, where the snow was much less deep, made a good camp. Small dead pines were not far off. We put our bed next to the tree after digging out a larger space with the snowshoes. We placed the fire on a snowbank several feet higher than the bed, since it would soon melt down to our level and below. It was dark long before we could eat, and it was growing bitterly cold. The sky was brilliant instead of overcast as the night before. Huge stars came out in the blue-black. The air was filled with the pungent odor of spruce boughs and smoke. We were wrapped round by the immensity of a forest at night. In all the world there seemed to be nothing alive but us and the glittering stars.

Once more J. slumbered peacefully on an icy bed. Once more I sat gazing into the red-gold logs, shoving them together when they fell apart, moving alternately closer and farther off. First I was burning from heat, then I was shivering from cold. Trees began to snap and crack. The temperature dropped and dropped. It must be at least 30 or 40 below, J. said, in one of his wakeful intervals. I made no attempt to lie on the bed or move away from the immediate circle of the fire. The high snowbanks threw off a tremendous heat, like a reflector oven; otherwise we could not have kept alive. I was numb and drowsy, and I did not watch the drying things as carefully as I should have. Once a mitt fell into the fire and a hole was burnt in the palm. But we could be home next day, so it didn't really matter.

When everything was dry at last and the fire had died down a little, I leaned back against the snow, and was rudely waked by rolling almost into white-hot embers. Several times J. got up to cut more wood, for the cold was so intense that we were burning twice as much as the night before. My most vivid impression of the night is of J. staggering into the circle of firelight with a log on his shoulder and dropping it with a thud, and then the creak of snowshoes and the metallic tinkle of hard snow, as he vanished into the dark again. Twice, we had brandy and hot cocoa. When one is awake in very low temperatures one needs food often. The hour just before dawn is the coldest and hardest of the night. So we had breakfast long before daylight.

A red glow behind black trees heralded the sun and when it grew light we packed, or rather J. did. Despite double mittens, my fingers were so numb on the instant I drew back from the fire that they were useless.

To get warm we traveled at a half run along the trail, now frozen rock hard. Could this short well-marked track be the one we had toiled over for long heartbreaking hours only two days ago? It seemed no distance at all until we came out of the woods into Hudson Bay Meadow, a dazzling world of white fields and mountains, blue sky, and sunshine. We were a mile from the cabin by noon and then our fluffy gray jays suddenly appeared from nowhere. This time there were no harsh scolding notes. They trilled and cooed and followed us in a most heart-warming welcome.

Bliss! To get out of clothes worn day and night for three days, to bathe one's body from head to toe in a basin of warm water, to put on flannel pajamas! As I lay in bed I could see, through the southern window, across the white expanse of Tetana and the black shadow of the forest, the Driftwoods shining silver under the stars. Through the west window I looked deep into the great wall of pines and spruces which shelters us. Did I ever say a rope-and-canvas bed was hard and cold? As I burrowed down inside my sleeping bags (I use the light one inside the heavier, warmer one) and hugged a comforting hot water bottle, it was borne in upon me how essential a certain degree of bodily comfort is before one can appreciate anything aesthetically or spiritually.

More and more I'm beginning to feel a sort of distaste for the Nature Poets — Wordsworth, Keats, Shelley, and Longfellow — whom I've always read ever since my first college English courses. Now I need someone stronger, more elemental, someone who knows firsthand the deep hardness and terribleness of a wilderness and, because of this, the greater beauty and wonder of it.

CHAPTER VI

Bear Lake

Bear Lake   *January 9*

The day after our siwashing trip, we lounged about the cabin, luxuriating in a paradise of warmth and rest. We'd had enough for a long time of winter camps and travels. In the afternoon as we lay sprawled in the easy chairs, and reveled in steaming cups of tea, a perfect babel of voices and barking suddenly shattered the world!

It was Chief Charlie, with two sons, sled, and five dogs, arrived after all to escort us to Bear Lake. He and his boys had tramped a trail in the soft snow, so that we could use the dog team and toboggan. A plane had arrived at Carl Hanawald's, the white trader's. If we reached Bear Lake in time we could send out mail and material for the Museum. Such a chance might not come again for a year. There was nothing for it but to pull ourselves together, collect camping food and equipment all over again, and once more start out for Bear Lake. In addition we had to pack specimens hurriedly in layers of moss dug up under six feet of snow. Since these occupied so much space in Charlie's toboggan, we could take no more equipment with us than we had before. But at least we didn't have to carry it on our backs. And I was somewhat cheered by glowing promises from Charlie that I should ride on the toboggan, though the sight of the small, badly kept sled dogs was not encouraging. Before we started, Charlie examined my snowshoes, which were still a bit damp because, in the flurry of packing, I had forgotten to hang them up inside to dry. Charlie muttered over them and fussed around me like an old hen.

"Officious old thing," I thought; "thinks I don't know how

to snowshoe when I've been doing it since I was six. I'll show him."

With moans of regret we locked up our cozy cabin again and started off, this time on a new trail. Charlie laughed to scorn the idea of following the blazed path that we had just been over. No one went that way in winter, he assured us.

"Snow too deep, trail too long. I make more better trail along river. I make fine trail. We go right to Bear Lake in one day — mebbe. White man not find good trail, but I good man. I know, see."

Thus escorted with much sprightly conversation from Charlie, we began our second trip in four days. With fresh memories of bitter cold nights when we had siwashed under trees, I dressed for this trip more warmly. But the weather had moderated again and I was uncomfortably hot. The snow was soon sticky from the morning sun and after the first few miles my moccasins grew wet and my feet were sore and rubbed by the damp harness. Snow clung to my snowshoes so that I lifted up pounds of weight at every step. The Indians cut light wooden clubs for each of us to carry, in order to beat our snowshoes so that we could free them of snow. But I found hitting my snowshoes now and again against trees was less trouble. I began to perceive what Charlie had been fussing about. His snowshoes were comparatively dry and light during the first part of the morning. We traveled at what J. and Charlie called an "easy pace" (I was almost running). I was frightfully annoyed at J., who was leading, for not setting a slower gait but, as the white woman, I was certainly not going to show any weakness before these Indians. The pace was also probably much too fast for them, but of course they must show the white man what great travelers they were. We all tried to show each other. The sled dogs panted pitifully, the sweat streamed from our faces, and the melting snow grew heavier and heavier.

Charlie's trail followed the course of the river. Where the ice was strong enough we traveled for miles along the flat winding surface, sometimes between high steep rock cliffs, at others through deep dark forests. Ahead rose the shining white Bear

Lake Mountains; on our left were the Driftwoods. At each turn of the river came a new picture of great peaks and wooded hills. Despite physical discomforts, we couldn't help rejoicing in this untouched land.

During the first few hours old Charlie discoursed on the country around us. The harder, slightly crusted snow of the river bed showed more signs of life than we had seen for weeks. Charlie pointed out the tracks and habits of different wild animals; and very interesting it all was, not the least part of it being his quaint interpretation of the English language. He pointed out how the moose tracks, the first we had seen since early December, followed willow-grown portions of the river-bank, as the moose browsed on young twigs of willow and red-osier dogwood. Twigs and strips of dogwood bark are used by the Indians as a scent for beaver traps. Where the moose go through deep snow, Charlie showed us how they rest their weight on bended knees and use these bent forelegs like snowshoes. Even the largest moose are unable to heave four-foot-high legs through six or eight feet of soft snow. The only way they can move at all is by leaning on their knees. Charlie shoved his axe handle down into the holes made by their legs. The hard tilted end of the hole shows the direction of the tracks because, as the moose moves ahead, his legs bend forward in the snow and the weight of his body packs it hard.

Here, near a patch of open water, where gushing springs kept the river open the year round, were otter tracks; open water where it may obtain food is essential to the otter. There on the banks were deep grooves, a foot wide, where otters had slid down into the river. Here were a few fisher tracks, soft rounded paws placed in pairs, two to three feet apart, closely resembling those of the marten, except that they were larger.

"That one, he too smart," Charlie told us repeatedly. "Ebery kind of trap I use, ebery kind of bait. Only sometimes I catch him."

Here was an osprey's nest, on a great tree high above a cliff. "That fish hawk, his cabin. That where he make his childern in the spring."

Marten

When a female grouse whirred up by a bank, Charlie said, "Woman grouse; he fly to man grouse inside the brush."

We are beginning to understand the Indian use of English pronouns, which at first was dreadfully confusing, for they use the masculine singular to denote any sex or number.

Charlie told us about his wife Selina, who is a young healthy woman though "he has many babies." We can't make out how many children Charlie and Selina actually do have. Charlie says "pretty near twenty mebbe," but when he tries to count them up on his fingers he can't remember more than about ten names.

The old man seemed to be delighted with J.'s and my interest in his remarks on natural history. At first he cackled away and talked incessantly in his funny, high, squeaky voice. But after a time he must have grown tired, for his words ceased, and we all plodded along in silence, William and Mac, the two quiet, efficient boys, minding the sled and dogs. The dogs, wearing the round simple type of tandem collar to which the traces fastened, were harnessed to the sled so that they traveled single file, not in the fanlike hitch often used in Eskimo country where snow is hard and the dogs can spread out. Here in the soft snow a trail usually has to be packed by several pairs of snowshoes before the sled can travel at all. Sometimes when we came to difficult spots along the river I had a breathing space while the sled was eased across. The trail would take an unexpected plunge down an almost perpendicular bank onto thin, clear blue ice; one could see and hear the rushing water. Old Charlie would hurry ahead, tap it with his axe, and shriek excited directions to Mac and William, as one encouraged the lead dog, alternately pushing or holding him back, and the other hopped wildly on his huge snowshoes behind the madly swaying toboggan, as he tried to keep it from plunging too suddenly down onto dangerous ice.

These Indians handle snowshoes rather differently from the white man. They walk in a sort of bowlegged fashion with knees perpetually bent. They never seem to vary this fashion of snowshoeing, or their gait, no matter what changes there are in the trail. The harness is arranged so that they merely step in and out of it without stooping down to fix it. I find their type of harness, made of long flexible thongs of moose hide, much simpler and superior to ours, but so far I can't acquire the trick of just stepping in and out.

During the early afternoon the river began to veer sharply to the west, and Charlie's trail headed north away from it toward the south end of the Bear Lake Mountains. For some time he had been assuring us that "very soon we see my cabin," but it was still miles before we reached his lake, which he calls "Bunshaw."

On a few old maps a portage, just north of Bunshaw, is marked by the words "Cache des Bon Jours." We wonder if Bunshaw may not be a corruption of the French. Charlie declared the word was an Indian expression. Be that as it may, I have pronounced and spelled it, just as we do all the various other localities, as it sounds to us in Indian.

J. and I looked around for "two lakes and a cabin on a hill," but there was nothing to be seen except the two-mile-long narrow Bunshaw, winding through partially burnt-over ridges; and it was not until we had climbed a long slope through dense growth that we came upon Charlie's little log lean-to type of cabin half buried in snow. So this primitive structure was the wonderful cabin Charlie had described to us on his visit to Tetana! Though he had politely admired our cabin, he had described his immediately after in glowing terms, which gave the impression that ours, though creditable, was definitely inferior.

There was no sign of another lake, or of Bunshaw, which we had left in the valley below. After walking through thick undergrowth back of the cabin, however, we did discover a second lake, though it was far from Bunshaw. J. and I smiled grimly over the way we'd been led about on our first trip, thanks to Charlie's elaborate descriptions, while Charlie cackled with amusement over our difficulties. Of course a white man could not find things in this country like an Indian, for "Indian he know how to do, see?" He also assured us that on his way down to Tetana he had several times "loosed off" his gun in case we should be anywhere in the vicinity. After some discussion we decided that in our search for Bear Lake, we must have reached a region some miles east of Bunshaw. Charlie thought he knew the big lake, with islands and winding points, which we described to him.

The snow around his cabin was littered with old bones, bits of fur, and messes from the dogs. The interior of the cabin, which Charlie hospitably bade us enter, was dark (there were no windows); we could see little. But I was only too thankful to be allowed to sit down anywhere. We made a big fire in an old gasoline drum which served as the stove. Soon we had hot tea. J. and I ate our own bannock, while the Indians chewed bits of smoked salmon. They politely offered us some of everything they had. Charlie wished to reach his second camp, which he called his "summer cabin," halfway up Bear Lake, by nightfall. Though he said it was a "short" way, he was anxious to be off again at once. I was beginning to realize what the old man really meant when he spoke of short distances. I wondered whether my raw and blistered feet would ever get me there. I had given up all hope of riding on the toboggan, for it was perfectly obvious that the poor thin little dogs had all they could do to pull it as it was. And Charlie was beginning to mutter about the heavy load we had brought and say "No use to kill the dogs."

Once when I could get J.'s private ear, I begged him when we reached the next cabin to put our tent up, so that we might have privacy for the night at least. J. replied diplomatically that we should have to see when we got there, but that he would put up the tent if he could.

We traveled two miles on Bunshaw, a mile along a valley, up another small lake, and across a short portage, where we struck the south end of Bear. Here we began a trek up the flat surface of the big lake through mile after mile of deep wet snow. The lake was two to three miles wide in places, at others it opened out into arms and bays which seemed to have no ending. Most of the shores and points and islands were densely forested. All along the west side rose the high gleaming peaks of the Bear Lake range. On the east, mountains as flat as a table fell in a sheer wall of gray cliffs over a thousand feet high. It was much more striking and beautiful than Takla or any of the other large lakes we have seen so far.

If I could have made myself conscious of anything but the pain of my legs and feet I would have been thrilled with it. As the afternoon wore on, a stiff breeze began to blow down from the north. This grew soon to an icy gale that chilled our sweat-soaked bodies and wet feet to the very marrow, and we had to fight and struggle with it in order to make headway. At last Charlie shouted and waved toward a point in the middle of the lake where his cabin was. It didn't look far away but, though we walked and walked, it just never got any nearer. I was certain that at any minute my legs would give way and I should just sit down, willy-nilly. I was hardly conscious of walking at all, until I stumbled up the point into the cabin and sank to the ground. I never thought of the tent. Nothing in the whole world seemed of any importance except to stop walking and get away from the terrible wind. When heat from a roaring fire, made in the cracked, rickety old drum stove, began to penetrate, I struggled to hold back silly tears which would come from the pain of my body and feet as the cold thawed out of them. It was partly the nervous weakness which follows physical exhaustion. I hoped that I successfully concealed my feelings from the Indians, who were on the other side of the stove. But J. saw (he always does!) and was stricken with self-reproach over what had not in the least been his fault. He said afterward that I had good reason to be tired, for, during that one short winter's day, we traveled some eighteen miles, at a pace to tire most men, and under trying conditions, when every step had been hard going. Moreover, he and I had traveled ahead much of the way to tramp the trail for the dogs.

We spread our marmot robe on our side of the stove. We couldn't see the earth floor covered with some old and a few fresh evergreen boughs. I managed to change socks and moccasins and doctor my blistered toes with pads of unguentine and cotton held on by a band-aid — a dodge which I always find effective. The Indians were drying their moccasins, and a great quantity of torn socks and old cloths from sugar and flour bags with which they wrapped their feet to avoid rubbing by the snowshoe harness. And then water was boiling and though I had felt too nauseated from exhaustion to want any supper, a cup of hot black tea set me up again. I was soon eating baked beans and bannock, the old stand-bys. Then I began to feel healthy again.

The wind howled, and blown snow beat in gusts against the logs. J. and I contributed our canvas bed sheet to hang over the open doorway and this, coupled with high drifts outside and the red-hot stove within, kept the cold out fairly well. There was one candle that swayed and guttered in drafts and threw weird shadows around. From time to time one or other of the two Indian boys stepped into his snowshoes, took an axe and disappeared in the dark, to return, staggering under a log of wood, which he heaved in through the doorway and chopped into small pieces by the flickering light from stove and candles. The poor shivering dogs were clustered outside as near the door as possible. Some were short-haired; even the long-haired ones had no thick coat like that of Eskimo dogs. They were so savage toward J. and me that I dared not go out except with J.; even then it was a risky business, and we could only step safely by them when old Charlie or the boys stood beside us.

We all sat on our beds, the Indians on one side of the stove, J. and I on the other. The space was some twelve by fourteen feet, and the log walls just near enough so that our figures, lighted by the candle, were thrown on them, in fantastic, swaying, gigantic black shapes. It looked exactly as though the cabin were inhabited by a company of goblins and ogres. The two boys muttered together and old Charlie, with a small willow twig whose end he had frayed into a sort of brush, scrubbed his teeth after the evening meal. J. and I, too tired to talk, listened to the guttural tongues of the Indians, and wondered idly what they were saying. After a time we all settled down for the night.

I've read a description in J.'s diary of the first night we passed in Charlie's cabin. After remarking that we had "a good trip up to Bear Lake on Charlie's winter trail, though the going was a bit tough because of soft snow," he briefly describes the cabin and then says, after we all turned in for the night, "there were a few snores and mutters — and it was morning." This is J.'s usual impression of a night passed under any conditions.

It always amuses and astonishes me to compare our two diaries. Experiences which seem thrilling or terrifying and about which I write pages, J. dismisses with a sentence. And things which do not seem especially interesting to me, such as different methods used by the Indians to set a trap, or the way they place their shots to bring down a bear or a moose, he writes up at great length.

The night seemed endless to me. We were lying over rough dead branches that had lost their needles. If I rolled too near the stove I sweated from heat, if I rolled too far from it, I was cold. And J., who, in uncomfortable positions, always snores vigorously, snored more loudly than Charlie, so that I was ashamed and considered it my wifely duty to push him into better postures. It seemed to me that I was awake every hour. Although I thought I knew almost everything about camping out in odd places, I still have much to learn about the art of relaxing.

The next morning we started out again around nine, just as the sun came up. The wind had died; great inky clouds, rimmed in red and gold, were rolling off high peaks. In the dawn light the pure white mountains and lake were a deep, lovely salmon. Charlie's cabin is not quite halfway up this fifteen-mile-long lake. We hoped to reach the north end, where the white trader and the Indian settlement are, by noon. It looked like such a good day we feared the plane might take off before we got there, though we hoped from what Charlie said that it would wait for us. The snow on the lake had frozen fairly hard and the dogs and men now traveled at what even they considered a smart pace. I was obliged to go at a steady trot, or run, in order to keep up with them. J., legs trained to the endless miles of flat northern barren country, thought the going was wonderful, and the Indians apparently agreed with him. My legs, accustomed to hills and the constant change of up and down grades, found the flat surface infinitely harder because I had to use the same set of muscles without a break. Hanging to one handle of the toboggan, I ran along beside Charlie, wondering how long I should hold out. J. and the two boys were way ahead of us.

After an hour or two, there was a sudden rumble which grew to a roar. The plane must be starting, but surely it would see us and might come down again if we signaled. It came sailing just overhead, gazed callously at our frantic waves and shouts, rose higher, and disappeared in a tiny speck far to the south, leaving us, insignificant black dots, standing on the white lake. Charlie said, "By gosh, too bad, you lose him," and we went on.

By the time we reached Carl's store around one o'clock I was just able to snowshoe in sprightly fashion up the bank to the door where Carl, having observed us coming on the lake an hour before we reached him, stood waiting to greet us. We were overjoyed to learn that he expected the plane back again in a few days with a load of supplies. No, neither he nor the pilot had been looking for us. He didn't know from what old Charlie had said whether we really intended to come or not. The plane would not have waited for us anyhow. It had brought the game warden and Indian agent, hunting a bad Indian responsible for a shooting affair. They had also made Carl a surprise visit, to see whether by chance he had any beaver furs, which are now out of season. Sure enough he had, and lost them all, and had to pay a heavy fine to boot. But what was a poor trader to do when the Indians owed him endless debts and brought the beaver furs to him? (Beaver meat, especially the tail, makes very delicious eating.) The beavers were already destroyed and there was no use letting the fur go to waste. So — there we all were, and we might as well come in and rest!

After hot water and sugar and rum I felt sufficiently revived to look about and take in our surroundings. The little room which serves as Carl's bed and kitchen and sitting room is partitioned off from the store, where he carries on his trades. Everything is spick-and-span and neat. We are out on a small point of the east shore facing west across to the sharp craterlike

peaks of Mt. Morice, over eight thousand feet high, south down
the lake where the Driftwood Mountains have receded into
distance, and north to the small cluster of Indian cabins at the
outlet half a mile off, where Bear Lake flows into the Bear
River.

Carl is most hospitable about asking us to stay with him, and
we have decided to wait here a few days, getting mail and Museum specimens ready to go out. We want particularly to see the
plane pilot, and make possible arrangements for having mail
and supplies brought in for us during the summer.

Bear Lake   *January 11*

We're having a real vacation. We eat nearly all our food out
of cans, which is a treat to us, though not to Carl. We had a
few fresh apples which he had got on the first plane trip. Since
we've had no fresh fruit for months, the sour little things
tasted heavenly. So do chocolate and candy.

We've enjoyed especially reading Carl's supply of good books
and old magazines, and listening on his radio to up-to-date
news and lovely music. Also bits from New York's famed night
clubs — some of the very ones we visited on a brief fling not
so long ago. Events in Europe sound bad, but it all seems too
far away to get worked up over. This is the first time, for almost five months, that we have heard any news from the outside world.

When we're not busy with mail and specimens, or reading,
we talk to Carl. It would be hard to imagine, as far as appear-
ances and manners go, a more typical German than Carl; he is
tall and blond with a heavy build, and he is hard and self-
disciplined. He is also a very interesting person, for he has
much time to read and think deeply. Having lived in these parts
for many years, he has acquired much valuable information
concerning the country and its inhabitants. Although he and J.
served in the last war on opposite sides, they talk about it im-
personally and amicably. One subject which Carl does not discuss amicably is the Indians! He has lived among them so
long that I should think they must have tried his nerves be-

yond endurance. He is, moreover, not the sort of person to excuse shiftless, lazy ways. These Bear Lake Indians are, we understand, a mixture of Tahltan tribes to the north, Sikanees to the northeast, and Babines to the south.

Carl has been telling us about an Indian baby, born in July 1936, on the mountains some eight miles out beyond Bear Lake. Several Indians just returned from a hunting trip came to the store one morning without one of the squaws who had been with them. When Carl inquired concerning her the Indians said, oh, they left her "back on the mountain" — she was having a baby. They'd left her a shelter and a fire. Her mother was with her. She'd be all right, she'd be in soon. And the next day, into Carl's store came the squaw with her tiny new baby strapped on her back. She was apparently quite healthy, though a trifle "pale around the gills."

And in 1931, when Carl was in charge of the Takla Lake post an Indian squaw gave birth to twins on Christmas Eve in deep snow out in the brush about seven miles from Takla. The men in the party, after leaving fuel and some sort of shelter, moved on to the post. Only the squaw's mother-in-law remained with her. A day or so later the Indian women and new babes arrived at Carl's, and came in to warm up a little after their seven-mile hike. We have all discussed the varying conditions attending the birth of Indians and Whites. Carl wonders whether white women, if they had the will power, could not have babies as easily as these Indians. Endless numbers of Indian births occur successfully in remarkable circumstances. But as little is apparently heard of the unsuccessful ones, there is probably a much higher infant mortality among the Indians than is generally supposed.

All these people up here, in company with most northern settlers who live by a body of water, dump old cans and garbage out on the lake ice during winter, and in the lake water during summer. This practice must have a bad effect on fish and other water animals. Apparently in the spring of 1936 when a large number of radio batteries were dumped in the water, all mink around this end of Bear Lake left the vicinity. Shortly afterward in near-by localities numerous whitefish, ling, and lake trout were found dead along the shores. Since then no mink have been seen or trapped around this part of the lake, although they were previously common.

At night J. and I retire to the store section of the establishment. I go first, with a basin of water, and take a bath on my side of the partition. I then sweep the floor and sprinkle flea powder liberally. This is provided by Carl in case anyone who comes to trade in the daytime should leave unwelcome insects behind. When our bed is laid out, I remove trousers, shirt, and moccasins and settle down, in company with the shelves of neatly arranged cans, the bolts of bright cloth, the masses of steel traps hung on the walls, the axes and guns, the rows of rubber overshoes and beaded moccasins, and candy bars. J. and Carl, unhampered by a female presence, sit up and talk till after midnight. Carl likes to wait up to get the latest fur prices over the radio.

The hardest thing in the world to sleep on, unless it is a rock, is a wood floor. One's body fairly groans all night. And, though everything is tight shut, drafts are freezing. No wonder pet dogs want to get up on beds or chairs. Carl kindly offered us the use of his two wooden bunks, but we could never let him sleep on the floor in his own house. One can't fit one's body to a floor the way one can to the ground. The earth may be hard and rough, but in its unevenness one can always find a hollow and, once used to it, there is a spring and strength to it that makes the most elegant civilized mattress insipid by contrast. Also the ground is the best kind of reducing agent; any excess fat gets rubbed off in short order.

There has been a bad storm. In contrast to the dead winter calm around Tetana, and the dense quiet snowfall, here wind and snow blow across the lake in mighty gusts. They whirl over Carl's point and bury his cabin in high hard drifts. We are forced to extend our visit, partly because we can't travel, partly because we hope that the plane may come through as soon as it clears.

I wonder whether Carl, in spite of his hospitable insistence, is really glad to have us here. Although we're a break in the monotonous loneliness of his life, it must be a trial to have two other people (even as nice and safe as we are!) cooped up with him day and night within the space of four small walls. We must curtail his freedom considerably and break into his fixed habits of living. A lonely life in the North is apt to follow definite daily routines, and if one is at all a methodical person, any deviation from that routine is frightfully upsetting. When white visitors turn up, no matter who they are, whether one likes them or not, they must be invited to stay in one's house. This is the law of the Northland. After the first excitement of their coming wears off, one begins to get frightfully fed-up with their perpetual presence. In wintertime especially they are with one night and day, and there are no bedrooms to retire to for privacy, no neighbors or towns or outside distractions to create diversions.

Several days ago J. and I, armed with stout sticks (Carl having warned that we should have to beat off savage dogs) , went to visit the Indian village. We stopped at old Charlie's first, wondering how he would receive us. We have seen him only once since our trip and then he and J. had had words over the price he had charged. J. thought that he had paid him handsomely, Charlie that it was not half enough. The business was further complicated by the fact that, since Charlie owes Carl considerable money, Carl said that some of the pay must go to him. Charlie did not wish to bother with past debts. He wanted to spend his newly acquired wealth at once on food and other items for his wife and children, who, he said, were starving. During all this bickering Carl formed a sort of gleeful third-party. For years the Indians have been such a trouble to him that it must have been a pleasure to see another white man in difficulties with them. Already we have grown to expect inevitable arguments over prices whenever we have dealings with them; perhaps eventually we shall learn how to manage with less trouble.

Charlie seemed willing to let bygones be bygones. When we approached his village cabin, a duplicate of the other two we have seen, though rather larger, he came out and greeted us affably. We also shook hands with his wife, Selina, and numerous other members of his family, children, grandchildren, and in-laws. If they all live in that cabin they must have to sleep two deep. As Charlie had previously told us, Selina is a fine-looking woman, remarkably young and well-preserved to be the mother of so many offspring. Charlie implies that she is like this because *he* has always taken such care of her. She is not like the squaws of nowadays, who are sick old women after they have borne a few babies. Selina looked as though she had considerable character; when she spoke, Charlie flew to do her bidding. Though she and I could have no conversation except through eyes and expressions, and though she is reputed to be something of a she-devil, I rather liked her. Her face shows strength and wisdom.

Michelle and one of Charlie's sons-in-law also talked to us concerning a dance they would instigate in our honor. Then Charlie came out chuckling, staggering under a great bundle which he set on a bench and "unveiled" with ceremony. There before our astonished eyes was a huge white plaster frog about two feet long. It appears that Charlie, and certain members of his family, belong to an Order of Frogs. They have all manner of superstitions concerning any kind of frog or toad. This accounts for the fact that they have always refused to look at our few specimens preserved for the Museum, and that Charlie's boys beat a precipitous retreat out of our cabin the other day at sight of the jars of pickled amphibians.

We took everybody's picture, including one of the White Frog, said good-bye, and moved on to the other cabins. There are about a half-dozen of these, some small huts, and a little frame house which serves as a meeting hall; also a partially completed little Catholic Church, visited once a year by a priest, at which time the Indians must acquire sufficient religion to last another twelve months. Charlie, though a sort of leader in the village, is not a real hereditary chief. He has gained his title from the priests who have apparently made him a kind of churchwarden.

As we walked past each cabin, hordes of snapping, howling, starving dogs surrounded us. Their respective families came out to yell at them, and to greet us politely. We talked with "big Kate," the prostitute of the village, who looked part white and must weigh over two hundred. She seemed to be quite a character and was very smiling and jolly, but she had that deep, unfathomable look in her eyes which always haunts me.

And we met "old William," a Tahltan Indian from up north. We were especially anxious to see William, for he has been said to possess small dogs which answer closely descriptions of the famous Hare Indian dog, a rare native race of North America. Reports of these dogs were written up during the last century by Sir John Richardson, various factors of the Hudson's Bay Company, and others, but in the middle of the nineteenth century the dogs were thought to be extinct. Recently, however, they were found and reported on by Dr. D. Jenness of the National Museum of Canada. The Tahltan or Hare Indians (so-called because hares at one time were supposed to form one of their chief means of subsistence), and others of the northern Cassiar District, were said to use a small, thickly furred dog for hunting. They also sheared these dogs to obtain fur for weaving into cloth. The dogs were always well cared for and highly thought of by the Indians. In general the Indians refused to part with them, and the whole business seemed to be surrounded with superstition and secrecy. Before we left for British Columbia we were told to be on the lookout for any stories about the dogs, and better yet for any actual descendants of them, even those with mixed blood. Our first report of one came from Ben on the trip across country from Hazelton. Several years before, he told us, a Tahltan Indian traveling down that way had with him a small dog, of which he took such care that the other men all laughed at him. He actually let it ride on his horse and fed it every day, a thing unheard of in that section. The dog was said to be a wonderful hunter. We pricked up our ears at this, and when we heard about William's dogs at Bear Lake, we were all agog.

Sure enough, as we approached William's cabin the other

day, we saw a small black-and-white bitch, with beautiful golden eyes, sitting by the door. She looked very different from the other Indian dogs, and coincided almost exactly in size, coloring, and general appearance with the specimen of the Hare Indian dog kept in the National Museum at Ottawa. Presently we saw another small dog, mostly black with heavy silky hair and curled-up tail, in much better condition, and a far finer specimen than the first. But when we admired the dogs and tried to sound out old William, he shut up tight as a clam. He was delighted to talk about his other dogs, or about almost anything else. We put out various tactful feelers concerning the purchase of a small dog from him — we said we had no dogs and liked the looks of his — but nothing has come of it. From the little we can glean from the other Indians, and from what we've seen ourselves, it seems that Hare Indian dogs are still in existence in fair numbers (though we have no means of knowing in how pure a form); also there is definitely some taboo or superstition connected with them, which prevents their owners from parting with them willingly, or giving information about them.[1]

Yesterday a young Indian, who came to the store, handed us a slip of paper which said, "Dance tonite 7:30. A. S. Wright." So, last evening, supposing this to be an official invitation, we walked across to the small frame meetinghouse. The best we could do in the way of dressing for the occasion was for J. to put on a clean flannel shirt, and for me to don a red sweater above the black ski pants. Wind and weather had made my face rosier than I cared to have it, but I did apply lipstick and powder and tied a handkerchief around my neck.

When we reached the dance hall, after braving the attacks of dozens of vicious dogs which surrounded us in the dark, we found the village assembled. As we entered they clapped hospitably, and we were led to seats of honor, two boxes placed in the center of the back stage, so to speak. One Simon, married to one of Charlie's daughters, and who has, we are told, been

[1] See article "Do Tahltan Bear Dogs Still Live in North America?" by John F. Stanwell-Fletcher, *American Kennel Gazette*, April 1940.

"outside" frequently and knows the ways of the world, had given instructions in the latest dance steps. He was Master of Ceremonies. He made us a very nice speech of welcome in quite fair English. Though most of the women here do not know English, the majority of the men and older boys speak and understand a very simple type. J. replied with ease and grace and told them carefully about our work and our reasons for being in their country.

I've always been thankful that my father and my husband, with whom I've traveled in odd parts of the world, are gifted with the power of impromptu speech-making. When I have warning and spend hours of preparation and agonizing thought on it I am sometimes able to give a fairly respectable informal talk, but things impromptu floor me completely.

After J.'s speech, the dance got under way. The three-piece orchestra was composed of accordion, violin, and drum. Our silent friend Sapolio was the violinist, and for one who has probably had no instruction, he did remarkably well. They played mostly fox trots and we occasionally recognized the familiar strain of a modern tune.

The girls and women wore hand-sewn skirts and blouses or cotton dresses. A few had on old leather shoes, but most of them wore moose-skin moccasins. Some had handkerchiefs around their heads, or bright-colored combs in their straight, oily black hair which was worn either long or in shoulder-length bobs. The men, except for trousers and short hair, were dressed in the same way. One handsome youth had a vivid light green scarf around his waist, and a long straight comb of the same shade stuck in his hair. If he danced too vigorously the comb leapt from its place, but he always caught it in mid-air. Older people and children sat on the floor. When a young squaw with a baby wished to dance, she deposited the baby on the lap of some near-by neighbor. Between dances she would return and nurse it. Men and girls took turns asking each other to dance.

The faces of the Indians were interesting. Some weak, some strong, but all quite individual. Their poise and dignity was universal. These people, even the smallest child, must be intimately acquainted with life — every detail of birth and death and passion. Beside this profound practical knowledge, what, I wondered, does all the culture of the white man really amount to? The essential underlying principles of living are so carefully wrapped up for us in medical aid and book theories. Shall we eventually lose completely the ability to ccpe with realities as many of us seem already to have done?

After some while the door opened and old Charlie and Selina entered with solemnity. Selina, carrying an empty coffee tin, followed Charlie; when he sat down she set the tin on the floor beside him. He at once spat in it. A spittoon was an extra piece of elegance; there was to be no spitting on the floor at this dance.

Thus far, the whole affair had been conducted with great gravity and decorum. Finally J. and I asked if we might not see some Indian dances and, after considerable consultation, they obliged. First, several sets of young braves performed a sort of hopping jumping affair, then two young girls did the same thing. It seemed to be hard work. They all grew red and out of breath, and very soon returned to mixed couples and fox trotting, which they obviously preferred.

Once Simon's wife drew him aside and talked to him earnestly. And all the while that she talked he cast a crucified sort of look in our direction. The look said, "This woman who is my wife, through no fault of mine, does not know what is proper. She has never been outside the way I have. She does not know the white man's ways, and she embarrasses me constantly by her primitive manners."

Presently she returned to her seat on the floor, took up her tiny brown baby, and began to nurse it. I wondered what she had said or done that had caused Simon to look so sad.

Incidentally, we are told, Simon has three wives, scattered in different parts of the country, each married to him by a different ceremony. One by Anglican Church, one by Catholic, and one by Indian rites.

Since we were not sure how we could adapt our mode of

dancing to the Indians' version of a fox trot, J. and I did not join in; we thought it would make things easier all round if we remained spectators. After a few hours, the dancers tired. This seemed to be a signal for refreshments, which consisted of a large box of chocolate bars which we passed around, and another box of the same kind which the Indians produced. We then said good-night and took our leave.

Although the weather is clear again, there is not a sign of the plane, and we have decided that we can't wait longer. As Carl says, out of years of experience of waiting for planes, it might come today, or it might not come for half a year.

Tetana *January 18*

We are home again, and I hope we won't leave our cabin and Tetana for months and months.

When we left Carl's we were once more escorted by old Charlie and the toboggan filled with supplies from Carl's store. This time Michelle and his wife Bella, with three tiny children, came along. Two children were tied with bundles into Michelle's small sled, which was on runners. Bella, who is a mere slip of a red-cheeked girl, strapped the other to her back by a blanket. Michelle apparently had to travel in our direction to examine traps and, lured by the promise of $7.00 a cord plus a bonus if he worked well, agreed to stop at Tetana and cut wood.

We had gone half a day's journey down the lake when there was a rumble in the distance. We all cried, "The plane!" and once again gazed helplessly aloft while it roared overhead, circled, and banked to land at Carl's point. There was no sense in going back, for even if we had wanted to, it was quite possible that the plane would leave before we could get there.

I said, "Damnation."

J. said, "What do you know about that?"

And proceeding once more along our weary way we resigned ourselves to the fates of the North.

On this trip we took two and a half days to reach Tetana. The going was better, and the journey homeward almost easy.

We spent the first night in Charlie's cabin on the point. This time, in addition to us and Charlie and the two boys and their dogs, there were also Michelle, Bella, three babies, and their dogs. The sleeping space was even more crowded, the dogs howled and the babies cried. Before we all rolled up in our beds, Charlie gathered together his flock and, pulling out his crucifix, bade them kneel and repeat after him what we took to be a prayer. The long ceremony would have been more impressive if it had not been an apparently uncustomary procedure. Charlie was ably seconded by Michelle, but the others looked blank and it was some time before they got themselves properly arranged.

The next night we stopped at Bunshaw, and while the Indians slept in Charlie's cabin on the hill, J. and I had our own camp down by the lake, with the added luxury of a tent. This was heaven! To possess private sleeping quarters once more, a clean soft bed of boughs, and above all, nothing but the wilderness to hear what we said, or see what we did. We ate pounds of moose roasted on sticks over the fire; we consumed cans of fruit and vegetables, because we convinced ourselves that it would be nice to lighten the load on Charlie's sled. Next day we traveled down the Driftwood to our own lake and the first thing we did, as always, was to drink, fresh from the springs, great drafts of Tetana, whose waters have no rival anywhere. J. says it is worth while going away, just for the joy of coming back to Tetana.

J.'s back is better after several weeks' rest from wood chopping. When we first got back from Bear Lake, old Charlie and William and Michelle, who, like us, needed fresh meat badly, went moose hunting. They got one some miles away across the river, and took what they wanted for themselves, leaving us the rest to pick up at our leisure. So our biggest worry — lack of meat — next to lack of wood is taken care of for a while.

When Charlie and the boys left, Michelle and his family stayed on. Michelle is doing good work. Though a prodigious talker, he is very efficient. Bella and the three babies, aged around four, two, and one, stay in a tiny canvas tent along the east shore. We have been having clear weather and sub-zero temperatures. Night after night, it has been 40 below. How she and those tiny children survive I don't know, but they all seem well and cheerful. We loaned them our small stove, several lengths of stovepipe, and a long strip of canvas which Bella sewed around the tent bottom to keep out drafts.

January 30

Michelle and Bella stopped here a week and got us three cords of wood; not nearly so much as we had hoped for, but still a great boon. J. thinks if he can do a little cutting often, he can keep a cord or so always on reserve. This gives us a feeling of security. The day they left, the two oldest children were tied once again on the dog sled and I gave them each a lollypop which they accepted with reluctant solemnity. Bella, the baby on her back, went ahead to break trail for the dogs. She will no doubt travel the ten miles to Bunshaw in one day, breaking trail through deep new snow all the way, and arrive quite fresh and cheerful.

We've had a visit from Vinson and Martha. J. gave them a commission to bring up important mail, by the middle of January at the latest. They arrived some weeks late, having apparently dallied considerably along the way — we know when they started by a letter from the Hudson's Bay man at Takla. They were even less polite than usual, and demanded commissions for more work, which J. firmly but politely refused. Vinson's talk then became openly unpleasant. In low sneering tones he recounted stories of white men in the North who have disappeared. No one, he said, could ever find out whether they had been drowned, lost, or killed by an Indian. To which J. cheerfully retorted that he, for his part, couldn't think of a single instance of an Indian's having killed a white man in the North without eventually being apprehended by the Mounted Police. Anyhow Vinson no doubt accomplished exactly what he intended; and he left me, at least, with a very unpleasant feeling and the ardent but useless wish that we may never again lay eyes on him!

CHAPTER VII

Wolves and the Aurora

Tetana   *February 8*

Where, we've been asking, are the timber wolves? This country is supposed to be one of the few places left in North America where the timber wolf still exists in fair-sized numbers. When we ask the Indians about them they all say: —

"By gosh, lots of wolf. Mebbe some day you see him, but not much I think. Wolf very wise, just like man. I think you neber see him in sticks [forest], only open country — sometimes."

They've told us various anecdotes which point to a remarkable intelligence on the part of the wolves. Their cleverness in avoiding traps, in hunting moose, how they follow human beings for miles, how they are able to distinguish an unarmed man from an armed one, in which case they are distinctly bolder, and so on. Though the Indians respect the wolves, apparently they aren't much afraid of them. They can cite no cases of men having been attacked by wolves, although wolves sometimes kill their dogs.

As a matter of fact, we have been able to discover no authentic instances in British Columbia, or elsewhere in North America, of ordinary healthy wolves (there are rare reports of rabid individuals) having ever attacked man unless the wolves themselves were hopelessly trapped or cornered. Although they're primarily flesh eaters, wolves do not evidently like human flesh. Bodies of men who have died in the wilderness are cleaned invariably by maggots and various insects, not by wolves or coyotes.

Do wolves ever come around Tetana or the Driftwood, we

asked? Oh yes, "lots, sometimes, pretty soon you see tracks, mebbe."

But it was not until a week ago that we found any fresh signs. Then, as we were taking a snowshoe ramble a quarter of a mile from the cabin, we came suddenly on new wolf tracks, so big that J., familiar with the smaller wolves of the Arctic, whistled loudly. The prints of a single foot measured five to six inches across. The tracks are more numerous now each day. Whether they're made by a few individuals hunting all over this territory, or whether they mean that the actual numbers of wolves are increasing, we have no means of telling. The snow, although much more solid than in December, is still so soft in most places that their long legs sink far below the surface, and it must take considerable strength for them to plow their way through.

A mile and a half northeast of Tetana is Wolf Lake, newly christened by us because it appears to be a favorite haunt of the wolves. It is a deep, narrow little stretch of water, bordered east and west by high hills and cliffs. The hill on the west sticks up from the surrounding country like a giant camel hump, and is higher and more open than any other hill within miles. One of our favorite trails leads to the top, where we can look over the whole Driftwood Valley and view six great mountain ranges. The wolves come down the high lake bank on the northeast, making long wide slides in the snowdrifts; their tracks cross and recross the flat lake surface in every direction. They also frequently climb to our pet lookouts on the hill.

February 15

Last night we heard the love song of the wolf! There had been fresh snow followed by clear sky and a full brilliant moon. Our thermometer stood at 24 below. I proposed a snowshoe hike to Wolf Hill on the chance that we might be able to observe wolves down on the lake. J. scouted the notion of actually seeing them, but the night was so beautiful that he couldn't resist the idea any more than I could.

We stepped out in a dazzling world. At least a foot of new powdery snow covered the firm six-foot snow level and made ideal snowshoeing. We traveled swiftly and silently through silver glens and black shadows. Our snowshoes kicked up feathery clouds that twinkled like quicksilver. Our breath froze over jackets and caps and hair so that we were dressed from head to toe in white crystals.

When we reached the top of Wolf Hill, all below us spread the Driftwood Valley, clear as noontime, lit by the moon for a hundred miles, still and primeval as in the days before the few men who know it now had ever seen it. Belts of dark forest were interspersed by willow swamps which, deeply buried, lay like open fields brushed with gold. To the south the mountains of Takla were faint blue in the distance. The jagged, tumbled Frypans jutted like silver spearheads into the deep amethyst, star-studded sky. The Driftwoods, our own mountains, lay serene and golden, so close that we could almost reach out and touch them. The glacial-covered range far behind to the west showed distinctly, and the Bear Lake Mountains stood sharp and shining all around the northern horizon. Finally we moved across to the east side where a rock precipice falls down to Wolf Lake, crisscrossed with fresh black tracks, and looked on the miles of forested hills that rise gradually to the rolling Ominecas.

Utter silence, a deathlike hush over the land, and then, from somewhere below, came a sound that made our hearts stand still. Like a breath of wind, rising slowly, softly, clearly to a high, lovely note of sadness and longing; dying down on two distinct notes so low that our human ears could scarcely catch them. It rose and died, again and again. A wolf singing the beauty of the night, singing it as no human voice had ever done, calling on a mate to share the beauty of it with him, to come to him, to love him. Over and over it sang, so tenderly and exquisitely that it seemed as if the voice were calling to me and I could hardly keep from crying. The whole wilderness was musical with it. After an interval — I have no idea whether it was short or long — from far away across the eastern hills

Wolf Song

came a soft, distinct, answering call. Three times more the wolf below us sang and was answered. Gradually the other voice grew nearer and nearer, until we thought that the two must have come together, for the sudden quiet was not broken again.

Then I knew that I was shivering like a leaf and my arm, which J. had been grasping, was almost paralyzed.

J. was cussing to himself and saying: "Gad, what luck! What marvelous luck! I've heard wolves howling in India and the Arctic, but I never heard the like of that! Let's go home — if we're not too cold to move."

On the west, Wolf Hill slopes steeply, almost perpendicularly, for several hundred feet, and is clear of trees. Spurred to recklessness by the height of our emotions, we did something that we've never dreamed of daring to do before. We sat on the crossed heels of our snowshoes and tobogganed down the icy slope at terrific speed. Powdered snow flew up in clouds and turned to rainbows where the moon shone through it. That we arrived, unscathed, in a drift below, instead of being smashed to bits against trees, was just a part of the magic of the night.

We reached the warm cabin after midnight, stoked up a roaring fire, and drank hot scalding cocoa. I hardly remember getting into bed and to sleep, but all night in my dreams I thought I could hear a wolf calling and singing and sobbing in a voice of exquisite tenderness.

February 21

"Bestial" is a commonly accepted term used by human beings to describe the lowest type of human behavior. I dislike this. To say that bad men are like beasts is an insult to the beasts. I doubt whether animals are capable of the rottenness of which some men are capable. Possibly because man has risen higher in his mental powers he is able, therefore, to sink lower. But this greater mental ability, and power to reason, should make low behavior on man's part far less excusable than low behavior in an animal.

The Indians of these regions agree with the scientists who say that in general wolves remain mated for life; a habit of behavior far above that of the domestic dog, which is notably promiscuous, and incidentally above a certain percentage of human beings. The male and female wolf may be separated for a time each year, but come together again at the mating season in late winter or spring.

J. now spends most of his time examining tracks of wolves and making sketches and detailed notes of everything he sees or hears. Wolves have been following us, even coming within three hundred yards of the cabin. They use our snowshoe trails and we've found places where they must have stood behind bushes as we went by. Careful examination of their tracks indicates that they were made exactly at the same time ours were, and the Indians, who seem to be almost infallible at trail reading, have confirmed this.

J. finds the power and endurance of the wolves remarkable.[1] Once, for twenty-seven miles, he followed the trail of two wolves. The bigger tracks, over the first fourteen miles, were obscured partly by the smaller ones. Then the larger wolf moved to one side, with no perceptible change in pace, and dropped behind the smaller one. The snow was some six feet deep and quite soft. The trail of the wolves was a shallow trough sixteen inches wide and a foot deep, with foot and leg tracks going still deeper. The leading wolf simply pushed its way through. After the change in leadership, there was a pause — not a rest — where both wolves sprinkled a dead tree. Then they continued on their way. Two days later J. followed the same tracks for eight miles in the opposite direction, and there was no change in leadership, no sign of rest being taken, just the same deep furrow made in the snow by a powerful chest. The dog wolf had apparently led for a total distance of twenty-two miles, breaking trail without a single stop.

[1] "Three Years in the Wolves Wilderness" by John F. Stanwell-Fletcher, *Natural History Magazine,* March 1942. My husband tracked pairs of wolves for some distances on several occasions in February 1938, but I have here used an instance described by him in February 1941, because his notes in this case were more detailed.

Wolf tracks are common where snowshoe rabbits are thickest. Sometimes we find places where the wolves have dug up mice or lemmings. But in deep snow, the light snowshoe rabbit can usually evade the heavy wolf. Nor can grouse be stalked easily by an animal that sinks to the belly or lower with every step. The moose, whose weight forces it to travel very slowly with bent forelegs, is the animal that can be hunted by wolves most successfully at this season. Moose have begun to come back again to our part of the valley; we've seen wolf trails leading through the forest near a moose yard where the moose feed on tall dead grasses under thick spruces. Here the ground is sometimes almost bare. Evidently the moose, as long as they keep in shallow snow, aren't often attacked. When the moose has firm footing, its hoofs are sharp and deadly. Though hunting moose at this time must be a necessity for the wolves, it must also be a precarious business.

From a son-in-law of Bear Lake Charlie, J. has bought the skull and skin of a beautiful, large, gray-black dog wolf which the Indian found alive. This wolf, with terrific wounds, broken ribs, and two shattered legs, had stood at bay against a tree surrounded by moose tracks, blood, and moose hair. He had been crippled in a great battle. Although very sick, according to the Indian, he fought his next enemy, the man, fiercely and bravely, never yielding an inch, until a merciful shot at last ended his life.

The Indians have told us of similar cases in which a wolf has alone attacked a moose. But in general, the wolves attack in families, outrun the moose, and surround it. They leap at the legs to hamstring them and force the moose down, when they finish it by tearing at the throat. This process has been described to us by Charlie, Sapolio, Michelle, and a plane pilot, all of whom claim to have seen it on open lakes or swamps. It must be a fierce and thrilling business.

On Sapolio's last visit to his trap line (he comes about once a month), he told us that six or eight miles north of Tetana, five moose have been recently killed by wolves. The moose are about a mile apart and very little of them has as yet been eaten. But Sapolio declares that later the wolves will return and finish each one off to the last scrap and bone. He says they never waste any.

You can't feel anger at the wolves. This business of killing is not deliberate cruelty. Wolves do not, like sportsmen, kill for the sake of killing, but for food. Unlike man, they apparently never waste meat or kill unless necessary. So far we have not found any instances or heard of any kills which have been made and then neglected. Every scrap of the dead animal, except the fur, is eventually used by the wolves. Even the fur is put to good use by squirrels, mice, and birds in nest building.

We have also heard reports of wolf bands having been seen on Bear Lake, and in the open plateau country farther north. Charlie's boys recently saw two packs of wolves crossing Bear Lake. In the first they counted thirty-one, in the other fifteen.

Scientists disagree as to the numbers of individual wolves in a company. Seton, in his *Lives of the Game Animals,* lists thirty-two as large for a single band. We find that the Indians here consider thirty in one group to be not especially large. Several trappers of the Hudson Bay country told J. of counting two hundred or more arctic wolves together in one bunch. On one occasion, J. himself counted a hundred and sixty-seven, following a large herd of caribou.

J. has made one thorough attempt to trap a wolf here, in order to obtain a specimen for the Museum. He hadn't much hope of success after what we've heard from the experienced Indian hunters, the most clever of whom are not able seemingly to catch wolves except on rather rare occasions. But last week he put a big number-3 steel trap on a point along the shore of Wolf Lake. Here the wolves that travel over the ice invariably go out of their way to sprinkle a mound. J. set the trap with greatest care — he wouldn't let me come anywhere near that end of the lake. He wore gloves and concealed the trap with snow, and covered his own snowshoe prints completely as he back-tracked away. Late that afternoon there was a wind, very unusual here in winter, and when we went back to Wolf Lake next day J.'s tracks, and the trap set, and all human signs were completely obliterated by hard-blown snow. New wolf tracks, made in the night or early morning, were all across the lake, but for the first time they made a wide circle around their customary stopping place. Nor have they ever gone near the point since the trap was put there, though they continue to frequent Wolf Lake and Wolf Hill as much as ever.

I'm glad! It has made me *sick* to think of catching some wolf with a beautiful voice, perhaps the very one we listened to on that wonderful night. It made J. sick too, for he finally took up the trap and decided hereafter to obtain any necessary skins or skulls from the Indians.

It's interesting to me to watch the transformation in J.'s viewpoint about trapping and hunting. Although he has trapped in the Arctic and been a more than successful hunter of big game, he now quite definitely dislikes trapping the larger mammals, or killing, except in cases of necessity. From boyhood he's been crazy about wild things, but since he's begun to study their lives and habits, he's acquired such a feeling for them as individuals that the desire to take life from them has become more and more distasteful.

If we feel a strong repugnance for the trapping of the smaller mammals like marten and mink and beaver, how much more strongly do we feel it in the case of creatures as highly developed as the wolves. There are various authentic instances, reported by reputable scientists and hunters, which show that wolves which have been caught in traps for a few days, or even hours, although in superb physical condition and very little hurt, died in a short time, apparently from sheer agony of mind rather than from any physical injury. The expression in the eyes of these wolves and their whole appearance have been so heart-rending that even the most hardened hunters have expressed wonder and pity. Nothing but a high order of intelligence could grasp so quickly the terror and hopelessness of such a situation.

Probably it is a mistake to compare the intelligence and

mind of an animal with the intelligence and mind of a human
being. Each has certain parts of the brain, certain gifts of understanding and feeling, more highly developed than the others.
Animals, especially wild ones, who depend for a livelihood on
their own wits and strength, possess senses and abilities which
man has not, just as man possesses mental powers which animals
don't seem to have, or apparently only in small degree. But
certainly a study of the wild things that live in a wilderness has
rather a humbling effect on one's idea of man's much-vaunted
behavior and faculties. Time and again one notes instances in
which the moral behavior of an animal is superior to that of
many a human being, or observes cases where an animal has
been able to cope successfully with a situation in which man has
been unable to survive.

Alec Bob, a young Bear Lake Indian, married to one of
Charlie's daughters, paid us a visit. He had an almost beautiful
face — not very dark — and a beautiful body. His voice was low,
his manners courteous. He did not use any of our seats or
chairs; he preferred to sit modestly on the floor. As he drank
tea, he answered shyly our questions about animal life. Rumor
has it that he is a direct descendant of a famous white man. His
Indian mother, the squaw of a Bear Lake Indian, is beautiful
too. She must have been wonderful to look at in her younger
days. Most of these Indians appear to be reticent concerning
any strains of white blood. Evidently they don't approve of
mixed races, although with their easy tolerance of traits among
themselves, they seem to accept almost any mode of behavior.

Alec is said by the other Indians to be the cleverest of the
hunters when he wants to be, and to know more about the
habits of animals than anyone. He brought J. a wolf skin. He
had caught the wolf by placing the trap under water at a favorite wolf feeding place along a lake.

We have also seen a dozen or so wolf pelts at the trading
posts, but apparently most of these wolves had been killed with
a gun in open country farther north or south of the Driftwood
and Bear Lake regions. Some of the pelts were eight feet long

from nose tip to tail tip, though the majority were six to seven feet. The larger wolves were said to weigh around one hundred and thirty pounds. There was a remarkable variation in color. They were gray-white, blue-gray, yellow, and occasionally all black. According to game authorities, more wolf pelts should be brought in annually because of the bounty, as well as the fur price, paid for each skin.

The occasional talk from some ignorant authority or, worse, a supposedly intelligent scientist, about an actual extermination of wolves here or in Alaska, on the ground that unless wolves are done away with there will be no game animals left, fills us with helpless wrath. *Control* of certain so-called predators, or bad individuals, in restricted localities, is one thing; extermination of a whole race or species is another. Long before man, himself the greatest predator of them all, came on the scene, wolves and big game — the deer and moose and caribou — existed in apparently healthy proportion side by side. You have only to examine certain areas in the United States where cougars and bobcats and wolves have been exterminated to see what has happened to the deer: overpopulation of the range, consequent overgrazing, and decimation of disease-ridden animals no longer kept down in the proper proportion by their natural enemies who destroyed the unfit and left the strong. It would seem from facts that man, in this, as in so many other fields, is not able to improve on Nature.

Moreover, by what right does man, who after all forms only one small branch of all the great world of vertebrate and invertebrate animals, decree that another form, because it must prey for its livelihood on other live things, shall no longer exist? Man who, himself, as William James puts it, "biologically considered . . . is the most formidable of all the beasts of prey, and indeed the only one that preys systematically on his own species."

And so J. and I, thinking of the many parts of the earth where wolves have been wiped out completely, rejoice that there is still this corner where they are holding their own, apparently living in normal numbers despite the unreasonable and selfish desire of man to upset the natural balance of wildlife in a wild land, and repopulate that land to suit his own whims and needs.

Here there is another factor which helps to safeguard the wolves. This is a superstition or taboo that prevents certain Indians of this region from killing or catching wolves. We don't clearly understand why this taboo applies to some Indians and not to others, nor how strictly it prevents them from obtaining wolf pelts if opportunity offers. Bear Lake Charlie is one of the tribe who dares not kill a wolf. This applies to his sons, except Michelle, the oldest, who is the inheritor on the maternal side, and whose mother, Selina, does not belong to the wolf taboo company.

"The gun that kills a wolf," Charlie told us, "will one day kill a man. I neber kill the wolf myself, see? And my boys, only Michelle, cannot kill the wolf."

It is interesting that this traditional respect for wolves, the taboo against killing them, and various other ideas are to be found among these North American Indians, as well as the ancient peoples of India and Europe. Perhaps all this has arisen partly from inherited fear and partly from admiration for an animal whose brains and personality have for centuries successfully contested man and his ways. Man's respect for the wolf comes from knowledge of the wolf's character and strength; the taboos may be a sop to man's ego.

February 24

We've taken a trip to Sapolio's hunting land, east of the upper Driftwood Valley and Bunshaw country. Sapolio's trap line leaves an eastern arm of Bear Lake, follows through until it hits the summer trail above Hudson Bay Meadow, and thence down past Tetana, along the Driftwood River to Kastberg Creek, six miles south. It takes Sapolio, making about ten miles a day, an average of two weeks to run his trap line. He does a sort of elongated circle from Bear Lake down past us to Kastberg, and then back up to the east of us toward Bear Lake again.

Lured by Sapolio's descriptions of the country north of us, especially of "two beeg lake with islands," we have tried unsuccessfully to find his trail. On his latest trip past Tetana, he suggested that this time we follow his snowshoe tracks while they were still fresh, and then "you find heem, sure."

We made up packs with equipment enough for three or four days and, since the weather was fair, started off before Sapolio's tracks were obliterated by any new snow. The country was all strange to us. Part of the eastern Bear Lake ranges, which we see from Tetana, and which are said to be good goat and eagle country, were close on the northeast. We traveled leisurely, because Sapolio had assured us that his cabin on a little pond, which is kept open by springs, was a short half day from Tetana.

We are, by this time, somewhat accustomed to the Indians' estimates of distance, but we figured that an allowance of four hours to Sapolio's two should be sufficient. To Indians, a familiar trail is about half its actual length; if unfamiliar, twice as far.

Once we found otter tracks leading along a bank to a deep slide where they tobogganed down to a small rushing creek, partly open. This, we thought, must lead from the springs of Sapolio's little lake. Otters, even in dead winter, could fish there in open water.

Presently we came to a small pond, less deeply snowed-over, where three otters had recently played. They must, as J. said, "have had a whale of a time!" The three of them, going side by side, two large and one smaller one, brothers and a sister perhaps, had started with a run and a jump, gathered their short little legs under them, and slid on their bellies over the surface, again and again, like human children. Each slide was anywhere from six to fourteen feet long. They had gone clean down the pond, which was about a third of a mile, then broken into gentle lopes, their oval feet placed in series of twos and fours, like a large mink; then their three tracks converged into one, which disappeared into the woods.

One could fairly see the whole thing: black impish eyes set in dark bewhiskered faces, under flat little ears and foreheads; slinky satin-brown bodies moving in the lithe graceful curves characteristic of the weasel family. Feet gathered up as they launched themselves into the leap which ended in the long slide across the ice. Getting up to do it all over again and finally trotting gleefully off, red tongues hanging, pushing at each other in sheer exuberance.

Many people seem to think that wild creatures lead a life which is largely a fearsome, bloody struggle for existence, but I *know* this isn't true. Much of an animal's time must be spent in the sheer joy of living, the sheer pleasure of physical sensations. Watch a bear basking on a rock in the warm sun of early spring; a moose plunging under cool water to rid its huge body of summer flies, and wallowing luxuriantly for an hour; baby foxes, ignorant of fear, playing hide-and-seek around a tree, and then coming out to somersault almost on one's feet; rabbits playing on a moonlit lawn in the dead of night. (One can do that even back in civilization.) There is bound to be cruelty and pain in a world where every living thing depends for its existence on the life of something else, but it isn't a deliberate cruelty, and there is every chance for joy in between periods of danger.

These were the first signs we've seen of a real otter colony. Occasionally there have been tracks of otter along the river, but either this country doesn't suit them or else they have been depleted by extensive trapping. We have had some difficulty in obtaining otter skulls from the Indians for, even when they do have the heads, they are unwilling to part with them. Charlie's boys have given us several, after refusing to sell them. If they part with a head for profit there is grave danger that the spirit of the departed otter will possess their mother and cause her to go insane!

Sapolio seems to be one Indian who conserves his otters as

he told us he did. Whenever he finds otters becoming scarce, he traps few or none for a period of years, or until he notes definite signs of their increasing again. Would that some of the other Indians had ideas about the practice of conservation; so far they've listened to our many talks on the subject with shrugs or skeptical silence. And there is considerable evidence of wasteful trapping methods. Some traps, because they've not been visited regularly, contain furs that have almost wholly spoiled; others have not been set with care and animals have escaped, leaving a leg or foot, and wandered off probably to die; whole beaver colonies have been exterminated, and so on. J. believes trapping here is carried on under more difficult conditions than in the Arctic, because of extreme weather changes which occur constantly — sub-zero temperatures are followed by ones barely freezing, so that a good trap set is covered with ice in no time. Or fresh snowstorms may in two days bury a trap four feet deep.

The trail from the otter pond continued to follow the partly open little creek, but daylight was fading in the thick woods and we were obliged to make camp without having seen any signs of Sapolio's pond or cabin. What a speed that man must travel, if, as he vowed, his cabin was two or three hours from Tetana. We fixed an unusually comfortable camp near the stream. J. found a supply of small dead pines and we had a huge hot fire; the night was mild — probably around 12 above.

The next day we left camp set up and decided to explore farther, thinking we must soon strike Sapolio's place and the first big lake which he had said was just beyond a hill. About a half mile along, sure enough, beside the partly open little pond which he had described to us, we found the cabin, built in the style of a log lean-to, with a hole in the roof to let out smoke from an open fire. Thinking that Sapolio would not object, we explored and speculated on how he managed. Inside, the earth floor was strewn with chips of wood from kindlings of many fires, a few half-burned logs, stretcher frames for fox, mink, beaver, and other skins, an empty tobacco tin and. in one or two niches, drippings of candle grease. Here and there were small pieces of bone, remains of long-forgotten meals. Cold, bare, and deserted, the place seemed to have no character, no warmth. It was just a shelter.

Since Sapolio's line leads down our side of the valley we often come across the remains of his little winter camps; we look at them with interest, wondering what he and the black pack dog, which he always has with him, think about as they sit at night by the lonely campfire. Except for the few charred ends of big logs and a small heap of boughs, there is nothing else to show that a man and a dog have lived and slept there for the long winter's night of some twenty hours.

I can, by this time, understand why the Indians take such intense interest in examining our tracks and the remains of our camps. It is exciting to speculate on the character and behavior of unknown people, to note how their living habits differ from ours. And if we, who have "outside" contacts and intellectual interests and memories of adventures in other lands, feel this intense curiosity about the Indians' ways, how must they, knowing nothing beyond their own immediate world, feel about ours?

We went on again for miles along a ridge, through a big balsam forest. The seven-foot snow level was not deep enough to cover the huge logs and fallen trees, many of which lay at angles eight or ten feet above ground. Sapolio's trail is the hardest winter one we have been over yet. There was no such thing as a level stretch. Up and down we climbed and fell and slid. J. cursed as his big snowshoes tripped him up and sent him headlong repeatedly.

"Where the hell are those lakes? If this is Sapolio's idea of one hill —"

It was past noon and we had no lunch with us, but as the chief object of our trip had been to see at least one lake, we pushed on. Finally, after descending a long slope, we came suddenly and unexpectedly out of the forest onto an arm of a big stretch of snow-covered ice. It was about four miles across, winding, and dotted with small islands. A new lake, in winter, is very satisfying; one can explore all over it and pick out campsites for summer, lovely views, open groves, good firewood.

By this time I was feeling a little faint, as I always do when I skip a meal. J. never will admit that he minds. One of his pet and most annoying theories is that it is good for our stomachs to have complete fasts once in a while.

We had been so absorbed in the lake that we had forgotten to observe the weather. But now we saw that the north wind had shifted south, where heavy cloud banks hung along the horizon. J. thought there might be snow before morning, and he was fired with one of his sudden and rather unreasonable desires to get back to Tetana that very night. I had been counting on another comfortable camp and a chance to examine the otter tracks further next day, but J. was uneasy about the weather, he had no wood cut for the night, he said we could reach Tetana on the now well-trodden trail before too late. He would stay if I wanted to, or if I felt too tired to get home, but he was anxious to be off. So I resigned myself. He would go on ahead to camp and have things packed up and ready to start by the time I got there. He said I could take my leisure and rest along the way and be "all fresh" for the return trip to Tetana!

"What I want is *food*," I said rebelliously, "I'm weak as a cat — "

But my remark fell on deaf ears, for he was already out of sight in the trees. As I climbed wearily up and down over the logs and drifts of that horrid balsam forest, I thought steadily and most unwisely of my favorite restaurant lunch — raw oysters, sea-food platter of lobster and crab and scallops, a green salad, hot rolls, fruit lemonade, an ice-cream meringue.

When I reached camp, J. had everything packed. There was just time to snatch a bite of food and a cup of tea. We had a few hours of daylight left in which to reach Tetana, and we must travel *à la* Sapolio if we were to make it. When we started on the homeward trip (a trip that had taken us five hours to do the day before and which we now proposed to do in two), I was already weary from the long trek to the big lake and back. The hasty snacks of bannock and cold tea, eight hours away from breakfast, were not the help they might have been. When I am tired, events always move in a vicious circle. I hadn't made up my pack with the usual care, or fitted the snowshoe harness exactly right. I had to stop and remake the pack several times. Then a thong of harness broke. Since only I could fix it to fit, I begged J. to go on and wait for me farther along. I wanted to be able to moan in private. The damn harness broke three times. Maybe it was because I didn't fix it properly. Maybe it was just plain cussed.

With J. far on ahead, the trail was utterly quiet and rather depressingly still. The snowy hills and little ponds were so hushed that my ears seemed to be covered with ear pads. Twice I had a feeling that some live presence, other than my own, was walking near by, but there wasn't a sound of any sort.

After I caught up with J., who had been waiting some time, I forgot it. When we were near Hudson Bay Meadow and some four miles from home, it was very late and dark. We agreed that J. should go on ahead, make up the cabin fire, fetch water, and start supper. The clouds which had been gathering had dispersed, it was clear again, and the well-broken trail wouldn't be hard to follow.

After I crossed the Meadow and entered the thick forest on the other side it seemed, at first, pitch-black. I tripped repeatedly and had to feel for the trail at every step. And then, suddenly, I *knew* I was being followed, and the first fright of it nearly shook me out of my weariness. I stopped dead. I couldn't honestly swear that I had heard or seen a thing, and yet if I hadn't gone crazy "bushed," I knew that something alive was there, close to me, in the deep snowy woods.

"Don't be silly," I said out loud. "Of course there are live things all around you. What about squirrels in their nests and mice and weasels under the snow, maybe a marten or two?"

But that wouldn't do, because I still knew that whatever was there was something big, and it wasn't just one "something," it was several somethings, on either side of me. I was sure then that it was wolves.

My greatest fear in this country has been not of wild animals, but of human beings. A bad Indian or a tough white man. I've not been much afraid of the wolves. But there was no denying that if these were wolves, they must be following me closely and boldly. I finally started on once more, stumbling and pushing stiff legs and ankles on and on, and I didn't stop again. Starlight began to slant through spruces in blue-silver patches, but the forest was too thick for light to strike the trail. Just because I could now see a little, I began to imagine moving shapes which I hadn't noticed before. I was only a mile from the cabin, but it seemed as though I could never make it.

J. was standing in the light of the open door, watching, for I'd been longer than he had figured on. Without taking off my snowshoes or answering his exclamations, I clumped into the cabin, sank down on a box, and sobbed.

J. looked at me aghast. Then he knelt down, undid my snowshoes, took off moccasins and socks and rubbed my feet, saying: —

"My darling, I shouldn't have let you do it. You're just played out."

And he so well *might* have said, "Why in heck did I ever bring a weak woman out here to bother me and hamper me at every step? This is no life for a woman anyhow!"

Credit is given the modern woman who dares the loneliness and hardships of pioneering adventure. But the man who dares to take the woman, be responsible for her well-being, and allow his own free movements to be seriously handicapped, deserves as much, if not more, credit than the woman. Quite a lot of people, believing great physical strength to be essential, wondered at J.'s undertaking such a life as this, so soon after a dangerous operation; and they also made remarks about my size and physique. Though average good health is probably necessary, the real factors which enable a man or a woman to cope with a wilderness existence are temperament and character. According to what one has within oneself, either one loves it and takes it, or one hates it and goes under.

The very next day Michelle and another Bear Lake Indian stopped at our cabin on their way across to Michelle's trap line over the river.

The first thing Michelle said was, "By gosh, Jack, we find your tracks other side Hudson Bay Meadow. Your wife come on behind you? He see wolves? By gosh, *seex* wolves. Gre-eat beeg ones. He walk same-time as your wife, all the way. We count the tracks, both sides your wife's snowshoe trail. All around he go. He come with your wife right to cabin. You neber see heem? *By gosh!*"

February 28

The other night, when the cabin was surrounded by the deep dark and snow of the winter evening, we were just sitting down to supper when a sound outside made us leap from our seats and fly to the door. Wolves again! This time there were many of them — a whole chorus — less than half a mile away. One voice after another — some deep, some high — caught up the song in perfect harmony. It was not the tender, longing voice of a lone wolf calling to his love, but a whole company — a family perhaps — singing together for the joy of making music. The song, starting low, rose ever fuller and higher, but always beautifully modulated.

One voice, singing on its own just before each big chorus began, was sweet and clear, exactly like a boy soprano. It started on a high, high note and slipped down, sadly and exquisitely, to a lower one.

Our supper grew stone cold and the open door chilled out the cabin while we listened, entranced. The only thing comparable to it was a stringed symphony, but the wolf voices seemed more full of soul and expression.

And each night since, this valley has become a concert hall filled with wolf music. No one who has really heard wolves at the time of mating could possibly describe it by any other term. The more familiar wolf hunting call is a very different sound and one which we occasionally heard here last fall. This appears to be always a prolonged series of high notes, persistent and savage. The movement of packs can be followed by their voices as they move along our valley. Undoubtedly it is the hunting and fighting songs, the idle calls, which possess the fearsomeness, and weirdness, or bloodcurdling quality commonly associated with the voices of wolves. Sometimes the wolf song comes from many miles away; it echoes and re-echoes melodiously up and down the hills. At other times it is close by Tetana, so that even when we are shut up warmly and tightly inside our cabin, we tingle and thrill at the first sound.

The wolves' singing seems to be definitely affected by weather; they are most active on beautiful nights, still, radiant ones lit by moon, or stars, or the faint glow of an Aurora, nights so lovely that we ourselves are drawn out of the cabin to look and listen even before the wolf choruses begin.

A high mound, half a mile from Tetana, is a wolf meeting ground. We judge from the tracks that about eight or ten wolves gather together to sing. They also use several small hills which we often climb, including Wolf Hill. The very spots where we linger to look upon the world stretched out below are favorite gathering places for the wolf tribe. Their tracks lead directly from one vantage point to another and there are many imprints of huge hind quarters, hard and encrusted, such as are left by a dog that has sat or lain in snow for hours.

Why, J. and I argue, should the wolves sit there unless it is because they too recognize and appreciate something that we call beauty? There is no food to be had on these hilltops. Deep, untouched snow covers mouse holes. Rabbit and squirrel tracks are scarce or absent, and dense forest hides any sign of moving game in the valleys below.

Oddly enough, however, when the Aurora comes with especial brilliance, the wolves are as silent as the grave. The owls and coyotes, whom we also hear frequently at this season, are noticeably quiet too. Perhaps they all know, as we do, that no sound should be made to detract from a miracle of sight and feeling. For, as February slips into March, we are being treated to another phenomenon of miraculous beauty. The Northern Lights, which we saw sometimes last autumn when they were not particularly spectacular, have begun to appear now in full glory.

The aurora borealis seems to precede great seasonal change. The lights appear on clear evenings around nine-thirty or ten. A saffron glow behind the forest on the east of Tetana grows gradually so bright that black spires of pines and spruces stand out sharply against it. Then, rising in tall columns of pale, glowing green, higher and higher toward the zenith, becoming suffused with vivid lavender and rose. Other columns begin in the north and northwest until they all meet, umbrella-wise, in the sky above Tetana. Never-still, ever-changing curtains of waving, swaying color — colors so intense that sometimes the snow across Tetana and the Driftwood Mountains is tinted pink, or green, or blue. Often as the colors bloom and die and bloom again, the air is full of sound. Something — actual noise or electric current — vibrates in our ears. This is what northerners mean when they say, "The Lights crackle." Something great and majestic is alive here in these night skies of late winter.

On such nights how can I bear to sleep and waste time in unconsciousness! But J. claims that Northern Lights are as common in his experience as sunsets and goes serenely to sleep at bedtime just as usual.

A feeling in the air makes one know spring is coming. The world is buried as deeply as ever in snow. Snowstorms still come and go. Snowshoes are as essential a part of moving as ever. Collecting sufficient firewood is a never-ending labor. The cabin roof and windows have still to be dug out, but snow on the ground is settling and crusts are forming. The sun is rising higher in the sky. The nights are as cold as ever. Temperatures still drop 20 or 30 degrees below zero, but we know that the hardness of winter is ended. The singing wolves remind us again and again of returning life and love. The throbbing colors of the aurora give warning of changing atmospheric conditions.

We've arranged to take a trip to Takla in early March for mail and to see about summer supplies. Traveling then is said to be good, and Michelle is to come with his sled to help us bring back some food.

CHAPTER VIII

Month of March

H.B.C. House, Takla Lake   *March 9*

We left Tetana on March first and reached here early on the third — having hiked about seventy miles in two and a half days. Michelle and young Mac, who must be around fourteen, came along with four dogs and Charlie's toboggan on which we loaded supplies for the journey and numbers of mammal skulls for the Museum.

The days were clear and hot, the nights bitterly cold. We tried to do most of our traveling from early morning to early afternoon, because after midday the snow grew soft and slushy. Around noon the sun was almost unbearable — the temperature must have been 70 or 80 degrees — and we could hardly stand our wool shirts and underwear. All of us, including the Indians, wore heavy dark glasses against the intense glare of crusted snow and ice. Even so our eyes watered constantly. J.'s and my skins are burned a deep red brown; on first sight the residents of Takla took us no doubt for two more Indians. By sunset it was so cold — down to zero or way below — that we couldn't get enough clothes on and, despite the usual six-foot fires of big logs, I could hardly keep warm enough to sleep. The first half day we estimated that we traveled fifteen miles; the second day twenty-five to thirty. We traveled on the flat surface of the long, many-curved, winding little river instead of by the shorter, up-and-down summer horse trail through thick woods. Because of soft snow, we were forced to walk all the way in the toboggan track. These toboggan tracks are just too narrow for snowshoes; we snowshoed mile after endless mile with our ankles turned constantly inward. Our moccasins were soaked through by melting snow and our feet rubbed raw by the harness. I tried the

Indians' method of wearing rubbers to keep my moccasins dry, but these made my feet extra sore. I thought I'd pass out (and earnestly hoped that I would) long before we reached the north end of Takla that afternoon. Near the swamps above Bulkley House we passed across fresh moose trails and the men, sinking in above their knees in spite of snowshoes, took extra side trips hoping for a shot.

On this trip Michelle has displayed the height of tact. Whenever I began to fall behind, he stopped the sled and sat down, saying that the dogs needed a rest. He has been courteous and considerate about our camps, and seems to enjoy working with us. If only he can stick to it.

During the second day, we stopped at Bear Lake Tom's Hunting Lodge. Martha and Vinson were staying there in a tent with old Tom and his wife. Martha was sick — it seemed like flu — and we administered aspirin. From Vinson we bought a coyote skin and a little Richardson's owl which had been caught in a trap. We gave him a note to the H. B. C. to pay him their value in cash or goods. We rather went out of our way to be nice, and he and Martha too were unusually polite. We hoped they just might have had a slight change of heart!

When we reached Bulkley House, where the snow was half as deep as at Tetana, we made camp near the winter cabin belonging to Johnny French. Johnny had saved a supply of good mammal heads for us — bear and marten — which J. bought for the Museum. As their agents, we purchase all the mammal skulls we can get. After the customary long exchange of gossip and courtesies, we were left finally to ourselves. We took off our soaked moccasins and socks, and about half the skin of my feet came off with the socks. I was convinced that my ankles would never straighten out again. Altogether, I felt so sick that it was some time before I could take even a swallow of tea. But my feet were nothing to J.'s. His were not only raw but bleeding. And I had supposed, judging by his rapid pace and cheerful shouts, that he had been enjoying the day to the utmost. But that is typical of J. The worse he feels, the faster he goes — to get it over with! And he always looks so fresh and gay I rather hate him until, at the end of a day, I see the condition of his feet.

The last day we traveled the twenty-five miles down the lake from Bulkley House to Takla Landing in five hours. All the way it was glare ice and the slightest tug from the dogs made the sled shoot almost on top of them. So, for the first time in my life, I rode on a dog sled. The dogs, tails held high, raced along. J. and Michelle ran or walked just ahead for the entire distance. And little Mac balanced himself on the rear runners. All day the ice moaned and boomed like a thunderstorm coming up, the sun shone and shone in a cloudless sky, the lake and mountains danced and glittered. It was wonderful fun.

Halfway along we stopped at the winter cabin of old Daniel Tegee, from whom we acquired our first moccasins and snowshoes. Daniel was very sick. J. thinks he is dying. Perhaps he has cancer of the stomach which is not improved by liquor drinking. Poor old man, with his pride in his hunter's skill and his beautiful moccasins.

When we got here, Mr. and Mrs. Holden of the Hudson's Bay Post, the young couple who have come to take the place of the Macintoshes (Mr. Mac is very ill with t.b.), gave us a warm welcome. Mrs. Holden, who is one of the prettiest brunettes I ever saw, cleared out her best room and has made us free of her house, even to the extent of allowing us to skin specimens and leave smelly skins and skulls everywhere. She has a baby boy, but finds time to entertain and provide us with lavish meals. Mr. Holden is quiet and reserved, fair-minded in his attitude toward the natives, and most helpful to us.

We've been to several meals with the Aikens, who are an interesting family and know a good deal about wildlife. Their two children especially are very keen on natural history; so we all had much to talk about.

Nearly everyone here has a cold. J. and I tremble for our perfect health record and wish we'd never come. I'd almost forgotten that such things as colds existed. In the wilderness we have never once caught cold from being wet or chilled. The Indians, too, inadequately dressed and nourished and exposed constantly to terrific weather conditions, apparently never have colds or contagious diseases unless they get "outside" to some settlement and pick up a germ.

We're rather hoping we may get back to Bear Lake next week by a plane which is taking freight to Carl. But one never counts on anything in this uncertain land.

What should we find here with our other mail, but a communication from the game warden of this district enclosing a letter of complaint about us from Vinson. It seems that we are trapping on Vinson's line without permission; that I, as well as J., put many traps out (I who have never set anything bigger than a mouse trap in my life!) ; that we haven't paid him for things we've gotten from him (i.e. a few mammal skulls for which we gave him last fall a letter to the Hudson's Bay Company for their equivalent in cash or goods since we had no cash on hand) ; that we threaten the Indians; that we are, in short, altogether bad, completely lawless characters! Since none of these Indians uses such good English, we are wondering who wrote for him. We've been obliged to indite a lengthy epistle to the game warden enclosing details of our many permits, explaining our business at length, and referring him to the warden and Indian agent at Hazelton, who heard firsthand about our work.

It seems that one of Vinson's favorite occupations is writing letters of complaint, especially about other Indians. We understand that the authorities are a bit fed-up. He is in a feud with another Indian over his trap line and if he doesn't stop making trouble his trap line here may be given to the other Indian altogether. According to the maps, Vinson's territory does extend up to Tetana, but it is quite likely that Sapolio also was told that his runs down past Tetana to Kastberg Creek. Sapolio's claims have not yet been marked on the maps.

This confusion over trap lines seems an inevitable and common occurrence. It may result from a lack of knowledge of the geography of a region. Shortage of staff makes it impossible for any one warden to get over the territory often. Due to language difficulties, there must always be a lack of clear understanding on the part of both Indians and white men. An unexploited, unsurveyed northern land remains free of the game warden except when he can travel by plane (too uncertain and expensive to be feasible more than once or twice a year) because he hasn't the time to spend months traveling hundreds of miles by foot even if weather conditions permitted him to do so. If we, living the year out with these Indians of the Driftwood region, acquainted with all the little natural boundaries that they know, find it impossible to make head or tail out of their trapline claims, what must it be like to the game warden who sees them only for a few days a year?

A lot of letters as disturbing as Vinson's, though certainly more flattering, have been piling up for us. These are from some of our most beloved friends. No less than five of them, apparently fired by our example, are desirious of taking to the wilderness — and our wilderness at that. One friend, unable to comprehend that we do not receive daily mail and telegrams, has written three letters followed by a cable from Europe — all many months old. Though all these people are, as far as we know, advantageously situated in the world of affairs, they are either fonder of us than we thought, or our few letters, which we have *tried* to make conservative, have filled them with impractical longings. Any white newcomers, however, especially collecting scientists, might have untold difficulties with permits, since the present authorities very wisely do not welcome outsiders and wish to keep British Columbia material for British Columbia. They might also have serious trouble with the Indians over encroaching on their lands. Furthermore, J. and I *don't want any other companions!* One of our chief objects is to see it through alone and discover just what it means to be alone. But perhaps the most important fact of all, which people unaccustomed to remote places never appreciate, is that only about two persons in a thousand are ever congenial enough to get on together in a wilderness existence.

We have sat long into the night trying to concoct tactful replies which will show how dearly we love them but how utterly unpractical and impossible it would be. Perhaps it would have been more pertinent just to quote them a tale of Mr. Macintosh's: Once at one of his far northern posts, Mr. Mac remonstrated seriously with a fine old prospector who, year in and year out, lived completely alone far off the beaten track. Mr. Mac urged him to take a partner, reminding him that as his age advanced he might become badly in need of help. To all of which the old man, looking him seriously in the eye, sorrowfully shook his head. He said, "No, Mac. Why Mac, I couldn't get on up there with old Jesus himself!"

Letters from Dr. Cowan of the Museum are enthusiastic over the mammal skulls and bird and small mammal specimens that we've sent. The skunk skull apparently extends the range of this species considerably, and there are some unusual subspecies of birds which they cannot yet place, and so on. They seem anxious for more material. Dr. Cowan, that delightful and versatile person, has been especially nice about writing us letters of information and just the kind of advice we need about everything, from the types of wildlife which might occur here to the best methods for preserving any kind of specimen.

In the short time we have been here we have heard an astonishing amount of gossip. It makes us wonder, uncomfortably, just what terrible things have been spread about us. For in the North, I don't suppose that anyone escapes the curiosity and speculation (so much more interesting if malicious) which inevitably arises in a world peopled by so few human beings that practically everyone for thousands of miles either knows, or has heard of, practically everyone else.

We've attended several social gatherings of the Takla inhabitants, and I felt exactly like a fish out of water. The few ladies of Takla sported silk dresses, thin stockings, and high heels, while I, because as usual I had been unable to carry any apparel with me except the clothes I stood in, was obliged to appear in baggy black ski pants, the old red sweater, and mooseskin moccasins, three sizes too large. After being accustomed night and day, for months, to the pure cold of God's fresh air, the heated crowded little rooms, plus the warm clothing, almost killed me off. My face was crimson, my clothes wet with sweat, and I had to step outside every few minutes in order to keep on breathing.

But be sociable we must, at all costs, for one of our chief objects in taking this trip has been to advertise our work and show people of this country that we really are perfectly harmless, ordinary characters, albeit we may have some unusual tastes about the way we choose to live. (The Indians who have seen us trapping mice on a large scale, have spread the report that we are obviously crazy.) I'm afraid that J. has given a much better illustration than I of the usual civilized human being. He never seems to notice temperature changes as I do. Men can behave more naturally because differences in clothes aren't half so prominent. At the party, clad in comparatively new pants and moccasins, with a clean shirt, and a new haircut (I have learned to cut his hair so becomingly that I think of setting up as a barber when I go back to civilization), J. looked so very respectable that I kindly kept away from his vicinity as much as possible.

Tetana   *March 14*

We came up on the eleventh by plane, landing at the south end of Bear Lake. The small Junkers plane carried a load of supplies weighing about 1200 pounds, not including our own weight; these supplies, supplemented with fresh meat, should see us through spring and summer. There are several hundred pounds of flour and sugar, dried fruit and beans, butter, tea, coffee, chocolate, sacks of fresh potatoes and onions, a crate of twelve dozen eggs (fresh eggs that have been dipped in preserving fluid), a few boards of lumber, wire screening for summer, and a roll of roofing paper (much too thin but all that was available) to nail above our leaking shakes. Since our diet is so restricted we find different kinds of flour and lots of spices and sauces — none of which add much extra weight to a load — a great boon. Michelle, who returned to Bear Lake some time ago, is bringing the things down to Tetana in two trips on his sled. The long haul by plane and short haul by dogs, to our surprise, makes the whole load at least four cents per pound cheaper than if it had been brought all the way by horse or dog.

Russ Baker, who flew us up, looks completely typical of one's idea of a northern bush pilot. He has the steady eyes which look on great distances, a big body inured to every kind of weather, and a ruddy face with lines drawn from making quick decisions meaning life or death. Mr. Baker has had much experience flying over the Northland, which he obviously loves. J. had heard about him even as far off as Hudson Bay. Like the other pilots of commercial airlines in this country, he is automatically a Dominion warden, entitled to act for the law when necessary. J. told him about Vinson, so if Vinson makes further trouble we shall have presented our side of the story.

The day we flew up, he made two trips to Bear Lake taking J. for a free ride when he went to deliver Carl's supplies. Then they returned and loaded in me and our freight. This was my second trip in a plane. Riding in a small heavily loaded freight plane through wild uncharted mountain ranges is very different from sitting at ease in a passenger plane over gently rolling cultivated country. Snowstorms whirled around mountain peaks and we flew off course, now and then, to avoid them. The mountains, gleaming in sun or darkened by clouds, were wonderful. We saw new spectacular ranges that we have never known about.

The plane was equipped with winter skis, and according to J., who has flown often, made a "beautiful landing" on the south end of Bear Lake. We climbed out stiffly, having been crouched in cramped attitudes on sacks of flour, canned goods, and lumber. They unloaded our stuff on the lake, the plane took off, and we were alone and quiet once more in the white stillness and clean air. Next morning, after carefully wrapping and storing the crate of eggs (which we had taken to bed to keep from freezing), we snowshoed the thirteen miles down to Tetana.

Just as we crossed the upper end of our "meadow" a mile north of the cabin, as luck would have it, whom should we meet but Vinson and Martha and a dog team headed for Bear Lake. J., ripping mad over Vinson's latest piece of mischief, stopped him and gave him a piece of his mind; told him we had reported him to the authorities, and never to darken our door again, etcetera. J.'s black beetling brows drew together in a straight line, his blue eyes glittered as they do when he is very angry; I wouldn't like to say he stuck his chest out, but his big body looked twice as powerful as usual. Had I been Vinson I should have been terrified. Martha stood somewhat apart; and I began to talk to her a bit, asking if she couldn't persuade Vinson to behave more sensibly. It sounded reasonable to me. She listened for a minute with averted face, then turned on me with such blazing fury that I jumped back about five paces. I was quite certain she meant to tear me limb from limb!

When Michelle brought our things, J. told him that in one day he had flown from Takla to Bear Lake, back to Takla and up to Bear Lake again (a distance that by snowshoe or dog team would, with luck in weather, and so on, take about three weeks), Michelle for once was speechless. He sat down heavily on a box, shook his head, and uttered no word for a considerable time.

While Michelle was in the cabin with J., I went outside to speak to his dogs. On the trip to Takla, we had been quite friendly with the savage little canines. Apparently regarding us as comrades of the trail, some of them had allowed us to pet them and showed every sign of pleasure. But when I walked toward them this time they suddenly bristled and with an awful roar sprang straight for me. The leader came within three feet of my throat. The only thing that saved me was the fact that they were held in by harness and the still partially loaded toboggan. At the din J. and Michelle rushed out, while I, red and breathless from fright and annoyance, tried to be extremely nonchalant. I suddenly remembered (what I should have recalled before) certain stories of women in the Arctic being torn to pieces by excited Husky dogs.

March 16

After weeks of brilliant weather the last of February and first of March, when pussywillows began to peep out and the snow level sank fast, winter came again. There have been three snowstorms, one on top of the other, and sub-zero temperatures. Our gay and charming dippers have all left, alas! alas! — we suppose for summer quarters.

Now it has cleared once more. Wolves and coyotes, silent when we first came back from Takla, have started up again. For three nights in succession, around dawn, we've been waked from sound sleep by howls and yelps. The wolves must be hunting, for their voices are menacing and fierce. I'm rather glad to be in a snug bed safe inside a cabin, and my warm feeling toward them is, I find, tinged now with new respect and a little fear. There are tremendous choruses of coyotes, their sharp staccato notes distinct from the smooth, long-drawn howls of the wolves. From far off they sound exactly like crowing roosters.

After the storms there have been wonderful displays of the aurora again. The snow is once more five feet deep on the level. It is still very cold, down to zero and 10 below at night. Except for Northern Lights and wolves and coyotes at dawn, there are still no signs of spring. We go along steadily each day attending to our chores, and waiting for a change in the winter-locked world, a change that seems just in the offing, and yet afraid to come. Above all other things, perhaps, the wilderness teaches patience and endurance.

March 25

We have a dog! At first J. and I were opposed to the idea of having dogs, since one of the primary objects of our new life is to observe wild things and we feared their presence might be a hindrance. But we're ardent dog lovers; it is almost the first time in our lives that either of us has been without canine friends of one kind or another, and we've missed their companionship terribly. Moreover we now understand just how useful and essential pack dogs are to the Indians traveling through this valley. None of them goes anywhere without a dog or two. And, although the Indian dogs are mongrels, no larger than small collies, and usually thin and in bad condition, each carries at least a twenty-pound pack. Forced to pack a large share of our equipment on his back whenever we took a trip away from home, J. especially had begun to think what it would mean to unload forty pounds or more on a couple of dogs. If we were to take long trips, we would need some way of carrying more supplies, since we much prefer to travel and camp without the Indians. Pack horses in this country during the cold season (about nine months out of twelve) are out of the question. There is too much snow and no horse food. So we at last decided to acquire dogs of our own if we could ever find any better than the Indian variety. But we had little hope of seeing a good dog until we went "outside" again.

Then, unexpectedly, fate landed one on our very doorstep. Last week Sapolio appeared suddenly out of the winter woods. Strapped to his back was a large radio which he set down without comment inside our door. To our astonished inquiries, he replied that it belonged to a white man named Brown who was on his way from Bear Lake, and points north, to Takla. Sapolio had left him back along the trail somewhere: —

"That man he have only one arm, he lame, and he go very slow."

But he thought Brown might reach our cabin by dark. He, Sapolio, was going on down the valley to see his traps. And he departed immediately, leaving us overpowered with curiosity about the white man and not too pleased at the prospect of an unknown visitor intruding on our privacy.

Around dusk, a bent little one-armed man, with white hair and a face red from cold, arrived at our back door, so tired he could hardly stand. But at first I scarcely noticed the man because of my intense interest in the three dogs that accompanied him. Here were no savage half-starved Indian dogs, but a beautiful Alsatian bitch and her two pure-bred little Alsatian pups. The bitch, whom Mr. Brown addressed as "Gyp," was one of the loveliest things I ever saw, with great stiff ears that quivered and pricked like a startled deer's, and eyes soft and tender and full of soul. Obviously this was a creature of high degree, a patrician of the canine world.

Mr. Brown seemed surprised and grateful when we welcomed his dogs into our cabin as cordially as we did him. He was so exhausted (he had come from Bear Lake in one day) that we fed him a hot meal before we began to talk. I sat down on the floor to make the acquaintance of Gyp, who, perfect lady that she was, responded with dignity and graciousness. The gist of Mr. Brown's story was that he had come from a mining camp some hundred and twenty-five miles north, that he had paid an Indian handsomely with a large supply of food left in the camp to bring him out by dog team to Takla, that the Indian had deserted him at Bear Lake so that he was obliged to travel the rest of the way on his own, and that Sapolio had brought the radio down to us because he was sure we'd like to buy it. He was completely incredulous when we assured him that we had purposely come in without one because we wanted to get away from radios and other appurtenances of civilization. He was positive that we would change our minds before he left.

That night we had disturbed sleep. The two pups, not yet housebroken, were restless; they made a few messes in the cabin and had to be let out. And Mr. Brown, on the bearskin on the floor, tossed and cursed in his sleep and talked a steady and amazing stream, so that I acquired a vivid picture of somewhat doubtful past adventures. Next day he told us he was snow-blind, so badly that he couldn't see the lovely view from our windows. And he was obviously too weary to travel; both his snowshoes were broken and were useless until they could be mended. J. said he had best stay with us for another night anyhow. J. also told me, in a private interval, that he didn't think Mr. Brown was nearly as blind as he claimed to be. J. has had too much experience in the Arctic not to know every symptom of snow-blindness.

With us, Mr. Brown was very courteous and interested. He looked often around our cabin and particularly at us. Once he said, "Well, I wouldn't live here in this Styx all the year round myself, but you people seem to be happy and that's what counts. Don't know when I've ever seen people that look really happy like you two do." And, "What d'ya do with yourselves when you *do* go out? Have a grand bust-up at cocktail parties and such, I guess?"

J. said, "Why no, as a matter of fact we don't go in for that sort of thing much. There are a lot of other things we enjoy more — "

But I don't think Mr. Brown really believed us. He talked of his dogs and said that he had been raising Alsatians for years, that he had never found a mean streak in any of them, and that as far as intelligence went no other species could hold a candle to them. He regaled us with remarkable stories of Gyp, who, I believe, was about eight years old and apparently gifted with almost more than human wisdom. She had had several pure-bred litters, but these two pups were the last she could ever have because, when packing for him recently on a cold mountain pass, her teats had been badly frozen and were now completely useless. His family, he said, didn't want her at home and when he got out this time he thought he'd shoot her; probably she wouldn't be happy with anyone else.

I *hated* Mr. Brown at this point, for Gyp had been listening and, from the look in her wonderful red-brown eyes, I felt sure she understood him. Despite what he said about loving her I didn't believe him; no real man would part with such a dog under any conditions.

The two pups were a male and a female; they had been born at the mining camp on Christmas Eve. All of the litter except these two had died. It had been bitterly cold and the pups had been moved near a red-hot stove. The contrast of extreme temperatures had perhaps been too much for them. The female was a dark-colored, sensible, friendly little thing, but the male was scary and skittish. He had never seen a white woman before, and he ran the minute I cast an eye on him. He had a tannish body mixed with dark, a black and white collar and ruff, and an all-black face. He was full of spirits and, I thought, much the brighter of the two. He spent hours watching the few wild ducks around the open water patch and never missed a thing that went on. When the other pup wouldn't play, he played with himself, chased his tail and turned somersaults with abandon and a wicked grin on his black countenance. He was Rex the Second. He had had a brother, Rex the First, who, according to his master, had been sold in Hollywood for a price and used in the movies. Mr. Brown did not know whether this Rex would make the dog his brother had — Rex Second was "bright" but "not very sensible." Here Mr. Brown remarked that he had promised the female pup to someone outside, but would give Rex to me if I cared to have him.

With visions of the big pack dogs we really needed and a knowledge of our slim food supply, I was a bit doubtful and said I must consult J. J. said by all means! It would never do to pass up a chance like this. Pure-bred Alsatians were valuable, he had always been wild to have one, and when Rex grew bigger he could pack a fair load. So Mr. Brown put Rex's hand in mine and told him that from thenceforward he was to be my dog and care for me. Little Black-face sprang off with a jump and a growl at the touch of that queer being, a woman, and Gyp growled at her son for his reprehensible behavior. Mr. Brown remarked that he had never seen Gyp take to anyone more than she did to us, and if he had not been obliged to have her carry his pack to Takla, he would have left her with us instead of Rex.

The next day, after J. had mended Mr. Brown's snowshoes and helped him pack, Mr. Brown departed with Gyp and the female pup, leaving Rex, to his horrified bewilderment, shut up in the cabin alone with me. Incidentally we had *not* bought the radio, though Mr. Brown had perforce to leave it with us. We don't want it on our hands at all, there are no batteries for it anyhow, and we mean to send it out the very first chance we get. J. took Mr. Brown to the main trail and started him well on his way to Takla, for, in spite of his assurance that he often traveled alone and would have no difficulty, we were rather troubled as to how a man with one arm would make out along the many miles of unfrequented winter trail.

When his family departed Rex made a few jumps at the doors and windows, but after a time he ate leftover beans out of my pan and then lay quiet by my chair, having apparently decided that he might as well be philosophical and accept me. After J. returned, Rex was quiet until bedtime, when it came over him with renewed force that his family had deserted him. In distress he performed on the cabin floor. We spanked him and talked to him and, seemingly, that is the only house training Rex is going to need, for not once again has he transgressed in his manners.

March 31

Rex has become my constant companion and guardian. When J. goes out, he tells Rex to stay and "take care of Teddy," and Rex never neglects his duty. One day I tripped on my snowshoes and rolled down a steep bank. J. was delighted because Rex hurtled after, trying to grab my sleeve and stop me as I fell.

Rex's presence makes a world of difference in our lives. At first, though we did not say this to each other, I think we both resented him — a little. It seemed too much like having a third person intruding into a world made for just us, a life which seemed complete as it was. But after all, a fine dog is not like a person, really. In his qualities of selflessness and utter loyalty, he is a cut above most human beings. He is the perfect companion (except that perhaps he spoils one), for he understands his master's moods almost before his master knows he has them, and he asks nothing better of life than to do whatever his master does. Above all he never talks back.

CHAPTER IX

A Northern Spring

Tetana   *April 4*

The snow is sinking fast and bare ground shows around many of the trees. But in the woods it is still six feet deep. We may have to wear snowshoes for another month. The Indians say that one has to wear them even in June in woods across the river. Tetana is the only lake anywhere around even partly free of ice. The open water patches should prove an attraction to migrating birds.

After a winter almost completely windless, except for a few short light breezes, high winds from the southwest are now sweeping up across the valley. They hurl themselves down the lake in mighty gusts and threaten to toss our cabin on the way. We're greatly alarmed about our roof, which has now some odd patches of flimsy roofing paper added to it. More than once we've climbed up on the roofing to hold it down by main force. Thus far we've been successful.

The jays and chickadees are coming less frequently to the feeding station. Necessity for food is less; they are absorbed in love-making and mating and nest building. An injured red squirrel has been around. One front paw hangs useless, and such a forlorn, thin little bunch of misery it is. One day it was creeping humbly about picking up crumbs, when a big healthy squirrel pounced on it and started tearing it to pieces. J., in a fury, promptly shot the attacker. The poor little hurt one, all bleeding and bitten around the mouth, hobbled away.

I suppose, by all the laws of Nature, we should have destroyed the weak and preserved the strong, so much better able to cope with life. Is man's instinct of chivalry toward the weak, unfit ones really a sign of progress and wisdom, or isn't it?

Old Bear Lake Charlie came yesterday. One of his little girls cut off the end of her finger with an axe. Her hand has apparently become infected and she is very sick. She "talk, talk, all the time and see bad things." He wanted us to ask Michelle, if he returned this way from his trap line, to hurry with the dogs to the Bunshaw cabin so that they could take the child to Bear Lake. He said to tell Michelle that he thinks "mebbe he [she] die" because "he dream about big chief long time dead and see him come." Charlie said he has "cut many people" and always put on beaver castors, which make the wounds heal. Now he has no beaver castors and is "very sorry."

Michelle and Mac arrived today. When we conveyed their father's message, they gulped and, tears in their eyes, hurried off without stopping to visit. These Indians seem devoted to their families and full of consternation and pity when any accidents or illnesses occur. We often wonder if they would have any real sympathy for us if we fell into bad circumstances. I believe that perhaps they would, just at first. Once at Bear Lake, when J. was stunned from a fall on ice and we thought that he might have been badly hurt, I was surprised to see tears and a spasm of pity on Selina's face. But pity, I imagine, would be short-lived. They would probably say, "By gosh, too bad that man [or that woman] he hurt [or he die], but I can't do nothing!"

J. claims that all natives are fatalists, far more so than the white man. When, in times past, he has been caught in dangerous ventures with the Eskimos, he says that after a time the Eskimo, convinced that he will die, lies down on the job and no longer bothers himself. The white man, on the other hand, will go on fighting long, long after there is no apparent hope, or until he is no longer capable of physical action.

We invite nearly every Indian who arrives at our cabin to come in for hot tea and bannock. Some white people of this country, with their strong feeling of racial superiority, believe this to be a bad precedent. Theoretically and ideally I think they are wrong. Practically, situated as most of them are, perhaps they are right. However, we do not live in a community, or run a trading establishment. We are alone, and acquire our livelihood from the wilderness as these Indians do. We are their neighbors and would behave as such. J., accustomed to the Far North where everyone is always given a hot drink, insisted that we do likewise here. At first it seemed to me rather unnecessary. Since I always boil cups and spoons to guard against t.b. or venereal disease, it makes considerable trouble. But now that I understand traveling in this country, I realize just what warm drink and nourishment mean at the end of a hard trip. J. and I would, moreover, like to return in some small measure the hospitality of the Indians. Wherever we have gone in this country these people have been invariably generous about offering to share their homes and food with us. In this respect, at least, they are more hospitable to the white man than the white man is to them.

April 8

The northward migration of birds has begun at last. Two days ago we went snowshoeing at 5 A.M. when the crust was still hard enough to hold us. The mountains had flushed dawn-pink at 4.30 and sunshine was coming out through spruces across Tetana. The temperature was 20. Life and warmth and spring were abroad. Down the lake in the still air, three wolves gave voice with soft lazy whines. One, with a yawn and a stretch and a good-natured howl to clear his lungs, was perhaps just waking. Another, which we now call "the boy soprano," gave suddenly the lovely, clear, high note which always drops down to the soft sad one. A male pine grosbeak, his body deep rose, was singing a rippling carol in the willow by our cabin.

Late on the afternoon of the day which had begun so still and clear and beautiful, the wind changed. In no time at all it rose to a gale, and driving, needle-sharp rain descended. At twilight, at 7 P.M., there was a loud, sudden flapping against the cabin wall outside, like a tent shaking in a gale. It was two American mergansers, a dark female and a gorgeous black-and-white male. With great difficulty they got down under wind and landed in the open patch of water below the bank. They must have been about to head down to the lake when a gust flung them against our cabin.

Yesterday, despite heavy wet snow all morning, followed by rain in the afternoon, a killdeer, calling plaintively, arrived at the edge of the water. At dusk, in hard rain, three mountain bluebirds came to the bank. There was just time, before darkness fell, to see the heavenly blue of their backs and their light breasts.

Today a robin was singing, and after the robin there came from the pine grove clear, metallic little sounds, like someone striking tinkly notes on a harpsichord. We crept out with glasses and found a varied thrush. Except for the rough dark band on its red-brown breast, it is something like a robin. There has been a pair of Brewer's blackbirds, also new to us, but easy to identify. The male has a purplish head, white eyes, and green metallic body, and the female is gray-brown. Tiny kinglets, yellow and orange crowns stuck up like jewels, are hopping on the shed roof and big spruce tree. A large shore bird, with streaked breast and long sharp wings, paused for one second on the willow bush and was off before we could get a real look at it.

The weather is so cold and dull it must be discouraging to the new birds. But longing for love and mating and the summer nesting ground is more compelling than all the difficulties of long flight through any dangers.

The little hurt squirrel which J. saved is still around. Now it looks as though it might survive and be fairly healthy after all!

April 10

For a week the weather has been atrocious. Rain every day; pile upon pile of dirty melting snow and unlovely debris are being uncovered all about us. We're completely confined to the cabin and to the few yards around it where we've dug snow away to keep from being flooded out. Getting wood and water and shoveling are our only exercise, but they furnish plenty. We can't go anywhere, even on snowshoes, without sinking through slush above our knees. Paths leading to wood and water have been packed so hard that they now stick far up above the rest of the melting snow. They look safe to walk on, but twice, when I've gone along them without snowshoes, which don't really seem to be much help, my feet have gone through. I've sunk to the waist and had a fight to get out.

One day when J. was in bed with lumbago, the first real illness either of us has had, and I was going for wood, one leg sank way down and my foot was caught tight. I tried to dig it out with my hands. The more I pulled and twisted, the more packed snow-ice formed around it. If I had had my big knife! But it was in the cabin. Who could think of desperately needing a knife in the fifteen yards between the house and the woodpile? Poor J., unable to straighten his back, crawled moaning out of bed and, though scarcely able to move, hacked my foot and leg out of its plaster cast with an axe.

Despite bad weather the spring bird migration goes on steadily. No need for us, in typical ornithologist fashion, to travel forth, build a "bird blind" to match the scenery, and squat for hours inside it in an agony of cramped limbs, watching birds from tiny peepholes. Our cabin, which most of the birds apparently now accept as part of the landscape, serves as a perfect blind and we can watch the water just below in comfort from our windows.

Tetana, with its open patches at the north and south ends, is still the only open water anywhere around, and is proving a favorite way station for the birds. The birds drift steadily now up the Driftwood Valley, new species by ones or twos, or even small companies. Many, having come hundreds or thousands of miles north, traveling successfully without calendar or compass by day or night through all kinds of weather, will arrive at their summer homes on approximately the same date as they have done for years. When the birds leave Takla, still icebound, thirty miles away, the first water, other than tiny patches on the river, is Tetana. Here there is space for water birds; even a small shore line, free of snow, for land birds. In the dark stretch of forest and snow-covered wilderness, bounded on two sides by an endless sea of mountains, Tetana must lie like a haven of rest.

Yesterday morning when we woke, we saw from our pillows

a Townsend's solitaire sitting on the clothesline by the open window. Though we have never before seen one alive, we knew it from the pictures. The large, soft gray bird, with slight yellow markings on the flight feathers, the thrushlike head and bill were unmistakable. One of our great ambitions is to hear the "heavenly music" of the solitaire, which nests in high mountain solitudes. Perhaps when we climb the mountains this summer it will be there.

Four male pintail ducks, their beautiful, cleanly shaped little brown heads striped with white, and tail feathers lengthened into long sharp points, have arrived; and for five consecutive nights around six-thirty, the same mergansers have come to our pool. We can set our clock by them. Tonight they were joined by another pair, and what a flutter they all fell into! The two males chased one female and then the other. And once the ardent lovers had a serious fight. They grappled each other with long narrow bills, and sank completely under water, the salmon pink of their undersides (which appears chiefly in courtship plumage) conspicuously gorgeous. Then the females turned the tables and chased them, spurning first one male and then the other. Such a squawking and opening of mouths and sticking up of defiant tails, one never saw. But they have finally settled it peacefully, for now, in the darkening twilight, they are sleeping calmly, four heads tucked under four wings, a male and a female side by side.

April 11

Last night was warm and still, with a gentle fine misty rain. The partly full moon shone with a watery light. Just as we were going to sleep, around eleven, we were surrounded suddenly by the music of trumpets, deep and sweet and melodious. We almost fell from our beds, and when we hung out the window, there in the shining silver mist were four great, white, graceful swans, long necks and huge wings lit by the moon. They were slowly circling our cabin and the pool. Now they were out above the water, now low close over our roof. In bare feet we padded from window to window, hushing little Rex, who was rumbling in his throat at this new sound. The swans almost decided to land. Perhaps the area of open water is too small, perhaps the cabin frightened them, for, after some little time, they floated like small white angels up into the northern sky, rising ever higher and farther till they had disappeared. Then came more trumpeting high up, and we saw the tail end of a "V" formation of a dozen swans flying northwest. Long after they had all melted into the white misty night we could hear the fairylike horns and trumpets receding into the distance.

We feel sure that these could have been no other than the rare, almost extinct trumpeters. For never was there a more perfect reproduction of professional trumpeting. The notes were so strikingly low and soft, so clear and resonant, yet exquisitely modulated.

Yesterday afternoon a lonesome female Barrow's goldeneye was with the two pairs of mergansers, who ignored her utterly. This morning, a male Barrow's goldeneye has joined her. There could scarcely be anything more splendid. We can hardly stop gazing at the royal purple of his velvet head set with topaz eyes and half-moons of white, the beautiful patterned black and white of his body and wings.

April 17

After the last few warm days, snow has begun to slide on the mountains. There is a sudden soft swish followed by a thunderous roar, like an express train hurtling by. Then an echoing, softer roar down the valley, succeeded by a shocking quiet. The old giant of the mountains is giving voice at last, and well that Tetana lies a good six miles away. No wonder the Indians give these mountains a wide berth in the months of melting snow. One of the great fears of their lives, in addition to grizzlies, rutting bull moose, and breaking through thin ice, is the possibility of being buried by a snow slide.

Often at night we're waked from sound sleep by the noise of an avalanche. In the dark the roar sounds greater and deeper and more terrifying.

Last night at 2 A.M., I saw a miracle! Great, bright scarlet clouds were rolling over the pinewoods. My first sleepy thought was of fire. Then I realized that such a thing couldn't be, for there is still a blanket of wet snow, feet deep, for hundreds of miles around. It must be a new manifestation of the aurora; but instead of the usual streamers and zigzag curtains, great rolls of cumulous clouds seemed to bear the lights. The crests were flame-red; the white Driftwoods and the white snow everywhere were painted crimson. Clear sky over the mountains was a pale, glowing green and yellow. The colors were too intense to be dimmed by even a brilliant full moon. Where snow has melted across the lake leaving bare ice, it was glittering gold, and the open water was half gold, half green and red. Black silhouettes of wild ducks (ordinarily so noisy and lively now throughout all the night hours) were passing slowly in complete silence in long lines up and down the water, leaving wakes of gold and scarlet ripples.

I could never have even imagined such a sight! It was all unbelievable, the sort of thing that happens only in fairy stories. But I know it was real, because I walked all round the house and moved a chair or two. J. was in one of his dead sleeps and refused to wake. But since he says Northern Lights are no better than sunsets, I wasn't sure that he deserved to wake anyhow.

Small companies of crows, which we haven't seen since last fall, have come back again. And sometimes there is the deep guttural *quauk-quauk* of a big raven, as it flies ponderously above the cabin. One day when we were crossing the meadow we saw an evening grosbeak on a tall spruce. The black and yellow velvet of its markings, the heavy pale blue bill, were unmistakable. We were wildly excited at this remarkable visitor, so far north of its range; and J. tried, without success, to collect it. At his first shot a whole company of shrill, yapping coyotes, who must have been following us closely, began to howl defiance.

Yesterday morning we took a walk down the lake at five, our snowshoes clattering on the hard lumpy crusts. Dozens of ducks were in the open water at the outlet. The mallards, heads gleaming emerald and violet in the morning sun, had their funny little black tail feathers standing coquettishly up in stiff, lacquered curls. Incidentally the Indians tell us that mallards are the only species of duck in this region which are sometimes caught in traps set for beaver and muskrat. There was a dainty green-winged teal, with a green and cinnamon head and white and gray body; and both the American and the Barrow's goldeneyes with green, or purple, plush heads and white and black velvet bodies. Pintails and baldpates arrived while we were there. The baldpates have white foreheads like bald old men, and pink and gray sides. When we got back to the cabin, a flock of violet-green swallows, newly arrived, gleamed like iridescent peacock-colored jewels, as they darted up and down over the water.

This morning was clear and still and we were off again at six over toward Trail Lake; then north to the meadow. Suddenly way down the valley there was music, for all the world like a traveling calliope, coming gradually nearer and louder. On the southern sky appeared a gigantic "V" of trumpeters — seventy or more — the dazzling sun lighting their white bodies as they passed low just above us, headed slowly for the northwest. Through the low, resonant trumpets and soft bugles came soft, short little notes, made, we supposed, by the young cygnets. A golden eagle swooped down and up in great wide arcs, but the lovely, eager swans paid him no attention as they sang their way along.

The antics and distinctive habits of the different kinds of ducks make royal entertainment. The most noisy and conspicuous are mergansers and goldeneyes. The additional Barrow's goldeneyes — there are now four pairs — have added complications. The males, in an ecstasy of showing off, stand straight up in the lake, weaving their purple heads from side to side and shaking their wings. When they fly through the air, or volplane thirty yards across water, their wings make a shrill whistling noise which distinguishes them from other ducks, even after dark when we can't see them. The little brown-headed lady goldeneyes remain quiet and demure, outwardly unperturbed by the antics of their passionate swains. *They* are not bold and aggressive and modern, like the lady mergansers.

The tiny green-winged teal surprise us by giving voice to a plaintive sweet whistling note, completely unlike the noises one commonly associates with a duck. The teal are busily employed gobbling up early insects — springtails and a tiny gnat — which are over snowbanks and above the water.

Pintails and baldplates, especially the latter, appear to have considerably less skill in flying and landing than other ducks. The baldplates land so clumsily and awkwardly that we can tell them half a mile away.

For the first time we have seen fresh skunk tracks, and smelled a strong skunk smell, on the north side of the meadow. We have been told that an average of twelve skunks are brought in annually at Bear Lake, and the Indians say that in every case the skunk is caught in a marten trap set. Whether this is owing to the bait or scent used, or the type of brush shelter under the trees where the trap is set, it is hard to say.

April 24

The lake is almost completely open at last. I had forgotten how lovely are reflections of blue sky, white mountains, and green forests. And we have a boat. It is one of Charlie's dugout canoes, hauled down on the snow from Bear Lake by Charlie's dogs. We bought it for $25 and are immensely pleased with it. It's thirty feet long and is made, as are all dugouts in this country, from the trunk of a huge balsam poplar. After a careful selection of the tree the Indians fell it, and then start a slow fire inside. When the fire has partially hollowed out the trunk, the rest of the shaping and cleaning process is continued by axe and knife until there is a smooth, shapely interior. Wooden stretchers are wedged across the two ends and middle, and it is ready for use. If the boat is badly balanced, big stones are placed in its bottom. We find our dugout is no more difficult to steer and balance than an ordinary canoe. The chief difference is that it is much heavier and harder to lift.

We are able now to explore the lake to our hearts' content,

and I suppose that my adventuresome husband will soon be off on the dangerous river.

Two pairs of little bufflehead ducks arrived last week. The males, with fluffy, pure white pompons on their heads, bear themselves as proudly as kings. Several large companies comprising seventy and eighty swans have gone over. We are sure these were the whistlers because of their distinctly higher, more whistling-like notes. Though some notes were lovely and musical, they completely lacked the deep resonant character so marked in the trumpeters. Grouse are beginning to drum back in the woods (we have suddenly begun to see ruffed grouse now as well as Franklin's). And there are marsh hawks, sharp-shinned hawks, a kingfisher, and a Lincoln's sparrow.

The tiny, striped, gray-headed chipmunks have waked from their seven months' sleep; they all appeared around the twentieth and are scampering about, tails erect as usual, as sleek and fat as if they had been feeding steadily for half a year. Now their favorite food is pussy willows. They climb up in willows along the bank and make a pretty picture as they sit nibbling at a pussy head.

May 5

We're all excited because Basil Holland, a Takla Indian with a trap line southeast of the Kastberg, brought a surprise packet of mail from Takla. Mother and Dad *may* take a trip west this summer and if they do will come away off up here to pay us a visit. Just at present we can talk of nothing but the joy of showing them this country. But if they come west, will they really surmount all the hazards of travel in this land and be able to reach us? We sent out, to be mailed by Basil next week at Takla, voluminous epistles of advice, and directions, and urging; all of which had to be written in the course of a few hours between lengthy conversations and eating and drinking, because Basil had to start back in the early morning.

This is so typical of this country. Weeks and months go by without our even remembering that such a thing as mail exists. Except for a visit about once a month from the odd Indian, who knows no more of the outside world than we do, and whose quiet coming and going scarcely disturbs the even tenor of our ways, we almost forget that there is an outside world. Then suddenly, completely unexpected and unannounced, someone arrives with a several months' (often they are four to six months old) batch of letters and business matters. And they all have to be decided upon and answered in a few hours, unless one wishes them to slide for another four to six months. The person who brings them is full of talk and news which we want to hear. So, only the most important business communications are answered, and those in such a confused and haphazard form that people whose aim in life is Business, carefully and accurately performed, wonder if we have taken leave of our senses and gone completely wild! The personal letters don't get answered at all (they've waited around for months anyhow) because most of our friends and relatives will have given us up entirely.

Open ground everywhere now, except in thick woods; and oh! the joy of being able to walk without snowshoes again and feel the ground under our feet. Little Rex, longing for spring greens, gobbles up every blade of new grass — and then gets sick.

The Driftwood, nearly freed of ice at last, is rising. J., strutting like a turkey gobbler, appeared with a six-pound Dolly Varden, caught in the river near Tetana's outlet after a thrilling battle with snags and currents. The fish are beginning to run. The tender, pale pink flesh of the trout tastes heavenly. We're heartily sick of stale strong moose meat.

Willow buds and poplars are showing bright new green, the mountains above the thick timber still shine with deep fresh snowfalls, but the lower slopes are green, laced with a thousand new white foaming streams. The limpid green and blue and purple of the waters of Tetana are a rest to eyes unspeakably weary from gazing on unsullied whiteness for seven months. More new birds arrive each day. It is the high tide of a far northern spring — doubly glorious and welcome because it has taken so long to get here. The birds and animals are obviously as thrilled with it all as we are. Today a mink played along a

Gray-headed Chipmunk feeding on pussy willow

log below our bank, and muskrats swim back and forth. When they're alarmed or nervous the muskrats swim with the tail almost erect and held up out of the water. At other times they use the tail as a paddle and rudder combined. J. talks at length to one big old grandfather rat. The rat swims toward him whenever he whistles.

May 20

The other day, in the pine grove near the cabin, I met a Franklin's grouse. Instead of flying off with the usual whir and cackle, he began to advance across the soft green mosses straight toward me — in fact right up to my feet. And then he started the most magnificent courtship performance exactly two feet away. I could have leaned down and picked him up any time. He dragged his wings, spread his tail, and puffed out the bright scarlet combs over the eyes till they stood out in arcs. He pirouetted and did little demure dancing steps. And all the while the black and brown feathers on his throat and hind neck were puffed into downy balls and he was quivering and shaking and whirring in the grip of a most ardent passion. Spellbound, I watched all this for ten minutes by my watch. And finally, his ardor subsided and he stood still.

"Thank *you*," I cried; "that was wonderful!"

The sound of my voice reminded him suddenly that I was a lady human and not a lady grouse, a fact which, in the ecstasy of his performance, he'd apparently entirely forgotten. With a highly indignant "Tut, tut, tut, tut," he was away in a moment. A short distance off I discovered the real object of his affections high up in a young poplar tree. It was a brown female, huddled close to the trunk, and she eyed me very coldly!

Willows and alders are alive with the flashes of color of dozens of warblers. Audubon's are the most common; such little beauties with yellow throats and topknots, blue-gray and black and white bodies. Redstarts, orange and black, northern pileolated, bright yellow with black caps, yellow warblers, canary bodies and breasts streaked with pink-brown, decorate the bushes like colored necklaces. They are never still a second.

Ruby-crowned, as well as golden-crowned, kinglets hang every dark green spruce with chains of bubbling, rippling melody. For such tiny things, only four inches long, the kinglets sing a gigantic song. Their olive-green bodies are hard to see in thick needles, but sometimes we catch a glimpse of a male, his crown perked up like a real ruby. A pair of red-breasted sapsuckers, heads, breasts, and hind necks a vivid rose, are, as they tap for grubs in branches of the willow tree, nearly the most beautiful of all.   .

Loons pass overhead, sounding clear, sweet, wild calls. These are the common loons whose relatives I've heard in Maine, but here they sound new notes — seldom the weird maniacal laugh. On dark storm-threatening days they give a high, ringing cry, which stirs one's blood like a bugle. The Indians say this is the call for rain; and they are right, for it's like the sudden burst of song from robins that always precedes a warm summer shower.

The lake is crowded with ducks; fighting and love-making far into the night, arriving and taking off. At evening we often count up to a hundred or more individuals on the water at this end of the lake. Dozens at a time shoot down over the cabin just at dusk, at terrific speed, with a whirring of wings and a tremendous splash as they land just below us. Sometimes they appear to miss the cabin roof by a mere two feet or so. Our days and nights resound with every variety of *quawk-quawks, quata-quata-quatas,* and shrill whistles. Goldeneyes, mergansers, pintails, buffleheads, baldpates; green-winged teal, scaups, gadwalls, shovelers, mallards, white-winged scoters, and ruddies; also horned and Holboell's grebes. The majority come in companies, stopping only for a rest and feed in their frantic haste to get farther north; others, which apparently nest around this region, like the mergansers, goldeneyes, buffleheads, and teal, are too busy acquiring mates and fighting rivals to have time at all for eating and sleeping.

We're catching more and more trout in the river. Beautiful fat things, eight- and ten-pounders. Most are Dollies, the pink spots on their silver bodies reminding one of the Eastern brook trout.

A few, which are rather like rainbows, are the Kamloops. They have much redder flesh and taste more "fishy" than the Dollies, but we enjoy them all.

Usually Rex and I sit up on the banks watching J. I can never get over the sheer joy of just being able to sit (now that the earth is warm enough again to relax on) and do nothing but absorb and think undisturbed, but with J. near enough to make me feel safe. Several times, however, I've gone fishing too. As the river rises, the current gets stronger; landing an eight-pound fighting trout, through the hazards of swift water and floating debris, is terrific. J. shouts with glee when he's playing one and bids me sternly to be quiet. But when *I* hook one he yells commands in a violent manner and, no matter how mad I am, I daren't waste breath or strength at such a moment telling him so.

Most of the fish that we catch have eggs or milt in them; right now is evidently the spawning season in these parts.

Numerous whitefish congregate in the deeper pools, but these are not at all interested in bait or flies. When the Indians at Bulkley House want whitefish for food they gouge out a deep hollow in the river bed, where the stream is sluggish, and lower into it a large piece of moose meat. Later they return to the spot with forked sticks and spear the masses of whitefish which have gathered there.

Two kinds of sucker, apparently both the large- and small-scaled, are also common here and at Bear Lake. The Bear Lake Indians have told us that they use the small-scaled sucker as bait for large lake trout. The sucker is skinned carefully, stuffed with pulped deer or moose meat, and with a large hook threaded through the entire length is lowered into the lake. The line is attached to a wooden float or sealed tin can, and left overnight. In addition to lake trout, Bear Lake also gets quantities of sockeye salmon in late summer, and steelhead trout are also said to occur in the Bear River.

Minnows, no doubt one of the shiners, are everywhere in the streams and ponds around Tetana, but so far we have seen no other varieties of small fish.

May 22

Clear, blue-green Tetana has vanished. Overnight it has risen fifteen feet and become a turbulent muddy mass. The only sign that it was once clear water is where the springs come out below our bank and shoot green streaks into the dark brown. We are hard put to it to get good drinking water. The river has risen so high that it has backed up into the lake, so that Tetana is now "The Lake into Which the River Flows." The flood is even pouring across the willow swamp on the west in broad swift streams. Lucky for us that our cabin stands thirty feet above the usual level. Exploring new shore lines in the dugout, and avoiding being swept off in some new swift current of the flood, are a thrilling pastime. The river has become thick brown soup and we can catch no more fish. They must be hiding out in backwaters or deep pools till it clears once more. We are out of meat again and are wondering how long the floods will last. Kastberg Creek, five miles south on the trail to Takla, has become a roaring river that can no longer be crossed by man or beast.

At night the rush of mighty waters troubles our sleep. We must be cut off from Bunshaw and Bear Lake. There have been no signs of the Indians for a long time. It seems that this country is quite literally inaccessible for a large part of the year.

When I stop to consider our situation with complete candor (which somehow I now seldom do, partly because I have become accustomed to accepting it, and partly because daily thrills and drudgeries and worries are so absorbing), I think I find it even more wonderful and more awful than I had supposed. There is always that kind of heartless loveliness and ruthlessness and serene indifference to one's welfare — and yet, more and more, I'm beginning to sense what I think must be a kind of kinship with it all. There *is* a secure way of life, and all manner of help and care for us, if we use the wilderness rightly, study it, work with it, not against it, accept its cruelties and uglinesses with its miracles and its beauties.

May 24

When we got up this morning at six-thirty, a strange Indian and a wet dejected black dog were sitting on our woodpile. The Indian said he was "George," a trapping partner of Vinson's; he had been at Bear Lake and had thought he might be able to float on a raft down the high waters of the Driftwood all the way to Takla. But last evening his raft struck a great whirlpool and was dashed against a log jam, throwing him and his supplies into the water. All his possessions were lost — gun, axe, furs, food, bed. He had kept a few matches above water by holding them in his mouth. The dog, tied to the raft, had nearly drowned before it could break free. They had landed on shore a few miles away and had been lucky enough to find the trail which led to our cabin.

All this was told far more briefly than I have written it, with a grin or two, and a shrug. Most of it was elicited by questions from J. We took George into the cabin and fed him a hearty breakfast and his dog a piece of bad old meat, so big the dog's eyes popped. Then we gave George a big tin can and some wire; out of these he made a cooking kettle. We supplied him with biscuits, tea, sugar, a little bacon, and matches, and directions about the Takla trail. All of which he received in uncommunicative silence. He then trod softly and abruptly out of the cabin, turned as he started down the bank, and said, "Well — thanks," and departed, a damp, silent, philosophic figure, followed by a reluctant, damp, and silent dog, who cast longing glances back at the place where he had miraculously been given food.

"Don't see how he'll ever get across Kastberg," said J. as we stood gazing after him, "but he doesn't seem to worry — hope he makes it."

The lake has risen still higher — it must have come up twenty-five feet, but perhaps has reached the peak because, for the last six hours, the level has not changed.

Rex has worms. They are not like any worms J.'s Husky dogs had in the Arctic, but we have tried various remedies. Very remissly, when we made up medical kits, we did not figure on dogs or parasitic worms. Therefore our medicine chest lacks a vermifuge. J. successfully wormed his Huskies with gunpowder. The Indians here told us they use soot and grease. So poor Rex has obligingly swallowed enough gunpowder extracted from J.'s cartridges to turn him into an arsenal, and enough soot to blacken his entire insides — without any ill effects either to himself or to the worms.

There are fresh signs of moose about. But since floods now make tracking impossible for any distance, we have no more hope than ever of actually being able to get a moose. We shall need meat badly, unless the river clears up and fish appear again soon.

June 2

Very early the other morning something big began crashing about in the underbrush on the east shore a quarter of a mile away. J. was up out of bed, into a jacket and waders on top of his pajamas, and out of the house with a gun, before I got both eyes open. About fifteen minutes later I heard his rifle go, more loud thrashing in the woods, and then a tremendous splash in the lake. The moose, for it was a moose, had lived just long enough to reach the water and it lay floating in weeds. J. shouted to me to come with the dugout and the clothesline. Rex, wild with excitement, came within an ace of dumping me in the lake by leaping on the very edge of the canoe just as I started.

When we paddled across, there was J. up to his chest in bloody water, trying to shove the huge moose hulk away from shore. We decided to tow it to a dry bank on the northeast corner not far from the cabin. Dripping blood and water, J. climbed in the tippy dugout, almost upsetting it. It took ages to lasso the moose and tow it laboriously to shore. J., standing in icy water up to his waist, bled it at once and took out the guts.

I had no idea how big a moose really is, nor how tough. With knives and axes, we hacked on and off all day, in broiling sun. Huge buzzing blowflies attacked the bloody meat in swarms and laid eggs on it before you could wink an eye. We shoveled up a big drift of snow back in the dark woods, and dragged great hunks of meat and bones to bury under it. We covered the snow in turn with moss to keep it from melting as long as possible.

We're still working on and off at the underside of the moose which is deep in water, and transferring the remainder to the snowbank. I've never seen anything like these flies. They get into seemingly airtight spots, lay eggs on the meat, and the eggs hatch into loathsome, crawling maggots in no time. We're all glutted with fresh meat, strong and well and happy. In between attacks on the moose J. is working at top speed to screen the cabin. We fear the flies are a foretaste of pests to come.

The lake is going down, praise be, and a wide arc of clear green at this end is reaching out and shoving back the muddy soup. Since the floods have subsided we've had a visit from Bear Lake Charlie, who has been attending to his beaver traps. He had a freshly caught large female beaver who must have led a life of hair-raising experiences. One of her upper incisors was missing, her left forearm had been cut off above the wrist long ago, because the break was well grown over, and one toe was missing from each remaining foot. At the posts we examined thirty-three beaver skins and most of them, like Charlie's, were a dark chestnut color. But there were a few very large reddish individuals, which the Indians say are the skins of old female beavers.

We spend the long bright evenings out on the lake, listening to the chorus of olive-backed thrushes and collecting toads to preserve for specimens. The olive-backs, which arrived last week, are the chief species of thrush around Tetana. Their deep contralto bells beginning in the evening around nine-thirty, when sunset comes and the other birds are growing quiet, seem to tone into perfection with the almost imperceptible falling dark of the northern twilight. We have counted as many as eighteen singing males just around the shores, and the water resounds from every side with their deep, peaceful benediction. Dozens of pairs of blackpoll warblers have also been here for a week, obviously starting to nest. We've collected several, thereby making an interesting new record for British Columbia, for blackpolls are said by ornithologists to be scarce in this province.

Toads, the most common amphibian form hereabouts, were swimming in the lake last fall. They vanished in early October and did not appear again until May 18th, before the lake began to flood. When, a week or so later, the waters subsided, they came out by the hundreds. Still nights are loud with their clatter. It reminds one of the noise of steady wood chopping. Dozens of mating pairs are swimming everywhere, the smaller, dark-colored males astride the large swollen females, which are either bright light green or reddish brown. The male, with thumbs interlocked below the breast of the female, clasps his lady with a death grip. In some cases it really is a death grip, for we've found females that have died, apparently suffocated, with the males still clinging to them. This tight squeezing process forces the eggs out of the females, and when the long jellylike strings are at last extruded, the males fertilize them.

We've collected many pairs that still remained clasped together despite the violent upheavals necessitated by putting them in jars. One pair were locked together the wrong way, that is face to face, but after they were put in a jar the male got around in the correct position. Eggs have been laid and apparently fertilized, for the tiny black balls have begun to turn white and expand and show cell division.

CHAPTER X

Summer Visitors

Tetana   *June 14*

Mother and Dad arrived the eighth. We still can hardly believe our eyes when they appear at the cabin door each morning for breakfast. They're sleeping in the tent, pitched where we first had it when we came to Tetana. J. has made rope and canvas beds for them. They seem very comfortable — except that the persistent all-night "pounding" around the marshes of numerous bitterns (big heronlike birds, sometimes called stake drivers, because their notes resemble stakes being driven into mud) keeps them awake. Sometimes the notes of these bitterns sound like water sucking out of a gigantic bottle.

The first week of June was harrowing because we had no idea whether or not to expect Mother and Dad. We'd heard nothing since April when we knew that they *hoped* to come and, *if* they did, would try to make it in early June. We had sent them numerous suggestions about how to get here — by horse if the floods were down, by plane to Bear Lake, by boat up the river. We also sent lengthy epistles to Mr. Holden at Takla, requesting that if they came, they be started with proper equipment, trustworthy guides, and so on. But we never knew whether any of our letters ever reached their destination. Twice, during early June, a plane flew over heading north, but each time it flew high without a sign. One evening, just at dusk, as we were paddling on the lake in the dugout, there was a shot over toward the horse trail. J. grabbed his pistol and fired in reply. It might be someone from Takla with messages looking for us. It might even be Mother and Dad. We beached the canoe and, in the gathering dark, hurried along the path to Trail Lake. But there was no sound or a sign of any human being. We crossed the marshes to the Takla trail. No footprints of horse or man, no turned-over stones, no new signs anywhere and no response to several more shots from J. Perhaps we had mistaken the direction or perhaps some strange Indian had been passing. (None of the Bear Lake Indians who travel this way ever go by now without taking a detour via Tetana.) We turned dejectedly home again, escorted by the lingering evening hymn of the olive-backs.

On June 8th, as we were eating supper to the accompaniment of the ecstatic singing and twittering of birds, I thought I heard something. I stopped eating, J. stopped, and we both heard it. Was it a plane far off? Although it was a whirring engine of some sort, it didn't sound quite like a plane. It stopped altogether and then it came again. A plane heading this way would have passed over long ago.

"What the dickens? What the heck is that plane doing anyhow?"

"That," said I, "sounds to me like an outboard engine — "

"No — by gosh, believe you're right! It's a boat coming up the river."

"Mother and Dad!" I cried.

"It could just as well be a message, saying they're *not* coming, or someone we don't know at all," retorted J., promptly dampening me.

Nevertheless we went to the canoe and started paddling furiously down the lake. Between breaths J. said: "Now, Teddy, don't get your hopes up! You mustn't; you may be frightfully disappointed y'know — "

There was a big fallen tree across the outlet. J. reached for his axe and began to chop with strong steady strokes, while I steadied the canoe and Rex crouched, shivering, in the bottom. The outboard engine whirred louder and louder. J. just finished chopping through the log as the boat came in sight — and there with three Indians were Mother and Dad waving wildly.

"Gosh, there they are — "

They were dressed in the good old khaki camping clothes which, from earliest recollection, I've associated with summer and glorious trips. Though over sixty, they looked as rosy and fresh as ever. Certainly not as if they had just traveled three thousand miles across country and up into the Far North, and topped it all by navigating eighty miles of a river supposed to be unnavigable — except for small canoes at certain seasons.

I have never known anything to be done on schedule in the North before, but by a series of miracles, Mother and Dad, from the time they left the railroad, forty miles away from Stuart Lake, made perfect connections and came straight through to Takla. Thanks largely to Mr. Holden, there they procured a boat with a reliable outboard engine, and Basil Holland to take them up the Driftwood River which is still in high flood. They had exciting times getting through log jams, breaking ropes, injuring the engine. Dad, along with Basil's two helpers, was more than once out in water over his waist, moving trees, while Basil and Mother held to the boat and supplies. But they made it — and here they are to stay two months.

As we had hoped, things are exquisitely beautiful. The mountains still wear fresh snow. Scarlet columbine and red and orange Indian paintbrush cover the open places. Beds of pink Calypso orchids — "fairy shoes" — are scattered through the woods. There are violets, yellow daisies, white Solomon's-seal in profusion. Feathery saskatoon and wild rose bushes cascade down the open banks. The most gorgeous of all are the acres of blue and purple and white lupines scattered through the poplar groves. It is all so much more colorful than forests in the tropics. These northern woods with their contrasting dark evergreens and light deciduous trees, their floors gay with brilliant flowers, are fresh and clean and good compared to the monotonous stifling jungles I've seen in Fiji and Java and Sumatra.

Rufous hummingbirds and bees zoom around the cabin all day long, feeding on wild strawberry blooms. Mourning cloak butterflies, purple-red wings trimmed with yellow, float in the sun, alight on flowers, or, incongruously, as beautiful butterflies do, settle on garbage and every dirty spot.

The long, long northern summer day, beginning with dawn

at 2 A.M. and lasting till eleven at night, gives a sense of life lived to its fullest by all living things.

At first Rex growled at Mother and Dad — so few human beings have entered into his life that every newcomer is highly exciting and suspicious — but now he finds his world enlarged by having two more wonderful creatures to love. He has gotten rid of his worms, thank heaven. They turned out to be the regular cast-off segments of a huge tapeworm. Mother and Dad actually received our letters and requests before they started, and so brought several kinds of worming medicine. The first dose of Pulvex did the trick.

In addition to extra food supplies, they brought big rolls of heavy roofing paper, which Dad and J. have been nailing over the shakes of our leaky roof. Now at last we shall be able to sit through storms undisturbed.

J. is off on a short, hard trip with old Charlie over the Driftwood Mountains. This time he could leave with a free mind, and go unhampered by a female. Today I think he's on the way home again. We heard a shot from a big rifle (none of the Indians have anything as powerful as his .348) on this side of the mountain.

Though seasoned campers, Mother and Dad have never before been quite so primitive or so far removed from the world. They're vastly impressed with the cabin. Dad, muttering and shaking his head, goes about examining things that J. has made. He hopes I realize what "a wonderful husband" I've got. In order to give us extra time for collecting and observing, my parents do all sorts of chores like dishwashing and water fetching. This, and having someone of our own kind to talk to, make a real vacation. Also, it delights my soul to see someone else going through the stages of greenness to pioneering that I went through. For instance, they are terrified of eating, just as I was at first, for fear of using up supplies.

Our old garbage hole was filled up and so swarming with maggots it made us sick to pass within yards of it. Dad volunteered to dig a new one. After a few essays on the stony ground with our one steel shovel, he said he must have a pick.

"But," said I, "we have no pick."

"What, no pick? Well, I've got to have one. You can't possibly dig a hole in this ground without a pick — "

"But a hole must be dug. We can't throw garbage around in
this fly season — "

"Then we've got to get a pick at once."

"Well, you'll have to hike seventy-five miles to Takla and
carry a big pack on your back with food and bedding to last
at least four days — and even if you get to Takla you probably
couldn't buy a pick in town. Takla's almost two hundred miles
from the Fort; you might have to wait there all summer before
they could get one in from outside!"

A capacious garbage hole was dug by Dad that day with the
shovel.

Dad knows such a lot about plants and birds that he helps
immensely with collecting and listing. Though I do think he is
a bit extravagant with flycatchers! Almost every time he sees a
flycatcher he's sure it's a new species and insists on its being
collected, thereby making me hours of extra work skinning
them in addition to the many other birds. Flycatchers *are* tricky.
Perhaps we do have five species here, but I doubt it!

I find that in addition to plant collecting I too can collect
birds quite efficiently with the small shotgun. This leaves J.
free to turn all his attention to the mammals.

As for my dear mother, she tramps the forests with me like
a girl of sixteen, looking quizzical when I whistle and shout
to warn off any lurking families of grizzlies. I don't think
Mother believes for an instant that there is the least danger.
But being a great lover of her fellow human beings she is a bit
distressed and appalled over our extreme remoteness. The fact
that weeks go by without our seeing even an Indian seems to
her an empty and useless kind of existence. But she thrives on
this existence anyhow. Her face hasn't looked so young and
rested since I can remember.

Recently she helped me with a big washing: her clothes and
Dad's, J.'s and mine. We carried and heated some twenty pails
of water (I have at last acquired water pails of average size and

strength brought by Mother and Dad from Takla). And we had clothes hung out on three lines and on every available shrub and tree limb before noon.

The "cellar," which in winter kept things from freezing, is equally good in summer. It keeps everything fresh and cold, and when I make jello, or other things that require chilling, it does the work to perfection.

June 20

Last night J. returned full of tales. The mountains, at six to seven thousand feet, were still deep in snow and he and the Indians waded to their waists. Down the west slope on the other side, Charlie showed J. tree stumps which had been cut by the Indians during winter at twenty feet above ground; the depth of snow must have been sixteen to eighteen feet.

J. took movies of a cow moose and her calf fording a stream which rises in the valley west of the mountains and is the beginning of the Driftwood River. Charlie watched anxiously to see that the baby got safely off with its mother. When the cow moose is alarmed, it is not uncommon for her to desert her calf. The little calf is located by its peculiar human whistling call, very different from the usual voice of a big animal. The Indians sometimes take the calf home if it is small enough, and feed it for a time, then kill it or release it.

They also saw a group of six mule deer in the same valley. Charlie told J. that deer are apt to occur there. Deer are apparently rather rare here, though we have occasionally seen their tracks. From recent reports, however, it looks as though they might be extending their range through this country.

Wolves chased Charlie's dogs, and he was sure that one of them had been killed, until it appeared again just as they were returning to Tetana.

Between five and six thousand feet, Townsend's solitaires were nesting and singing in full glory. Loud and liquid and crystal clear, the song rang from every side across the mountain. But J. says he is quite incapable of really describing it, for he thinks it the most wonderful he ever heard. Even the

Indians, who know it of old, stopped long to listen. Charlie's young William said, "That bird, I like heem *bad*."

Just below timber line J. collected a Tennessee warbler and its nest, and a big dusky grouse. He also brought back a huge reddish mouse, as large as a chipmunk, which we think must be the rare tawny lemming, almost unknown in scientific collections.

When we first came to Tetana there were scattered rows of young pines dying, because bark had been peeled off them in huge strips. There was no reason, that we could see, for this wanton destruction (nor would the Indians tell us any). If they girdle trees to kill for firewood they choose those with a fairly large diameter. But when J. returned from the mountains this time, we caught the Indian boys in the act, stripping new young pines and stuffing great bites of the tender white inner bark into their mouths. This, Charlie explained, is for the "sugar." It seems that when sap runs at this season the inner bark is full of a sweet jellylike substance and provides an element in the Indians' diet often lacking and consequently much craved.

We have had visits from Martha and Vinson, separately. Michelle and Charlie told us that Martha had left Vinson and gone back to her father. We hardly believed this, until one day she actually appeared with her father, old Peter Haimadam, quite a notorious character, outlawed for some years for a killing affair, then tried and acquitted. He also had quite a reputation as a guide and hunter. Now he is an old man, mild and quiet, and seemed to me less formidable than Martha! Martha apparently came bearing peace offerings — a big red tawny lemming and an albino hoary marmot skin, obtained from mountains north of the Bear Lake country. She said nothing about Vinson. Rex was unusually ferocious. Whenever she and Peter came within yards of the cabin he followed their every movement, nose pressed to their insteps, each pressure proclaiming: "One step too far and I bite!"

Michelle and Charlie reported that Vinson was at Bear Lake living with a squaw. He wished to see J., but dared not approach because he feared J. would shoot on sight. Mother and Dad thought this highly amusing. J. and I, now somewhat acquainted with the workings of the Indian mind, understood that he was probably in dead earnest. J. asked that a report be circulated that he had no intention of shooting if Vinson behaved properly, and that Vinson might approach with safety to say what was to be said. Four days later Vinson, with several protecting friends in the background, appeared on horseback. He and J. talked long outside the cabin while the rest of us hovered anxiously on the outskirts, wondering if there would be blows. But no, their voices came low and soothing, they shook hands. Vinson, the picture of meekness, was invited into the cabin, Rex repeating the performance he had used with Peter and Martha.

Since the water of Tetana is too icy even to wade in (still 38° F. just as it was all winter), we sometimes go across to Trail Lake for a swim in the deep water off the north marsh. The path to Trail Lake these days is a thing of beauty. All along the dark aisles of the deep forest, soft to the feet with the needles and mosses of hundreds of years, are the flowers of the far northern Clintonia — little white lilies with hearts of gold. And there are endless carpets of the pale pink, tiny bells of Linnaea trailing over logs and mounds, and white and pink Pyrolas of many species. The pure whites and pale pinks are set off by the dark greens and blacks of the deep forest.

The marshes and bogs of Trail Lake are all white with little rein orchids and cloudberry, and bright with the tender reds and greens of young leaves of Labrador tea and wild rosemary. The wettest portions are carpeted with clouds of feathery masses of buck bean, whose white petals inside are covered with sticky curly shreds. From a distance they look like a floating mist. This is a new plant to us, but we are sure we have identified it correctly, for no other flower here possesses this unusual structure.

Around dusk each evening some small bats appear (so far they all look to be of one species), and nighthawks begin their "zooming" in the pine woods and around the cabin. The peculiar buzzing noise made by the males as they dive down is said to be part of the courtship display. It sounds rather like the deep, stertorous breathing of some large animal. At first, before we learned to associate it with nighthawks, J. and I spent some hours trying to locate the bear or moose that we thought must be wandering in our woods. And Dad, after he came, refused to be convinced that it was not a bear, until he actually saw the birds diving and heard the noise simultaneously.

June 23

The mosquitoes have begun! Hordes of roaring, suffocating, stinging insects are here. For about five days they have been hovering ominously about, but strong breezes kept them down. Now we are having a spell of real heat. Under a broiling sun that shines sixteen hours out of twenty-four, the cabin grows stifling hot despite four open windows and two doors. During early afternoon the thermometer goes up to 88 or 90 in the shade; but by 10 P.M. it is down to 60. In the early mornings, before five, it is 48 or 42 degrees. So that, no matter how exhaustingly hot the day, we are refreshed and invigorated by the cold nights.

It is impossible to clear the cabin of the mosquitoes, which gather in mats on the outside of screens and burst through the doors in swarms every time we go in or out. J. and I will have to put up a tent to sleep in. Mother and Dad seem able to clean their tent out effectively every night by means of a smudge fire or Flit. Also a tent cools off far more quickly than the cabin does. But we are all forced to spend many hot daylight hours inside the cabin to avoid being literally bitten to death. We can't go out at all without head nets and gloves and every inch of flesh tightly covered.

Dad and I have given up our morning bird collecting and observing. From five o'clock on, the thrum of mosquitoes drowns out all bird song. Even when, through stifling head-nets and the black clouds of insects, we can observe a bird a few feet away on a bush, though we see its throat moving in song, we can't hear it. The willow swamps are a roaring hell. J. and I wonder why we ever urged Mother and Dad to come

in June. Telling them and ourselves that mosquitoes here are
nothing compared to those of the Arctic tundra doesn't help
at all. Stories of insect life in the Arctic, which we have recounted and which our family formerly heard with derisive
hoots, they now listen to with respectful moans and groans.

July 3

The weeks and weeks of clear weather, which we rejoiced in,
resulted in terrible drought and dryness. At first it seemed impossible after the countless tons of melting snow and the roaring
rivers and streams that this world could ever be dry again. But
the gravelly rocky heights of land, especially in open pine and
poplar groves, became dry as tinder. The soft oozy mosses were
hard and crackling; and then, from the south, arose an ominous
signal — smoke clouds and the acrid smell of a forest fire. In one
short day small clouds became big ones that rolled and rolled up
our valley, till the sky and the sun and the mountains were
smothered, blotted out. The mountains, their white tops a pale
pink through the hazy smoke, were enormous. They seemed, until they faded away entirely, to have become thousands of feet
higher. Then a west wind shifted south, and the end of the
lake was lost. Mosquitoes and singing birds vanished, our eyes
smarted, and we gave up all occupations other than eating and
necessary chores, to watch and listen.

We had no means of knowing how near the fire was. It might
be thirty or ten miles away. Our beloved wilderness seemed
doomed. Then we even ceased to agonize over the wilderness
and began to wonder whether we could survive, if the fire
reached us. It was useless to try to head north for a big body
of water like Bear Lake, as the fire might overtake us before
we could reach it. There are no accessible lakes larger than
Tetana between us and Bear. Our only chance, J. and Dad
decided, would be a hide-out on the big marsh that juts out
into this lake. J. cut long logs of dry wood and built a large
raft, which we anchored to the bank by the canoe.

The great dangers of fire are not only actual burns, but
also suffocation from smoke and fumes. We might be able to

bury ourselves sufficiently well to survive in the marsh if the fire passed over. There was no hope that the cabin would stand, surrounded as it is on three sides by forest. We all toiled up and down the lake bank storing valuables, books and specimens and food, on the raft, leaving the canoe free to paddle in. Almost everything else was placed on top of the bank, ready to roll down into the lake at a moment's notice.

Two horrible days went by, and then came a third, when the smoke was noticeably worse and we expected to see flames and hear the roar at any hour. We watched steadily for a sudden exodus of animals. That night, as we sat at supper and said a silent grace, the same prayer must have been in all our minds. I wondered if this were to be the last meal I should ever eat in our cabin. J. stayed up all night. The rest of us might as well have, for we couldn't sleep. The wind was strong from the south, the smoke so thick we could hardly breathe.

Red-eyed and pale, we gathered in the cabin for breakfast. Was this to be the day?

"At least it's no worse and we are still here," we said.

And then, about ten o'clock, it began to rain. At first a gentle mist which gradually strengthened into a hard, steady, blessed downpour. We worked all day hauling things back up the bank to the cabin again. By nightfall the smoke seemed almost to have vanished, birds were singing once more. Tetana and the wilderness are still ours.

July 15

J. and Dad have been on a trip to Bear Lake, and Mother and I have been alone. It took some persuading to convince Dad that it was all right to leave us; but he finally trudged off, a gray-haired, youthful figure, his rather large sleeping bag strapped to his back. J. carried a huge pack consisting of tent, food, and the big gun.

Mother and Rex and I escorted them as far as Hudson Bay Meadow. This, and our own meadow, have been magically transformed into big blue and purple seas, dotted with bright green islands. For all the grassy parts are now completely cov-

ered with acre upon acre of tall monkshood and luxuriant del-
phiniums. In between are the clumps of green-leaved, yellow-
stemmed willows, and the Driftwoods, dark green and white, are
the background.

During the time Dad and J. were gone Mother and I filled
our days with chores, and talking, and trying to escape the mosquitoes which, after the smoke died down, returned in greater
force than ever. Nothing, short of actual burning, will ever
discourage them! Before he left, J. wove a big fish net with a
homemade shuttle *à la* Hudson Bay Eskimo, out of a ball of
twine; and each day Mother and I paddled down the lake to the
outlet to set the net. Setting it across the swift current and
fastening it securely without upsetting the dugout was quite a
trick, but we caught several good trout. The air out on the
lake was slightly less filled with mosquitoes.

We spent hours watching a family of young Barrow's goldeneyes. The male parent was very little in evidence, the female
apparently doing all the training and guarding of the young.
The mother duck cared for her sweet fluffy babies with unfailing watchfulness. If we got too close she herded them toward
the bank, putting her body always between them and the
canoe. When we stayed perfectly still, at a respectful distance,
she began to teach them things. How to scatter out of the
straight lines which they always form like soldiers when they're
following her any distance. How to crouch still and camouflage
against a log if a mink or an eagle or a hawk appears.

Dad and J., exuding health and spirits, returned on the fifth
day. They had gotten through to the south end of Bear Lake
in one and a half strenuous days. Since Dad couldn't travel as
fast as J., he stayed, on the second day, in the rear, taking his
time to stop and rest. J. was to wait for him farther along. It
seems that after J. had gone five miles on ahead he left his
pack by the trail, and went some ten yards off to sit down near
a small pond. He waited and waited and waited; when there was
still no sign of Dad he grew anxious and started back to look
for him. He went all the five miles back without meeting him;
he got wilder and wilder. He shouted and fired his pistol. Sweat

Little Brown Bat

JF '38

Young Barrow's Golden-eye

streaming from every pore, he returned over the five miles for the third time, so excited he never realized that he had been carrying his sixty-pound pack the whole way. When he got a mile north of his resting place, he found, in a soft spot along the trail, a footprint of Dad's headed toward Bear Lake. In about five more miles he caught up with him. Dad, bent under his pack, was plodding wearily along, having passed J.'s pack on the trail without ever seeing it or him. He heard the shot but, as it came from the rear, supposed it must be an Indian.

"Gad," said J., recounting this little incident, "I haven't been so scared for years. I lost twenty pounds!"

When they reached Bear Lake, as they had hoped, they found old Charlie and family camping near the south end. They then went, by Charlie's boat, the fifteen miles up to Carl's point. They would never have been able, with the time and equipment at their disposal, to follow the long winding shore on foot, cutting out every step of the way, for there is no trail. They visited with Carl and took a trip up on the east Bear Lake Mountains. The hike up on the mountains with Sapolio was apparently about the worst Dad has ever had. First they climbed up nine miles; then, before they turned back again, Dad hiked another six miles along grassy slopes collecting plants for me. On the return trip Dad fell far behind, so that he could push his aching limbs along and moan in private. When he reached the little Indian settlement, not knowing which leg moved after which, about thirty Indian dogs sprang at him, and he was too exhausted even to kick. Most of the Indians were away, so he had no help. But he got through the dogs unscathed; maybe because they saw that he was too weak to harm a fly!

Dad and J., learning that a plane is coming up to fetch Carl out the first part of August, arranged for Dad and Mother to fly out with him. This will cut expenses two thirds for each one. But J. and I dread the day of departure.

Yesterday, J., on a hike to country east of Beaver Lake, came suddenly on a grizzly digging for grubs in a small clearing. He and the bear were about a hundred feet apart and as J. had only the small .410 bird gun, he looked about for a climbable tree to use if necessary. He was sure the bear saw him, but as is, apparently, the habit of grizzlies, it refused to budge at the presence of a mere man. It took its own time to finish the grubs and eat some berries before it finally ambled off with an irritated snort. J. has sketched it, one front foot and head uplifted, just as he first saw it.

The Indians have some new tales of grizzlies. A week or two ago Selina and her children were traveling along the farther bank of the Driftwood not far from Tetana when, in a clearing, they unexpectedly met a huge grizzly. The little Indian dogs held it at bay while the others got away safely.

July 21

This summer is not monotonous. J. has had to depart suddenly and may now, for all we know, be some three hundred miles away at Prince George. For a week he has spoken, casually, of a bad tooth. Several days ago he arose in awful pain with his jaw swollen to gigantic proportions; he could hardly open his mouth, and it was obvious that he had an abscessed tooth of the worst variety. Through closed lips he managed to announce in my ear that he was going to Takla, and from there to the nearest dentist if he had to walk all the way. Providentially, though we had previously been annoyed to see them, Michelle, Bella, and family were camping at Tetana.

A few days before J.'s abscess began, Michelle stepped on an old board near our cabin. A rusty two-inch nail went through his light skin moccasin, far up into his foot — so far that he had to call J. to come and pry it loose. J. washed the wound with warm water and poured iodine into it, while I administered a drink. Michelle, though a trifle whitish under his brown, never turned a hair, never moved a muscle. I admired him heartily.

It was arranged that Michelle, whose foot was much better, but who could not yet walk any distance, should go with J. down the river in our canoe and bring it back, while J. should catch the weekly freight boat, if there was one, from Takla to Stuart Lake. Michelle would only consent to go, and Bella to be left, if she and their children and all their dogs could camp "right by" our cabin. After considerable tactful discussion, her tent was moved to the edge of the pinewoods twenty yards away and hidden from the cabin by a clump of bushes, so that we are all, unfortunately, within speaking distance.

These Indian women may be able to chop huge trees, and travel thirty miles a day, and bear babies in a snowbank, but when it comes to having guts about staying alone, I do believe I can beat them!

Bella is a sweet little thing with her red cheeks and her sparkling eyes; and it must be tough to be shut up all day in a tiny tent with three babies. They are really well-behaved, for we hear little noise from either them or the three dogs who are tied to trees close to the tent for protection against prowling beasts. Bella knows only a few English words and it takes some time for me to understand her, but she does seem to comprehend most of what I say. Apparently she can't understand a word of Mother's or Dad's conversation. They haven't yet acquired the Indian version of pidgin English.

As I have to provide her with food, our twice-daily parleys take considerable time. She is obviously overcome when I bring her food for the dogs also, and old cans for them to drink out of. If I could get just one of these Indians to care for his dogs in a reasonably considerate way, I should be happy, but no doubt any efforts along this line will continue to be fruitless.

In the late afternoons, Mother and Dad and Rex and I have fallen into the habit of walking over the mile-long trail to pools above the river log jam. Here is a long strip of sand and gravel. Breezes cooled by the water suck down the valley and blow away mosquitoes which are at last beginning to die down considerably. There are mighty spruces to shade us from the hot sun, and charmingly framed views of the Driftwood and Bear Lake Mountains. Dad fishes for trout in deep pools, while Mother and I take breath-taking, scream-producing, icy plunges, and Rex chases his tail along the sand bars. I don't think I shall be able ever again to enjoy swimming in a bathing suit. Even my proper mother has, for once in her life, discarded this cold and hampering garment. When we cook supper — a fresh trout perhaps — we congratulate ourselves over having escaped from the too populous vicinity of poor Bella and family.

Life went along peacefully in this manner for about five days when, lo and behold, just as we were about to undress for our daily bathes, who should appear at the gravel bar but Bella, three children, and three dogs. We tried to explain to her that this was a sort of private family bathing spot. She smiled and nodded, but has appeared regularly each day since, though she keeps at the outskirts of the bar. It gives us a sort of hunted feeling, and we pray for the return of Michelle.

Having extolled the virtues of an existence unhampered by the presence of other human beings, I am annoyed excessively that my parents should not be having the chance — the only chance of their lives probably — to experience it.

Camp at South End of Bear Lake   *July 26*

We have finally arrived with all Mother's and Dad's summer equipment, tent, sleeping bags, duffels, and boxes of specimens for the Museum. But for a while, without J.'s stern and commanding presence to deal with Charlie and company, I thought we'd never make it. Michelle returned from Takla, and Charlie and the boys appeared, supposedly ready to take us to Bear Lake. Prices and ways and means had been previously gone into with J., who hoped to join us by special plane trip at Bear Lake the last of the month. We had supposed everything settled. But four days of exhausting efforts on Dad's and my part were required to effect an agreement all over again. The baggage we wished to take was more than they had understood; they would have to increase the price. They could not carry so much stuff. They did not feel very well. Their pack dogs were "sick," and so on, ad infinitum. Each morning, noon, and evening a new difficulty was brought forth. At first I left it to be dealt with by Dad, the man of our party; but Dad, though now exasperated to the point of heavy curses (he has, formerly, thought us much too "unsympathetic" with our Indian friends), was too credulous of the obstacles that seemed to have mounted by leaps and bounds, and much too "appeal-to-their-better-nature" sort of thing. Then I tried, but being of the weaker sex was too gentle and easily talked down.

Through all this Michelle, who was to escort us on the trail, was the difficult and rather ugly one. Finally Dad had a long, long talk with Charlie, alone. *He* said he appealed to his better nature! *I* think he got really mad and told the old man he ought to be able to control his son better and set the example. But whatever happened, it was all agreed upon at last, after we had raised the price above J.'s estimate but kept it below the Indians'.

One day when the Indians were all off hunting, there came a woeful howling from their camp. I went across to look and found that one of their dogs had been left behind. Thin as a skeleton and matted with dirt, it was fastened by a piece of wire two and a half feet long to a bush, and, in broiling sun, was panting its life away. I went back to the cabin and got water and biscuits, and since I couldn't get within reach of its bared teeth, I threw it the biscuits and lumps of moss dipped in water. And while it was occupied with these I pushed a can of water up to it with a stick, and stuck a spruce branch in the ground for shade. On winter trips these dogs have appeared to be fairly well fed and treated. (They would be no use if they weren't.) From what we have observed so far the cruelty to the dogs does not seem to be a deliberate act — we have not seen them beat one, for instance — but the complete callousness and indifference to their welfare is inexcusable.

We are to camp here about a week, hoping that J. may turn up. If he does not, we will go on by Charlie's boat up to Carl's in time to meet the plane due to arrive there.

This end of the lake has jutting peninsulas and little winding bays. Parts of the forest on this side have been burned in years past and, though this does not make for the beautiful scenery of the blackly wooded opposite shores, it is rather an asset for living purposes. It is open enough to walk through and allows strong breezes, sweeping down the lake, to blow away flies and mosquitoes. The shallow little ponds and backwaters are black with swimming tadpoles, which we suppose to be the

aquatic stage of the northern toad. Oddly enough, though there
were thousands of mating toads in Tetana, we were never able
to find any tadpoles there. But the swampy pond back of the
cabin was swarming with them. Dad suggests that the water of
Tetana, which must be 15 or 20 degrees lower than any ordinary
water, is too cold for proper development of the tadpole stage.
I can think of no other explanation. But why then do the toads
go there to mate and lay eggs every spring? The Indians say
they are always there in May and June.

Numbers of loons are out on the water. Still evenings echo
with their clear wild calls, but songbirds are scarce and mostly
silent. They had almost ceased singing at Tetana by the end of
June, when their nesting season is finished. By the middle of
July they were beginning to flock together and make ready for
the southward autumn migration. The little bats had begun to
disappear and had apparently started their migration.

Bear Lake   *July 29*

The other afternoon we took our supper to an open point a
mile up the lake and were preparing to eat, when we heard a
plane. It came over very low, roaring just above our heads.
Thinking that it might be J. looking for us, we climbed up on
rocks and waved frantically. But no, it flew on up the lake
and we were sitting down again disappointedly, when it turned
and came roaring back. After circling a few times it hit the water
about a mile up and then taxied slowly toward us over rough
waves. A stiff breeze was tossing the water about at a great rate.

The plane came to within twenty yards of a little sandy
beach, and there was J., climbing out on a wing, and Russ waving from the window. J. waded ashore, but he might have
saved himself the trouble, for the plane washed almost up to
the beach; he and Russ began passing out bundles and throwing things from windows. In ten minutes the primitive wilderness beach was covered with an assortment of articles it had
certainly never known before, Russ had waved a "So long," and
the plane was turned about and heading off into the wind.

We stood buried in food. Dozens of fresh peaches and cantaloupes and squashed tomatoes were rolling about. Pounds of fresh steak and new potatoes and peas and strawberries and pears. There were pies, cakes, and candy. Two quart bottles, one-third full of fresh cream (the remaining two thirds were on the floor of Russ's cabin, having been expelled over a rough air pocket), were rescued before they were slapped over by waves. And we all stood about grinning at each other.

For two days now J. and I have done nothing but eat. I, because this is the first time for nearly one year that I have tasted any of the aforementioned articles of diet; J., because it's the first time for two weeks that he has been able to take anything but liquids.

J. has acquired a new haircut, his hair in back shaved to a straight line so that it looks like a wig. Very distressing to me after the sleek cuts, shaped nicely to his head, which I always give him. Apparently the Prince George barber and I totally disagree as to what is good-looking in haircuts. The first thing the barber said when he examined J.'s head was, "Who the hell has been cutting your hair?"

It took J. and Michelle, in the tippy little dugout, two exciting days to get down the river to Bulkley House, where they discovered that the great fire which had threatened us had burned all round the head of Takla and on the northwest. It had gotten to within eighteen miles of us. They spent another half day paddling the twenty-five miles down to the Landing. Luckily some Takla people were out on an excursion and towed them about ten miles by launch. At the Landing J. waited a week for the mail boat, his jaw in a frightful state, but as there was no other way of getting out (no plane came near the place while he was there and there is no telephone or telegraph) there was nothing else to do. When he finally reached Prince George, some two hundred miles south of Takla, a shocked dentist extracted his tooth and treated the abscess, and J. was again able to look about and take notice. By great good luck he ran into Russ Baker, who was making a trip upcountry to a point east of Bear Lake, and Russ said he would take J. along and drop him at Bear. It seems that J. then raided the stores for food and, after describing my year's diet to amused and sympathetic shopkeepers, was offered quantities of delicacies at extremely low prices.

When J. was at Takla he bought, for fifteen dollars, a huge dog which Russ has promised to bring up when he flies in for Carl. I simply don't see how we will feed another creature, but J. says that "Wahoo" (where on earth did he get that name?) will give him more free time for hunting by relieving him of packing and heavy work. The dog is *not* to be treated as a pet (with a lowering glance in my direction), but is to be kept tied up and used strictly for working.

Camp at North End of Bear Lake
Near Carl's Point   *August 9*

Mother and Dad are gone, as suddenly and surprisingly as they came. We had been up here two days, having arrived four days ahead of the expected plane. We thought, since planes like everything else in this land are wholly dependent on weather and are apt to be weeks late, that we should probably have some time to explore this country. Dad and J. had delectable schemes for thrilling salmon fishing up the deep canyons of the Bear River, as the sockeye are now running in countless thousands. Bear River flows into the Skeena, which in turn empties into the Pacific. Hence spawning salmon run up into Bear Lake each summer; and the Bear Lake Indians are able to net and smoke any quantity for themselves and their dogs. As far as we can see, they have no excuse for allowing themselves or their dogs to be in the half-starved condition which most of them seem to exhibit before winter is even half gone. The probable truth is that they just get bored with catching and smoking fish after a while and never put up a sufficient quantity.

I had planned to get Mother up on at least the slopes of the mountains back of the Indian village, so that she could have a taste of the heights. But early yesterday afternoon, just as we were all setting forth on various expeditions, the plane arrived two days ahead of schedule. Russ said a spell of bad weather was brewing and he must go right back. Mother and Dad and Carl had one hour to get ready. In all the frantic excitement of packing and receiving our new dog — the picture of abject misery as he was unloaded from the plane — we had no chance for sad leave-takings. Mother and Dad were hoisted into the plane on top of duffels before they had time even to kiss us good-bye. Carl, also departing with great speed, gave J. the keys of his store and hasty directions to supply some of the Indians for whom he was to provide food before he went "out" for his customary summer and autumn vacation. We promised to stick by the post until various Indians, who are off fishing, have showed up, and then to lock everything securely and keep the keys with us until Carl can send for them.

J. and I, surrounded by Indians and each holding a frantic dog with gigantic efforts, stood on the little beach as the plane took off. It went with such a rush that the wind nearly knocked us over. Rex broke his leash, and Wahoo, held by a chain, nearly pulled J. off his feet.

Wahoo is chained to a tree beside our camp, as we dare not let him go free just yet. He is a huge, ungainly, yellow and white creature (good pack dogs are usually bred for size and strength rather than pure strains), just a pup, but three times as big as Rex. He is very thin, his coat is in bad condition with the fur coming out in patches, and his great big floppy white feet with huge transparent nails don't look as though he had ever been allowed to use them. At first I thought him rather homely and, mindful of past experiences in this country with seemingly friendly dogs, I was wary of approaching him too closely. But the first hour after he arrived, when I took him a bowl of water, he wagged his tail so violently and gulped the water so gratefully that I rather loved him. Rex, obedient little gentleman that he is, has never once, so far, seemed to resent his presence. This evening I unchained Wahoo and took him and Rex to walk, wondering if, at any minute, they might tear each other limb from limb. But, except for a few growls, they got along perfectly.

Wahoo is like a child just learning to walk. He trips all over himself and can't negotiate the smallest log without falling. He tries so hard to follow lithe, sure-footed little Rex that my heart boils with indignation at the way he must have been kept perpetually tied up. He will be useless as a work dog until he can learn to use his feet.

Now that we have two dogs, especially one as stupendous as Wahoo, the Indians are already cautious of approaching our camp too closely. I foresee this will mean a new and welcome privacy.

Tetana   *August 12*

After we cleaned and boarded up and closed Carl's cabin, trying to leave everything in the spick-and-span order worthy of Carl, Michelle and Alec took us down the lake in Charlie's boat. As there was a brisk north breeze we hoisted our ever-useful canvas bed sheet and sailed part way, thus taking about half the usual time to reach the south end. We brought back some new provisions. With those and Michelle's dogs and our dogs, the boat was overflowing. Wahoo and Rex, squashed together almost on top of each other in the bottom, which was several inches deep in water, behaved with exemplary manners. So did the Indian dogs at their end.

During the night at camp we had a strange visitor, who gave the Indians, at least, a tremendous scare. As J. and I were sitting over the evening fire there came from up the shore a queer cry, almost like a child's. We wondered whether it could be an owl, or a lynx, or just possibly a cougar. Around midnight, we were waked from deep sleep by a terrific noise from Rex and Wahoo, and from the Indian dogs, camped a little way beyond. It was the first time I had heard Wahoo give voice to the deep belling note that rose out of his great chest. Soon, close by our tent, came Michelle's voice out of the dark, asking if our dogs were tied, because he had let his loose.

"What's the matter, Michelle? What's happened?"

"By gosh, Jack, I dunno. Something come round. I neber see nothing like him before. You hear the dogs? Something big come right up to our camp. He creep around, *soft*. Jus' like a man he creep. We jus' see his shadow. Like a ghos'. By God, we scare. We let the dogs go, but he neber chase him. He come back, he scare too. I neber see him that way before."

"A cougar!" cried J. in great excitement. "It must be. It won't hurt you, Michelle. It doesn't attack man — wish we'd seen it. Which way did it go?"

But Michelle didn't know and I don't think he was reassured, for, when he went back to his camp, he and Alec built up a huge fire. We could see it and hear their voices all the rest of the night.

Although cougars, or mountain lions, are not uncommon around Hazelton, they have apparently never been seen up this far north, and they are an unknown quantity to these Indians. Michelle's descriptions, plus the weird cry we heard in the evening, make us almost certain that we have a new record for the northern range of the cougar.

Next day, on the shore just across from camp, I saw a large bear moving through undergrowth. Though I'd like to think it was a grizzly, according to my few glimpses it was dark, so probably it was only a black. Black bears are common through the Driftwood and Bear Lake regions, and the Indians tell us that some brown bears (doubtless a color phase of the black) have appeared during the last three years around Bear Lake, although they were previously unknown.

Wahoo is justifying J.'s predictions and proving himself a noble pack dog. Twice at Bear Lake, J. practised him with small loads, but it was not until the trip home to Tetana that he did any real work. He then carried, without difficulty, a pack of about thirty-six pounds, all the fifteen miles. He takes to packing with perfect naturalness; stands still as a lamb while the pack is being roped on, and then, waving his tail with pride and immense good nature, struts slowly off. As soon as he feels the weight of a load, he falls immediately to pacing, a method which does not shake the pack nearly so much as a regular walk. He seems to know instinctively just how to use his great strength to the best advantage, an instinct which Rex, though the brighter and better guardian of the two, lacks entirely.

Rex, however, carried a twenty-five-pound pack all the way

home, and, once he got actually started and because his first aim in life is to serve, did nobly also. But roping on Rex's pack is an ordeal; he whines and moans at the mere sight of it, won't stand a minute, and blows himself out like a balloon, so that each time after we have started and he has unswelled, J. has had to pack him all over again. Rex is just too much of an aristocrat to make a worthy beast of burden.

When we got back as far as the little pond where Mother and Dad had camped on the way up to Bear Lake, we were horrified to see that fire, undoubtedly spread from our own campfire some weeks before, had burnt over the whole point and was still smoldering underground. Now Dad, impressed with the careless handling of fires by some of these Indians, had gone back purposely to our campfire, and I with him, to make doubly certain that it had been thoroughly extinguished. We had watched Michelle beat it out and pour water on it, but as an extra precaution we had fetched another pail of water from the pond ourselves. I begin now to perceive a good reason for the dirty, unoriginal habit of using old campsites and the same fireplace year after year. A deep bed of ashes is perhaps the only real safeguard against fire spreading underground.

The dog packing went well until we reached the deep narrow little stream that separates Hudson Bay Meadow from the woods leading down to Tetana. Across this stream three small, slippery logs are stretched for a bridge. J. and I passed over, then sure-footed Rex with never a slip; and then, since we had no way to help him, we held our breaths for Wahoo. Trembling and squeaking he started. The more he trembled the more his pack swayed and the more unbalanced he grew. As he reached the very middle, the pack gave one awful sway, and down he went with a gigantic splash, clean under water and began to float off slowly, his heavy pack retarding his frantic efforts to reach shore. We rushed along the bank after him, caught his tail, then the pack rope, and hauled him out with one titanic heave. We had to take his pack off and wring out bedding and clothes before the pack was anywhere near light enough for him to carry again.

J. has made a log kennel for Wahoo near the back door, and here Wahoo is to be chained, against my will, much of the time. When he is loose he plays with Rex, and the two appear to be fast friends. The courtesy of the dogs to each other is amazing. Of course we discouraged any ill feeling at the start, but both possess manners of gentlemen born. They never quarrel. They take turns eating out of the same pot or pan with perfect amicability. If we offer them a drink each is so polite that he is reluctant to be the first to take it. When they wrestle together, beautiful, strong, well-developed muscles are brought into play; the grace of their movements as they melt from one position to another is a lovely thing. Each teaches the other new tricks and tactics. Wahoo's strength and size are balanced by the speed and sureness of Rex.

Yesterday noon, when we got here, we found the whole place overgrown with weeds feet high. Plants as tall as we were growing up through cracks in the cabin floor. It looked as though we had been gone a year instead of one month. Our screened meat box, built onto the outside wall, has been torn down; a ham and the remains of bacon and cheese have vanished. A black bearskin, nailed to the wall, has been pulled off and dragged as far as Mother's and Dad's tent site. Bear droppings are scattered about. An irate bruin has evidently been entertaining himself with our property. How, we wonder, did he feel about the bearskin?

CHAPTER XI

Autumn

Tetana   *August 16*

Today when we reached the Driftwood River, after not hav-ing seen it for weeks, we were struck dumb with surprise. From a distance it looked as though the water had turned to gold. It was crammed from shore to shore with little fish, about seven inches long, struggling violently against the current. They were a bright scarlet with peacock-green heads and, in the pale green crystal water, with sun shining on them, were one of the pret-tiest sights I've ever seen. Talk about tropical fish in the tur-quoise waters of a warm sea! We have here a red-gold river flowing through forests of deepest, darkest green with moun-tains rising, snow-crowned, in the background.

The fish must be some kind of tiny salmon running up the river to spawn; a few, already beginning to die, were so feeble that we caught them in our hands. We rushed home to look them up in the Fish Books. Possibly they're kokanee, a dwarf landlocked form of the sockeye. But none of the books mention such fish as ever getting up into these regions. The coming of the kokanee in such gigantic numbers has apparently driven off the trout; since the kokanee are beginning now to die, the whole river is fouled with their decaying bodies, and a frightful stench pervades the country for miles around. When the wind sets in that direction we can even smell it at the cabin. It reminds me of Singapore and other odoriferous places of the Orient.

Every day now across the still green waters of Tetana, we hear the voice of the Pacific loon — that ghostly, haunting, wail-ing "oh-h-h-h, oh-h-h, ooh-ooh." Like a woman crying hope-lessly, endlessly. Like a baby bear who has lost its mother. Like the faint far-off foghorn of a ship at sea. Like the mournful sigh of wind in a pine tree. We have a pair of these loons — which are the American form of the Arctic loon — staying with us for a time. And because we have heard them on tundra ponds of the Arctic, we were not unduly startled when the ghostly voice rang over our waters. The loons are quite tame and sometimes allow us to paddle within thirty feet of them. Then we can see their exquisite black and gray velvet bodies, barred with white, and their ruby eyes. When they're separated they begin calling and answering in those voices which haunt one day and night and of which, somehow, one can never hear enough. Since they have been regular visitors here on and off throughout the summer, it seems that they must nest somewhere near by; perhaps in this valley or in surrounding territory.

August 27

For the first time in eleven months, this country looks almost colorless and rather unlovely. There is hardly a flower to be seen; poplars and willows have lost the vivid green of early summer; the Driftwoods are almost bare of snow. Mornings white with frost, flocking of birds, calling of the jays, squirrels dropping spruce cones, all say that August in the Driftwood Valley is the beginning of autumn. It now grows dark at the respectable hour of 8 P.M. and the nights are clear and cold. Last night the temperature dropped to 26 degrees. August stars are almost as wonderful as those of winter. We've been sleeping out on the open bank above the lake, with nothing between us and the heavens. Night after night, frosty air full on our faces, we lie looking up at the glittering pageant of other worlds moving steadily and throbbingly and imperceptibly from east to west. And we know again that man and his works are a very small part of something very great.

Flies and mosquitoes have almost vanished, and we can breathe freely and enjoy Tetana once again. But, just to remind us that we can't expect life in this country ever to be really easy, we now have yellow jackets around in angry dangerous swarms. They attack all meat and garbage in buzzing masses.

If we want a dirty mammal skull cleaned we have only to leave it out for the yellow jackets and, presto, in an hour it is white and clean as a whistle, far cleaner than we can make it after days of odorous boiling and picking, airing and drying.

We also have another new pest. Whenever we put fish or other meat in Tetana to keep cold, it's covered almost instantly with a form of small black leech about a quarter of an inch long. None of the other lakes seem to have these tiny leeches, though some possess a few large common ones. Something about the cold spring-fed quality of Tetana must attract this special variety.

The six-by-six-foot garden we planted with radishes and lettuce in early June, and which we have hung over all summer watering and shading, actually has lettuce in it. (The radishes never got beyond the stage of green shoots.) Each plant is composed of two or three lettuce leaves two to three inches long and one inch wide. Since the nights are frosty, we have decided to eat it all now. This won't take long. It tastes heavenly! We had hoped that the long hours of burning sun might counteract the cold nights and produce vegetables, but the sun was so hot we had to shade the plants constantly and even the short nights were apparently too cold.

Days are also much cooler now, which is a blessed relief; though yesterday the thermometer went up to 110 in the sun. With the dying down of the kokanee run, trout are beginning to appear in the river again. J., who has now to supply himself and me and Rex and the capacious tummy of Wahoo, spends long and earnest hours fishing, while I keep the dogs at a safe distance so they won't scare the wary old trout. The trout are fighting fiercely. Several precious spoons have been lost, but J. has made new, quite successful ones out of coffee-tin lids, and with these he has caught ten- and twelve-pound Dollies. I find that the stomachs of all the biggest trout are stuffed with two or three dead kokanee, indicating that they have been feeding largely on these.

My job as usual is to clean the fish, and I have by this time cleaned such countless numbers that I could do one blindfold.

If I can clean them when they're freshly caught and easy to handle, I don't mind it a bit — except for the worms. Just inside the body cavity and outside the stomach and intestines are great balls and mats of slender white wriggling worms, several inches long.

When I'm eating the fish later, I always, always remember the worms. And the fish becomes much less appetizing. Just as a piece of nice red, juicy meat which seems to be perfectly fresh and sweet becomes almost unedible when one discovers, suddenly, that maggots are disporting themselves gaily around inside it. In vain I remind myself that maggots have been found to be useful members of society; that, when they have been introduced into horrible wounds, they have eaten the unhealthy tissue and saved many a life. I still don't like them in my meat, and I don't know anything that requires greater strength of character than to go on calmly eating and *digesting* a wormy piece of meat. But what's the use of getting weak and pulled down by not eating the most important article of diet? I pray for the winter when worms and maggots are no more.

We keep finding reminders that make Mother and Dad seem not so far away. Stones which Dad piled near the trail to mark a junco's nest. A row of colored pebbles on the gravel bar by the log jam where Mother played with Bella's children. A long, flat, flexible little piece of whalebone near the spot where we used to undress for our swim.

Said J.: "Last remnants of civilization discarded here by Mother!"

We've planned a trip to the Driftwood Mountains, following the ascent at the lowest point that J. took with Charlie in June. Since Wahoo can carry forty pounds and Rex twenty, we figure we may be gone a week. For dog food we will take smoked salmon which we got from the Indians at Bear Lake. This salmon, as well as being very light and practical for carrying on long trips, appears to be excellent for the dogs. Small pieces are quite satisfying and keep them in fine condition.

J. has been cutting a mile-long trail through the dense willow swamp to the west, so that we can ford the river at a spot where an old canoe track of Charlie's (which it took us days to discover) heads towards the foot of the mountains. The willows across the swamp grow above our heads; trunks and branches are interlaced in mats; water and deep oozy mud surround the roots. Getting through these swamps in summer is no fun, but one has to do it the minute one strikes across country, for they cover the valleys.

Tetana   *September 6*

We left for the mountains on August 29th by J.'s trail across the swamp to the river. There we forded a wide pool of water still foul from dead kokanee, wading in over our waists and carrying Rex's and Wahoo's packs in addition to our own, while the dogs swam. Fresh grizzly tracks were in the mud and bits of half-eaten kokanee lay along the banks. Charlie's canoe trail consists of small poles laid crosswise at intervals. These once formed rollers for the canoe, which he made from a balsam poplar near the foot of the Driftwoods. Now they are so overgrown with moss and bushes that in many places we couldn't find them at all. The dogs stepped in a yellow jackets' nest and turned into raving maniacs as they dashed about against trees. The more the yellow jackets stung Rex, the madder he got and the more he insisted on chasing them. When things calmed down again the dogs' packs, which had been carefully roped on fifteen minutes before, had to be undone and put on all over again.

J. has become quite proficient at dog packing — he has adopted the single-rope hitch of the Indians' that goes clear around the pack and the dog's chest, then once under the body and up over the back. But even so whenever we start on a trip we always stop at least once or twice early in the day for readjustments. The packs may be fastened a little too loose or too tight, they may be slightly heavier on one side than the other. A perfectly balanced pack tied on the dog's back well forward, so that the weight comes primarily on the shoulders, is essential if the dog is to travel any distance without undue strain or sores.

Soon we struck endless stretches of that indescribably awful devil's-club. It's a big shrub, covered from root to crown with sharp stout thorns; scratches are unavoidable when walking through it, since the shrub grows as thick as a wall. The scratches nearly always fester and make bad sores. J., with his axe, had to cut out every step of our way. It took us two hours to make one mile, and our chances of reaching the mountain pass before night vanished. The scent of fresh bear and moose was everywhere. High logs were strewn in all directions and, because of constant swampy mudholes, we could never proceed in a straight line, nor could we see the sky above, nor the mountainside directly ahead. The air was as close as a tropical jungle. While J. cut, it was my job to hoist the dogs with their packs over logs, and my pack, which included the .22, J.'s nine-pound rifle, the cameras, and two pairs of field glasses. Half the time we slipped and fell off into bunches of devil's-club; the dogs' howls and my groans brought no response from J., who, with sweat and blood streaming off face and arms, was chopping grimly on ahead. With all the climbing and falling the dogs' packs again got hopelessly disarranged and one-sided so that the ropes were cutting into their sides and throats.

I might as well draw a veil over the rest of that afternoon and evening.

Just before nightfall we reached the high bank of a roaring mountain stream. Here the devil's-club gave way, thank God, to a dense growth of alders, azaleas, and thimbleberry. This was the beginning of an almost perpendicular incline that marks the real ascent to the pass. There was barely time, before darkness dropped, to make a small bed of boughs on the narrow precipitous little bank and cook supper over a tiny fire.

By afternoon of the next day we at last reached the top of the pass which is around six thousand feet. The ascent up the mountainside which, from Tetana, looks so easy and open was one of the steepest I ever negotiated. As the trees had been burned over years ago, dead logs were tumbled in every direction. We climbed on hands and knees and hauled the dogs up over high logs. But every panting effort was worth something and when we came out on grassy meadows above timber line, it was so lovely that the hard ascent was completely blotted out. Against a background of thick stunted balsam we set up our small tent fly which we made ourselves out of lightweight canvas. It is completely open on one side and is much smaller and easier to carry than a tent. A cold little stream, containing apparently the same species of small leech now in Tetana, trickled along near by; far below spread the whole Driftwood Valley, and across to the east were the big Ominecas. On left and right rose high black and red-brown peaks; behind, for several miles, stretched a swampy meadow, in wet places very green, studded with yellow and lavender daisies and a few other late flowers.

We spent three days wandering over open peaks that rose some two thousand feet above camp. Miles and miles of steep grassy uplands stretched to high rocky peaks and, in every direction, falling and rising in blue sheets so vast the eye could scarcely compass them, were views undescribable of great new ranges, wooded valleys, countless lakes. Never a trace of man, or of anything made by man. A whole country, untrod by man, unknown to him. The peep of glacial-covered mountains, which we see from the hill back of our cabin, is part of a great range, some fifty miles long, covered with mighty ice fields that shine and gleam in changing lights. This is probably the beginning of Pacific coastal ranges. On the maps it is just blank space.

The Frypans, rising up beyond green slopes of the Driftwoods, were most wonderful of all. Their peaks, glittering with eternal snow and ice, were fantastic and oddly shaped like a painting in a fairy tale. We spent hours sprawled on dry, sweet yellow grass, bathed in hot, hot sun and cold pure winds blowing fresh from the snows across the western valley. Lying on this high narrow Driftwood range that stuck up all by itself was like being rocked in a cradle hung alone in the vast canopy of the clear, clean blue sky. Here and there were bright pockets and basins, with flowers and little springs and rills coming out of old snowbanks. The dogs, free of packs, went wild with joy as they dashed and tumbled from one soft mound to another. When they were resting Rex would lie placidly close beside us, but Wahoo wandered off by himself a little and, from a special vantage point, would gaze solemnly and steadily and fascinatedly at the view. Wahoo is, we have come to understand, a philosopher.

J. was disappointed not to find mountain game, but there must be plenty there at certain seasons, for numerous old goat tracks led along the rocky slides and bear droppings were down below. The goats were evidently off in a different part of the mountains, the bears fishing in valley lakes and rivers. Except for small flocks of white-tailed ptarmigan and clouds of sweet-voiced larks there was hardly any bird life at this late season. We're determined, another year, to get up there in late June as soon as snow has gone, when summer birds are in full song and the mountain meadows in flower. J. had sores on his legs from that wretched devil's-club, which prevented him from climbing around as much as he would have liked.

When we were heading home from the foot of the mountains, in order to avoid the worst devil's-club, J. tried blazing a new trail for about six miles across to the river and hit, within a hundred yards, the exact spot from which we had started six days before.

September 18

We have a new addition to our family. J. has lately been down the river to visit a small mammal trap set near a sand bar where we have seen fisher tracks and droppings several times this summer. (Altogether, counting those at the Takla and Bear Lake posts, besides a few freshly caught ones, J. has now seen twenty-five fisher skins. But since the fisher is so notoriously wary, we have no more real hope than ever of being able to watch one alive.) The other day J. came paddling up the lake *shouting* "Teddy" at the top of his voice — a most unprecedented procedure! At his feet reposed a big sack full of something warm and lumpy. But not till he had dumped it out on the cabin floor, with doors and windows shut and two frantic dogs on the outside, did I know that what he had was a young coyote. He had found her, caught in his trap by the forefoot.

Though a little odorous, as J. puts it, she is quite the prettiest thing one ever saw. About the size of a young collie dog with thick golden gray fur and a huge bushy tail, she has a fine delicate little head with the most enormous stiff, prick, white-edged ears, and pure amber eyes which tone in perfectly with her fur. She must be three and a half or four months old, and does not seem to be vicious. Her teeth are only partly grown, and by holding the scruff of her neck we can handle her quite easily. In fact she stays quietly and apparently contentedly in our arms with her head on our shoulders. She eats milk and fish out of a spoon, though she won't touch food from our hands. Her foot does not appear to be badly hurt.

We are so in love with her that we've decided to keep her for a short time to study and photograph. J. has built a little cage pen with remnants of screen wire — heavily reinforced by numerous poles and stakes.

The dogs became accustomed to her in one day and, beyond an occasional growl at her cage, don't seem to bother much about her. Every night since she's been here, we've heard strange noises outside the cabin and wonder if the mother coyote is hanging around near by.

September 25

The little coyote began chewing her injured foot so much that we feared she would bite it off, so, after several days, we set her free in the woods some distance from the cabin, and have seen her no more.

We've been more than busy lately, enjoying the good weather, freedom from insects, fishing in the river, canoeing on the lake, laying in a store of winter wood, rechinking the outside of the cabin, trapping mice and shrews, and last, but not least, mending shoes, moccasins, snowshoes, and the dogs' pack sacks. Moose sinews (from muscles along the backbone) are stronger than any kind of ordinary thread, and are used largely by these Indians just as Eskimos use caribou sinews. We also use them for mending shoes and moccasins, et cetera. The dogs' canvas pack sacks, where they lace together, have had to be reinforced by strips of moose hide which is much more durable than canvas.

I have also spent long hours arranging the plant collection which I've been making for the Museum. I have several specimens of every kind of tree, shrub, flower, fern, and Lycopodium which I could find growing around Tetana and throughout this valley. It's been a man-sized job carrying an oilskin bag around all summer to keep the flowers fresh till I got them home, putting them in the plant press, and writing notes about each one. But I have now about a hundred and eighty kinds and hope to complete the set by getting more from the mountains another year.

After weeks of peace, we've had a few visitors. Johnny French came with mail from Takla, and then Michelle and Charlie and a young Indian from Bear Lake. According to their quaint custom of addressing everyone by his first name, they call my parents, who evidently made a favorable impression, "Mother" and "Daddy." Johnny asked if Daddy is coming back again next year. Michelle remarked, "I suppose Mother and Daddy are long way away by now?" The young Bear Lake Indian said, "Why doesn't Daddy make trade store here? Good man that, lots of Indian come to his store!" Charlie is tickled to death because Dad, in addition to giving him a present or two, wrote him a letter. Charlie said, "Lots of white man he make me present, but neber he write me, Bear Lake Charlie, a letter. Always I remember that man Daddy!"

Once again autumn is burning in waves across the valley. Gold and orange and scarlet of poplars and willows against the dark evergreens are as marvelous as before.

Yesterday we took a trip miles down river in the dugout canoe. J. roars at me, but I vow it was one of the most hair-raising experiences I've ever had! I've often canoed on lakes, sometimes in "high seas," but shooting a swift, shallow, rock-strewn river in a dugout canoe was new to me. Taking the place of a strong man in the bow was also a novel experience. Flying down small rapids, avoiding logs and rocks, keeping the dug-out from going over, provided hours of breath-taking excitement and hard work. We would fly by banks and trees at a dizzy rate, to come out into some deep quiet pool, where gold leaves, spires of black-green spruces, red-berried shrubs, clouds and sunlit mountains were reflected in still waters. No sooner would I recover from one rushing passage than the canoe would be sucked off again down another whirlpool. J.'s shouted, completely incomprehensible directions as to what to do with my paddle, and his annoyance because the directions weren't always carried out on the second, kept me panting. I was fairly trembling with fatigue by the time we reached our stopping place.

Rex and Wahoo, those angelic dogs, crouched motionless in the bottom of the narrow canoe the whole way down, but when we did come to a halt they almost upset us by frantic leaps for the bank. Our stopping place was a great deep backwater of the river. While J. fished I made a fire for noon tea on the high open bank. Wide views spread out across the autumn-lit valley to the cloud-shadowed Frypans and Driftwoods. Although J. was not especially successful at fishing, the air was so spicy and warm that we lingered for hours.

I had fondly believed that, since the trip down river was safely accomplished, the up trip would be easy. What a lot I don't know! While J. poled in the stern, it was my job to keep the bow pointing upstream. When we went up rapids, even though they were small, it took every ounce of strength and wits to keep the bow from turning down. A stroke made a fraction of a second too late, around swept the dugout, almost capsizing, and we would be headed downstream again, having lost all the progress we'd gained. J. is really a fine teacher and his directions are usually clear, but in this case I found them hard to follow.

"*Left, left!*" he would shout. "Push to the left," and I would shove obediently to the left.

We'd then swing all wrong, and he'd yell, "No, no, I mean right. Jumping Joseph, can't you see yourself which side to push on? Do use your own initiative!"

And later when we'd gone wrong again he'd say, "Why can't

you just follow my directions? Next time do *exactly* as I say."

My eyes bulged, my heart nearly burst, and when I'd suppose I hadn't an ounce of strength left, we'd get up a swift stretch at last and come to the blessed calm and straight paddling of a long pool. How J., doing double work without adequate assistance, was faring, I dared not inquire.

When at last we pushed through the outlet of Tetana and once more reached the haven of a lake, I leaned back with the virtuous feeling of never having worked harder in my life and exclaimed: —

"Phew, what a workout!"

"Well, I do think," said my sweating husband, "that you might have put a little more *pep* into it!"

October 15

We've been on a short camping trip to the Kastberg Creek country. Just as we were making camp on the south bank of the stream the first afternoon, it started to pour. When J. began to chop tent poles, he cut his right hand with the axe. It wasn't a very deep cut, but it must have struck a vein, for blood poured out so fast that I had to tie on a tourniquet, and his hand was useless. I, therefore, had to put up the tent and start a fire with the already wet wood. It all took me about twice the time it does J. What with great splotches of blood about, rain pouring down our necks and wetting our supplies, and my struggles with tent and fire, we felt completely demoralized. This little experience showed me that I am still far too dependent on J. I must hereafter practise camping on my own.

We spent three nights and two days at Kastberg, exploring up and down stream along the Takla trail. We put out dozens of mice traps along the gravel bars and across extensive bogs down toward the river, in the hope of getting new species. The usual white-footed and red-backed mice and the cinereus shrews were by the stream, but on the bog we actually saw, though we failed to catch it, a tawny lemming. We were thrilled, since these lemmings are exceedingly rare and observations on their habits few. It set a new range record because they are supposed to occur only on the mountains. Their runways and green droppings, distinctly larger than those made by the other mice, were everywhere through the sphagnum moss of the bog. J. also collected a large hawk, either a Cooper's in immature plumage, or possibly a goshawk, as the two are said to look much alike. It took me two hours to skin, it was so tremendously tough and strong.

Inspired by the lemming signs on the Kastberg bogs, we have been out looking for them all around Tetana and have discovered enough to exceed our wildest hopes. The first were two only half-digested bodies that we took from the stomach of a trout in the river. (We examine the stomach contents of nearly everything we collect, for in this way one acquires accurate knowledge of the food of animals, and one is apt also to find an interesting record occasionally.) The next tawny lemming was one that, with the help of Rex and Wahoo, who ferreted it out, I captured by hand on one of the high little wolf lookout hills by Trail Lake. Mindful of the ferocious teeth, I first put my foot on its back. The lemming let out a loud scream — exactly like a rabbit in the clutches of an owl — and I was so startled I very nearly lost it.

Since then we've discovered a whole colony of tawny lemmings on the rock slide of Wolf Lake, and here, by putting traps directly across their runways (they don't take bait apparently), we've caught several more. We are now convinced that these lemmings have reached plague proportions, that in order to obtain sufficient food they have been obliged to spread from their usual mountain habitat down into the valleys. They must have been swimming across the river since we've taken several more from trout stomachs.

Except for my being unable to conquer the fear that something may happen to J. when he is off hunting, everything about life is nicer this year than last. All the little hills and valleys and swamps around Tetana are old familiar friends. Rex and Wahoo are unspeakably comfortable companions — though I've been in terror all fall lest they get mixed up with a bear. The Indians are scared to death of the dogs, and since

Muskrat

they won't come near the cabin without first making certain they are tied up, I have a much greater feeling of security. Certainly at mere sight or sound of a stranger, the dogs present a ferocious appearance. The hair on their backs rises as stiffly as pigs' bristles, and the roars that issue forth, especially from Wahoo, should be enough to deter the stoutest-hearted.

But apparently the Indians also have the greatest respect and admiration for them. Tales of their prowess as watchdogs, their obedience and obligingness as work dogs, and their intelligence as pets appear to be spreading throughout the country.

Both dogs, despite a low food supply at times, are in beautiful condition. The ugly patches of loose hair on Wahoo have disappeared, his gold and white coat is smooth and shining. He has lost his awkwardness and filled out (he must weigh around a hundred pounds). With his mastiff-like body and a head something like a Newfoundland's, he is altogether a stunning-looking dog. Rex too has grown fine-looking with all the points of beautiful breeding, except for his ears which, though very large and lovely, have never become completely stiff. He is exceptional in his intelligence and obedience, and has remarkable comprehension of human speech and character. But in a way he is difficult to handle because of extreme sensitivity; he is like a high-bred race horse that requires consistent patience and gentleness.

November 6

We've been on another trip to Bear Lake. This time we heard that Russ Baker was expected in with several loads for Carl, and we wanted to make arrangements for flying out with him this winter.

We have, at last, made up our minds that we must "go out," go back for a time to so-called civilization. This decision is made for the sake of our family and our work and not because we've grown restless or fed up with our wilderness existence. For, in spite of its hardness, I believe we like it more deeply than ever. The thought of leaving it, even though we are determined to come back, fills us with dread.

We've planned to go the end of December, which will be the earliest date when winter traveling by plane is possible, when ice on the big lakes will be thick enough for a plane to land safely on skis. After trying every mode of transportation offered by this inhospitable land — pack horse, pack dog, dog sled, canoe — we are convinced that for long distances, the plane is not only quickest, but cheapest. Its great drawback is, of course, the perpetual hazards and uncertainty of bad weather. It has been agreed that Russ will pick us up at Bunshaw "on December 31st or as soon thereafter as weather permits." Though he does not know Bunshaw, after talking with J. he considers it long enough for a safe landing. Since it is so much smaller than Bear it will more certainly be well frozen by midwinter. We shan't be able, after this, to communicate with Russ until he can collect us two months from now. I hope he won't forget us!

On our way back, after rowing down with Charlie's boys in the face of a blinding snowstorm, J. and I camped at the south end of Bear Lake. Making camp in the dark in wet snow was miserable business. When we woke in the morning a foot of snow was on the ground. The boys, who were afraid that they might be storm-bound, had started home in the boat before dawn. J. and I cached our tent and small tin stove and some winter food in trees by the trail, and started posthaste for Tetana. The boys were to ask Michelle, or whoever next came down our way, to bring the stuff that was cached in the trees.

November 12

Michelle arrived on a trapping trip and brought our tent — but no stove or winter food. It seems he reached the south end of Bear Lake a few days after we had been there and found that our tree caches had been pulled down. The tent was lying on the ground, but the stove, stovepipes, and food were there no longer. Since there had been no new snow, Michelle found tracks of an Indian leading off to the west through the gap of the Driftwoods and Bear Lake Mountains. He and the boys followed the tracks for some distance and made certain that they belonged to one Gunanoot, member of a famous family of law-less actors from over Hazelton way. Several of these Gunanoot brothers have been mixed up in shooting affairs, one had recently broken into Carl's store and robbed it, and it has been thought that one, two, or possibly three of them are hiding out in the mountains. Obviously one had either seen J. and me make camp, or had found our camp shortly after we left. Our light little stove and the food must have been a godsend. Doubtless he contemplated taking the tent too, but found it too much to carry.

We've had a visit also from old Charlie. We returned to him his crucifix which we discovered recently hanging on a tree here in his summer camping place. Charlie chuckled mightily when he saw it. He had never missed it.

Just as Charlie was leaving he said in a chastened voice, "Jack, you got any dried fruit? My little girl, he sick — too much meat, flour, he get — he want the fruit — " And his words trailed away with unusual meekness.

J. grinned at him. "What, Charlie! You going to make home-brew again? Thought you just had some."

Aware of what usually happens to dried fruit, we gave him an extremely small quantity. Whenever Charlie can gather together a sufficient amount of fruit he and Selina make a very potent home-brew. Carl does his best to keep home-brew materials from reaching the Indians in any quantity. Although it is unlawful to supply Indians with liquor, it is thought that they must have some hidden away which they mix with the fermented fruit. When all is ready, so we are told, Charlie and Selina invite the inhabitants of Bear Lake; and because they recount how very hard they have worked to prepare the feast, the others are shamed into contributing a little revenue (which is taken in charge by Charlie and Selina) for the general good.

The home-brew doesn't seem to make Charlie, at least, particularly happy! He's apt to go clean berserk at times and the other Indians have more than once been forced to flee the village until he regains his right mind.

One of the Catholic priests who came to Bear Lake on a

yearly visit was highly entertained one day when, inadvertently, he overheard Charlie, the Church's greatest Bear Lake supporter, wishing ardently that the priest might depart from Bear Lake before his (Charlie's) good behavior gave way completely. For, as Charlie told Carl, he had not once during the priest's stay of several weeks been able to make home-brew. He doubted that he should be able to hold out much longer. And if he couldn't, not only would his status, but also that of the Church, be woefully upset.

As the winter trapping season comes round once more we hear the usual discussions among the Indians of fur prices and the relative merits of different posts and traders. It must be fairly easy for a trader to cheat the Indians if he so desires, especially those farthest from the large settlements. The trader may name the current price of a certain fur, but when it comes to supplying the Indian with the equivalent of that price in store goods, he can make a more than handsome profit. A marten skin is, for instance, worth some $18. The Indian wishes shells for his gun, new traps, a wool jacket, cloth for his wife, flour, tea, tobacco. The trader, while supposedly supplying him with his $18 worth, in reality may give him only $12 worth of goods. The trader may claim that prices of certain commodities are higher than they really are, that it has cost him so much to transport them to his post. The average Indian cannot check up on prices outside, nor can he add figures accurately.

Indians who get about and meet with Indians from other regions can and do compare prices of both furs and goods and, if they become too dissatisfied, may take their furs to the post which, at the time, appears to give the most desirable bargains. This serves as a check on the trader, but not a very serious one. How can the Indian prove, for instance, that his marten was as good a fur as the marten which brought a far larger supply of goods at the other post? Nor is the Indian liable except under great provocation to carry his furs to a place some eighty or a hundred miles distant when he has a post near his own settlement.

In justice to the trader, however, it must be said that he is obliged to protect his own interests. Because he is not supposed to let any native actually starve, he is forced to carry many of the Indians at a constant loss. The Indians cannot by law be forced to pay their debts. So, in order to make his own livelihood, the trader must often squeeze the Indian where and how he can. Whether or not he abuses this necessity must depend on his integrity, or on the trading company with which he is affiliated.

Every so often, in addition to dissertations on the vast importance of conservation, J. gives the Indians what he calls a "pep talk." We have tried again and again to impress them with the fact that all white men are not alike. That, because one white man has treated them badly, it does not signify that we shall. That, until they can prove otherwise, they must give us the benefit of the doubt.

The Indians are always greatly interested in tales of the Eskimos, their near cousins, and J. frequently uses the Eskimo behavior as a sort of yardstick by which to measure theirs. He points out the value of the Eskimos' reliability, trustworthiness, and gratitude towards those who have helped them. He recounts stories of Eskimos who in times past, when they have been in dire need, have broken into his arctic camps and taken food and supplies, but who never failed to leave a foxskin or some other fine fur in payment and apology.

Whether any of this makes the slightest impression on these people it is difficult to tell. If they were subjected to such ideas for a sufficiently long time, it might perhaps have some effect. If only we could stay in this country long enough to try.

So far we have not gone beyond the discussion of generalities of behavior. We never touch upon Indian morals and customs. For one thing we know too little about them. Matters of sex we can judge only superficially from the relationships of the few we know. We suppose their views on sexual behavior to be quite elastic. Charlie and Selina appear to respect each other and to be a united and devoted couple. Michelle appears to be a dutiful husband and father; Bella an obedient wife. But there have been stories lately that relations have been considerably upset because Bella and William have had an affair, have been going off alone together, and so on. When this happens Michelle is, according to reports, one day angry enough to kill William, the next friendly and forgiving. Martha, though once seemingly devoted and loyal to Vinson, has now had enough and separated from him. There seem to be no outward ill feelings on Charlie's part toward Simon, who, when he married Charlie's daughter, was reputed to have two wives already. Charlie and Selina apparently encourage all their children to marry young and raise families of their own as the best safeguard against loose behavior.

None of the Bear Lake Indians have ever been disrespectful to me, though some are considerably more courteous and considerate than others. How they would behave if J. were not at hand, I don't know, but I have always the feeling that I could handle a tough Indian more easily than a tough white man.

I have never observed any of these Indians to be anything but polite and decent in their private habits. In this respect, they appear to be utterly different from natives of the Old World.

CHAPTER XII

Rex and Wahoo

Tetana   *November 15*

This evening, as I write, Rex lies stretched in dead sleep on the floor, his head, as usual, against my feet (at night by my bed his pillow is my slipper or shoe), so that if I move ever so slightly, he will know all about it on the instant. J., reading, sits on a hard box, his back propped against the log partition near the stove, for *Wahoo,* if you please, reposes in J.'s easy chair!

Wahoo is at last living in the cabin. Thanks to my repeated urgings, arguments, and entreaties, J. succumbed and has allowed him to fulfill his rightful place as a member of the family. J. said that as I always get my way sooner or later (this is base slander), he supposed it might as well be right now, but he just hoped I'd realize that if Wahoo turns out to be useless, *I* am responsible for the ruin of a good dog.

J. is used to sled dogs of the Arctic and has trained and driven Huskies for years. He was sure that if we made a pet of Wahoo, as we have of Rex, Wahoo would be useless for working. I have maintained that if the two dogs associated together, it wasn't fair to make a companion of one and not the other — that the more Wahoo loved us and was on terms of intimacy with us, the more willing he would be to work for us and the more easily I, at least, could handle him.

Unless Wahoo is on a chain he never stays tied up, anyway. After vain attempts to break him of the habit of chewing through ropes and leather by repeated lickings, at which he howled and sobbed so heartbreakingly that I cried (and I believe J. almost did), and by useless applications of mustard and pepper on the chewable portions, J. has finally given up.

I think he also anticipated that we shall have to bring Wahoo in at night in very cold weather, since his comparatively short hair would probably not enable him to survive 50 or 60 below.

Wahoo has never had to be housebroken. He came by perfect house manners from the start and, though at first rather nervous of the cabin and our approaching him too freely, he soon adapted himself and has become as great a pet as Rex. And no one is more indulgent with him than his master. J. will sit on a hard box the entire evening rather than disturb Wahoo, who, with sighs of bliss, has miraculously curled his huge form into his master's one soft easy chair. There, like a gigantic cat, he sits purring and rumbling in his great chest; or swallowing one foot after another until he nearly chokes, which is his idea of a nightly bath. Never have I seen a more particular dog than Wahoo. Not only does he wash every part of him within reach before lying down, but after each meal he dashes out to clean face and whiskers with scrupulous care by vigorous scrubbings upon the ground. When his toilet is satisfactorily completed, or when pleased with anything or anyone, he invariably puffs and blows his cheeks in and out in a completely irresistible fashion.

For such a big creature he is most gentle and careful; he practically never, even in the most narrow confines, disarranges or upsets anything. Nor will he ever, any more than Rex, even when extremely hungry, touch food left upon ground or table unless given permission to do so.

Once, in order to teach the dogs the danger of traps, J. baited a small number 0 trap with a tempting bit of meat and put it out of sight around a corner of the house. It was left there for a week, but neither dog ever would go near it.

Although good manners and obedience to commands are usually common to both, the actual characters and personalities of the two dogs differ as widely as those of people. Wahoo possesses certain traits characteristic of Husky dogs and their near relatives, the wolves. For instance, there is his tendency to find high lookouts and gaze for hours at the view. Another is his peculiar sensitivity to sound. At the ringing of a bell, or the playing of J.'s mouth organ, Wahoo raises his nose to heaven and begins to sing. Sometimes the smooth howls are interspersed with barks and his voice doesn't compare with that of wolves in its ability to express real music. Wahoo, though he now loves us devotedly, always retains his own independence and a sort of untouchable quality. On trips he chooses his camp site a short way off from ours, where he can ruminate or philosophize, or whatever it is he does, without interruption. He extracts the maximum of comfort from the toughest terrain. When he lies down, he relaxes in every inch of him. He curls his paws like a cat, draws his toes in and stretches them out. Even on the stoniest ground his whole body is composed and at rest. It makes one relaxed just to look at him.

Wahoo is surprisingly aware of weather conditions and responsive to them. On a fresh, clear day, who so merry and carefree and alert as Wahoo? On a rainy one, who more excessively dull, sleepy, and lazy? Curled into the warmest, driest, most secluded place that can be discovered, he whiles away unending hours in deep sleep.

Rex's whole being, on the other hand, is bound up in us — our habits, our moods, our behavior are his. Except on the hunt he does not care to wander by himself. His living quarters are as close as possible to ours. Changes of scenery interest him only slightly. So long as he is with us, it apparently makes little difference whether he dwells in human habitations or wildernesses. Weather affects him scarcely at all. He is as lively on stormy days as on clear ones. Even in deep repose, he sleeps with one ear open, ready to leap at the slightest hint of danger for us.

The Indians admire Rex excessively, because he will never allow them to touch even the meanest of our possessions. J. must hand them anything we give them, for they dare not pick it up themselves. I am unable to approach any of them closely, even with a cup of tea, without Rex's interposing his body between me and the recipient. Nor can the Indians approach me so much as to return an empty cup.

Nowhere is the difference in the dogs' respective characters better illustrated than in trips along the river ice. Much of the river is still wide-open, but quiet water now has thick enough ice to make it safe walking. J., who did so much arctic traveling on the treacherous sea ice of Hudson Bay, is expert at gauging the depth and safety of new-made ice. He always seems able to distinguish the danger spots by tapping with his axe. When we walk on the river Wahoo is nervous beyond words and feels every step with his nose and front paws. Sometimes we can hardly induce him to follow us. He trusts J.'s judgment not at all. Rex, on the other hand, trusts it implicitly and goes across the thinnest ice as close to me as J. will allow him. (If ice is doubtful, J. makes us all separate in order to distribute the weight.) Rex says, positively, that it is necessary for him to be at my heels every instant. If the ice is bad and I go through, his job is to go through too.

Since Rex and Wahoo have come to live with us, our old friends the jays and squirrels and weasels are more wary about approaching the cabin closely, but I don't suppose that the dogs' presence affects the larger wild creatures, who are probably less shy of them than of us. Certainly tracks of moose and wolf and coyote come as near the cabin as ever. For the past month, wolves have been fairly common. Though we never hear them now, we often see their trails. As soon as the snow gets really deep, they will be off again to other climes — farther south or to open plateaus of the north, where winds blow snow hard almost as soon as it falls.

Sometimes J. goes on a short trip and takes Wahoo with him. Wahoo, though he loves us both, if he must choose prefers J.'s society, just as Rex does mine. Rex is left to "stay and take care of Teddy"; and if ever a human figure approaches, he knows it at least a quarter of an hour before I do. If it happens to be a stranger, he rumbles fiercely; if J., he whines and wags his tail. This peculiar gift of being able to perceive the approach of a distant figure is common to both Rex and Wahoo. Sometimes the two dogs are left at home with me. How, when they're shut up tight in the cabin and J. is still a mile off, do they know that he is on the way home? They can't smell or hear him. Yet they never fail to make it clear, fifteen or twenty minutes ahead of time, that he is coming.

When Rex and Wahoo have been separated even for an hour, they growl and bristle when they meet as though each were an utter stranger. Wahoo leads in this distinctive behavior, Rex is amused, really, and highly entertained, but if Wahoo does it, he too will give growl for growl, bristle for bristle. After the first greeting, which Wahoo decrees must for form's sake verge on the ferocious, they are warmly affectionate and pleased to be together again.

And if one be chastised or even reproached ever so gently, the other is as upset as if he were the culprit. When Wahoo has chewed his rope or disobeyed and run off for a bit, Rex, with closed eyes, retires to a corner or otherwise effaces himself as completely as possible. When Rex has been naughty, Wahoo's tail beats a humble, anxious, and constant tattoo, and he becomes at least two sizes smaller.

November 20

Over three feet of snow are on the ground, and snowshoeing is fairly good. We have been feeling sad because last week J. found in one of his traps east of Tetana what we are sure was our little coyote. Although she had probably been dead some time, her body was still in good condition and the same foot which had been caught in the trap before was well healed up. It seems strange that after having been caught once she did not avoid the trap, for she had seemed to us to be very intelligent. Perhaps she got caught when she was excited and running fast, and it was just an accident.

Rex and Wahoo are surely pure-bred northerners, for they have perked up amazingly since winter has come. They adore the snow and imbibe great scoops of it in preference to drinking water. They are contributing largely to the winter wood supply, for they are now learning to haul big logs on a new sled which J. has made. With Rex in the lead they begin to make a promising team. But in harness, Wahoo had at first to be handled with as great care and patience as Rex. At the slightest scolding or sign of annoyance he became abject and useless. Perhaps he was mishandled when pulling a sled before we got him. At any rate, he is now getting over that and willingly uses his great strength to pull heavy loads.

The Indians claim that their dogs never have fleas or lice and our dogs, though they've been in close contact with the Indian dogs on more than one occasion, have never caught anything from them. This is interesting in view of the fact that other animals in this country seem to possess the usual number of parasites. We find lice on many of the bird specimens, and fleas are often common on the small mammals, especially squirrels and weasels.

The dogs not only make possible longer trips around the country, but also, the additional warmth from their bodies as they lie one on either side of our bed enables me to sleep out comfortably in winter for the first time. This year we are so much better equipped, so much more at home and aware of all conditions. We have a dry roof over the cabin, a good stack of wood to start the winter. Never have we loved our life so deeply. We are, I believe, complete idiots to have been persuaded to leave it at all for any cause whatever.

Every day when we're not actually on trips, I take the dogs to explore old and new haunts. J. has decreed that we take short walks separately. This is real wisdom, for, when we go in different directions and have been away from each other for a time, each has something new to tell, and we're happy to be together again. Seemingly unimportant little customs and habits, which one acquires from experience and a little straight thinking, are vital in relationships of people thrown together in a lonely wilderness. Most good northerners agree that when two men are partners they avoid unpleasantness, sometimes serious consequences, if they live separately and meet only on occasion. On one famous sled trail it was once customary to station two men at intervals to keep shelter and food on hand for dog teams that came through. But such violent and frequent altercations, even murders, occurred that two men are no longer allowed together. The authorities now advise a man and wife instead.

Not that couples of mixed sex get on to perfection either. J. and I have plenty of lapses, some hours now and again when we're scarcely on speaking terms! But thanks to J.'s years of experience in the North (not to mention the fact that he has a wise wife), we've probably avoided many a serious pitfall. Above all, there are no inquisitive neighbors to make unnecessary comments. This lack of a restraining third party can, of course, work the other way too. If we stayed steadily in the wilds without a break, we might turn, as certain highly respectable citizens of the North have done, into uncontrolled murderous creatures with no one to say us nay.

Since fish are under ice again, acquiring sufficient food for the dogs is a serious problem. Rex and Wahoo, between them, need four or five pounds of meat per day. They can subsist on large quantities of cooked flour and corn meal mixed with lard, but our supply of these commodities is not inexhaustible. So J. has been hunting moose again.

A large part of life seems to be composed of a quest for moose in winter, a quest for fish in summer. A moose is large enough to supply us with meat for a month or two (it took many dozens of seven-pound trout to keep us this fall), but somehow a moose will seldom allow itself to be killed within miles of Tetana. If J. or one of the Indians succeeds, after a twenty-mile chase, in making a kill five or six miles away, we count ourselves fortunate.

Just recently, by a happy providence, Sapolio shot a moose some five miles east of Trail Lake. He had taken all he could carry and said that we might have the remainder. So we've been over there twice, armed with all available sacks, canvas, and packs, in order to bring meat home before wolves or coyotes demolished it. A cold snap has frozen the early ground snows more solid than usual. As this condition won't last and everything may, at any hour, be buried deep in soft snow again, we're making the most of it.

Yesterday when we started out it was 32 below. Rex and

Wahoo were allowed to run free; J. and I carried their empty packs in our knapsacks. J.'s snowshoe trail to and from the moose kill was frozen hard and the dogs raced along it like demented creatures. J. and I, on our large snowshoes that slid all over the slippery trail, raced too. The sparkle of the cold was in our blood and we were full of vigor from the fresh meat J. had brought home the night before.

The dogs especially enjoy their freedom as they begin a hike, for freedom, when they travel in this country, is a rarity. Either they're obliged to carry heavy packs, or we're stalking game and they must stay quietly at heel for miles. And woe to either of them if he slips up under J.'s rigid eye! This discipline is an excellent thing for the dog, and a very necessary safeguard. Imagine the consequences if the dog, carrying all one's food and bedding, breaks away on the chase and becomes injured or lost. Both dogs have now learned to "heel" very creditably, though Wahoo, if a new smell is just too enticing, occasionally goes off on a short dash before he is brought up, trembling, at the tone in his master's voice. Rex is almost perfect in his obedience to the command "heel," but when nervous or excited he whines and moans, and nothing on earth will suppress him. Whenever this happens J. swears that next time Rex shall be left tied at home. But even this awful threat, which Rex understands perfectly, can't make him control his nerves.

Through thick forest the snow was soft to the feet, but out across swamps the crust and hard ice cut our snowshoe webbing and the dogs' feet. In the open, the sun was so strong that we sweated and unbuttoned our jackets. When we passed through a grove of black spruce along a swampy area, temperatures were so low that we were numb and had to rub cheeks and noses continually to ward off frostbite. Once, in a small opening in a belt of spruce, we looked up into the azure of the sky and saw, just overhead, a little half circle of colors, a kind of sundog formed by sun shining through hoarfrost in the air, which is often seen in the Far North. This was a miniature rainbow, so vivid that it held all colors of the spectrum. We snapped a picture of it on color film.

Half a mile from the moose kill we came on tracks of three big wolves. These headed in the same direction as J.'s trail and crossed and recrossed it everywhere. Judging by the freshness of the prints and the excitement of the dogs, we thought they must have been made that morning. Perhaps even now wolves were at the dead moose. We called the dogs to heel. But though we moved with caution, it was impossible to make our approach completely noiseless because of the creak of snowshoes. The wind, however, was in our favor and there was just a chance that we might surprise a wolf. J. cocked his rifle and I stared fiercely at the trembling dogs crowding against my legs. We left the dazzling world and warming sunshine behind as we clambered over high snow hummocks formed above fallen trees and entered a belt of dense balsam. It was dark and eerie and bitterly cold. J.'s pace diminished to a crawl. I hoped and feared to see a great shaggy head, lifting bloody jaws from the moose carcass. But no, there lay the moose and there was neither sight nor sound of a wolf, though meat and bones lay pulled about in many directions. Fresh tracks were everywhere, and the dogs growled and whined and shook in the cold.

Perhaps wolves were watching as we bent above the moose, but it was too cold and time too pressing to worry about them. Hours of work were ahead for J. before he could get enough of the meat, frozen hard as stone, chopped off and made into packs for the dogs and ourselves. My hands were not strong enough to be of much help, but I *could* make a fire to keep J.'s hands from freezing as he worked. The temperature in those thick trees must have been 40 or more below.

By this time, I've had considerable practice in making fires in winter woods without paper or kindling or dry leaves and twigs. In fact I have been rather proud of my skill along this line! But I had never had to make one in a forest of solid balsam, so much denser and damper than any other. I located a dead tree and chopped pieces out of the trunk, and with these I thought to start a fire. I wasted nearly a dozen matches, an unprecedented extravagance, and J., hacking furiously at the bones and icy meat with aching fingers, wanted to know what in heck was the matter? How he could continue working at all

I couldn't imagine, for my hands, even in heavy double mitts, were so stiff and painful that I could scarcely handle firewood, let alone lumps of meat the temperature and consistency of cakes of ice. There didn't seem to be a bit of burnable wood in the whole forest. In all our travels through this country we have never yet seen signs of an Indian camp in balsam forest.

By this time, despite frantic efforts over fire building, I was so numb that I deserted J. and made a dash for the open and sunshine a quarter of a mile away. Rex, chewing a meaty bone, left it promptly and, faithful to his duty as always, escorted me. But Wahoo, shivering and biting aching paws every few seconds, never looked up from his ecstatic gorging of big moose ribs. I found a long sunny open meadow, really an extensive swamp buried under snow. Here was a different climate; I was soon warmed enough to notice things again. A mile across to the east, rocky cliffs rising to a dry flat-topped, pine-covered ridge marked the rise of land toward the Ominecas.

Around a small hummock two great dark birds rose heavily from something on which they were feeding. One lit in a tree not far away and I could see perfectly the golden brown of the hind neck, the dark body and feathered tarsus above the yellow feet; all of which, coupled with the huge size, proclaimed it a golden eagle. The wing spread of these eagles is often eighty-four inches. The birds had been eating the moose head which had been dragged by wolves to a patch of soft drifted snow. Around the head was a maze of animal tracks: wolf and coyote, fox and mice and weasel, all mingled with the footprints and wing marks of the eagles.[1]

The eagles were angry at the disturbance of their banquet. One circled, screaming, overhead in the dazzling golden air. The other, from his perch on the tree, still guarded their property. Through the glasses I could just see the gleam of his wonderful, untamable, fierce dark eye. It was the finest and nearest

[1] A somewhat similar instance of golden eagles feeding on a moose carcass in April 1941 is mentioned in our Museum paper, "Some Accounts of the Flora and Fauna of the Driftwood Valley Region of North Central British Columbia." Golden eagles appeared to frequent the Driftwood Valley especially in spring and autumn when snow was not too deep for game.

view I've had yet of the golden eagle, but of course this was the first time for months, since we knew that we must carry home as large quantities of meat as possible, that we had gone off without the movie camera.

We often see golden, as well as bald, eagles over Tetana and along the Driftwood River. Sometimes a golden eagle has swooped low over a flock of ducks but, other than scattering slightly, the ducks did not appear to be alarmed. Evidently wild duck is not a usual item of the eagle's diet. Old Charlie and Sapolio and Michelle have told us that in summer golden eagles keep primarily to the mountains where they prey largely on hoary marmots that live in the alpine meadows. The eagles also eat young mountain goats when they can get them. Old Charlie claims to have witnessed on several occasions their catching young kids and has described this procedure to us in detail. The eagle waits until a kid gets near the edge of a precipice. At the right moment, the bird swoops and strikes, and the goat falls hundreds or thousands of feet onto rocks below. Then the eagle flies down and begins to feed on the still warm, tender, broken little body. There is nothing more delectable than fresh young kid. We know, for we have tried it too.

In winter, when snow is deep on the mountains, the eagles apparently go to the valleys or far to the south, where they feed on rabbits or act as scavengers at moose or deer kills.

Finally we abandoned all hope of making a fire. J. stopped work on the moose and tried for a bit, but his fingers were too numbed to be effective. For hours I tramped back and forth between the bright world of sun and the dark icy world of forest. Every so often I took the knife or axe from J. and continued the meat hacking, while he warmed his hands inside his shirt. The big bones, hard as rocks, had to be chopped with the blunt edge of the axe head. But my fingers, in ten minutes, were useless from cold again. I didn't see how J. stood it; the pain in his hands must have been very bad. He'd started with gloves, but as they became bloody and slightly moist they froze stiff as boards, so that much of the time he worked without them.

When we finally got all the meat we could carry, we made it up into four packs to suit our respective sizes and strengths, loaded up, and started off. In the sunshine again J. began to thaw out and was able to smoke. The dogs plodded happily along under their heavy, well-balanced packs. They knew perfectly that they were carrying food for us and for them, and they didn't mind how heavily they were burdened. From time to time they turned their heads to lick the packs. Heat from their bodies was melting the frozen meat, and delicious blood made appetizing smells as it oozed through the canvas.

When we reached home, J.'s back and clothes were soaked in moose blood, the odor of which still reminds me of disinfectants in a hospital ward, and my clothes were badly stained in spots. J. was wringing wet with sweat. We weighed all four packs. J. had carried sixty-four pounds (plus axe and rifle), Wahoo forty-five, Rex twenty-six, and I thirty-two. We now have on hand a hundred and sixty-seven pounds of frozen meat.

December 6

Some time ago I made up my mind that I must try camping alone in winter. Not because I really wanted to, but because I wished to see whether I have actually learned enough at last to manage by myself. If I could once prove that I was able to travel and exist alone, even in winter, I felt that this would help lay the spectre that still haunts me as to what will happen if anything goes wrong with J.

J. encouraged this plan, partly because he knew how I felt about it, partly because it would be good practice and, a little I think, because, having himself been completely self-reliant for so long, he didn't quite realize how hard it would be. I was rather irritated, as a matter of fact, because he showed so little anxiety! I suppose I should have been flattered that he considered me so capable.

I spent several days hiking to favorite haunts, examining them with an eye to the three essentials for a winter's camp: shelter, drinking water, and dry, dead trees that were small and accessible enough to cut and carry alone. I narrowed the choice down to Wolf Hill or the southwest end of Tetana, a mile away from our cabin and near the river. The balance swung in favor of the latter; the forest near the lake afforded more shelter and it *was* a little nearer than Wolf Hill. Actually I gave myself an unfair advantage in having a place picked beforehand — the real test would have been to find a camp in strange country at the end of a hard day's trip. But for my first venture I thought I wouldn't have things too difficult. Even the Indians always choose, whenever possible, to stop at old well-tried camping spots.

So two days ago, when the temperature at 10 above was warmer than it had been (the snow is over four feet deep), we packed up the dogs. I left the cabin in early afternoon so that I should have the two hours of daylight requisite to make camp, and J. waved me a very cheerful good-bye. He was not to know where I was going.

When I reached the thick belt of spruce that stretches between the southwest end of Tetana and the river, I set to work in the usual routine — unpacked the dogs, then hunted firewood. I went after small dead spruces, but, little as they were, it took so long to chop one down, carry it to the camp site, and cut it up, that I was afraid dark would come before I put up the small canvas tent fly. So I stopped to do that, having first dug with my snowshoes a space in the snow under a big spruce. The snow was about six feet deep compared to the four out in the open, probably because it had not melted. By the time the fly was up I was already tired and cold, though I had come only one mile from home! Everything had taken about twice as long as I had figured. I wouldn't have time now to cut more spruce trees before dark, but plenty of wood I must have. Small dead willow trees near by would have to do. After I started the fire I got spruce boughs for the bed — I had to skimp on these too — and I fetched water from a hole cut in lake ice (no convenient open springs here) and set it to boil for tea.

The dogs, watching forlornly, evidently thought all this a most unnecessary and improper performance without J. But they cheered up when I fed them and settled down resignedly on the edge of my bed in the firelight. The temperature was dropping and the willow logs didn't throw out a quarter of the heat that J.'s big fires always do.

My supper was not the well-ordered peaceful affair I had pictured. As the small willow logs burned fast, I was obliged constantly to get into snowshoes and go for more. I decided finally that the best thing to do was to leave a few for morning, let the fire die down, and crawl into bed with a dog either side in the hope that I should sleep till daylight. Stars glinted so brilliantly through the great spruces that I knew we were in for a bitter night. A little silver slip of a new moon was going down in the west; through openings in trees, I looked across to the pure outlines of the Driftwoods, their white peaks etched sharply under the setting moon. There was not a sound in the whole world except the hiss and crackle of a red log as it died in snow, or an occasional boom of ice on the lake. Rex and Wahoo had become by now tight unconscious balls of fur on my sleeping bag; I had to push and haul them around like sacks of potatoes before I could get in bed. For the first few hours, when heat from the dying fire still blocked out the cold in front of the fly, I was fairly warm. But it grew colder and colder. The one thing I could think of and long for was the feel of J.'s warm body that I had always been able to snuggle against on all our camping trips. Now I missed not only his heat, but also the extra bedding which he is able to carry. Rex and Wahoo missed the extra warmth too. They shivered all night; sometimes Wahoo tried to crawl right on top of me! I've spent unendingly long, uncomfortable nights in this country, but none much longer than that one. I was never warm a second, but at least, I told myself, I was apparently not cold enough actually to perish. I wondered if the thermometer was really around 30 below as it felt, or if I was too cold to gauge it.

Long before light in the morning I got up to start the fire. I couldn't stand the icy bed another second. After I'd thawed out, had breakfast, and sun began to slant across the south end of Tetana, I felt better. At least I *had* kept alive out of doors through a bitter winter's night, entirely owing to my own exertions. While I was breaking camp Rex and Wahoo played endless games on the flat surface of a tiny swamp pond near by, where snow was harder and less deep and they could get about without being buried. I lingered over the packing-up process — I was ashamed to appear at the cabin too early. But I needn't have worried, because getting packs on the dogs took ages. In the first place the fire was too small to keep me properly warmed (all the dead willows were gone) and my fingers were so cold I couldn't handle things. I'd thought I could do it all perfectly, because I had helped J. so often; but it's mighty different with him attending to the hardest parts.

There was a glorious morning when we emerged out onto the brightness of the lake. Frost crystals dazzled my eyes. When we rounded a bend there was the cabin way beyond, smoke pouring from the chimney. And then J. was greeting me at the door and I was in the warm, safe, sun-filled room again; he was handing me hot coffee and unpacking the dogs. I was astonished and chagrined to hear that our thermometer had registered only 12 below during the night.

J. doesn't know yet the location of my camping place. But I heard him rather boasting to Michelle about how "my wife she leave me and camp all alone [something Michelle's wife won't do anyway], and I never know where she go." But until he reads this, or unless Rex and Wahoo tell him, he'll never know just what kind of a night I really spent.

We've been watching a duck hawk (a rare visitor in these parts for we've seen only one other) feeding on a large freshly killed snowshoe rabbit out on the middle of the lake. The rabbit had reached the center of the ice when the falcon, like a flash of lightning, swooped down on it. From fifty yards away we watched it tearing at the rabbit's flesh, and then as we slowly snowshoed to within thirty feet of it, it looked around at us with bright angry eyes, and raised its long sharp wings; it tried repeatedly and unsuccessfully to lift its prey and take off with it. But the rabbit was too heavy and the hawk finally left. It returned on and off for three more days, however, to feed until the carcass was demolished.

CHAPTER XIII

Snowbound at Bunshaw

Tetana   *December 28*

With heavy hearts, we have been packing for the past week. Tomorrow we close the cabin, say good-bye to Tetana, and go up to Bunshaw to wait for Russ and the plane due the thirty-first. The nearer the day of departure, the colder the feet we get. If we'd had any way of sending word to Russ during the past two months, we would, I am positive, have put it all off for another year. We try to cheer ourselves with thoughts of food for we are a bit sick of our rather primitive diet, and memories of good food grow more and more potent as the possibilities of actually having it come closer.

J. keeps saying: "The first thing *I* have is a *green* salad. Green beans and radishes and spring onions, and endive and tomatoes and celery and watercress and lettuce — "

"Be quiet, we're not there yet. *I'll* have a salad too, and fresh spinach, and a sundae with hot fudge and marshmallow and nuts, and sausages bursting from their jackets. . . ."

But if we must go, we'd like to get it over with. Some unlucky event at the very last could so easily mar our record of perfect health. We vowed that we could come safely and happily through a year of complete isolation in a northern wilderness, and we've done better than our vow, for we've made it nearly a year and a half. Possibly the fates have been kind, but we believe that our well-being has been thanks largely to our own efforts.

Today J. remarked, "Surviving in this country is about 90 per cent good management and forethought, and 10 per cent luck."

I think that 75 to 80 per cent good management plus experience is more accurate, because here there are so many things over which man has no control. But J. believes that by careful thought and figuring, one can anticipate most or all of them, be prepared for their occurrence and be armed against them. Nature, he says, is sometimes cruel, but never deliberately or purposely so. On the whole she serves man marvelously well.

Man talks much about serving his fellow men, very little about serving the earth which has served him faithfully throughout the centuries of his being, and without whose co-operation he could not even exist. It is very humbling to learn how much better a natural area gets on without the inevitable interference or exploitation of man — to realize that while birds, for example, can exist perfectly without man, man, because birds keep down the insects which might otherwise dominate this earth, very possibly could not exist without birds. And it is rather appalling when one has watched the manifestations of a primeval land and its wild inhabitants to realize the depths of the arrogance and ignorance displayed by most human beings toward the character, mind, and behavior of the animals.

Prince George   *January 9, 1939*

At Bunshaw I tried to write in my diary a dozen times; in fact I did write a few sentences every so often, but it's so confused and badly written, owing to our tough situation there, that I'm going to do it all over in greater detail.

Early on December 29th, Michelle and one of the boys helped us move our gear to Bunshaw. J. wanted to be a few days ahead of schedule in order to tramp a solid runway at least a mile long on the snow of the lake, so the plane skis could land and take off without accident.

When J. was packing up the dogs just before we started, Michelle, after watching him for a bit, burst out: "By gosh, Jack, too bad you go. This country good for you. You just like Indian! You know how to do, see? You pack dog, make camp, travel just like Indian. Other white people he not know how to do in this country, see?"

The ten-mile winter trail that follows upriver to Bunshaw

was, by this time, so familiar that it seemed short. J. and Wahoo and Rex and I, each loaded with good-sized packs, made it in a few hours, well ahead of Michelle and the toboggan. We set up a good camp in shallow snow under a big spruce on the south shore of the lake.

In addition to making a runway, we laid out a huge cross of evergreen boughs, about twenty by fifteen feet, so that Russ, at four or five thousand feet up, could see it and be sure to locate the right lake. Locating one small lake in a country dotted for thousands of miles with unnamed lakes of every shape and size is not so simple as it sounds.

We spent two whole days tramping up and down along the center of Bunshaw. The snow was deep and very soft; since each ski track on the lake was a mile long, we figured that between us we must have snowshoed about twenty miles on the first day. The deadly monotony of it was far more wearing than tramping twenty miles through a tough country — twenty miles that at least got one somewhere.

The first day we began to look anxiously at the weather, for there were long cirrus clouds in the bright sky. If the weather turned bad and the plane didn't get through on schedule, or at least soon after, we were going to be out of food. In our anxiety not to leave any to be wasted, or stolen from the cabin, we had calculated perhaps a little too closely. Except for a few heavy canned things which had been cached, we had almost finished our supply at Tetana and had with us only enough to last for a few days at Bunshaw. Michelle had gone on to the Bear Lake settlement with the understanding that he was to return at once with a little food from Carl's. If the plane came meanwhile and we had gone, he was to have the food himself in payment.

It is always possible during the first half of winter that, while some lakes in the country may have frozen over, others, especially large ones like Takla and Stuart where Russ starts from, will still be open. Even though Russ might safely land on Bunshaw, he might not have been able to take off from Stuart.

On the evening of December 29th the sky became solidly overcast, a breeze came from the southeast, the thermometer

hung on the spruce tree by our tent went up to 14 above, and
we resigned ourselves to a storm. The next morning thick snow
was sweeping over the land and it lasted on and off for four
days. Another four feet was added to the three-foot level already
on the ground. Due to the huge spruce our tent was somewhat
protected, but it was hard work to keep the fire going through
the heavy snow that filtered constantly down on it. Our bed
inside the tent was unusually warm, thanks to a grizzly skin
that was going out to the Museum.

This skin, recently taken by the Indians, is wonderful. The
fur, a rich golden-brown, is half a foot thick and the skin meas-
ures over nine feet from nose to tail. The bear, a male, must
have weighed around eleven hundred pounds. The adult male
grizzly of this country is usually a dark-colored animal with a
well-marked cross of buffy grizzled hairs over the shoulders and
part way down the back. Its head is the antithesis of the female,
having a long narrow skull as compared with the bulging fron-
tals of the latter.

But because of the constantly sizzling, dying fire it was hard,
when we were not wading about, to keep warm during the
daytime. Most of the dry dead trees around that part of Bunshaw had been already exhausted by Charlie's family in years
past. We had to travel a mile or more up the lake to find dry
wood. And each morning, storm or no, we plowed up and
down through deep wet snow to keep our runway open.

When we were not getting wood or tramping the trail on the
lake, the hours were deadly monotonous. At first we hadn't
dared to go far from Bunshaw on the chance that Russ might
appear ahead of time. Now, when he couldn't possibly come,
the storm was so bad that we couldn't go anyhow. There was
nothing to do but hug the smoking fire, and, in the intervals, go
for firewood; there was practically no food to cook, no books
to read. We played with cards spread out on the bed, but our
fingers would soon grow too numb to hold them.

To me nights were the worst; it grew dark long before four
and there was no earthly thing to do after our meager and un-
satisfying snacks of supper but go to bed and keep warm in

order to save strength and firewood. By the light of a stumpy candle, I tried reading a tiny edition of poetry; it was so cold that I couldn't read for long. But at least it gave me fine thoughts to sleep with. Since daylight didn't come until after nine in the morning, we were hunched up in our narrow little bags for fifteen hours out of every twenty-four. The only break during those fifteen hours was when one of us got up to shake snow off the tent so it wouldn't cave in on us. I could no more sleep more than eight or nine of those hours than I could fly. If J. had been awake too during the remaining six or seven hours, it would perhaps not have been so bad. But J., like a sensible animal, long ago learned how to accept the inevitable and while away time by sleep when nothing else can be done. Wahoo, the old philosopher, slept hour for hour along with J. Sometimes, when more than ordinarily vigorous snores woke me, I found Wahoo's head on top of J.'s and what issued forth was a sort of snoring duet. Rex, because he is always alert, and because his moods chime in with mine, slept lightly and for shorter periods. Waking on a perfectly empty stomach in the morning hours, long, long before it was light, was the worst of all.

January 2nd came and went, and still it snowed and snowed. We composed a poem about spending New Year's beneath a tree, to send to the family if and when we ever reached a post or telegraph office. Needless to say Michelle had *not* returned with any food (he couldn't have traveled in the deep soft snow through such a storm) and my stomach was so hollow that I could think of nothing else. Nothing in the world seemed important any more except food. We had left eight pilot biscuits, enough split-pea powder for four servings of soup, a very little tea and cocoa, but we ate such small quantities at a time that it seemed to me my stomach felt worse after eating than it did before. J., I knew, tried to skimp on his share so that I should have more, and I tried to skimp on mine because he had a bigger body to nourish, and must retain his strength in order to get firewood.

The dogs had nothing; and this seemed the hardest thing of

ail. At night we could give them only crumbs and licks of soup or cocoa. We had never before failed them. We could hardly bear to meet the eyes which looked into ours anxiously and wistfully and always so lovingly. The first day at Bunshaw J. killed six grouse out of a flock of ten for dog food, but the little birds had been gobbled up raw, even to the feet and bills, in two days. And we saw the live grouse no more.

And then, worst of all, Rex and Wahoo, the dear, clean, pleasant-smelling companions of our days and nights acquired in their hunger a horrible habit. No matter how carefully we buried our refuse, though there was now hardly any, they found and ate it. I realized then why deserted Indian camps appear to be so clean. The starving Indian dogs never leave any scrap of refuse to decompose on the earth. The discovery of all this on top of the nasty feeling now always present in my tummy very nearly made me sick.

So, this was what it meant to be hungry. And we weren't starving — yet. This was nothing to what J. had experienced in the Arctic when he and an Eskimo were snow bound in an igloo during a terrible storm. They ate their sealskin boots and some of their dogs, and very nearly died before they finally reached home. I understood why men who are really hungry steal and kill, why women sell themselves. *We* had no reason for despair. We expected the plane would come when it cleared; we had other loopholes. But if I were hungrier than this and had no hope, no one to keep up for, I should have no more scruples than the lowest of the low.

Life in a wilderness seems always to be one of endless physical — and mental, for without the mental one would never have the guts to endure the physical — struggle and endurance. It's a great mistake to separate the virtues of moral and physical courage, to say that moral courage is greater than physical. (I believe only sheltered people who have never known the meaning of physical hardship and agony, unallayed by medical aid, think this.) To stand up under great physical pain or stress requires a high kind of moral fortitude and bravery, and must be a very fair indication of moral strength.

Although the heaviest snowfall had stopped by January 3rd, the weather showed no signs of clearing. We decided to wait one more day and then, if it was still bad, someone would hike the eighteen miles to the north end of Bear Lake and get food from Carl. The short trips we had made hunting for game had been unsuccessful. Now there was not a sign of an animal or bird anywhere and we knew that these months are the least productive of the year when it comes to hunting. We had no real hope that Michelle would show up until traveling grew far easier; or, as so often happened, he might have delayed to visit some trap line, and never have reached the settlement. It would take two to three days to get to Carl's and back again in such heavy snow. But we couldn't afford to go hungry much longer and something would have to be done before we were too weak to do it. I had noticed that J. no longer carried any big logs. We talked it over and agreed that if it became necessary, J. and Wahoo would hike to Carl's while Rex and I remained at camp. Staying alone under such conditions was rather a nasty thought (suppose J. got caught in another storm, for instance?), but if J. went now there would still be a bit of food for me. He could travel at twice the speed I could — I didn't in fact feel sure that I could travel those eighteen miles at all — and we didn't want to risk losing the plane, if and when it came. Another snow might cover all trace of the cross and runways and our camp, and if we were both en route to Bear Lake, Russ might not be able to trace us or get word of us.

That evening, as we sat gloomy and shivering and hungry over our smoking fire, there was a sudden breath of wind. Which way? Could it be north or west? We stepped into snowshoes and stumbled up onto the snowbank above the fire, looking and listening. It *was* from the west. Even as we watched, it grew stronger. In an hour there were rifts in the clouds, the first opening in the heavy sky for five days, and a few stars began to prick through.

J. said, "Jumping Joseph, it's going to clear, sure as eggs," and we went to bed with hope in our hearts. Three times in the night, just to be sure, we got up and looked out; each time more stars were shining and a moon appeared through rolling clouds; the air was cold and dry and fresh, instead of damp and stifling as it had been for days.

We woke to a bright morning and went out to open the runways and shake snow off the big spruce cross. We didn't really hope that any one would come that day. But suddenly, around noon, we heard something. A rumble in the distance — a real noise after days of suffocating stillness, a noise that grew louder and louder.

"Gosh, it's a plane!"

Perhaps it was not our plane at all, but it was heading straight for Bunshaw. Yes, it was coming lower. It must be Russ looking for us. It began to circle slowly above the lake. Then it headed into the north, turned, came low and hit the upper end of our runway to a nicety, roared down to the spruce cross, and stopped.

"He'll stick in slush, sure," J. moaned.

This was exactly what happened. The ice, which had been firm and hard when we first came to Bunshaw, had sunk under the tons and tons of new snow; the added weight of the plane had caused an overflow of water which, mixed with snow, made a thick slush. When the plane tried to move again the skis stuck as fast as if pinioned in sticky clay. Russ climbed out, and then his mechanic and another pilot. We would all have to wait until the temperatures of night, which promised to be cold, had frozen the slush again.

"I brought lots of food," said the angelic Russ. "Thought you might be hard-up — ?"

And out came potatoes and bread and eggs and all sorts of things. They would be hard to cook over our fire and would freeze solid in no time, but we could eat them raw if necessary. And there were canned things too. We'd have a big feed, the men said, looking toward me complacently. I, knowing the difficulties of preparing food under present conditions, could only grin feebly. The temperature was by now far below zero.

"I'll just let them try cooking a few things themselves," I thought, "instead of telling them it can't be done! I'll take along the canned things — "

We all gathered around our campfire, now about six feet long and sunk into a pit five feet below the last snow level. The airmen set up a radio transmitter close to the fire with an antenna attached to a high tree, as only within the immediate circle of the fire could they keep their hands warm enough to operate. They must send out word immediately that they had reached Bunshaw, that we had been found safely, that their skis were stuck in ice and they couldn't get back to the Fort that night, but hoped to be in next day. Russ and the other pilot took turns working the set with hands so numb they could hardly move them: —

"CFABK calling Fort St. James, CFABK calling Fort St. James — CFABK calling Fort St. James — — "

At last, after an hour, they contacted headquarters. Russ even added a message to tell Madge, his wife, to have a roast in the oven and put a big feed on for the next night.

All this time J. and I were a highly entertained audience of two. We had been cut off for seventeen months; for weeks at a time no one had known of our whereabouts or, for that matter, whether we even still existed. And these men, who expected to be twenty-four hours behind schedule in arriving at a destination, were required to spend hours of painful effort sending messages about it to the outside world.

For supper they wanted French-fried potatoes and fried onions, and so on; so I gave one potatoes, another onions, and busied myself opening cans into the frying pan. It was four o'clock and quite dark; the thermometer on the tree showed 26 below; and the usual clouds of sparks and smoke poured up into our faces as we bent down over the huge fire. Tears streamed down the men's cheeks; they cussed and muttered and milled about trying to escape smoke and flames. A pair of mittens got burned, their feet got wet, their hands froze or scorched, and I, with inward glee, observed that not even the peeling of the first potato or the first onion had been accomplished. With

some difficulty one boiled a pot of water for tea without upsetting all of it.

In the meantime the big pan of canned beans was ready and
we began to eat without more ado. The men started to pass
them around on tin plates, but, after finding that the beans
froze fast to the plates before they could get them to their
mouths, gave up and took turns dipping out of the frypan the
way J. and I were doing. We demolished the yeast bread before
it had frozen and crumbled away, and a few other items like
jam, which didn't have to be cooked, provided by the thought-
ful Russ. To J. and me, it was manna from heaven! I followed
my customary procedure of melting and heating a pot of snow
in order to wash up dirty cups and spoons; as usual the water
on them froze into brown ice before they could be dried.

One of our visitors, a silent spectator of this, burst out:
"By —— , just wait'll I get home and tell my wife a thing or
two next time she fusses over washing dishes in a nice warm
kitchen!"

It had become one of those brilliant, magical, northern
nights, with stars and quicksilver moonlight. Mountains, shining and quiet in the blue-white light, towered around us. The
fir trees and the surface of Bunshaw were draped in glittering
powdered snow, soft as feathers. The little plane, an alien
factor on the wild frozen lake, like us was swallowed up in the
silence and majesty of the winter night. And it was the night
of my birthday and wedding anniversary. Once again I was
spending it, with J., in a camp in the deep snow of the northern
wilderness. A last memory of perfect beauty and utter unspoiled
serenity was to be ours to carry with us from one world into
another.

The three airmen slept close to the fire just outside our tent.
They had sleeping bags which, though good ones, were not very
adequate for this kind of climate. We gave them our grizzly
rug to put under them and they rolled up in a huge tarpaulin
from the plane, but only one of them would admit that he slept
at all.

As soon as it was light the young mechanic was up and off to the plane, where he worked for long hours thawing out the engines with a blowlamp. The temperature was 35 below. The ski runways had, to be sure, frozen hard, but the skis of the plane were frozen in solidly also. It took four men all morning to chop them free.

Our gear had been moved out onto the ice on Michelle's sled. (Michelle had arrived soon after the plane did!) Wahoo, inspired by his first meal in five days, to the admiration of all beholders had alone pulled an estimated eight-hundred-pound load a quarter of a mile on the trail from camp to the plane. As the men, tired and chilled, were resting against the waiting plane, J. offered them the brandy flask which had been stored in a knapsack. Russ, rubbing his lips so they wouldn't stick to the metal, took a swig and said, "H'm'm, tastes like water!" Then the brandy suddenly warmed up inside and exploded. His heels and eyebrows rose and he registered the funniest expression I ever saw. Everyone had to try it after that.

Early in the afternoon we loaded up and I climbed in, Rex leaping at my heels. Wahoo, who had had one horrible experience of a plane and had no notion of having another, bolted every time he got near the door; it took three men to lift his huge and struggling form in beside me. Then they banged the door on us and the engines roared and roared as they tried to move the skis under the heavy load. J. and the mechanic were hanging onto either wing to keep them down while the plane turned. I thought Wahoo would tear either me or the plane to pieces, or at least smash a window. Between him and the roaring, jerking engines, there wasn't much left of me by the time we did get up half an hour later.

We rose straight toward high cliffs, out above Bunshaw again, then away toward mountains on the other side. The angle and speed at which cliffs hurtled by reminded me of a nightmare of the worst order.

In a few minutes we were over Tetana gazing down on our cabin. It looked like a doll's house, an incongruous touch in a completely uninhabited land. Will it still be there, I wondered, when we come again? Or will it be swallowed by a wilderness where the works of man seem always so unimportant and impermanent? Now it was gone and we were flying on and on through a universe in which we seemed to be the only living things. The country below spread out like a relief map. These mountains and lakes were not the wild and imposing and beautiful ones we knew so well; they were just little and unreal, without sound or scent or feeling, lights or shades, or movements.

As we headed farther south we ran into storm clouds and the plane seemed to be tossed as insignificantly as a feather in whirling flurries of snow. Sometimes we struck an air pocket, so that we lost five hundred feet altitude in a second, and went down with a horrid drop like an elevator loose from its cables. Wahoo no longer thrashed about, but crouched in J.'s arms. Now he seemed less terrified than Rex, who was having the first flying experience of his young life. Rex's eyes were as green as new grass and saliva dripped from his jaws, but at least he was not sick. For once he was utterly unresponsive to my voice or hand. Shouting in his ear never stirred him out of his terrified trance.

When we got near the north end of sixty-mile-long Stuart Lake, we ran into dense fog. Fort St. James, for which we were headed, lay at the south end. And we'd have to land, I thought, because Russ had said we had just gas enough to reach the Fort.

I peered at the faces of the men. J.'s and the mechanic's, who sat beside me, expressed nothing, although they kept looking out. I couldn't see Russ or the other pilot up in front because of the pile of baggage between us and them. It seemed like hours, though I suppose it was only a few minutes, that we went on and on through the dense cottony white. And then suddenly, just below, there was a jagged hole in the solid floor of mist, and through the hole, as though we were looking through an old spyglass, appeared tiny buildings and a church spire.

"Fort St. James?" I shouted, unbelievingly, to J. and he nodded.

And down we went, right through the hole, like the fairy-tale Jack with the giant at his heels, climbing down through a hole in the sky, to his own house and garden.

We hit the ice in a nice landing, taxied to the shore, and stopped, just as dark was falling.

Out of the plane, on terra firma again, Rex went clean crazy. He howled and ran in circles till I was really scared and had to beat him with a leather leash to bring him to his senses. We walked along a snowy road to the house of Russ and Madge. The door flew open and, in a stream of light, Madge, whom I had seen once before a year ago when we were on the visit to Takla, rushed out bareheaded, flung her arms around me, and kissed me! It seemed so good after all that time to be hugged by a girl, a real live talking girl, to be gathered into a warm honest-to-goodness house, to be petted and made much of. Madge and Russ gave us a wonderful feast. They had planned a New Year's party for us if we had arrived per schedule instead of six days late.

That night we drove, with Joe Huffman, the efficient and delightfully urbane taxi driver of Fort St. James, eighty miles on to a hotel in Prince George, where we hoped to pick up our trunks of civilized clothing and get a train. Twice along the way Rex was sick all over me and Wahoo and the back seat. The feed he'd had at the Fort, plus excitement and the up-and-down icy road, was just too much for even his tough insides. When J. and I, two raggedly clothed individuals, more or less blackened, smelling evilly of fire smoke and Rex's un-digested fish, and two very large, lean dogs, stumbled into the lobby of the Prince George Hotel sometime after midnight, we must have given the proprietor a bit of a shock. But he wel-comed us and the dogs (I shall always love him for not object-ing to the dogs) with as much consideration as if we were royalty, and showed all four of us to a large front "room *with bath*." Imagine a hot bath at 1 A.M., when one's in a state of exhaustion, half frozen, and hasn't been in a bathtub for a year and a half!

For the first time in my life I went to bed with the steam

heat on and every window shut tight; and J., who is always complaining bitterly of the drafts I subject him to, crowed over me. Some hours later I woke to find Rex and Wahoo panting on the floor like steam engines, J. tossing and moaning, and our bed and pajamas wet with perspiration. I flew up and opened three windows wide and very nearly froze the plumbing before morning.

While we are waiting here a few days for the proper train connections, we have spent our time having the clothes, which have not been worn for seventeen months, taken way, way in. I had been thinking how elegant it would be to step into a real dress again, but when I donned my very first one I had a rude shock. It was one foot too long and hung on me like a potato sack. I weigh a hundred and seven, having lost eleven pounds; J. has lost about fifteen. But, though lean, we are both in perfect glowing health.

With considerable apprehension we introduced Rex and Wahoo to the civilized world of Prince George. So far they have been perfect gentlemen. J. strolls casually along the streets with them, not even bothering with leashes. And they, just as they did in the wilds, walk along at heel superbly indifferent to the many strange sights and sounds of a great town. Strange dogs and cats and yelling children now scarcely disturb them, though cats and cows, two unknown quantities, stirred them, on first view, to growls and barks; the town dogs dash out with roars, but are generally brought up short at close sight of Wahoo's majestic proportions. Rex and Wahoo walk politely and quietly with us into restaurants and lie entirely still during the whole meal — this is something they have been carefully taught to do in the wilderness. We have also taken them into beautifully furnished houses to afternoon tea, and each behaved in the manner of one born to it. Every evening we hold a sort of court in the hotel lobby, when admiring crowds gather round the dogs. The dogs accept every kind of caress from strangers with courtesy and never a growl. Apparently they instantly grasped the fact that this is a different world; that here they have no obligations to guard property, and that strangers are not to be treated as they were in the wilds. Everywhere that we go the dogs are welcomed. One lady said, "They're so clean they don't even smell like dogs!" People continually comment on their superb condition and ask what we feed them. To which we reply that at times they fared well on moose meat and trout, at others they subsisted for weeks, sometimes months, on corn meal, flour, and lard.

Part Two

CHAPTER XIV

Blue Lake

Tetana   *February 18, 1941*

J. has already been here over a month repairing the cabin roof which fell in last winter under an unprecedented depth of snow. The Indians cut a mark on our tree at eleven feet, six inches, where the level came to. It is as high as our chimney. There are two reports from Bear Lake of twenty-foot snow levels. And J. found a new thermometer, which he had left wrapped in layers of bedding in a barrel *inside* the cabin, registering 61 below zero. J. flew in with Russ, but as Russ had only a small Fairchilds plane available, J. could take nothing but the thousand-pound load of lumber and roofing for the cabin. So the dogs and I came later, bringing our year's food supply.

I had not, of course, been able to communicate with J. since he went in to Tetana a month before, but when he left Fort St. James he sent word for me to leave Pennsylvania toward the end of January and try to reach Tetana during the first week of February. Owing to the usual inevitable difficulties of weather and other things, Russ was not able to fly me in from the Fort till a week behind schedule. But I hoped and prayed that J. was alive and well and would greet me at Bunshaw.

This time, though we were reluctant to bring a disturbing element into our wilderness peace, we decided to take a radio. The war, though still confined to Europe, is becoming more widespread and imminent. We may have to return to the U. S. earlier than planned. On this radio J. can receive short-wave messages. The Canadian Airways operator at the Fort had called J. on the very morning of February 14th when Rex, Wahoo, and I were actually on the way. So I had a faint hope that some sort of message, confirmed by the brilliant weather, might inform J. of my impending arrival.

On this plane ride Rex was a calm, interested observer. He gazed out the window and wagged his tail gently. But poor old Wahoo shook like a leaf and clawed Frank Coulter, the mechanic, and me at every "bump." In a few hours we were over Takla. Up in front Russ was speaking in his radio tube to the operator back at the Fort, making the regular quarter-hour report, now required, back to headquarters.

"CFAWV calling Fort St. James, CFAWV calling Fort St. James; five thousand over Takla Lake, heading north, ceiling unlimited, moderate winds, north northwest."

In another half hour we were above Tetana, making two half circles to tell J., if he was below, that I was in the plane. There was a tiny, slanted glimpse of the cabin and, yes, there was certainly a roof on it, so J. was probably still alive! And now Rex, who up to this moment had been quiet and mannerly, began of a sudden to howl and wag his tail and wriggle from end to end.

"Sure knows where he is, doesn't he?" shouted Frank in my ear.

He certainly did, incredible as it was. Rex hadn't been to British Columbia or seen Tetana for two years — couldn't see it now at all in his humped-up position at five thousand feet in the air — and had meanwhile traveled some six thousand miles by plane, bus, boat, and train to Pennsylvania, and all the way back again. (Never once, except when Rex was sick on his first car ride, has either dog made the slightest mess or trouble.)

In no time we were losing altitude and circling over Bunshaw. I peered down for a sign of J., but could see only one tiny figure which I took to be an Indian. Then we had landed and my heart sank a little, because J. was not there to give me the big hug he had promised. But out across the lake came three people: Bear Lake Charlie, Selina, and a small child, beaming and chuckling and shaking hands all round.

"By gosh, Missus, you come back again, ha! ha! Hello, Rex and Wahoo! We kill the moose for you on the river, just one mile from Tetana. Rex and Wahoo, you and Jack eat lots now!"

In the northern wilderness, no greeting sounds pleasanter to the ears than the one which says fresh meat is at hand.

"Jack, where is he? He not come yet?" I asked anxiously.

"Oh yes, by-em-by, pretty quick now he come, I think. He know you come. He tell me, 'Charlie, my wife, he come to Bunshaw soon now. You fix the tent there, Charlie, you meet him; by-em-by I come.' "

This, though vague, was comforting. And I had a tent to shelter in. Russ was anxious to see Jack and, as he didn't want to leave me alone, said he would wait a while. But I knew he couldn't stay long. He must leave time enough to return to the Fort before dark. We hoped that J., if he had not received any radio message, would have seen our plane, and even if he had only then started for Bunshaw, he might make it before nightfall. We made tea by the tent on the shore, and several more Indian figures appeared suddenly from nowhere, just as they always did. The same silent Sapolio and several of Charlie's boys. Evidently I was expected, if they had gathered here from their widely separated trap lines. In a little over an hour from the time we landed the boys began to talk and point southward.

"Jack, he come, Missus," Charlie shouted, "my boys he know."

Russ and Frank looked surprised as we hadn't heard a thing, though we had been listening and looking for some time. These Indians have either a sort of extra sense like an animal, or maybe a greater development of other senses, which often enables them to tell of approaching figures long before the white man can. Sure enough, about twenty minutes later a man emerged on the south shore half a mile away. I knew it was J.; so did Rex and Wahoo, for they let out dog shouts of gladness, hurled themselves down the lake, and nearly knocked him over. When J. reached me his heavy woolen shirts were wet with sweat. He had made the ten-mile trip from Tetana to Bunshaw in the record-breaking time of one hour and twenty minutes, having apparently run most of the way. Between pants he told us that, contrary to all northern laws of conserving the heavy batteries that have to be carried in, he had had his radio tuned in all day because the weather was so good he thought we might come. But he had gotten nothing from the Fort and had given up expecting us. And then that afternoon, he suddenly heard Russ's voice saying "Five thousand feet over Takla heading north." J. was half a mile along the trail to Bunshaw when we circled above Tetana.

The plane took off, Charlie and the other Indians retired to his cabin on the hill with promises that the boys would be down next day with a tobogganload of things, and J. and I were alone again on Bunshaw buried in snow, just as though we had never left it. We had an hour or so of daylight left and instead of camping there decided to snowshoe down to Tetana carrying with us the cameras, new medical kit of perishables, heavy game rifles, and my sleeping bag. It was a swift trip, for we must make it by nightfall. At first we had much to say. J. must hear all about our darling Patricia (named after two British grandmothers) who, having been born in October '39 on the very date we planned for her, is now a year and a half old. She has been left behind in the easy world to grow big enough and strong enough to survive a northern wilderness, temperatures of 60 below, ten feet of snow, and twenty-mile hikes. Because of Patricia, this time our stay here is to be limited to nine or ten months. But soon we settled to the steady pace of the trail and complete quiet just as always. The valley around us had darkened, but the mountaintops, bathed in sun, still shone on. Rex and Wahoo, after wild excitement, had quieted too, noses and ears and tails erect and eager.

Every glance of bright eyes and those gently waving tails said, "Ah, we are back again. We are real dogs once more. This is the life!"

I had thought that perhaps I should be soft after being so long in a soft world. But no, we were over halfway and I felt not a particle of fatigue or chill in the 20-below temperature. It seemed to me that I was less tired than I had been for years.

Four miles from Tetana the faint twilight, through which

we had been walking, faded out. We were feeling for the trail with our snowshoes and traveling in darkness under the faint, high, starlit roof of the forest. At times we stumbled or stepped off the firm trail and were submerged in soft snow.

Now I recognized, though I did not see, the willow thickets and meadow north of Tetana, then each familiar twist of the trail. We were by the Frog Pond, then out in the open with the black shape of the cabin, almost hidden in heaped-up snow, just ahead. There lay Tetana and the Driftwood Mountains below the winter night sky.

"Perhaps you have changed," they seemed to say, "but we have not. We are here just as we have always been, long, long before man trod the earth, long, long after he treads it perhaps, serene and changeless."

We stood very still, looking and listening; and then we stumbled down through the snowbank to the door and into our cabin, still warm, because J. had left it only a few hours ago. Home again. Moose steak and onions in a hot pan sending forth the most delectable odors in existence, the yellow, mellow light of the little old oil lamp, and a very spiffy-looking clean new roof overhead.

"Just finished rechinking last night, or rather at two this morning," J. told me. "Must have known you were coming! I wanted everything finished and in place for you."

February 22

Thanks to William and Mac and Alec, who have made three trips down from Bunshaw, about eight hundred pounds of a year's food supply and duffel have arrived safely. J. paid Charlie well for this, and we gave each of the boys an additional present — a pair of shoes, pants, a shirt.

When old Charlie arrived for his pay, we had much lost time to make up, past events to be told, fresh gossip to be retailed. One of Charlie's daughters has died. Alec Bob cut his leg terribly with an axe. It had never healed, and he had been taken out by plane to see a doctor; the doctor had said the leg must be taken off, or Alec of the beautiful face, the best hunter and woodsman of them all, would surely die. But Alec would not consent to the amputation. If he had only one leg, he would, he said, die anyway. He wished to take his chance. It is now thought that he has t.b. in the wounded leg, but otherwise he seems better. He may possibly recover.

Martha and Vinson are now said to be legally divorced. Vinson's trap line in the Driftwood area has been divided between Sapolio and Johnny French. Vinson lives on Babine. Michelle no longer lives at Bear Lake. He and his family have moved to Babine because, according to Charlie, who does not seem to be pleased about it, Bella found life at Bear Lake too dull and confining. And Simon has left Bear Lake and Maggie, and taken unto himself still another wife. Maggie, apparently with perfect amicability, has taken unto herself a new husband, a young Bear Lake Indian.

"By gosh, Jack, Missus, lots of bad thing he happen. I get old man now. Lots of pain. Pretty soon I die, mebbe," and Charlie shrugged and chuckled merrily.

In this world it is hard to remember the war. The Indians are almost unaware of it. Even back at the settlements the white people seemed uninterested. Many of them apparently didn't even bother to listen to the war news on their radios. Few of their men or boys seem to be in it. Coming across Canada I saw plenty of troops, but as I left the railroads and headed up into the North all signs of war, except for a rise in prices of canned goods, vanished.

We've arranged to go with old Charlie early in March on a long trip around the south end of the Driftwood Mountains, up along the valley on the west side, back across the mountains to Tetana. In the summer of '39, when J. worked out here alone, he saw from the summit of the southern Driftwoods a lake in the midst of the spires of the Frypans. Although it was probably twenty to thirty miles away as the crow flies, the shape and color and setting so caught his fancy that he has talked of it ever since. When I saw the tiny Kodachrome photos showing the lake, like a turquoise, set in sharp white peaks, I was as fascinated as he was. Long ago, we made up our minds to get to that lake somehow, someday. Old Charlie knows the lake and Michelle has been there as well as one or two other Indians connected with Charlie's family; but apparently no one else knows of it at all. Charlie and Michelle call it "Blue Lake" because "the water just like the sky, only more blue I think."

Whenever J. mentioned any particularly pretty place both Michelle and Charlie would say, "By gosh, Jack, you like that one, but I wish you see Blue Lake. No place pretty like him, I think. You like him, sure."

The Indians don't enthuse over beauty — we are not even sure that they recognize beauty. So the fact that they have spoken of Blue Lake in what, for them, are glowing terms has made us more anxious than ever to see it. Charlie said if we go south around the Driftwoods he can take us to Blue Lake "easy." "March month," since the deep snows will have settled, is the time to go.

William is now fully grown and appears to be the brightest and most pleasant-spoken of the boys. Since Michelle has gone, William, Charlie says, is the man of the family. He is to go along on the Blue Lake trip, and we gather that Charlie intends him to take Michelle's place as a guide and helper.

We had various reports from outside about the Indians. One was that Michelle and Vinson and another Indian and a young squaw spent some time living in and enjoying the luxuries of our cabin. Anyhow, whoever has been here has stripped it well of the few possessions we left. My yellow curtains and a pair of snowshoes have vanished (lucky I brought in with me this time material for new curtains and two new pairs of snowshoes) ; old clothes and bedding and most of the cooking utensils have also disappeared. Some of the latter, however, are reappearing slowly; Charlie informed J. that he had been "keeping" them for us.

So, when he's missed some especially useful article, J. has said, "Charlie, next time you come, please bring the big knife [or the stewpot, or the frypan]. I need him now." And Charlie, full of smiles and self-praise over his thoughtfulness in keep-

ing them safe, brings them sure enough. This time he brought
the big bread knife, pointing out that it is completely unrusted
and its blade very sharp (and well worn).

March 18

Last week Charlie and his toboggan and William and Mac
appeared, not much more than a week behind schedule, all
set for the Blue Lake trip. We started from Tetana in the
early afternoon, heading south down the valley toward Te-gai-
une-lee, "Lake of the Silver Fish" ("Beeg trout in there, by
gosh, just like silver they look"), which is one of Charlie's
chief trapping and hunting areas. We proposed to make our
first camp there.

Old Charlie's big bent figure snowshoed ahead. There were
the same familiar trousers of two years ago, or if they were not
the same trousers, they bore patches of the same material, and
they were pinned carefully in front with safety pins, a safety
device insisted upon by Selina, which Charlie cursed loudly.
There was a new heavy wool jacket obtained from Carl's, there
was the old silk handkerchief tied around his iron-gray hair.
Behind came the loaded toboggan and five dogs escorted by
William, smiling and talkative as always, and Mac, still and
withdrawn. J. and I and Rex and Wahoo brought up the rear.
It was considered an easy half day to Te-gai-une-lee from Tetana
(about ten miles). The trail on the west side of the river led
along fairly level ground through pine forests and across
swamps. It was entirely strange country to me.

Sometimes when one is doing something quite new, it seems
that one has done it before. Or one sees a place already seen in
a dream world so clearly that it has partaken of reality. As we
traveled the trail to Te-gai-une-lee I had the oddest feeling.
It seemed exactly as though I had traveled every turn of this
very trail before. There was the musical tinkle of a dog sled
and snowshoes on hard snow, completely silent Indian figures,
and a man I loved walking with me through the winter stillness
of a great flat stretch of spruce and pine. There were the same
glimpses of white mountain shapes, a river under ice, frozen

lakes, cold pure air. It was all just as I had known it. It was the fulfillment of my childhood dreams, the strong determination of adolescence, something that had always been meant for me.

On the toboggan we had tea and sugar, dried fruit, flour, powdered milk, and beans enough to last five of us a week, but we were depending on killing fresh meat along the way. Charlie assured us (as he always does) that in *his* hunting country there "is all time meat, lots of moose." But if this, like many of his other pet ideas, did not turn out to be true, we should just have to return earlier than planned. When we reached Te-gai-une-lee shortly before dusk, the sky was solid silver-gray and light snow was beginning to fall.

"By gosh, Jack, I dunno, I think we get big storm mebbe. March time now. No storms in March month. Dunno what's the matter. Mebbe we stay here long time. No meat, no dog food. William, he hunt the moose right now."

And turning to William the old man fired rapid and emphatic orders in his own tongue. William and Mac picked up their guns without a word and vanished into the woods, followed by the customary volley of excited parting directions from their father.

"Poor things," I thought, "how can he expect them to hunt moose at this time of night? They must be dead and won't go far once they get out of his sight."

The afternoon trip had seemed much more than ten miles. And those boys had gone an added ten miles that day, before they had started from Tetana with us. But I reckoned without complete knowledge of these Indian boys. J. and I have by now acquired a real respect for their abilities. From the time he is ten or twelve and strong enough to wield an axe or fire a gun, the Indian boy is the slave of his parents. This state lasts until he marries and sets up a family of his own, when he is no longer answerable to his father. It is he who does the family hunting, gets firewood for his mother, is ever at his father's beck and call, attends unceasingly to the hardest ends of living. On trips through the wilderness he drives the dogs, visits the trap that is five miles off while his family proceeds in leisurely fashion along the main trail. He does the hardest things around camp. While his parents set up the bed and shelter, he cuts and hauls big logs of wood. He feeds and beds down the dogs. He has the outer unsheltered portion of the camp bed. In the morning he gets up first to rebuild the fire. If he happens to be on a trip with the white man, the Indian boy is the one to help the white man get his wood and run his errands. On the daily trips he carries on his back the extra impedimenta, such as guns and cameras, in addition to driving and managing the dog sled or pack dogs, which is no mean feat on an unbroken trail. If fresh moose tracks are seen, he follows the tracks or chases the moose, to come back and pick up his party on the main trail perhaps after many hours and a run of an extra ten or fifteen miles.

By the time he is fourteen or fifteen this Indian boy can exist alone successfully in the wilderness, under almost any conditions; he could care for a family of his own if he had one. He knows how to find a camping site near dry wood and good water in unknown territory, he can make a camp that will keep him safe through storms and 60-below-zero temperatures. If he is out of food he knows where to look for a moose habitat, how to trail the moose, head it off, and bring it down with a single well-placed shot. Or he can snare snowshoe rabbits, find beaver or muskrat, dig a hibernating bear out of its den. He knows how to bleed a moose and cut it for meat, how to skin the hide, cure it and fix it for tent, clothing, and shoes; and he has learned what parts of it make good medicine. If his old snowshoes break, he can shape the wooden frames and weave the complicated patterns of moose-hide webbing to make a new pair.

Time probably never hangs heavy on the hands of an Indian boy. He is seldom bored or in need of entertainment or occupation. If his morals are poor, if he steals from, or lies to, the white man or his fellow Indians when occasion offers, it is, after all, only what he has seen his elders do. No one has illustrated a different life for him.

In the fast thickening storm over Te-gai-une-lee I set about, a bit gloomily, to make camp, while J. and Charlie were laying in firewood. When we camp with Bear Lake Charlie we always have some arguments over the camping place. J. and I choose one with an eye to beauty, Charlie to practicality only, and the old man fusses and squeaks about if he thinks we've picked a bad site. Moreover he is quite apt to put his own camp right beside ours, because privacy doesn't seem to mean much to him. I always maneuver to get him to say first where he is going to camp, so we can have ours as far away as possible.

This time, in the fading light and whirling snow, we had no time to pick and choose camp sites. We couldn't see any view and, following Charlie's directions, put our tiny tent by a high bank, with our door facing the bank and our fireplace dug into it. Charlie's tent fly was placed in the same position about twenty feet away. The fire on the bank could not melt down below our tent level and consequently threw heat directly into the tent — also quantities of blinding smoke, but then smoke never affects the Indians! They are simply immune to it. The Indian dogs were tied to trees around Charlie's camp some fifteen feet away from us. But Rex and Wahoo, though allowed their freedom, adhered strictly to their own territory, so there was never any trouble.

Well after dark the boys returned and when J. came back from talking to them I inquired, more in fun than in earnest, if they got a moose.

"Oh, sure," said J., but I supposed he was being weightily sarcastic, until William appeared in our firelight with a fresh, bloody moose heart.

The next morning it was still snowing, a wet heavy snow, and there was nothing in the world to do but crouch inside the tiny tent and weep and choke in clouds of smoke from the damp fire. We had to raise the back of the tent, thereby letting cold air and snow blow in on us and our bed, but that was better than suffocating to death. That day went by, the snow continued, and the boys were off cutting up the moose which they had killed two miles away. We were all quite cheerful because we had plenty of fresh meat. By nightfall the snow had let up somewhat; we prepared to feast heavily on moose, now that we could cook over our fires again without being stifled by smoke and wetted from snow which melted to rain in the fierce heat of the logs.

William, as a special treat, brought us the moose nose. This is considered a delicacy by the Indians and was a part which I had never tasted. Speared on the end of a stick, it had to be roasted slowly over hot coals and, though I had been crazy to try it, my ardor was a bit dampened as I watched the huge, bloody, hairy thing that slowly blackened on the outside without getting done inside. We had also been boiling the tongue for hours, but it did not really get soft enough to chew because it was the tongue of a bull; bull moose at this season are especially tough. Finally, however, we could eat parts of the nose. It was a spongy sort of material with the consistency of gelatin. Though J. pronounced it delicious, I wondered why the Indians are so crazy about it and suggested returning part of it to them as a polite gesture.

Charlie and the boys had steaks from various portions of the moose body roasting on sticks all around their fire. It looked as though they were cooking meat enough for a regiment. The old man was eating the raw intestines and stomach lining which he declared was very good medicine. Almost no part of the moose body is wasted by these Indians. They even eat the horns roasted over hot coals. J. sampled them once, and thought them excellent. The Indians also sometimes eat the fresh stomach contents, which are a sort of undigested vegetable fiber. In this way they get a well-balanced diet. They never seem to need fruit or vegetables as long as they include all parts of an animal in their meals.

"By God, Jack, I think I eat all night," cried Charlie gleefully when J. called out to know how he did. Before I went to sleep, the last thing I saw in the bright red circle of their firelight was old Charlie's handkerchief-bound head bent steadily over a hunk of moose. William and Mac were sitting barefoot on the bed, their dark intent faces silhouetted against the fire as they bent over their snowshoes, patching new tears that must be mended before they could travel on them again. Torn socks and wet moccasins and numbers of old cloths which are always wrapped round their feet were steaming to heaven as they dried on sticks stuck in snowbanks around the fire. An apparently undiminished supply of meat was still cooking in pots and pans and on sticks.

By noon the next day a wind began to blow and clouds moved fast across the sky from the west. Patches of blue appeared, to vanish again in flying mist. Charlie, after a prodigious sleep and fed to the brim on moose meat, was in fine fettle as he watched the sky.

"Now," he said, "the wind he come, make him all clean up there."

The clouds lifted slowly and revealed first the long narrow snowbound surface of the "Lake of the Silver Fish." This was the place where, two summers ago, J. killed a moose on the opposite shore eight hundred yards away. He did it with one shot, and the Indians still talk about it. The south end of the Driftwood range shone out, high and imposing, close on the west of Te-gai-une-lee; and the Frypans nearer and grander than I had ever seen them. The mountains appeared, vanished, and reappeared through flying clouds. The great stretches of fresh white snow, the peaks, here gleaming brilliant in dazzling sunshine, there purple and inky under passing cloud banks, were magnificent. J. and I were about to expose all our color film on the spot, when we severely reminded each other that the trip was only just beginning.

We wished we could be off at once, but the snow was much too soft to allow traveling. The boys — those ever-useful boys — were to spend the afternoon breaking trail ahead so that it could settle and freeze hard during the night. On the morrow we would all be off again at an early hour.

The next day was cold with high wind and flying clouds, fitful gleams of sunlight, and snow flurries. We headed directly for the Frypans. Charlie pointed out one of the dozens of deep clefts in the jumbled peaks which he said held Blue Lake. Between the Driftwoods and the Frypans was the great canyon and waterfall of which he had sometimes told us. No white man had ever been in any of this country before, he assured us.

As we proceeded along the trail, tramped down a little by William's and Mac's snowshoes, we had all we could do to keep our own dogs and the Indian dogs from bolting, as very fresh moose tracks were everywhere. The old man must have been telling the truth, for nowhere else in this whole country have I ever seen so many moose signs. Charlie kept pushing his axe handle down in the tracks to judge of their freshness and see which way they were heading.

One of our ambitions has been to get motion pictures of Indian dogs attacking a moose and holding it at bay. So when we crossed a particularly fresh track, and Charlie thought the moose only a few miles off, he said if he loosed his dogs they might catch it and hold it for J. to make pictures. It was decided that I should remain on the main trail with Rex and Wahoo, make a fire, and boil water for tea. Some months before Wahoo had cut his leg at the ankle so badly that it was still not perfectly healed. If he chased a moose it would be reopened and he might be unable to travel the rest of the trip. Moreover, I understood as well as the rest, though they were all too polite to say so, that I couldn't possibly keep up with the men when they started running miles across country after a fleeing moose. I resigned myself to a long cold wait and to holding onto Rex and Wahoo — quite a job, as they were greatly excited — until the others got out of hearing. From time to time we heard the yelping of the Indian dogs as they grew hot on the chase, but I didn't suppose J. would really have the luck to get close enough for a picture. After several hours there were voices and I hurried to tie up Rex and Wahoo so they wouldn't get into trouble with the returning dogs. William, grinning from ear to ear, appeared first.

"By gosh, Missus, we make lots of fun," he called; "we catch the moose."

"Did you really? Did Jack get any pictures?"

"Oh yes, by gosh, lots, he make picture all the time. The

Bull Moose

dogs he hold the moose just right. Then we kill him, oh, by
gosh, lots of fun we make!"

Then the others returned, triumphant and panting, and J.
said he had taken some thirty feet of a cow moose kicking at
the dogs and holding them off. He prayed they were good.

"Why did you have to kill the poor thing when we already
have all the meat we can carry?"

"Charlie wants to store up all he can get. Says it will keep
frozen a couple more months till they can come back and cut
it up and smoke it for summer."

We were off again, still toward the Frypans. Then the trail
veered west toward a pass on the south end of the Driftwoods.
It was afternoon. Presently we came to a deep little swamp below the trail on the right. And there, just below, were two huge
moose. Before they even lifted their heads from feeding on
the willows, William's and J.'s guns were out and they had
fired at the near one. But for once they didn't bring it down,
for it had only been hit in the leg and started to run at that
instant. In a twinkling, before anyone had said one word, the
Indian dogs were loosed from their harness and had vanished
down the bank, followed by the boys and old Charlie, who,
as they ran, scattered packs and jackets and axes all along the
trail. Then J. disappeared with Wahoo at his heels before I
could grab him, and even Rex, beside himself with excitement,
had departed. It was too much for me and I ran. J. shouted back
that, judging by blood on the trail, the moose couldn't go far
and would soon be brought down; now was a chance for me to
be in at the kill. But I couldn't travel like J. My calls to Wahoo
were fruitless and I panted on, way in the rear, with Rex now
beside me again, though he was quivering and squeaking at the
great splotches of fresh warm blood in the snow. After a time
I noticed that where J. sometimes veered from the moose trail,
Wahoo's foot was bleeding badly. I shouted myself hoarse, but
J. either didn't hear or didn't understand; and we ran on and
on and on.

After a long time of this he at last waited for me to catch up.
Wahoo's foot had opened and he was losing blood steadily.

There was no sound of the Indians or the wounded moose. I said that I was completely done and if either Wahoo or I went another step we wouldn't be able to make camp that night. J. thought he knew where the trail and toboggan were, but we had circled around so much after the moose that *I* hadn't the faintest idea. There was nothing for J. to do but give up the chase and take me and the dogs back to the trail. Which he did, in disgust. I knew that this was one of the times when he was remembering that I was a woman who had no business being in this country at all. In half an hour we had hit the trail about half a mile from the loaded toboggan.

We set about making a fire and tea and, in less than an hour, the Indians were also back. They had killed the moose a mile or two ahead of where we had abandoned the chase. For once *they* actually seemed tired. So we made camp a few miles farther on.

I gathered spruce and balsam for our bed, while J. and the two boys went to get a big supply of logs for the fires. No matter how weary we were, we all had to go on working harder than ever to make secure camps for the night. It had cleared completely and promised to be very cold. I carried in one load after another of boughs. The more boughs, the warmer the bed, and the better the chance of getting rested for another day's travel.

Old Charlie had disappeared again; he wanted to break trail on ahead and see the condition of the country. When it grew dark and he still hadn't returned, J. and I began to wonder if someone ought to look for him.

But just then the two boys appeared by our fire. William was worried. "I think we go look for my father. Mebbe that old man he lose himself and get hurted."

"Fire your gun two times, if you need help," shouted J. as they vanished into the night.

We had eaten our favorite supper — moose meat and slices of dried onion fried in a pan, and a potful of hot tea — and we had leisure to enjoy our comfortable camp as we turned steaming socks and moccasins and mittens and snowshoes in the fierce heat of the fire.

Then above the roar and sizzle of the burning logs we heard a noise. We sprang into our snowshoes and climbed on the snowbank away from the fire. Either it had been real voices or an echo. Presently, from far away, it came again, a mourning, heartrending cry that made little prickles go all along my body. We were almost sure it was wolves and not, as we had thought at first, the Indians calling for help. So we went back, shivering, to our fire. After another interval we heard human voices again, and there were old Charlie and the boys. Charlie told us he had gone a long way, "five, seben miles, mebbe" to the beginning of the canyon on ahead. The boys had met him coming back.

He said: "By gosh, Jack, I hear something in that canyon. Something funny. I not know, see? I scare. I think a man down there, mebbe, but not like a man. How a man get down in that place? I neber hear that thing before. By God, it scare me, bad. I come back quick." And he cackled uneasily in his high squeaky voice.

No, it was not wolves. He had heard them too, off in another direction. We suggested it might be an echo of water or the falls, but old Charlie shook his head and, followed by the silent William and Mac, went off to his own campfire, muttering to himself. I was sure he thought it was a ghost or spirit but didn't know how to say it to us in English. Several times that night I woke, hearing the wolves; either the wolf cries or a thought of the mysterious voice in the canyon troubled my dreams.

The morning dawned icy and sparkling; we were soon off on the trail again. The farther we followed Charlie's tracks of the previous night the more I marveled at the old man's strength. The day before we had gone at least fifteen miles along the main trail and, in addition, he had chased two moose at least another ten. While we made camp he had, as he had said, gone on five or six miles ahead and back to camp again. And he keeps telling us that he is so old (he is probably something over fifty — men and women age quickly in this country) that he can't work any more and "pretty soon now I die, I think!"

"If I was as strong as you, Charlie, I wouldn't worry about dying yet a while!" J. often tells him.

We headed toward a low spur of the southern Driftwoods. It was well Charlie knew the country, and that Michelle and his dogs had traveled that way some time before, for the trail was scarcely blazed at all. Apparently only members of Charlie's family ever use it. Along a swamp we kept passing by trees where great bunches of thick sphagnum moss were hung.

"What's all that moss for?"

"I think Bella, Michelle's wife, he put him there to dry. Last fall mebbe. Mebbe my wife. He use him on the baby, under his legs. Sometime he tie moss in old sugar bag. He make baby clean that way."

"Diapers!" said J. "What do you know about that?"

As we began slowly to ascend the mountainside, tiny Grinnell's chickadees followed us from tree to tree. In contrast to the brown-headed Columbian chickadees so common around Tetana and the valleys, these seem always to haunt the mountain slopes from three to five thousand feet.

"When we see that little bird," Charlie told us, "always he say we meet a man pretty soon. Sometime that little bird he say right, sometime he lie I think! Mebbe we see that man I hear in canyon last night!"

It was hard going up the steep incline. The sled dogs strained and yelped, and our Wahoo, with his heavy pack, sank down way below the level of the soft snow. More than once he was completely bogged and J. and I had to get before and behind to pull and push while the others dug around him. We saw great sweeps of wild mountainous land, but it was the peaks of the Frypans that always caught the eye. Such height and space and majesty. Such lights and shadows and shining snow fields — so enticing and cruel, so beautiful and terrible.

We passed down through heavy balsam forest to a long flat plateau which bordered the canyon. Here we made tea together around a fire and when Charlie observed that J. and I had no moose meat with our lunch kit, he offered us generous pieces of theirs which Mac had fried in a pan. Mac is the cook ("Mac, he neber talk, only hunt and trap — by gosh! good hunter that boy — and cook. Always he want to cook things!"). We had

not expected to need anything at midday except the usual tea
and bannock, but after the hard climb of the morning, the red
meat set us up again and revived us wonderfully.

Charlie told us that once, on this spot, some time after he
and Selina were married, they had made a camp. For some
years they had had no babies and Selina had traveled all round
the country with Charlie just as I do with J. When they were
camping here Charlie had chased a moose way over into the
mountains towards Blue Lake, so far that he couldn't get back
to camp that night. But as he was worrying over what might
happen to Selina and wishing he had their camping things
right there, she and the loaded pack dogs appeared suddenly at
his fireside.

"Fine woman that one," said Charlie with a reminiscent
chuckle; "he track me all over and then he come just right and
bring camp along beside. By gosh!"

After we had eaten we went to the edge of the great canyon,
a half mile away, and looked and marveled. Streams from Blue
Lake and other valleys converge to fall in two great cataracts,
the biggest of which, as nearly as we could judge from a distance
of a quarter of a mile, was a thousand to twelve hundred feet
high and seventy-five to two hundred feet wide. Both were
completely enclosed in ice, but underneath was a deep muffled
roar of mighty and gigantic waters. In late spring, at floodtime,
the volume passing over them must be incalculable. J. and I,
as far as we knew, were the first of our race to gaze on this
awesome spectacle. Above the canyon, tossing forested ridges
rose steeply to the dazzling whiteness and spearhead peaks of
the mountains.

From the canyon we looked across the ridges directly to the
depression that held Blue Lake. As we started back to the main
trail J. began to ask the old man how we were to get there.

Charlie said, "Now, Jack, you see. Blue Lake too far. No good
we go there, I think. No trail. Very rough. Dogs can't go there.
More better we go my cabin other side mountain."

J. and I looked at each other in horrified dismay. After our
experiences with Charlie and his family we have come to know

that their interest, patience, endurance, whatever it is that they *don't* have much of, usually gives out after a certain interval of time — three days to a week at most. But on this trip, when we were so far from home, we'd thought it safe to count on their sticking until at least we got round the Driftwood range and were heading north toward Bear Lake country again. But in our ardent desire to see Blue Lake, and because of Charlie's apparent enthusiasm, we had forgotten that, viewed from a distance, any feat seems possible to an Indian, any place easy of access. The difficult or impossible is always quite possible until it becomes necessary to put words into deeds. Either Charlie was telling the truth and getting into Blue Lake was impossible with the time and equipment at our disposal, or else he was just tired and bored and home, which he had been delighted to leave, now seemed most desirable.

I was not going to give up Blue Lake, though, without a struggle. Why, our whole trip had been planned especially for this! The moose and the waterfalls were all very well, but they were nothing to what I pictured Blue Lake to be. I was, however, really discouraged to note that the more J. surveyed the country and listened to Charlie, the more he was inclining to believe him and think that perhaps it really was too difficult a trip to be feasible.

Once, when I was on ahead with Charlie and the others were well behind, I reminded Charlie of what he had said about our getting to Blue Lake, that this was supposed to be the best season of the year for it, and so on. He replied with grunts.

I then said: "Charlie, if way to Blue Lake too rough for toboggan why not leave toboggan on main trail and take a few dogs with packs? If we can get there on our snowshoes, surely the pack dogs can come after us and carry a little food. Jack and I we want to see Blue Lake *bad*. One time you say some rocks there. You don't know what they are. Maybe gold. Maybe something good. If we see them maybe we take them out to be examined for you."

To this he condescended to say: "Mebbe."

I didn't know whether I'd made any impression, and was

ready to cry with disappointment and rage at Charlie, and at J. for giving in to the old man too easily. But being mad didn't make it any better because if Charlie made up his mind we shouldn't go to Blue Lake, no words or threats of ours could persuade him, and we couldn't get there without him. It would have to be decided at our camp that night because, by tomorrow, if we were going to Blue Lake at all, we must turn off the trail and head in a new direction.

Once we came suddenly on fresh snowshoe tracks. We all stopped dead; Charlie and the boys examined them excitedly. They told us they were made by one of Charlie's sons-in-law from Babine. The Indians can nearly always tell to whom a snowshoe track belongs; they apparently know certain marks left by the snowshoes of every individual in the country, just as a detective ferrets out the track of a man with a certain kind of shoe. They thought he must have come up to camp with Michelle in Charlie's cabin on the other side of the Driftwoods.

Charlie cried, "By gosh, Jack, Missus, what I tell you? That little bird on the mountain he say we meet a man, ha! ha!"

I stopped along the way to take a picture or two and when I caught the others, around sunset, they were already making camp.

J. said, "I picked our camp this time without any help from the old man. He didn't approve of this stopping place, much less our tent site. How do you like it?"

We were in an open grove of young balsam and spruce that grew on an incline which sloped gently down to the banks of a stream lined with big trees and heavy timber. Our tent door and fire faced a picture that took my breath away. Framed by high luxuriant green firs, two peaks of the Frypans rose so near that they towered into the very zenith. They were cut marvelously into pinnacles, shaped and colored like a Maxfield Parrish painting. Their feet lay in violet light beyond the black spires of forest along the stream. Their white breasts were deep salmon, their jagged crowns etched with brilliant gold from the setting sun. We delayed to watch the changing colors and lights, so enthralled by what lay before us that much of our camp had to be fixed after dark, and we did not get it as well arranged as usual.

In utter defiance of the view Charlie and the boys made their camp against a tree that faced *up* the slope and now sat stolidly beneath a fly with their backs deliberately turned on heaven!

After supper J. went over to confab with Charlie, while I tried vainly to keep warm by our fire which had now not only sunk below the tent level, but was also gradually receding a little farther downhill away from us. After all, though Charlie's back was turned to the view, his fire was sending heat down on him and he could relax and keep warm. How much was even the most gorgeous scene worth, if one was too uncomfortable to look at it?

When J. returned he said, "What do you know? Now the old rascal thinks we can get to Blue Lake in half a day from here, if we leave the toboggan behind, and get back here to camp again for the night! I can't make out for the life of me how far it really is. Don't believe the old cuss remembers himself — it's so long since he's been there."

Next morning we arose in darkness and ate breakfast by fire-light in order to start the minute day broke. It was bitterly cold and our fire had now sunk far away from the tent door; I was stiff and shivering and could hardly get my snowshoes on. But the thought of Blue Lake was so strong that being desperately sleepy and numb all over didn't seem to matter. The sun came up as we started. Rex and Wahoo came with us, but the poor little Indian dogs were left tied along a felled spruce tree from which the boys had lopped off branches here and there for them to bed on. Their howls of anguish at being left behind followed us for a mile.

We traveled across wide bogs and swamps buried seven feet below the level of the white crust. The world was made of diamonds; from every direction frost crystals along the surface, over twigs and bushes, flashed colors. Behind and before, white, sharp-cut peaks towered straight up into a sky of deep indigo. But soon we began climbing up into one of those dense jungle-like balsam forests. Even the deep snow couldn't cover the huge fallen trees and masses of trunks. I understood now some of Charlie's hesitation. We climbed over icy mounds and jagged surfaces. J. and the Indians, on their huge snowshoes, tripped and fell and were caught up repeatedly. But I had never traveled better or been more sure-footed. This was probably due to my smaller snowshoes. Maybe it was plain luck, maybe the excitement of anticipation.

In two hours we were heading downhill again to an opening below and, before we had time to comment, there was a sudden sharp termination of the dense forest. And there in front of us was Blue Lake. For once Charlie said not a word but looked at us curiously. I said nothing at all. J. began to talk fast, delightedly: —

"Jumping Joseph! Look at that. Get your camera *quick,* Teddy. Use the light screen. *You didn't bring it?* Hell's bells. I never heard such carelessness. We may never see anything like this the rest of our lives — to miss getting good pictures of it — what in heck ailed you!"

I was frightfully annoyed at myself for forgetting the color screen, but I never have thought it as essential as J. does (as a matter of fact I have taken as stunning pictures without it as he has with it). And I was furious at him for making such a fuss and swearing at me, at a moment like this, and in front of the Indians!

But as we walked out onto the ice of Blue Lake we forgot to worry about the screen or anything else. We'd arrived at the outlet which flowed into a little river thirty feet across. It was open and free of ice for several hundred yards; fresh-water weeds bent over in silver waves beneath the swift current. The water was the glass-clear blue-green that we have seen in only one other place in this country — our own Tetana. The lake itself was like a precious jewel, perfectly proportioned, perfectly set. It was some three and a half miles long by a mile wide, and, because it curved from point to point, looked much larger than it actually was. It was completely surrounded by solid luxuriant forest which grew from its very edge for several miles up the mountains. Out of the dense black belt rose glacial-covered peaks in a shining circle. Saw-toothed rims, needle points, conelike domes tumbled at every angle, with glaciers in between glittering like fire in the brilliant sun. We judged the mountains to be eleven or twelve thousand feet high, the altitude of the lake itself to be around five thousand.

Noon tea was made on a point halfway up the east shore. Since we were only three hours away from camp it was decided that Charlie and the boys should return at once, pack our things, and go on along the main trail to Charlie's cabin about "three miles" beyond. J. and I were to linger and explore the lake, waiting till the lights grew soft enough for good photography. We thought we might get back to the camping place and on to Charlie's cabin in some two hours, since a good trail would be already broken. This arrangement suited everybody. J. and I, because now we could be alone to exult in what we saw, the Indians because they were interested, above all things, in reaching the cabin where they could eat and sleep in comparative comfort.

As the sun sank a little, lights and shadows filtering between peaks and points lit up the loveliest place in the world. We drew up wild schemes for making it our own forever. We might have it surveyed from the air and purchase it! Whatever happened we wouldn't tell anyone much about it. Its very inaccessibility might save it from invaders by land or air.

Once when J. was ahead of me around a long point, he saw a big gray wolf come out suddenly onto the lake a hundred yards away. It gave him a long look before it melted back into the forest again. J. wondered if it had ever seen a human being before. We imagined that the mountainsides just above timber would, in summer, have grassy slopes and be good bear country. Charlie vows that they abound with grizzlies. The Indians also say that there are fish in the lake. If this is true, the bears are a certainty. Our fondly preconceived idea of making a long summer's camp, or building a cabin, on Blue Lake is not so good, however. But for its enchanting beauty, it would not be an easy place to explore or live in. Guarded by its ramparts of cruel mountains and perpendicular banks, the dense tangles of forest, and the dangerous swamps below, perhaps it will keep safe from marauders by land or air.

Some day I hope, I believe, we shall visit Blue Lake again. I should like to see it free of ice when its waters — "blue like the sky — only more blue I think" — contrast with the green forest and white mountains. Wonderful as it now is, all black and white in winter, it should be doubly so in summer. It is left now to the bears and the wolves and the trout, for I think that even the two or three Indians who know of it seldom visit it.

After leaving a record of our names and the date on a big tree, we made the trip back to the camping place in good time. We were more tired than we had expected, doubtless owing to the many extra miles we had tramped over Blue Lake. But we fondly hoped that Charlie's cabin, our tent, and firewood which William had promised to prepare would be only a few miles farther. We hiked and hiked until we had covered twice the distance stated by the Indians, and still their trail went on and there was not a sign of the cabin. Sunset faded into starlight and moonlight. As our trail passed across an open plateau, which was mostly free of forest, the whole range of the Frypans stood clear on our left and a great new valley unfolded itself to the west. But my legs, alas, had reached the point where I couldn't distinguish them from the rest of me and I was not sure whether they were moving or not. We found the cabin long, long after dark and our tent some way beyond (for William is a bright lad and knew we liked privacy).

William reported that old Charlie was asleep. He said, "When he get to cabin my father he lie on floor and sleep, no blanket or nothing he put down. He neber wake up yet."

Michelle and several sons-in-law, including the one whose snowshoe tracks we had already seen, were, sure enough, on a trapping trip up the valley and were also stopping at the cabin. They appeared promptly at our fire for a visit, to my dismay, for I wanted to go to bed. I finally got into bed anyhow, with my clothes on, because I couldn't sit up another minute.

And when this didn't budge them (they are quite used to anyone's lying down and sleeping anywhere) J., who was also dropping from weariness, said, "Well, I think we go to bed now."

At this they said good-night and turned away, dejectedly. It was too bad. The appearance of a white woman and a white man in this vast uninhabited valley, much wilder even than the Driftwood area, must have been the event of years.

When we woke in the morning we ached all over from the cold, hard, lumpy bed. William had put up our tent over huge tree roots, and his idea of the proper number of boughs for a comfortable bed was not the equivalent of ours. Old Charlie, whose previous day had been far less strenuous than ours and who had had twice as long a sleep, was ready to be off at an early hour. Now that he was headed back toward Bear Lake he was, as we had anticipated, eager to get there without more ado. The promised trip up over the Driftwood range was all off. The dogs and toboggan could never get up there! But it was arranged that J. and I and William, with our dogs, should hike over it, while Charlie and Mac and the toboggan went on to Bunshaw.

The tiny ten-by-twelve-foot old log hut with its curl of smoke, surrounded by giant spruce trees, was set up against the perpendicular white walls of the Driftwoods. In '39, when J. had his first view of Blue Lake, one of his two pack horses, the little mare Lassie, had had an attack of colic somewhere on the summit which towered far above us, and almost departed this life. All one night, in snow flurries and high ice-cold winds, J., with the help of Michelle and young Mac, had worked to save her. They surrounded her with a circle of fires, put their own bedding over her, and forced hot lard down her throat. And Lassie survived and is still alive and healthy.

We were to travel that day up the valley along a small stream. This stream flows north till it reaches the gap between the Driftwood and Bear Lake Mountains, whence, reinforced by other streams, it turns east through a canyon and, by a series of rushing rapids and cataracts, flows south to form the main Driftwood River. When we reached the foot of the lowest point on the Driftwoods, a saddle six thousand feet high, William,

J., and I, and Rex and Wahoo, were to climb up over the pass, spend a night there, and then go down the other side and across to Lake Tetana. We'd all have to carry heavy packs and the going, without Charlie and Mac and the toboggan to break trail and transport our things, would be tough. But J. and I were determined to see the view from the summit of the Drift-woods in winter.

The valley trail passed almost entirely through open country, as much of the land here was covered with willow swamps. The timber began at the base of the mountains. At first it seemed wonderful always to be out in the open and away from forest. This is the Indian idea of Paradise! Ugly burnt-over land, provided it is free of trees, is the ideal country. But as the cloudless sun of March rose higher and hotter, we began to long for the restful darkness of trees. It had been far below zero in the night, but the beat and glare of the sun were now intense. The low saddle of the Driftwoods seemed to get no nearer. Even J. fell way behind the Indians and we lost sight of them entirely. We were still tired from the strenuous day before; the unmerciful glare exhausted us as storms and dense forests had never done.

Noon came and went and the toboggan with our tea and food and all other possessions, was still out of sight, and we grew more and more furious at the Indians for not waiting for us. It was late afternoon before we finally caught up to them placidly drinking tea under a spruce not far from the foot of the pass. J. was mad as hops and showed it. Rex, nose in air, trotted up and sprinkled disdainfully on Charlie's pack sack. This was a habit in which Rex, though on excellent terms with the Indians on this trip, occasionally indulged. Whenever it happened, Charlie naturally yelled and cursed. J. and I, chastising Rex loudly, couldn't help chuckling a bit in private. Charlie, who perhaps had a guilty conscience for going so far without us, was quite meek. He helped us assiduously to make camp several miles on ahead before he and Mac and the toboggan departed.

After supper I melted a teakettle of snow, heated it very

hot, and with washcloth, soap, and toothbrush, had a bath on the balsam boughs in front of the flaming six-foot logs. I took off socks and washed my feet as well as most of my body. On this trip, at the end of each day, I never once neglected my bath. Feeling cleaned-up that way kept me in trim and was worth all the effort. When we first camped out in winter, despite J.'s well-founded advice about how to keep comfortable in the Arctic, I thought it impossible to bathe with any real thoroughness out of doors in sub-zero temperatures; I used consequently to reach a miserable state of grime and mustiness.

But this trip, our longest winter trip of all, was a good one. I seemed to be hard as nails and recuperated after a tough day in a way that surprised even J. I have learned so many little useful wrinkles — such as forcing myself to wash in snow water each evening — which make winter camping a hundred times easier and pleasanter. I can get rested now at night, no matter how hard and cold the bed, by lying close between the warm bodies of J. and Rex. I was sorry when this trip was nearly over — though I'm usually eager to get back to the bliss of the cabin.

Early the next afternoon, after climbing some four thousand feet through soft snow which we estimated to be about fourteen feet deep, we reached the top of the pass and made tea. We then traversed a sloping series of meadows some two and a half miles across to the east side and our old summer camp site. There was not a track or a single sign of a mountain animal anywhere over the whole open white expanse. Except for marmots, mice, and lemmings that stay far beneath the snow, the Indians have told us that all mountain animals move down in winter to the belts of timber and the valleys; bears to hibernate, wolves and caribou to feed in the lowlands. Mountain goats descend to the first line of trees where they subsist on bark and shrubs not completely covered by snow.

William and J. began to hunt a camping place, and I thought how wonderful it would all be under the full winter moon. But after some time, J. said that both he and William believed we could get down the mountain and across the valley to Tetana that night; there was really not enough dry wood here, there was no good camping place, the snow was too deep, we had seen everything — in short, why not make a final effort and get back to the cabin, good food, and warm beds? I gave him and William one stare, saw that they were both in earnest, and quite obviously determined.

"You're just like the Indians," I said to J. bitterly; "the minute you turn your nose toward home you've got to get there, no matter what!" And I stalked off, too angry and disappointed to bear the sight of either of them.

Besides having long wanted to spend a moonlit night in winter on the mountains, I really didn't know whether I could climb four thousand feet down the mountain again and six miles across country by night. But J. came after me and was so sweet and persuasive that I made up my mind I'd do my darnedest to make home without further fuss. Then William appeared suddenly, dragging a huge black bearskin. It was one of the grandest I've ever seen, purple-black, glossy, in perfect condition. He had killed the bear on the mountain the previous summer and left it pegged out on a stretcher. He was, he said, making me a present because I was tired! I couldn't see how we were to carry it on top of our already heavy packs. Since it had been safe there all winter, I thought we might leave it until spring, but J. wouldn't risk anything happening to such a wonderful fur, and said he would handle it. In addition, he and William were also taking the material from Wahoo's pack.

Off we went, starting at once down the almost perpendicular open slope. Though William, who charted the trail, made zigzags, they were so steep that it was almost as bad as going straight down. I couldn't keep my balance standing upright. The only thing to do was sit and slide, using the snowshoes as a sort of toboggan.

I don't think I have ever been more scared! Time and again, I thought I was going to fly straight off the mountain. I went so fast that I could hardly ever pause and recover at the end of a zigzag, or listen to shouted directions from J. way down below me. The full moon, gold and enormous, had come up and was shining straight in our faces, but the silvered valley far below, and the flying snow, were more like something in a nightmare than in reality. I don't think I did see them until we reached the first line of timber some thousand feet below. Rex and Wahoo were also there safe and sound, though we had never once been able to think of them or see how they fared.

As we started down through the timber there came a soft "hook-hook, hook, hook," and there, just ahead on the bare, slim post of a small dead tree was the little black figure of a pygmy owl, silhouetted against the moon. William was pleased. He said, "We see that little owl here sometime. Lots in Caribou Hide country. Lots of story about him. He bring good luck."

How J. and William found the way, six miles across country through dense forest, without trail or blazes or adequate light, I can't imagine. The trees were thick; most of the time we traveled in darkness, though brilliant moonlight filtered through high branches and made ghostly shadows. It was not light enough to see our snowshoes and we stumbled repeatedly. J. and William, consulting on directions, climbed occasional trees to watch the position of the mountains behind. In two hours we came out on the banks of the river and there (why yes, it really was) lay the old log jam, every stick of which is familiar. We had struck the river just right and were a bare mile from home.

By our watches it was 11 P.M.; *I* thought we'd been traveling just about all night!

Well, it had been a wonderful ending to a wonderful trip — the most wonderful trip we had had thus far in all this wonderful country. . . .

CHAPTER XV

Camping on the Driftwoods

Tetana   *April 1*

We left on March 25th for a short trip to the central part of the Driftwood Mountains, where the great, deep gorges and indentations lie. This has always looked to be the most precipitous section of the whole range, and it was a part that neither of us had visited. On the return from Blue Lake we saw wolf tracks along the mountainside at five thousand feet and thought there might be a chance of seeing wolves themselves in the open.

To take actual photographs of the great timber wolf in the wilds is one of the foremost objects of all our trips this year. We haven't the slightest idea whether there's any real chance of success. The Indians haven't thought so. Many wonderful close-ups of nearly every other big game animal have been taken, but none, as far as we know, of the North American timber wolf. If we could get them, it would be the best feather of all in our caps.

In summer this section of the Driftwoods has looked difficult or impossible to reach, for below there is an extra wide belt of willow swamp and a jungle-like balsam grows on all the eastern slopes. But by going before the snow began to soften, we could travel on snowshoes above the impenetrable undergrowth. We wanted to camp part way up, above the deep forest and just below the big wall of precipices. We had to be off at once because, by April, the snow slides begin and from then until June the Indians avoid the vicinity of all mountains.

After crossing the river and traversing endless numbers of steep, thickly forested ridges we began really to climb. Hard crust made it very slippery. Rex and I, the most lightly loaded members of the party, managed fairly well. By digging a foothold with my toes at each step, and clinging with both hands, I succeeded in getting up; but J., with snowshoes and pack twice the size of mine, could scarcely find footholds at all. After violent exertions, he would get halfway up a slope only to slip and go down again, backwards. Wahoo climbed by dashes. He almost would reach the top, then, squeaking and moaning, back *he* would slide all the way to the bottom. More than once I dumped my load and went down to help haul both J. and Wahoo. When we finally got up through the thickest timber, the slopes leveled off a little and we came to a belt of open trees, wonderful balsam, towering far over a hundred feet, the biggest that we've seen in this whole country. And in years past there had been a race there of real giants for the ends of very old fallen logs measured five and six feet across.

As soon as we reached this belt, which was about a quarter of a mile wide, black-headed jays (a subspecies of Steller's) began to follow us, their metallic, dark peacock-blue bodies glittering in the light as they flew from tree to tree. They seemed to be nearly as curious and as tame as their relatives, the whisky-jacks, but the calls of the black-headed jays are hoarse and raucous rather than clear and musical.

We came at once on the perfect camping place in a small open meadow just above the belt of balsams. Under dense sheltering branches of a big fir was an open space, almost free of snow, large enough to hold our tiny tent and a good-sized fire, and still leave space to stand without snowshoes. In front, twenty feet away, an open mountain brook purled along through snow mounds six feet deep, that looked like gigantic white iced cakes. Just behind, sheer thousand-foot rock precipices rose into the sky, but our particular meadow was not in direct line with the steepest parts. A little hill joined onto the mountain-side directly back of us would, we figured, cut off slides from our camping place.

Huge, apparently stable slides — mixtures of snow and rocks and earth — spread out fanwise from the mountain at regular intervals. Our meadow was just midway between two of these and, from the condition of the trees, one could see that there had been no big slide just there for many years. It seemed, that slides occur almost always in definite fixed spots.

As we sat cooking supper, we were surprised and charmed to hear a familiar little tinkly song along the brook. We left the steaming frypan near the fire and went to look. There, sure enough, were two tiny winter wrens, with perky upturned tails, hopping merrily along the huge snowbanks. First heralds of the spring migration.

We spent the next day exploring the mountainside and looking for wolves. Several huge tracks, very fresh, were along the edge of our little meadow. Wolves had evidently been viewing our camp in the night or early morning. Much of the surface snow here was hard enough so that Rex and Wahoo, to their surprise and delight, could run freely on top instead of having to follow our snowshoe tracks.

In June '39, some miles south of there at a lower height, J. found the damaged skull, hair, bones, and toenails of a wolverine. These were surrounded by the skeleton of a moose. It is questionable whether a full-grown wolverine could successfully attack and kill a full-grown moose, but the position and condition of both wolverine and moose remains indicated that the animals must have died at about the same time. Possibly both died from wounds, or possibly the moose was finally killed by wolves. However, the condition of the moose bones and skull, which had been left undisturbed, did not seem to bear out the latter supposition. Wolverines are apparently rare in the Driftwood Valley, but not uncommon north of Bear Lake, especially in the Tatlatui and Thutade districts; the majority of wolverine skins that are traded at the posts around here come from these areas.

One small rounded peak, jutting out a mile south of us, didn't appear to be impossibly steep. If only we could get up to it, I thought, we could see down into the deep gorge which, from Tetana, looks so fascinating. J. preferred to explore lower down, so he and Wahoo wandered along at five thousand feet, while Rex and I began to start slowly up. Before we could climb the little peak we had to cross one of the fanlike snowslides, a sort of miniature glacier with irregular ridges, and hollows in between almost like real crevasses. It seemed firm enough, but I was scared of something giving way and tested every step. We got safely across but found that, in order to reach even the foot of the peak, we'd have to climb up a long steep slope through thick stunted trees. The snow through these trees had slid down and piled up and hardened into a slippery perpendicular wall. It looked rather impossible but, having come this far, I wasn't going to give up that peak without a struggle. Hanging from tree to tree, I hauled myself and my big snowshoes up and up. Rex, at my heels, was climbing like a little goat, but I had occasionally to give him a pull to keep him from going over backwards.

We were halfway up and the top was well in sight, when *the world moved under us*. It was the most sickening feeling! I almost let go my hold. Was the whole mountainside going to slide? The sharp movement stopped, but it seemed that the great wall of snow and trees still quivered. I thought no more of going on up. My one idea was to get down, away from this awful, unstable wall of snow before it moved again. I kept telling myself that I had trees to catch if the wall did give way, but how could I hold to Rex?

We both got down, somehow, though getting down was far more precarious than getting up. I was never more thankful in my life than when, after going halfway across the bottom of another fan slide beyond the snow and tree wall, we saw J. and Wahoo not far away.

"I knew you couldn't get far!" said J.

"Well, for Pete's sake, if you knew what it was like, why did you let me go?"

J. grinned at me. "I have some faith in your common sense! Anyhow when you're bound to get somewhere, you never listen to me. The only way to convince you is to let you see for yourself."

That night was brilliantly clear. But it was mild, and a sweetness in the sharp mountain air spoke of spring. As we lay on our bed by the warm fire, we watched the stars flashing above the sheer wall of cliffs. Once, far to the south, there was a deep thunder that echoed and reverberated along the mountainside. The warm sun of the previous day was melting snow; slides were beginning.

"We'd better go home tomorrow," said J. I was reluctant to leave our comfortable camp, but I agreed.

Long after dark, as we all lay close together on the hard pungent bed, a hardness and a pungency which I have learned to like and welcome, we heard bird voices below us in the eastern sky, passing north along the mountainside. They were not far off; and we could distinguish the separate high clear notes of two whistling swans. Odd to hear birds in sky *below* us. Two more heralds of the spring, we said, and went to sleep, happy and secure.

The next day as we traveled slowly down through the thick balsam belt, we heard the familiar little "hook-hook" of two pygmy owls. We spent an hour calling them and trying to get them close enough for pictures. From the way they came almost up to us and followed us about, we were sure they must have thought two more owls had joined them. But they kept high up in the giant trees and never once could we see them clearly enough to photograph. They behaved like a mated pair and we're almost convinced that pygmy owls breed on the Driftwoods below timber line.

April 30

Once again we're living through a far northern spring, and the wonders of the migrating birds. Most of the same species have been coming through that came in 1938, but there is considerable variation from that year in the dates of arrival, a much greater variation — say several weeks — than is found usually in migrants of the Eastern United States, where the same individual birds often arrive at the same place on the same date year after year. Since this is only our second early spring here we have no way of telling whether this variation is normal. We should be here for five or six springs at least.

The same kinds of ducks that we saw in 1938 have appeared

in approximately the same numbers, but the swans have
dwindled seriously. So far we've seen only four trumpeters,
which came through on April 11th, as against several hundred
in '38.

The four trumpeters landed on Tetana over toward the west
marsh and stayed for an hour. Their gorgeous white graceful-
ness, shining in the early morning sun against the background
of black forest and white mountain, seemed like a fairy tale.
Somehow I am still not quite able to associate the actual sight
of white swans with a dark northern wilderness. When we
tried to steal close enough for a picture, they were up, rising
slowly and beautifully, shaking great, sparkling showers from
their big bodies, sounding their soft, deep, exquisite trumpets.
I'm glad that I have heard again the music of trumpeter
swans.

Our dugout canoe is stored at Takla. When J. left here in
'39 he arranged for Michelle to bring it back up the river, but
of course it was never brought. Since we must have a boat, J.
has made a new one, a little skiff, out of exactly five boards
of lumber that were left over from the roof. It is barely large
enough to hold the two of us, but it is quite watertight and
otherwise efficient. J. also made good lightweight oars out of
dry seasoned pine.

May 12

We've just returned from a quick five days' trip all the way
to Carl's and Bear Lake, having gained nothing but a cracked
rib for J. — our first casualty. We heard some time ago that a
plane was expected at this time to take out Carl. We had
important mail to send, and we particularly wanted Carl to try
to get us some dental cement for mending teeth and fillings.

Several weeks ago the whole cap which had covered a badly
broken tooth of J.'s broke off completely. Recalling the awful
abscess which had once forced J. to go three hundred miles out
to Prince George and knowing what it would mean if we both
had to go out now, we were wild. But no terrible toothache has
developed, the worst result being that the sharp edges of the

broken tooth keep cutting J.'s cheek. We tried to fasten the cap on again with cement used for mending things. The cap came off at the first bite. Finally I suggested liquid solder which we use for filling holes in pots and pans. And this works, with moderate success. That is, the cap stays on for some days at a time, or until J. forgets and bites on something hard. At any rate we never take a trip now away from home without including solder in our essential equipment.

We reached Carl's in a day and a half, traveling all the way up Bear Lake on soft bare ice, only to find that he had been expecting the plane in long ago, but it had never come. He didn't know what had happened; he might have to hike out or go by canoe, but, if and when he ever did get out, he would try to procure some cement for J. and bring it back with him.

We camped for two nights on a point half a mile south of Carl's. This was mostly free of snow and had on either side of it two small streams dashing into the lake. Everywhere, the ice for some ten yards off shore was soft and partly under water, so that in order to reach firm ice out on the lake we had to take flying leaps on our snowshoes through water and slush. On one of these leaps, the toe of J.'s snowshoe went down through several inches of soft ice and caught, the heel sprang up to his side, and his body was given a terrific wrench. He stood knee-deep in water clutching at his chest, and for fear of our both going clean under, I dared not go out to him. When he got back finally to the tent he said a rib, already broken several times, had snapped again. But he'd traveled with a broken rib before and could get back to Tetana. If he had to be laid up for a bit he infinitely preferred to be laid up in our own cabin.

So the next day we started back, camping for one night at the south end of Bear Lake. J. seemed able to walk sufficiently well, but suffered much in the night. His side is very painful and sore to touch, but he is sure it's not a clean break. Probably only a crack or slight fracture. Now that he has been several days resting at home he seems almost recovered again, except for great local soreness.

June 2

We've had about ten days of floods but they have now begun to subside and, almost before we thought of expecting them, Johnny French's boys and Charlie's William, who had been at Takla, arrived with the two horses, Baldy and Lassie, which we are going to use on the mountains this summer.

This is the second time in this country that anyone or anything has come on schedule (Mother and Dad appearing in early June three years ago was the first). We become so accustomed to giving every event at least several weeks' leeway that when it does occur on a planned date, we have the annoyed sensation of a guest arriving inopportunely way ahead of time.

The boys stayed a day or so, and when they left we began to adjust ourselves to the two new additions to our family. Baldface is large and tan and rawboned ("A bit too thin," J. said to the boys when he was paying them off) ; he has one blue eye and one brown, and his big, almost white, face accounts for his name. But I think that if we can get him fattened up, he may be rather handsome. There is something beautiful and noble about his poses and the way he tosses his head when he's startled. Lassie is small and black and fat and has several raw places on her back from carrying a pack when the boys brought her. Apparently the Indians have hardly used her at all, she is so skittish. They claimed she was so nervous they could hardly get a pack on her. J. was annoyed at the sores because sores mean that a horse shouldn't be used again until they heal, and sometimes this takes weeks.

He began at once to feed both horses tidbits and put salt out by the back door, but he left them loose to graze. They apparently remember him and this place perfectly. Leaving them free seemed rash, but as J. says, they couldn't possibly get enough to eat from the rather sparse grass if they were tied. He had no trouble with their running off during the previous summer. Baldy never went far and Lassie was so dependent on Baldy that she never left him.

The first day, while J. was off woodcutting, I was to watch the horses who were grazing round the cabin, and head them off if, by any chance, they started along the path toward Trail Lake. Once, leaving them placidly feeding on top of the bank, I went to the cabin to get something, and when I came out they were headed east, Lassie leading and Baldy following, and they were moving slowly, feeding as they went, down the path toward Trail Lake and Takla. It was an awful moment! If I started behind it would just drive them on in the wrong direction. Since the path is bounded on one side by Tetana, on the other by the high steep bank leading up to Teddy's Hill, there was nothing to do but climb the hill, cautiously so as not to startle them, and come down beside or in front of them. As I climbed, they moved faster. I called; good old Baldy paused, lifted his head, and looked at me, and then I got down the bank just in time, caught his halter, and started leading him toward the cabin, trusting that Lassie would follow — which she did.

When J. came back we decided that it was too risky to leave them loose near the cabin again and J. took them to the meadow. There was so much good grass there he thought they'd stay. Anyhow, if they didn't, we'd hear Baldy's bell coming back and could go out and stop them. Lassie had no bell, but certainly wouldn't go without Baldy.

I had an uneasy night, half listening for the bell. Every so often, when the wind set in that direction, it would tinkle faintly in the distance. The next morning when J. went to the meadow there was Baldy, but no Lassie! We waited all day hoping she might have just wandered off and would hear Baldy's bell and come back. Baldy raised his head and listened and whinnied anxiously, but there was not a sign. Finally, that evening, just to confirm our worst suspicions, J. followed the path all the way to the Takla trail. It was dark when he got back.

"She's gone all right," he called. "Saw her prints a couple of times before I hit Trail Lake; then I went farther and saw them heading straight south along the Takla trail at a smart clip. She must have gone by the cabin in the night. She's at Takla now, if she hasn't been mired in a mudhole or mauled by a bear. Hell's bells! The little fool — !"

We can't now, with the time at our disposal, take a trip of some hundred and fifty miles to Takla and back. We can only trust that someone will see her, *if* she got there safely and, hoping to get good pay out of it, may bring her back eventually.

At our cabin Baldy comes to the back door every few hours to visit and get a rub and a tidbit. He eats anything — bread, meat, fruit, and above all sweet things. He especially likes the dogs' food of corn meal and flour and trout. And when I go out with the big pot of their supper, Baldy almost treads on me or knocks the pail out of my hand. With him and the dogs all pushing and milling about, neighing and barking, the evening meal is a precarious business. When we eat, he comes to the door and stands puffing and blowing gently, soft nose wedged against the screen. Sometimes he gets his front feet in over the doorsill, and once when we let him come in all the way, he behaved with perfect propriety. Baldy and the dogs have become great friends and, on occasion, rub noses together. Baldy is scrupulously careful not to step on them, even when, as frequently happens, they come dashing out of the bushes right under his feet.

When Johnny's boys came they brought word that a plane is expected to go up to Carl's around the twelfth. We sent out a list of orders to replenish our food supplies, requesting that if possible the plane bring them in when it comes for Carl and dump them at the south end of Bear, so we can pick them up with the horses (!). By William we sent word to old Charlie that we expect to be camping at the south end of Bear around the twelfth; if he sees a big smoke to come down with his small dugout, for which we will pay rent if he'll let us use it for the week or so that we're there. We want to explore along Bear Lake, trap for small mammals and collect any new birds, frogs, fish, and plants. William said the whole family at that time might be in the "summer cabin" up the lake. We also arranged with William for him and one of the other boys to go with

us up on the Driftwoods three weeks from now and stay there
to help hunt and collect. He seems glad of the prospects of a
job.

South End of Bear Lake   *June 14*

We reached here the eleventh, J., Rex and Wahoo, Baldy
and I, and are camping on the old site. Though black flies are
here, there are hardly any mosquitoes. Either they don't breed
much or the winds, sweeping down the big stretch of water, are
too strong for them. Mosquitoes were just beginning around
Tetana, much earlier than our previous summer. If our supplies come in by plane we may have food enough to stay here
for a week or more; and then, when we get back to Tetana,
we'll be starting soon from there for the mountains. By
these maneuvers we should avoid the worst of the mosquito
menace.

Although the Indians have always said that there's "plenty"
of grass for horses at this end of Bear Lake, we found the little
grass plot was barely enough to feed Baldy for a night. We've
scouted the country, and there is no other big grassy place anywhere. So we have had to leave him in a swampy meadow down
toward Bunshaw at least two and a half miles away. Worst of
all we have to tether him because we can't risk his wandering
off in a strange country or going back toward Tetana. Every
day one of us takes the five-mile walk there and back to visit
him, let him loose for a while, and then tie him in a new place
where he'll get feed and be able to reach water, and yet not
tangle his long rope around stumps or bushes. We're more
than uneasy about him because if he gets into trouble we can't
hear his bell; and if bears or wolves go for him, it would be
difficult for him, tied as he is, to defend himself.

Baldy, we have discovered, is an expert botanist. In addition
to grass, there is a definite list of certain plants which he eats in
large quantities — lupine, Solomon's-seal, horsetails, certain
species of Epilobiums, and buttercups. These he will pick, with
unerring accuracy, with dainty pink velvet lips, out of a mass
of other plants, and he never apparently makes a mistake!

Already he seems a beloved friend to us all. In his wisdom and ability to carry a load without getting into trouble, he is like Ben's old Bill, but he is more responsive to human beings, far more affectionate and companionable.

Johnny French's boy said, "That horse he pretty near talk! He haul logs for my father. That horse he know everything; he do everything hisself. My father, he only put the rope round the log. Then Baldy bring it in all hisself. Then he come back for more. Even, he know what logs to bring!"

As soon as we made camp the first day we went to the jutting rocky point a mile up the lake and started a big smoke fire. That very evening after supper as we sat on the bank watching the mountains towering up across the lake and enjoying the lovely, long twilight, to our pleased surprise, around a bend drifted Charlie and Selina and their three youngest in Charlie's big boat which was towing the dugout.

They all got out and sat round our fire for some while. Charlie and J. talked; Selina and I smiled and nodded and enjoyed the antics of the children, whose brown merry faces peeped at us from behind trees. They are much less shy of J. and me than they used to be. They were all chewing wild parsnip. Selina, who had a big bunch of it, peeled the green, purple-splotched stems and handed them one by one to the children. She also put some by our tent for us to eat if we wanted. And Charlie gave us two big lake trout, caught on the way down, which were most welcome. They have not been back to the Bear Lake settlement for weeks and knew nothing of planes or supplies for us.

Charlie said we might keep the canoe as long as we wanted. He told us to make another smoke the evening before we left, so that he would know when to come and get it again. He politely waived all question of rent, but we'll give him a big present next time he comes to Tetana, or send it up by the boys.

Charlie and Selina have never been nicer or more friendly. Perhaps now we are all really beginning to understand each other.

Bear Lake   *June 18*

We're taking today off from Natural History to recover from quite an adventure. Yesterday we decided to paddle up the east shore and explore all the bays and backwaters that we have heretofore seen only from a distance. Charlie's dugout, though as big as ours, is considerably more tippy and, since we always take Rex and Wahoo, we have to be extra careful not to upset. We took food for a light meal, meaning to supplement it with fish caught along the way. During the morning, the dogs lay still in the wet bottom of the canoe and we fished for lake trout. We had a late lunch on a tiny island. While J. continued fishing (we need fish badly for dog food) I cleaned one that we already had, roasted it on a stick over a fire, and made cocoa. Then we went on to a large point where Carl, when he first came to Bear Lake years ago, built a little store and cabin. But now, except for a framework of logs sticking up through gigantic weeds and bushes, and the fact that there is a slight opening in the endless miles of forest, man might never have been there.

As the afternoon wore on the weather looked far from settled. If we had been sensible, we would have started on the three-hour paddle back down the lake to camp, cooked late supper, and gone to bed. But there was the great unexplored eastern arm of Bear Lake, five or six miles wide, opening up just before us. And from this eastern arm led a narrow fiord winding back among the mountains. This fiord was a place we had long wanted to see. None of the Indians, except Sapolio, seemed to know it. We had come at last to within a few miles of it. The northern June twilight lasted till eleven-thirty. What matter if we didn't get home till late and went without supper? We could always paddle in the dark. Baldy had been visited that morning.

So we went on, following the shore line for miles until we reached the entrance of the little fiord. And then we must paddle along it for a short way anyhow, and the farther we went the more we wanted to keep on. For it was magnificent, an

utterly new type of scenery for this country. It was like a little
arm of the sea, narrow (about a quarter of a mile across), and
deep and dark and wild. It wound toward the south for miles
between high steep hills on the west, covered to the water's
edge with jungle balsam forest and devil's-club ("Looks just
like parts of Alaska," J. said), and, on the east, endless forma-
tions of sheer rock cliffs which rose about fifteen hundred feet
straight up to the flat-topped southeastern Bear Lake Mountains. Two pairs of eagles screamed overhead. The ones farthest
up along the cliffs we took to be golden; those just above the
fiord were the bald. They had a nest with young eaglets in it
at the top of a huge balsam poplar leaning out over the water.
As our canoe passed silently below the tree, both parents
hovered anxiously just above, their great spread wings and
white heads catching the afternoon light that bathed the rock
cliffs but which never reached down into the deep, winding
waters where we were. We took turns paddling and watching
through field glasses for goats on the cliffs, and soon we located
a whole family of them. An old billy was feeding by himself a
short distance from the nanny goat and two tiny kids who
were on a ledge just wide enough to hold them, that dropped
for hundreds of feet into the narrow belt of forest along the
water's edge. Though the cliffs looked near and perfectly clear,
as though one could step out of the canoe and touch them, they
must in reality have been far from us, for we could barely see
the goats with the naked eye.

We had constantly to caution the dogs, who were trembling
with excitement, to lie still; two wet quivering black noses were
lifted high, as new scents came at every breath. Constant movements and cracklings were in the thick forest on our right, and
J. got his big gun ready. But the growth was so dense we never
saw a thing.

"We ought to turn back," said J. warningly, "you'll be too
tired to paddle home; don't think I could make it paddling
alone — "

"I'm not a *bit* tired! We can paddle all night and stop and

Mountain Goat

J. F. Nov
1937

rest all along the way. We just can't turn now! I'm sure the next bend is the last — "

It was two more long bends, and then we were looking at a spectacle that made us cry out. A great, foaming, tossing, leaping cataract of white water, hurled across a sloping incline of rock into the end of the fiord. The cataract came from a lake just above. Below it, in eddies and whirls which flattened into quiet water, the biggest lake trout we had ever seen were leaping clean out in great silver arcs, snapping at insects which hung low over the surface in the still evening air.

J.'s eye glittered. He began reaching for his rod. And he said no more about going back. Nor did I, knowing our need of meat. But I persuaded J., before he started fishing, to land so that we could walk above the cataract and look out on the new lake. Landing, without upsetting in the swift water, and climbing up into dense undergrowth, was quite a trick. The growth was so thick everywhere that we could catch glimpses of only one arm of the lake, which appeared to be large and winding. We thought it might be one which Sapolio crosses by snowshoe on the way to his trap line and winter camp. Judging by the mountains it lies well north of the lake J. and I reached when we had followed Sapolio's trail.

J. would not let me or the dogs linger. We could smell bears everywhere. Thickets like this, where one can't see a yard and the noise of a roaring cataract shuts out all sounds, are dangerous, especially at a place where bears obviously congregate to fish. The dogs were scared and stuck to us like leeches. When we were all safely back in the canoe, we paddled to the edge of the swift water, and in no time at all J. had caught three trout, eight to ten pounds each, one right after the other, by casting at spots where the fish were leaping. I was just getting ready to try a cast or two when it suddenly began to pour, a hard pelting shower that lasted half an hour and soaked us all to the skin. When it cleared again clouds of mosquitoes descended and almost smothered us. The dogs began to grow restless — they had been miraculously patient sitting dead-still under the hard rain and only moving slightly under the onslaught of insects that settled on their ears and eyes and noses. We too began to realize how tired we were and decided that if we were to reach camp at all that night we must start back.

We paddled north along the little fiord (it must have been four to five miles long). Soon we should reach the last point and then we would have to cross five miles of big open bay before we could start down the lake again. Black, heavy clouds were piled in the north, but it was perfectly quiet in the little fiord. We rounded the last sharp point and, before we could even turn, struck head on into the full force of a terrific squall — a rush of inky-black water and a white swirl that lifted the canoe.

"*Keep her head on!*" shouted J.

In one minute we were out from all shelter in a big sea of high, wicked waves. No time to turn and head for shore, no time to do anything but paddle for our lives, to keep the bow from turning and the precariously balanced little dugout from going over. Nothing to do but keep on heading out into the bay farther and farther from shore. Every ounce of J.'s powerful body went into each perfectly timed stroke, every ounce of my strength went into holding the bow straight. We shouted at the dogs to keep still. One single, panic-stricken move from either of them, and we should be done. We should be done anyway, if we couldn't head for shore.

It seemed that at times there was a lull in the fierce wind, but there was no letup in the waves, higher than our heads.

"If the wind dies a second I'm going to try to turn her. Be ready!" J.'s shouted words were tossed off by the gale so quickly I only just caught them.

"Turn," he yelled, just as we got in a wide trough between two waves. With one gigantic sweep he turned us and we were almost around when the wave was on us. The edge of it washed over us, but we were fully about before the crest came, and were heading diagonally toward the shore line a half mile distant. A new squall from a slightly different direction came behind and drove us heavily toward the steep rocky shore.

We were almost there. Wahoo, his control suddenly at an end, stood up . . .

"Jump, Teddy."

I was out, over my waist in ice-cold water, and had caught the bow just as it hit a high rock partly awash. At the same instant Wahoo leaped, though Rex, absolutely obedient, stayed motionless till we called him.

J., in up to his chest, was pushing the canoe through rocks toward the bank.

"Just in time," said he; "Wahoo'd have had us over in one more second!"

It had started to rain again and was almost dark. One of our watches had stopped, but the other said ten-thirty. We grabbed up the axe and gun and cameras, a fish, a nearly empty can of cocoa, and headed up into the forest. We couldn't have struck a much more inhospitable spot. We were on a fairly steep incline covered with balsam and devil's-club and all manner of dense bushes. We tried to push up as far inland as we could, away from the force of the wind. It was dense black in the deep woods. Shivering from cold and fatigue we stopped on the lee side of a huge tree and began to grope round for dry wood. We both had matches in waterproof cases. I couldn't feel a dry stick anywhere, but J. came back dragging a dead log which, though dripping wet, was dry inside. With his big knife he cut hunks and chips and we had a fire, feeble and sizzling at first, but gradually brighter and warmer. We made a sort of windbreak of branches and bushes, undressed, and wrung out our clothes. At first I was perfectly sodden. But gradually I began to feel as if I were made of firm flesh again. While J. was crashing about and looking for firewood I groped my way down to the shore and filled a kettle which I took back to boil. By the uncertain light of the sizzling fire, constantly wet with new gusts of rain, I partially cleaned a fish, speared it on a stick, and set it to cook. We had enough cocoa left for four small cups. One each now, and one for morning.

Between struggles with the fire we ate as much as we could of the half-cooked unsalted fish and gave the rest to the shivering dogs. Hot cocoa, without sugar or milk, was better. A small old stump, laid across the fire, had caught at last and was sending out a feeble but steady heat. Though the rain had abated into a drizzle, the wind seemed as high as ever. The great trees creaked and moaned and roared far above our heads. It was midnight and we figured that before dawn the wind would die for a while. As soon as it did, we would start and cross the bay. If the storm rose again we should then be headed down the lake and could paddle close off shore with wind at our backs. We must reach food and shelter and go to Baldy as the storm might last for days. We were to take turns feeding the fire and watching the wind.

But before we knew it, we were both fast asleep. Had anyone told me that, cold and wet and aching all over, I could sleep soundly on a sickeningly empty tummy, suspended head down over a tree root, I wouldn't have believed it. But, after several hours, I woke in this exact position. J. had fallen partly over a stump; his limp body looked as though it were dead. As I struggled back to consciousness, I realized that I could see forest around me. Daylight, after two hours of the short northern summer night, had come again. Though I could hear waves washing on the rocks, there was a deep quiet in the trees. The wind had stopped.

"Jack, the wind has died — we must go — "

In a second, J. was up, reviving the fire, and collecting our few possessions. I heated water. We had the last of our cocoa, and were loaded in the canoe in half an hour. There were still big waves, but they were not nearly as high, and there was no wind. Nevertheless, we had to paddle with care until we got three miles across the southern end of the bay. It was not raining but was still heavily overcast. The wind began to rise again just as we got headed down; J. thought we had time enough to get the two miles clean across to the west side of the lake where we should be more sheltered.

It took hard paddling, but we made it, and started down the six-mile stretch to camp. I paddled as much as I could, but had to rest every few minutes. So J. had to do a large part all on his own. Instead of having another strong man to help he had only my nearly useless self. He must have felt as rotten as I did, but he only talked cheerfully, and paddled steadily, never ceasing watch on the big following waves, looking ever for rocks and submerged logs, for we kept close off shore.

We reached camp at 5 A.M. Though tempted to go to bed on the instant, we forced ourselves to cook a good meal — hot coffee and our last can of beans. And then, in the dry warm tent, all four of us slept like the dead. It was almost eleven when we woke, and J. was off at once on the five-mile hike to see how Baldy fared. When he came back some two hours later, he reported Baldy O.K., but exceptionally glad to see him.

We have taken stock of our food. If the plane and supplies do not appear we must go home in two more days. That is, unless we wish to live solely on saltless fish. Personally *I* never want to see a lake trout again.

Tetana   *June 24*

Home again but not, I trust, for long — the mosquitoes are devilish. If William arrives on schedule, we should be off to the mountains this week. We had an uneventful trip back. The plane never came and there is still no sign or word of Lassie. We should have food enough to last through the trip on the Driftwoods and then, if no supplies come to Bear Lake for us (though how we'll know whether they have or not is a mystery), we shall have to go to Takla to get enough for the rest of the summer; and also find out the fate of that wretched Lassie. J. says if we don't get her back, our trips will have to be curtailed considerably, because we shan't be able to take the extra two hundred pounds that she would carry. In view of the fact that we have only three months to complete our work on the mountains, this will be a very serious handicap. We expect to go out in September.

In camp on the Driftwood Mountains
at approximately 6000' — *July 2*

William, with Alec, arrived at Tetana last week, full of news
of a number of things.

The first was that a Bear Lake Indian had seen an unknown
white man — said to have come from Takla — heading into
mountain country east of Bear Lake, leading two pack horses,
one of which was "Jack's Lassie for sure!" It was a small black
horse with a white star on its forehead, and very fat. In short,
the horse had all the earmarks of Lassie, and, as horses in this
country are not at all common, it certainly was Lassie. The man
had undoubtedly seen her wandering loose somewhere around
Takla and had just walked off with her. So thought William,
and so thought I. J., more inured to rumors of the Northland,
was noncommittal.

Second, William had recently killed a grizzly and wondered if
we would like to buy the skin? No, they did not have the skull
because it was all smashed. They had seen the grizzly, a female
of medium size, swimming across Bear Lake, had chased it in
the canoe, and, because they had no gun, had killed it by hitting
its head with the axe and chopping into its back and neck.

"By gosh, big fight that. Almost the bear he upset us. He
fight like hell. He try to climb in the canoe. We chop his head
and pound his back. We cut him like wood. The water just
red all over with blood. That bear he neber die long time."

And William smiled and shrugged. I looked at his smooth,
serene, young boyish face, and felt sick.

The third thing was that he and Alec had not brought food
enough to go all the way up on the mountains with us. Worst
of all, they had only one pair of moccasins each and no rubbers
to protect them with; and we knew that no one in this country
can go far in summer on one pair of moccasins. Moccasins used
continuously in rocky country wear through in a day. They wet
through in a few hours; in less than a few days the wearer has
bad feet and is totally unable to travel.

Now all this meant one thing. For some obscure reason, im-

portant or unimportant, the boys, although formerly full of
enthusiasm, just didn't want to go up on the mountains. This
was serious because we could never without their help get
enough food up to enable us to work there the required time.
Since getting to the mountains has been our chief object this
year, we had to take drastic steps.

It all ended, as these affairs usually do, with considerable advantage to the Indians. By supplying all their food, two brand-
new pairs of J.'s own moccasins and socks, with which he could
ill afford to part, and a tent fly, it was finally arranged. The
boys, now full of smiles and interest and obligingness again,
were ready.

They spent a day cutting a trail which Baldy could negotiate
across to the foot of the mountains. New heavy rains had made
the river, which had subsided from spring floods, rise way up
again. Baldy had to swim and the rest of us cross by Charlie's
new big dugout, recently obtained at Takla, and providentially
left at Tetana for a while. About the least dangerous place
seemed to be across the river just above the outlet of the lake.
The two boys, Rex and Wahoo, and I, got in the canoe. We had
to go two hundred yards upriver against the current to land at
a safe place and the start of the recently cut trail. The boys
poled the canoe and I held the end of a long rope to which
Baldy was fastened. J., wading in up to his waist, talking gently
and persuasively, led Baldy slowly out into the deep current, got
him headed upstream, and we were off.

I was petrified. Since J. could not safely climb in the canoe
in deep water, I must hold to Baldy and keep him from being
carried off downriver. It took all of the two boys' strength, and
then some, to pole against the current. In half a second we were
out in cruel fast water, I braced myself and held on with every
ounce of strength as the rope grew taut and good old Baldy,
listening eagerly with pricked ears to our encouraging shouts,
was swimming for his life, straight up the current. William and
Alec worked furiously, their hard young muscles swelled in
great ridges under their thin shirts, the sweat pouring from
their brown faces. Baldy's nostrils were red and distended. He

was going backwards. He couldn't make it! We were across! Baldy's feet had found bottom and, with heaving flanks, he climbed out, shook himself mightily, stood still to catch his breath, and began calmly to nibble at grasses. The panting boys watched him in admiration.

"By gosh! Some strong horse that! He swim right up current; he neber scare, or turn back, or nothing. By gosh, good horse, that one."

The canoe started back for J., and I went to hug Baldy. He pushed at me with his great white nose, and looked at me with a calm, wise, and (was it?) an amused eye that said: —

"My dear girl, you don't suppose, do you, that that's the first flood I've swum? Of course I knew what I was about!"

Up to now I have not really mentioned the mosquitoes. They have been as unspeakably fiendish as ever, but we kept thinking complacently that when we reached timber line on the mountains they would all be left behind. After we left the river and began to cut across through interminable swamps and undergrowth to the foot of the mountain, swarms of mosquitoes, the like of which I never remember, even on the arctic tundras, attacked us. The air was stifling, hot and sticky, and we couldn't breathe through head nets. Mosquitoes settled on us in mats and stung like red-hot needles. We toiled grimly on, each of us carrying a heavy pack, Baldy and the dogs floundering and struggling through mudhole after mudhole. At last we began the steep ascent, following roughly the old, mostly obscured, blazes. The dogs and I, in the rear, fought and struggled with our packs and mosquitoes.

I was afraid Baldy could never get up the nearly perpendicular stretches. At one very bad spot J. climbed up ahead, took Baldy's rope and began to haul hand over hand. Baldy went up in a series of bounds while I, with bated breath, held the dogs and watched from below. Baldy was up the worst, he was turning on a zigzag, he stepped on a rotten log, he struggled agonizingly, he turned a clean backward somersault, and crashed down, down, down, down over rocks, and stumps, and trees, out of sight.

Oh God, oh God, it had happened! I braced against the mountain, hanging on to the whimpering dogs, sobbing and saying I don't know what. J., his face white as a sheet, began to climb down after Baldy. William, tears streaming down his cheeks, crouched on the trail high above.

If Baldy were not already killed he would be suffering horrible injuries and J. would have to shoot him. I waited for the shot. But no shot came and J. was shouting for the boys. I too climbed down, dreading what I must see, but unable not to look. There lay Baldy, on the very brink of a three-hundred-foot drop into a canyon, wedged up against a huge old fallen tree. He had fallen about eight hundred feet and was lying head down at an angle of 45 degrees; his eyes were tight shut; he seemed to be hardly breathing. J. had felt all his legs and said they were not broken. Perhaps he was badly injured inside. If only they could get him up.

"Lift his head," I said, "so the blood won't all run into it —"

J. promptly sat down and lifted Baldy's head onto his knee, talking and patting him lovingly. Then, leaving Alec to hold the dogs out of the way of Baldy's feet in case he started kicking, I went down to him. I had talked to him so often and he had always seemed to like my voice and respond to it —

"Baldy darling, get up. It's all right, you'll be all right, Baldy boy —"

While J. still held his head up William loosened the pack ropes. I spoke to him again and this time he opened his eyes. He looked at me, he kicked. William sprang to the log behind. He and J. heaved and pulled, and Baldy was up. He stood there, quivering.

I held his head and put my face against his and talked and talked, while the men took his pack, already half off, and began feeling him all over. He had one deep scratch far up on one leg, but outwardly showed no other sign of injury. If we could get him to eat that would steady him and perhaps show whether anything was wrong inside. I picked lupine and Solomon's-seal, two of his favorite articles of diet, and held them to his nose.

At first he wouldn't touch them, but presently he began to nibble, then he ate a big bunch. He shook himself mightily, he began to move and hunt food himself.

The two boys, with a greater display of emotion and affection than I have ever seen in any of these Indians, followed him about, hugging him and laughing and talking.

Baldy's pack was terribly ripped; food and tents inside were in a bad state. Strong cans had been bent, some torn open. But it was the pack which had probably saved his life and taken the full force of rocks and trees as he fell.

After a time J. put the almost empty pack back on Baldy, and each of us added various articles to our own loads, leaving the rest to be fetched by the boys later.

Alec surprised me by taking several of my things to add to his already huge pack because, he said, they were too heavy. Alec is a boy whom we have somehow seen less of than the others. When we've gone on trips with old Charlie, Alec has generally been the one to stay at home and care for the family. During the summer when he was out here alone, J. had some trouble with Alec, for he caught him, redhanded, taking things from our cellar. Charlie was apparently surprised and grateful when J., instead of making any great fuss about it, suggested that he send Alec out to school the following winter. This Charlie actually did, and Alec apparently benefited. As J. said, the boy had probably merely done the sort of thing he had seen his elders and betters do — only he was not clever about it and got caught.

Except for the period when our cabin was closed and we were far away, we've had practically no trouble with thefts. When things are actually put in their charge on a long trip, these Indians appear to be scrupulously careful of them. Once a big can of honey disappeared on a trip to Bear Lake. We thought it had probably been taken by a Bear Lake boy who was not a member of Charlie's family. But J., before us all, read Charlie a lecture which the Indians apparently remembered for a long time. J. said that he held Charlie responsible for all our things; that if any of them, even the smallest possession, ever disappeared again, there should be no more work or pay for any of Charlie's family.

After a long tough climb, we reached the top of the pass safely and spread out in the swampy meadow. J. and I made camp in our old spot by the little stream, with the balsam clumps and high peaks at our back. The boys made their camp in another clump of trees beyond the stream. Baldy was turned loose to graze. We were just at timber line. There were strong refreshing cold breezes, *but* the mosquitoes, though not as thick as lower down, were still there! And they have been with us ever since, everywhere, except on high bare peaks.

Baldy feeds uneasily on the poor marsh grass and when the mosquitoes get too much for him comes galloping down the marsh, bell ringing wildly, takes a flying thundering leap clean across the stream, and lands at our tent door. We're always terrified he'll get tangled in the tent ropes, but he never has so far. He always stands full in the heavy smoke from our fire. He sleeps here part of the night, or across in the boys' camp. J., who keeps close watch on the quantity and appearance of his daily stools, says Baldy is not getting enough to eat and that we can't stay here as long as we planned lest Baldy get too pulled-down and in poor condition. After his terrible fall, all of us, even the two boys, seem to love him more than ever and take a profound interest in his welfare. From the way Baldy behaves at night when he's out feeding, bears or moose must frighten him frequently. J. always gets up at dawn to look across the meadow in the hope of seeing game.

The songbirds here are wonderful. Hermit and gray-cheeked thrushes throw their notes like silver bells all around us every dawn and evening. The hymn of the hermit thrush is, as ever, the most supremely beautiful of all. Dozens of winter wrens, along the mountain streams, pour out icy, tinkly strings of music all day long. Big, bright, red-brown fox sparrows, which I have heretofore known only in migration, are nesting everywhere. They have a loud, rich, clear, whistling song.

Well above timber line Gambel's and golden-crowned sparrows, with their achingly sweet, plaintive calls, nest around every clump of stunted little trees. And, surprisingly, the common robin nests there also. But only a few Townsend's solitaires are in evidence and we have never once heard one singing. After J.'s descriptions of the glorious music of the solitaires which were common here in '38, I'd been looking forward to them especially. Possibly it is too late in the season for them; but since other birds are still in full song this seems unlikely.

Above the last clumps of bushes, in the open rocky meadows, are the flocks of white-tailed ptarmigan and the little larks. All the bright green grassy pockets, watered by tiny mountain streams or melting snowbanks, are gay with color. There are beds of deep pink Epilobiums, purple lupines, blue forget-me-nots, and yellow Potentillas. Many, like the deep blue gentians, bluebells, pink moss campions, and thick leaved red-flowered Sedums, grow in drier places and peep out along rock crevasses.

We've been exploring the northern ridge which, though much less high and precipitous than the southern one, is very satisfying. Passing through a dense belt of small balsams along the mountainside, one comes suddenly every half mile or so into a grassy, flower-filled little meadow with a crystal stream flowing through it. Through openings everywhere are mountain peaks, close and high and colorful under the dazzling sky.

We've looked everywhere for dry upland meadows that might be good for Baldy. But none of them is big enough to supply more than one good meal.

Every afternoon is devoted to skinning specimens and pressing plants. This means hours of back-breaking toil, crouched inside our tiny tent, smoke blowing through and smarting our eyes. No matter how careful we are with the netting, a few mosquitoes and flies always get in. Flies attack the smelly bloody skins; mosquitoes attack one's neck, or ear, or arm just as one reaches the crucial and most difficult part of the job. So far we've caught mostly meadow and white-footed mice. J. does bird collecting while I collect plants. Since many of the birds congregate in the densest part of this dense and mosquito-filled upper forest, bird collecting is a far from pleasant occupation. The tiny winter wrens, unlike winter wrens at home, don't stick to stream banks and low brush heaps. They all seem to do their singing from the very top of thick tall trees. After hours of stalking, J. has killed three, only to have them fall and get caught somewhere in high branches without ever reaching ground.

We'd been here just four days out of the ten days or two weeks allotted for the Driftwoods, when the boys said they must go. This time it's their mother! She's alone with the younger children, their father's away, she has no food. William and Alec must go home to hunt for her, or she will die, maybe!

There is nothing on earth to do but let them go, unless we tie them down by main force. We will just have to carry on by ourselves and get Baldy back down the mountain without help. It's bad for J., who will have to do the work of two strong men. This vacillation on William's part augurs badly for the bigger and harder summer trips to come. William *was* to have been our chief helper and mainstay. There seems to be no one else.

Hunts for game had been fruitless. We had to have meat, or else *all* go home before our collecting was half done. So yesterday, knowing that they would probably be gone in another twenty-four hours, J. insisted that the boys go with him on an extensive all-day hunt along the precipitous south peaks. The dogs and I were to climb on open lower peaks, keeping an eye through field glasses on Baldy in the swampy meadow far below. We were to stay well away from the section where the men were hunting, for in these deceptive mountain atmospheres moving human figures can easily be mistaken for game.

The dogs and I, free to roam at will in the steep uplands, had a marvelous day. We kept to high knolls where winds were strong and cold, and the sun was hot. We ate a few biscuits in the shadow of a big rock and drank from an icy rill. Stretched at full length on dry grass we were just drowsing off, when the mountains around, in every direction, echoed with a deep muffled roar. A shot! Then another shot and another and another and another. The whole mountain range reverberated with a steady thunder. First the shot and then the echo, passing from peak to peak, like a cannon ball bouncing and rolling on, and on, and on, until it receded gradually into distance. The effect, after the great calm wind-swept silences, was terrifying. I counted at least eight distinct shots. Surely nothing but a grizzly would need so many shots from J.'s great rifle or William's .30–30. My glasses, as they swept all round the horizon, drew nothing but motionless peaks. In spite of what J. had said about not going anywhere toward the precipitous part where they meant to hunt, the anxiety and temptation to get a little nearer and perhaps see and hear more were too great. I made the dogs heel and we walked slowly toward the eastern ridges, keeping well down behind the rises.

For fear of being blown off by a sudden gust of wind as we neared the top, and in case guns should be pointing in this direction, I lay flat, and made the dogs lie flat. We all wriggled slowly and cautiously up to the very edge. I peered fearfully over. There was nothing there but the great old mountain with wall-like cliffs and precipices dropping straight down under me for thousands of feet. My glasses showed no sign of figures, dead or moving.

There was a sudden call of "Teddy," so faint it was almost swallowed in the immensity of space. I looked wildly around and then I saw them. Three tiny figures which, even through glasses, looked no bigger than ants. They were at the foot of a snowslide and they were bending over something. All the way down the snow patch was a path of red blood. It must have been a goat. No bear could have been up along those sheer rock walls.

After an hour or two the three little black things, each bent under a load, began to go slowly across the great gorge. The size of the gorge, which had been undiscernible to the naked eye, was now revealed by the tiny moving figures. Through the glasses I watched their steady progress. It took them nearly an hour to get across. Then they disappeared and had begun to climb, I supposed; though how they were to get up out of there I couldn't imagine.

After another hour, when I was beginning to think they all must have fallen and been killed after all, they emerged one by one at the top of a ridge half a mile farther along.

They were loaded with the meat, skin, and head of a large goat. I made comment on the number of shots; said J.: —

"Did you ever try to hit a goat running up a rock wall and leaping through the air from crag to crag? William and I were both shooting! We don't know now whose shot it was that finally got it."

As soon as we were back down at camp we all began to cook meat; we had an orgy of eating. We were so hungry we ate, at one sitting, as much of the goat as we'd intended should last at least two days. Fresh mountain goat meat, unless from a kid, is very tough — think of the muscles required to enable a goat to leap all day up and down mountain precipices — but it has a most delicious flavor. It is a light-colored meat and looks a bit like veal.

The boys have just left. J. and I plan to stay on another five days or a week, according to how our food supply holds out and how Baldy seems. William said if we stay that long they will get back in time to help us down. We all know perfectly well that they won't, but it made possible a graceful exit! They're to pick up any cached supplies that we are unable to take with us, and bring them back to Tetana. When these are all safely brought, they will be paid off for the entire trip!

CHAPTER XVI

The Ominecas

Tetana   *July 14*

Our longest, hardest, and most important trip of the summer is to be on the Omineca Mountains. J. went to the Ominecas in the summer of 1939, and it was there that he got our first really good pictures of big game — some rather remarkable shots of mountain goats, a grizzly bear, caribou, et cetera.

In defiance of a solemn promise made to me, he took, alone and unarmed, fifty feet of a grizzly feeding four yards away. The day before he had shot a mule deer at the foot of the mountains. When he went back to get the meat, there was a brown grizzly, which must have weighed all of nine hundred pounds, lifting a bloody, fly-covered snout from the deer carcass. J. didn't have his rifle (only a small pistol), but he did have the camera. Naturally he took pictures! The bear paid no attention to him and continued its gorging unperturbed. It was very fat and wallowed somewhat in the manner of a tame pig. Every so often it ceased gnawing and gazed at J. When it did this he stopped the camera and looked for the nearest tree. Either the bear was too dazed from the swarms of flies and mosquitoes that attacked it to bother with J., or else, as usual, since it was a grizzly, it refused to be disturbed by just a man. Although grizzlies feed heavily on berries, grubs, and fish they are evidently fond of a red-meat diet also. We have seen considerable evidence which shows that grizzlies dig up marmots on the mountains, and this is confirmed by the Indians.

When Mac and Alec came at last bringing the things down that had been cached on the Driftwoods (William didn't reappear at all — we learned that he had been busy getting married!), we sent a note to Carl inquiring his opinion of Sapolio

Mule Deer

as a possible helper during the Omineca trip. Could he be counted on to stick with us for some weeks? If Carl was at all favorably inclined, and if Sapolio was at all interested, would Carl send him down as soon as possible?

To our pleased surprise Sapolio soon appeared, apparently quite willing to go. He brought a letter from Carl who decidedly recommends him, and since Carl has few good words to say about most of these people, we feel quite hopeful. Now, if we could only get Lassie back (J. is sure he can pack her even if the Indians can't), we may have the chance of making a really successful trip.

It has been decided that J. and Sapolio and Baldy will go to Takla, leaving me and the dogs here. They will make as quick a trip as possible, load up with the necessary summer food supplies, and get hold of Lassie, always supposing she is there to be got hold of! All this will probably take at least a week. And as soon as they return we'll be off for the Ominecas.

For a while, knowing the gamut of feelings which my mind runs through when J. is gone for even a few hours, I believed that the rigors of an exhausting trip to Takla would be preferable to being left alone here for a whole week or more. The reasons that have made me decide against the trip, aside from the fact that I don't in the least want to go to Takla, are that I need a breathing space after the Driftwood trip if I'm to be fit for another, and I'm not able to travel as fast as J. and Sapolio. I should make the Takla trip much longer, and hence seriously delay the Omineca venture. Last, but by no means least, I would pass up my best, perhaps only, chance to know what it really means to live alone.

July 21

J. and Sapolio have been gone six days. Any day, beginning with tomorrow, I am to look for their return.

Always, until now, I've waited to write up an adventure until it was safely over. I'm not really superstitious, but I don't see any sense in taking unnecessary chances. However, this once, I am going to describe an experience while it is actually going on. Except that in the back of my mind during most of my conscious hours there is a nasty nagging little fear, I have not minded being alone at all — so far! It is perfectly astonishing how, without any other human being about, one can adjust one-self to the tasks and events of every day, and like it.

The very fact that I've known I couldn't expect J. for a week at least, plus the fact that he was traveling a well-marked trail, accompanied by a human companion instead of plunging through uncharted country by himself, has made me, for once, almost comfortable about his welfare. And there has been the rather dubiously consoling thought that if he does not come back, I could perhaps travel safely to Takla on my own as I couldn't do in winter or floodtime. Before he left J. made me promise that in case of emergency, I would first try, since it is so much nearer, to reach the south end of Bear Lake, and make smoke fires just on the chance that they might be seen at the settlement fifteen miles up.

Just at noon I always tune in the radio on the short wave to the Takla H.B.C., where, this year for the first time, they have a sending and receiving set. J., who knows quite a bit of Morse code, is often able to understand the messages which Takla sends to other H.B. Posts around noon. I've also learned a little. Before he left he promised that each day while he re-mained at Takla, he would ask the H.B. man at the end of his own message to tap out "J.O.K." three times. In this way I should know that he reached Takla safely. When I ceased hear-ing the letters it would mean that he was on the way home again. But though I've listened each day for a good half hour till I was sure the official Takla business was finished, I have not, until today, been certain that I heard J.'s message. This time I got the letters unmistakably, three times. I feel vastly comforted.

Yesterday was quite exciting. Over by the river log jam where the dogs and I go every afternoon to escape the heat (the temperature has been 96 degrees in the shade), I caught a fish, the first we have caught since early June, and a plane came over. The plane had flown north up the valley earlier in the day, and just as I was wading up to my waist in J.'s big rubber boots and casting in deep water, it came back. It followed the course of the river till it got opposite Tetana, then turned at right angles and headed for the lake, circling very low. It came back toward the river again, flying directly above me, and seemed barely to clear the trees before it rose and was off to the south. And, just before it got over me, I had a strike. A big, lovely Kamloops trout over eight pounds leaped clear of the water three times. In desperate excitement I played him, fearful every second that he would get off and that I should lose him. But I landed him just as the plane came back from Tetana. With the struggling fish under-foot, I waved wildly, convinced that the pilot must certainly have been looking for me. Perhaps he heard at Bear Lake that I am alone, or possibly he even saw J. at Takla and J. asked him to have a look at me; perhaps it was some pilot whom we don't know at all (he didn't waggle his wings as Russ does), and he was merely curious at sight of the cabin.

Anyhow the plane, and my successful battle with the much needed trout, and the radio message today, have been very cheering.

July 23

On the eighth day J. and Sapolio returned from Takla. It was around seven in the morning that I heard the jangling of horse bells over toward Trail Lake, and presently two figures, each leading a loaded horse, came down the path out of the woods. There was Baldy and there was Lassie! And there was Sapolio and there was J.! They had camped at Bear Lake Tom's place, leaving at dawn.

My own little adventure of living alone was over. It didn't seem very big or important after all.

Among other supplies J. brought a case of eggs and while he and Sapolio were consuming, between them, eight fried eggs in a sort of belated breakfast, I recounted my adventures, or rather the fortunate lack of them. Sapolio then retired to make his own camp, and J. told his story.

The heat, after they left Tetana, almost knocked them all, including Baldy, off their feet. They were obliged to travel in the evenings and early mornings and lay off completely during the day. They found no one at Bulkley House, where they turned Baldy loose in Johnny French's big meadow. And the only boat they could discover was an old, very leaky, dugout canoe.

Rather than hike the forty-five miles around by shore to the Landing, they decided to chance paddling. Before they could even float the canoe, however, they were obliged to patch up and seal the large open cracks. This they did with pitch gathered from spruce trunks, which they cooked in an old lard pail and mixed with pieces of cloth torn from their shirts. The dugout still leaked considerably, but they managed to keep going by taking turns at paddling and bailing. It took them all day and part of a night to get the twenty-five miles down the lake in the waterlogged canoe. The only thing that saved them from heat stroke, during some fifteen hours of broiling sun, was a constant wetting of their arms and necks.

When they reached the Landing they learned that Lassie, unharmed, had arrived there the end of May, a few days after Johnny's boys, and she had been running loose with a bunch of horses sixteen miles out of Takla all the rest of the summer. Two days before the plane had gone up to Bear Lake they had a terrific storm — a sort of miniature hurricane — that uprooted huge trees and tore roofs off buildings. J., fearful that we might have had a similar blow at Tetana, had asked the plane pilot (it was not Russ), who had stopped at Takla, to have a look at our cabin and see if he could locate me and the dogs. The pilot reported the cabin O.K. (we had gotten only the very edge of the storm, which had lasted a mere few minutes), but had never seen me or the dogs at all. Thus far Sapolio had proved an excellent and tactful helper. There was no talk of his having to leave for home. Lassie, handled carefully and gently, would make a perfectly good pack horse. She had already carried a big load from Takla without causing difficulties.

This summer a big potlatch and funerals were held at Takla for old Daniel Tegee, and several others, who died last year.

There were games and feasts and much celebrating. It seems an odd time to hold a funeral, but also a practical one, for it is the one time when all the Indians, from a hundred miles around, can gather together. And while they commemorate the dead, they must also have some kind of rejoicing to pay for the arduous journey from such distances. Babine and Takla seem to alternate each year in having the honor of a potlatch and games.

J. attended the one which was held at Takla in 1939, or at least he attended the public games, which he found vastly entertaining. The Bear Lake Indians knew nothing of baseball and such like, but in the tournaments of a game which appeared to be something like poker (except that men were bet instead of cards), the Bear Lake team, of which Sapolio was star, carried off all honors.

J. traveled to the Takla games in company with Charlie's family and others from Bear Lake. Bella had just come through a dangerous confinement which had lasted three days. As nearly as J. could make out, it was ten days after the difficult birth that Bella, on foot, with the tiny new baby on her back, traveled about fifty miles from the south end of Bear Lake to the north end of Takla. It stormed almost every day and J. watched with extreme interest, how Bella managed. After a day of pelting rain the baby was soaked to the skin. As soon as they made camp Bella removed all its clothes, laid it naked by the fire, and allowed the rain to wash it off. After which she wrapped it in dry clothes secreted somewhere about her person, nursed it, and then put it to sleep under a fly or tree. J., who despite wool underwear and shirts was thoroughly chilled by the cold wet nights, noticed that the child was clad only in thin wrappings made of sugar bags and cotton cloths; he asked Bella if in all this cold and wet, she did not want woolen clothing to dress it in. To which Bella replied, with decision, no. Her baby must never have wool about until it got big! Wool would make it weak and would keep it from growing strong.

The baby apparently thrived on this Spartan treatment and is today well and husky.

Camp on the Ominecas at 7000'   *July 28*

On the twenty-fourth we were all off for the Ominecas. First we went down to Kastberg Creek, then turned off the Takla path and struck up along the old Ingenika Mining Trail that passes to the west of the Omineca range and, in its early stages, follows the Kastberg.

J. has especially vivid memories of the Kastberg. Traveling alone with the two horses in 1939, it was near the Kastberg that he had had another of his wild adventures with Lassie. Lassie trod in a yellow jackets' nest and, clean demented, had run for miles and miles through the forest, scattering the contents of her two-hundred-pound pack over every one of the miles. It took J. all that day, and part of the next, to recover not only Lassie but also his possessions.

Mountain maple was growing all along the first part of the dry rocky trail. I have also found this maple east of Hudson Bay Meadow, and at the northeast end of Bear Lake. These localities are far north of its known range.

We made our first night's camp by a big stream that comes from "Basil Holland's Lake," some distance southeast of the Kastberg Creek country, where Basil has a winter cabin and trap line. Just above camp there was a gold-brown, sun-flecked pool, deep enough for swimming and diving. It was the first water I've struck in this country really warm enough to enjoy. I made the most of it and over and over again reveled in "the cool silver shock of the plunge in the pool's living water."

The next afternoon we reached the foot of the lower slopes of the Ominecas. The going was very tough for five or six miles along the Ingenika track, before we turned off it. The entire trail had been gouged by a freshet and was washed into a deep ditch full of big rocks. It was like walking up a narrow rocky stream bed. Since there was dense forest on either side, there was nothing to do but keep along it. We also crossed some bad bogs and occasionally lost the trail.

Lassie, who is behaving beautifully, like Baldy, shows great courtesy to Rex and Wahoo. The Indians told us that she kicked their dogs but I think, because ours behave politely toward her, she treats them with equal consideration. Courtesy and respect in one animal seem to beget courtesy and respect in another, except for the case of the odd bad individual. Animals appear to be quite as considerate toward each other as human beings are — sometimes much more so! They certainly accept each other's oddities and peculiarities with a far greater degree of philosophy and poise. Thank God, they aren't reformers! It must be this which makes their society so restful to that unrestful creature, man, who is forever trying to stir up his fellow comrades and induce them to behave differently.

Once, at an old camping spot in a clearing, J. and I let Sapolio and the horses go on while we paused to read old "letters" written on trees. One, written by J. himself in July of 1939, when he had passed through en route to the Ominecas, was addressed to a man from Vancouver who had come up that summer to take a trip around the mountains and, in the company of an Indian acquaintance, look for gold or other minerals. He had stopped with J. for a day or two at Tetana. Though a tenderfoot and soft from his city life, he was completely enthralled by the beauty of our territory and our "ideal life." J.'s "letter" invited him, in case he returned by way of Tetana when J. was absent, to stop and make himself at home.

On another tree the gentleman from Vancouver had written a letter to J. The letter said that he had gotten thus far in safety, though this "hell of a trail" had just about done him in. Both letters, done in pencil two years before, and well weathered, were as clear and legible as if written yesterday.

J. neither saw nor heard from his Vancouver acquaintance again, but, from various reports of Indians and citizens "outside," he pieced together parts of the man's summer adventures. It seems that though he did not find the desired minerals he did run into experiences aplenty. Rather more than he had bargained for! He had had serious (what *he* thought were serious anyhow) disagreements with his Indian so that he had ridden for days, bearing all the firearms of the party on his own person. They had gone smack into a grizzly and the horses had run; and they had escaped serious consequences only by a miracle. But the climax occurred when, in a spot northeast of Bear Lake, they had come suddenly and unexpectedly on old Peter Haimadam (Martha's father of whom I have written) sitting up against a tree, stone dead, with maggots crawling from his eyes and mouth.

The Vancouver gentleman had finally arrived at Takla in such a hurry to reach the outside civilized world, from which he had formerly been so happy to depart, that they had had much ado to persuade him to wait for the freight boat. He wanted to walk to Fort St. James without delay. This, said he, was a "wonderful country, wonderful country, but my God, let me get out of here!"

What really happened to poor old Peter is still one of those unsolved mysteries of the North that for years provide an endless amount of fascinating conversation and speculation. In the late spring of 1939, Peter, in company with several other Indians, one of whom was Sapolio, had been returning to Bear Lake. But he had decided to delay a bit and come on by himself. When he did not show up after many days they had gone back to look for him and been unable to find him. As the river was in high water it was generally supposed that he had been carried down in the flood. After reports of his dead body came in many weeks later and they had gone to examine it, several more theories had presented themselves. Old Charlie told us that Peter's skull looked as though it had had a heavy blow, and, since there were old shots found in trees in several directions, it was Charlie's opinion that he might have been attacked by a grizzly, that the bear had bashed his head in, and that old Peter, as he leaned dying against the tree, had fired the shots at random. Some of the other Indians didn't think it was a bear. They thought he might have fallen and hit his head, or just died from old age, and that he had fired the shots to bring help.

There was another perfectly legible "tree letter" on the other side of the clearing. This, apparently addressed "to all whom it may concern," was signed by a strange Indian. It read: "i trap here one year i get no nothing i go now to babine."

We had delayed over the letters for some ten minutes when we heard the sudden jangle of a bell. And there was Baldy come all the way back, just like a faithful dog, to look for us!

Soon after this we approached what appeared to be the foot of the lowest and most open ascent of the Ominecas. Here we were obliged to leave the Ingenika Trail and blaze one of our own. In '39 J. and Michelle had made the climb, starting at approximately this point. It was late afternoon, but the summer twilights were still long, and it was essential that we get the horses up to good feed and pasture. Somehow we missed the easier ascent which J. had used before, and the higher up we got, the more impassable the going became.

Years ago this section of the mountain slope had been burned over. Probably due to the gentle incline, the forest had been very thick. Tree trunks, broken four or five feet above ground, were strewn in every direction. The dead trees were thickly overgrown with briers and all manner of dense shrubbery; and huge rocks were scattered about everywhere. Getting the already tired horses through this became more and more of a business. Their legs, at times, were so tangled up that they apparently couldn't go backwards or forwards. On several occasions Baldy refused point-blank to move, a most unusual attitude for him. Since Lassie always follows his lead, it looked for a time as though we might be really stuck.

Finally I climbed over beside Baldy, gave him a hug, and said, "I know it's awful, old boy, but you must go on and not give up. Don't you see we're trying to get you up to good grass? We can't stay here. Look, no water, no food for you. Please go on, darling, and try your very best. Look up at those grassy slopes."

I vow he understood every word! Because at once he made a mighty effort, extricated himself from the seemingly hopeless tangle of logs and rocks, Lassie followed suit, and not once after this did we have serious trouble with them. We reached the top four hours later, the ascent having taken at least twice as long as we had figured. When we emerged into the open, we had still several miles to go until we arrived at the meadow where J. intended to make camp.

In the deepening cool mountain twilight, we straggled along, three jaded human figures, two drooping horses, two sad dogs, scarcely able, any of us, to push one leg after another, too completely played-out to give voice to a single noise of any description.

It was 10 P.M. and pitch-dark before we got the horses and dogs unloaded, a hasty camp put up, and supper on to cook. Sapolio ate with us before he retired to his own little shelter. When we had eaten and drunk several quarts of hot bitter tea, and observed that the horses were sufficiently recovered to start feeding, J. was able to make a few observations.

Sapolio contributed one sentence. He said: "Hard trip that; well, good night."

When I woke next morning, sufficiently revived to take things in, I saw why J. has raved about the Ominecas. This whole section of mountain, for as far as one can see north and south, is divided by dozens of clear, splashing little mountain streams into lush-green, flower-filled meadows. And every stream waters a flower garden of surpassing beauty. Many of the same species are here that grew on the Driftwoods, but they are far more luxuriant and colorful and widespread. Masses of low Epilobiums turn the banks rose-pink. Great clusters of purple monkshood and lupines and white saxifrage and starflowers cover the flat places. Giant blue forget-me-nots, wet all day by cold spray, lean over into the water. Purple bluebells and gentians, scarlet columbines, and star-white grass-of-Parnassus stud the rocky outcrops. Buttercups and yellow daisies light the shadowy places like sunshine. Lower down near timber line are acres of red, orange, crimson, yellow, and white Indian paintbrush.

Our tent, close by a splashing stream, is sheltered on three sides by a dense wall of stunted balsam. It looks down over a whole field of deep lavender daisies, blown by winds into white waves, to the valleys, falling away in blue-green sheets of forest.

rising again from a distant purple sea to the rock masses of the Driftwoods, dwarfed now against the great glacial-covered lines of the coastal ranges.

All this gently sloping part of the range, for a distance of eight miles, is three or four miles wide. Behind to the east, green and yellow meadows rise gradually to steep slides of loose rocks and red shale, in places to high rims.

Clouds are wonderful. It is like living in the sky. Mountainous masses of them, fluffy as cotton, roll across the meadows, the blue of the sky between each mass intensified and deepened. They roll over us. We are enveloped in cool, damp, thick mist, shut away from winds and sounds. But in five minutes the sun is there, bright and hot, and the winds are blowing again, the clouds are repiling themselves on the peaks and meadows beyond. Valleys and mountains below and above are radiant with sunshine and shadow, the colors of grasses and flowers, wetted by the fresh mists, are even more vivid than before.

"Surely," as my beloved Kim once said to the lama when they reached the first ramparts of the Himalayas, "the gods dwell here. This is no place for men."

Although mosquitoes do gather about and blowflies are bad around sunset, there is usually so much wind that we are fairly free of them. Then, too, this camp site is far more open and farther above timber line than the one on the Driftwoods.

Most of the summer birds have already gone, or are flocking for migration. But there are still many Gambel's and golden-crowned sparrows about the little tree clumps and, a bit farther down, families of winter wrens (of which we have at last collected several) and a very large species of dusky grouse. Loveliest of all are the flocks of mountain bluebirds, their backs like the sky, their breasts like the clouds. They shower us all day with tender warbles. They are a much lighter, more real sky blue than the Eastern bluebirds. Sapolio is a keen observer of bird life and apparently familiar with all the common birds, but he had never seen a bluebird until he came up here. Flocks of white-tailed ptarmigan are on the rocky slopes higher up. Big red-tailed hawks, dark brown or almost black except for bright reddish tails, swoop low over the meadows, often pouncing down upon mice and lemmings.

Every acre on this part of the mountain supports a family of hoary marmots. Their shrill whistles, as they pop down into holes one by one, mark the line of advance of every approaching figure. Sometimes, as we walk along, whistles come from a dozen different directions. This drives Rex and Wahoo to the verge of distraction. They run round in circles, completely unable to decide which way to go.

Golden eagles, one of the chief foes of the marmots, seem to be fairly common also.

My chief job is to be plant collecting and bird skinning; J.'s, trapping for small mammals and, with Sapolio's help, locating mountain goats and caribou for both eating and photographing. And we still have some hope of seeing wolves! Here, if ever, on these long open plateaus there may be a chance of observing them, at least in the distance.

Omineca Camp   *August 8*

The first day Sapolio climbed a high peak. Almost as soon as he reached the top and looked down on the other side, he saw a flock of fourteen goats at a little mountain tarn. He sneaked down closer and got one at once.

We have also lived on marmot and porcupine, both of which are delectable. Their meat is tender and delicate and, except for a higher flavor, is much like chicken. Porcupines, about twice as huge and ferocious as the ones of Pennsylvania, inhabit the deep canyons and are found also just below timber line. Because of their slow waddly gait, they are easy to kill if caught in the open. Skinning one for eating is not so difficult as it sounds. Merely lay it on its back, open it along the fat little belly which is free of spines, and gradually turn it inside out. Clean out its intestines and internal organs, cut off its head, and then the legs at the ankle joints, put it in a stewpot with a few onions and potatoes (if one is lucky enough to have them — dehydrated onions and rice are almost as good), and put it on in a little water to boil gently. We often add a handful of dried beans and barley, both of which are easy to pack on long trips, and a few cubes of bacon. In about an hour there is the most appetizing of stews.

Stews, since they combine in one pot all the necessary elements of nourishment, are the most practical dishes on camping trips. Occasionally when we have fresh goat which is tender enough, we vary the stews by roasting special cuts on sticks over hot coals. Such a diet, supplemented with fresh eggs (of which we brought several dozen wrapped in paper from old magazines and packed in kettles and pots), dried fruit, and bannock, which I bake each morning in a frying pan, is excellent. We have lived well on this trip, for we have been constantly supplied with fresh meat and, owing to the two horses, have been able to carry plenty of other things.

The horses always have to be tethered (the first time we tried letting them loose, Lassie promptly headed south at a brisk trot). But they fare well on the unlimited supply of lush grass, and already are so fat and full of pep they're hard to handle. Every evening we turn Baldy free to drink, after which he thunders across the field at a gallop, leaps like a two-year-old over the stream below our tent, and lands neatly on top of the steep bank. He even has the nerve to kick up his heels and snort when we offer him the customary tidbit.

The weather has been pretty fair, though I am very tired of the almost incessant winds. We had one really bad storm, lasting for almost twenty-four hours. In the night a mighty wind arose, and I was waked from sound sleep by the wild flapping of the tent and the noise of running, pounding hoofs in the little meadow where the horses were picketed. I woke J., who, battling in pitch-dark with the heavy gale, found Lassie almost frantic. She had wound herself up in rope and her stake was nearly pulled out of the ground. He had to call Sapolio to come and help. While J. was gone, Wahoo, who hates winds and flapping things, wormed himself clean down inside J.'s place in bed and had to be forcibly ejected.

All next day the wind was high and there was whipping, biting rain. We worried about the horses, who were without shelter — the stunted clumps of little firs provide poor wind-breaks — but, standing close together, heads down, and tails toward the wind, they seemed to be riding out the storm success-fully. (Ordinarily they have a quaint custom of standing with the tail of one by the head of the other, so that each tail does double and effective duty in keeping flies away.) Every so often we went out and rubbed them down and talked to them. They were so marvelously patient and steady through the endless hours of icy rain and wind. The loyalty of dogs and the pa-tience of horses are very big and touching things.

J. and I enjoyed the storm. We agreed to take time off from perpetual skinning and plant-pressing, and just read. J. had tucked into our packs a few pocket editions of detective stories, acquired at Takla. With the dogs stretched beside us, and our good old tent tightly closed against rain and wind, we lay on our bed and read all day in one of those silences that are delicious and companionable, because they last, undisturbed, for hours.

J. and Sapolio have been on several goat hunts. J. has needed a few more heads and skins for the collections; and we have been drying and smoking a supply of goat meat to take back to Tetana. First, we hang the meat where the smoke of the fire will blow over it continually. Then, after a day or two, when it has become hardened on the outside, it is hung in a huge bag of netting suspended in a shady windy place. This all has to be done with greatest care, for, until every spot of its outside surface becomes hard, blowflies get in and lay eggs.

Since J. has wanted more good goat pictures, he has taken over fifty feet of Kodachrome. Among other goat views, he procured close-up shots of a nanny and her kid, which, un-fortunately, had to be taken during a series of wild snow flur-ries. The precipitous places that he and Sapolio have been across on their goat chases make me shudder. One day, high above the canyon which lies four miles south of our camp, they followed a herd of thirty-five goats, the biggest number that we have ever heard of in this country; and at the same time, not far away, they counted a herd of eighteen others. Out of one bunch they killed two full-grown ones and one kid.

At the time, I had been off with the dogs, collecting plants a mile northeast of the canyon. Sometime after the shots, we encountered Sapolio going back to fetch the horses so that they could carry home the goats. Sapolio, full of glee over their thrilling hunt, said: —

"Gee, lots of goat in this place. Neber I see so many at one time. We chase him all over. We run and climb just like the goat. By gosh, we make lots of fun! Goat jump and leap. Neber he stay still. Hard to shoot that one."

"Sapolio, did you ever see a goat slip and fall?"

"No, that one he neber fall. All my life I watch goat. Neber I see one fall. Nobody ever see one fall. Goat he jump and run on wet rock or in snow — very slippery. Neber he slip that one. *Gee!* — Jack he want you go to canyon and see goat we get and help skin — "

He was off, at the easy, graceful stride that always covers twice the ground I can; the dogs and I hurried on to the canyon, climbing down into it at the upper part where it was much less steep. This canyon is a spectacular place. It cuts deep into the eastern slopes of the Ominecas and is about seven hundred feet deep by four miles long. Its bare rock sides are red and orange-brown, its slides of shale a dark rose. A swift boulder-strewn stream, filled by many old snowbanks, waters vivid green grass and gay flowers. Under bright sun and blue sky it is as brilliantly colorful as the canyon country of Arizona and New Mexico.

After much hallooing, I located J. skinning furiously at the two big goats which had providentially rolled down close to a patch of old snow. Seeing the body of the little goat lodged under the precipice four hundred feet above, I volunteered to climb up and get it. The dogs, worked into fits by shrill marmot whistles coming from every direction, were sliding frenziedly hither and yon, but Rex promptly left Wahoo and the exciting chase and came swiftly up after me as I began to climb.

The slide was steep and I went on hands and knees. In a few spots it was so nearly perpendicular I thought I might topple over backwards, but Rex climbed merrily about exactly like another goat. When I reached the still warm body of the dear little kid, I found it too heavy to lift; the only way to get it down was to start it rolling. About thirty feet below, it promptly caught against a big rock and I had to climb down and get it started all over again. Once a whole rockslide slid under me and I went with it for about fifty feet. But finally we all arrived at the bottom. I don't really like mountain climbing!

With special interest, I examined all the goat feet one by one, wondering if they had some peculiar non-slip quality. Inside the little hoofs are resilient tough cushions like very hard rough rubber. These would act like suction disks. The ankles, just above the iron-strong, graceful little feet, were the most flexible I've ever seen. They bend backwards or forwards or sideways with equal ease. No matter how the goat runs or leaps, no matter what object he lands on, he could surely keep his balance on ankles like those. And the tough rubber pads would hold him right where he landed. The two dewclaws above the hoofs were large; these are said to act as most efficient brakes when the goat slides down a steep incline.

One wonderful clear cold evening of the full moon, J. decided that he would spend the night alone up on a high little peak some miles back of camp. This peak looks over a deep valley on the other side; just below are several small mountain lakes that make good watering spots for game animals. J. hoped, from this perch, to be able to observe goats if they came to drink at dawn, and also — just possibly — wolves.

In 1939, he had seen wolf tracks and a freshly killed kid below a rocky incline near one of these same small tarns. Sapolio, in his tent on the other side of the meadow, and I in ours, minded the horses and dogs and camps. Soon after breakfast next morning J. returned, very stiff, after many icy hours of inactivity. Sapolio hurried over, and J. gave us an account of his night.

"The night," said he, "was freezing, but it was worth it! Jumping Joseph, it was cold. Wish you'd seen what I saw this morning around dawn. A whole flock of goats came down to drink — eleven of 'em — and they were just starting slowly up a rockslide on the other side when blest if two wolves didn't come out and start driving 'em. And did they go! The whole bunch was up the slope out of reach before you could whistle. The wolves never had a chance — "

"Oh Jack, did you — "

"Nope, never got a picture! Light too weak and anyhow they were too far away even for the telephoto. I watched them all the time through the glasses."

Another day J. and Sapolio saw a great shaggy wolf silhouetted on the skyline of a ridge behind camp. "Biggest wolf you ever saw," they said. "At first we both thought it was a caribou!"

But it had vanished before any of us could get up there. We have at last, I think, almost given up hope of ever seeing a wolf close enough to photograph. We have also been disappointed at not encountering mountain caribou, for though we heard several going by one night, and have found fresh tracks of a few, there are no small bands of them as there were in '39.

We have a fine collection of small mammals, however. Tawny lemmings, meadow mice, deer mice, shrews, marmots, and one which J. thinks may be the rare Phenacomys; this closely resembles a meadow mouse and is difficult to determine. It was caught almost in the same spot where J. took one in '39.

The tawny lemmings seem particularly common here this summer. They occur most frequently along grassy banks of the small streams which come from snowbanks. The mounds of large, noticeably green droppings are a sure guide to their burrows. Their underground runways connect and wind for yards in every direction. Green cuttings of grass cover the floors of the deeper recesses of the burrows, which are also of considerable length. One of the burrows measured over eleven feet long.

I have learned something about the real extent of these mountains. Deceptively broad and rolling on the west, they are on the east, where they fall off as sharply as if sliced with a knife, entirely different. One day the dogs and I climbed a small ridge which looked more accessible than the others. But when we got less than halfway up, I began to be more and more scared. Though ascending gradually from the direction of camp, it fell sheer for thousands of feet on the other side. There was rather a high breeze. J. had told me how, two summers before, in a sudden violent gust, he and Michelle had come within an ace of being blown off a very narrow ridge near this one. J., dropping flat, had grabbed Michelle by the hair just as Michelle swayed perilously toward the edge. Luckily only their two caps vanished in the abyss. Now I too dropped flat and clung to the dogs till the hardest blow had swished across. I should turn back, I thought. But having come this far, I must go on the short way to the top. It would never do to leave the Ominecas without at least one high view.

When we reached it, terrible precipices and gorges fell away on every side. Beyond was an endless sea of bare tumbled rock mountains stretching away as far as the eye could see — the nearer reds and browns and yellows turning gradually to blue and purple in the distance. It was grand and wonderful but not, I thought, really beautiful. There were no deep green forests and shining lakes, no whitened spires like the Frypans, no long glittering glaciers.

The Ominecas are, possibly, a spur of the western edge of the barer eastern Rockies. They do not, as the Driftwoods, stick up by themselves out of forested watered valleys. There are not the breath-taking lovely views which appear from every peak of the Driftwoods. But the flower gardens of the Ominecas, the miles of meadow, and little lakes and streams, their wide plateaus, make them far more pleasant and comfortable and safe to live on, and, on the whole, more interesting to explore.

When the dogs and I left our high outlook, we climbed down onto a new plateau lying some four miles north of our camping meadow. Here a whole series of exquisite cobalt-blue, deep tarns were laid like jewels at the foot of a long black rock ridge. A big splashing stream fell away from the last one, down, down, down, into the green wooded valley far below. The banks of the little lakes were carpeted with acres of pink Epilobium, which, in the distance, exactly resembled wet Scotch heather when the sun shines on it.

The water was so tempting that I took a swift and icy plunge, but the sunshine was too weak and the stiff breeze too cold to make it fun.

After a bite of lunch and a long series of Kodachrome snaps, I climbed back up over a high ridge, down through the meadows, and home to camp. On the way I found a small outcrop of strange rock that looked like hard molasses candy. We often pick up odd rocks, but we have never found anything really valuable like gold or copper or mercury (no one in this country will believe this — they're always certain we're concealing some wealth-producing minerals). But fortunately for the wilderness (and for us), the Driftwood Valley has in bygone days been more or less prospected and nothing of great value discovered.

We've had many interesting talks with Sapolio around our campfires. Discussions about Indian customs, the country, and the weather. In particular we've talked about the Indian treatment of dogs, a subject which always hangs heavily on our minds. Sapolio claims that the Tahltan Indians up north, for whom he has apparently considerable respect, take care of their dogs and treat them differently from the Bear Lake people. He says that here, only he and old William, the Tahltan Indian who owns the little Hare Indian dogs, bother to feed their dogs throughout the year. When we asked Sapolio what season he liked best he replied instantly, "Winter! Gee, summer no good, flies all the time, meat bad, lots of dirt. Wintertime cold, very hard. But winter clean, good time to live and hunt."

The trapping season will begin soon and Sapolio should return to Bear Lake, but he says quite definitely that he will wait until we are ready and then help us back to Tetana, although if he cut directly across country from here, he could reach Bear Lake in half the time by traveling one side of a triangle instead of two. For almost the first time on a trip in this country, J. has been comfortable and carefree, and consequently, so have I.

We are beginning to wind up our work and consider starting for Tetana, perhaps next week. I believe that we have a touch of mountain sickness, for we all seem to long for the lowlands. We have been living at an elevation of seven to nine thousand feet, and though at first it was wonderfully bracing and refreshing, now, without having anything really wrong with us, we don't seem to feel quite up to scratch. Our eyes are tired from looking perpetually into vast distances; our heads ache a little from the never-ceasing winds. It will be good to get down to quiet forest paths and still lakes, just to see mountains instead of feel them.

CHAPTER XVII

Our Wild Comrades

Tetana   *August 25*

The autumn trip to Blue Lake, contemplated in the spring, has been given up, for we've been having the most thrilling and longed-for experiences right here on our very own doorstep! The day after we got back to Tetana, Sapolio left for Bear Lake. Some hours later, J. and I were surprised to hear a tremendous chorus of coyotes barely half a mile away over toward the river. Their shrill barks were mingled with a few smooth wolf howls. The noise waxed louder and louder until eventually the wolves drowned out the coyotes. What in the world had happened to call them forth and make them give voice so lustily at this season, and so near our cabin? Had they cornered a moose?

Seizing cameras and guns we hurried off. When we had gone only a little distance, the noise was shut off with sudden and complete abruptness, nor could we find any trace of them or a moose, in the thick spruce and swamps next the river. A few well-posted sentries had obviously announced our start and progress and, at the proper moment, bid the others shut down. When we got back to the cabin J. prepared to pole up the river in the skiff, thinking that a more roundabout and silent approach might yield better results. It was then three in the afternoon.

As the skiff is too small for two of us on such a dangerous trip, and as the horses had to be watered and taken to the meadow for the night, I, alas, had to be the one to stay home and attend to evening chores. Later, leading the horses, with Rex and Wahoo running ahead, I was halfway to the meadow when I heard wolves howling again — no coyotes this time — from the same direction over by the river, and I wondered anxiously

if J. had reached there in time. After a laborious hour of hunting for two places where Baldy and Lassie could find a sufficient
quantity of the late grass and would not get tangled in bushes,
I tied them both. I was just leaving, with many an anxious backward glance, hoping they would be safe, when Wahoo, chasing
Rex in a wild game of tag, barged into me from behind and
knocked my legs clean out from under me. One knee must
have been put almost out of joint, for it hurt frightfully.

As I rolled, moaning, on the grass, with Wahoo's huge pink
tongue darting out contrite kisses from above, from somewhere
along the river a loud shot from J.'s big rifle rang out. This
scared me stiff, for I knew that he would shoot only if he were
being attacked or was dangerously cornered. I thought at once
of a grizzly.

The spot where I supposed J. to be was, as the crow flies, a
mile and a half from the cabin. To get there by boat it was
necessary, after leaving the lake outlet, to turn northwestward
up the river and follow the shallow rapids, deep eddies, and
winding willow-bordered stream to a V-shaped bend, where
tall spruce hid the mountains on one side and dense willows
overhung the bank on the other.

At the shot, the wolf chorus had stopped dead. I was just
starting toward home when, on the still sunset air, there came
a sound that made me cold and almost stopped my heart. It was
the horrible, low, wailing moan of something or someone in
mortal agony. It sounded exactly as J. had at the time of his
accident at home when, after a terrible operation, he had been
wheeled up from the operating room. Could it be the cry of
a wolf? If a wolf, it was unlike any wolf note I'd ever heard
before, and I thought I had run the gamut of all wolf noises.
In the gathering dusk I limped slowly along the path, stopping
now and then to rub my knee and listen. Just as I reached the
cabin the cry came again, repeated twice. This time, because it
was nearer, it was even more horrible. And then, most terrifying of all, the loud, wailing, always musical chorus of wolf
voices began again. They had not even been scared off by the
shot. Were they singing over J.'s dead or mangled body?

I'd had a faint hope that during the hours I'd been gone J. might have returned, but the cabin was dark and empty. There was not a sign of him or the boat. I crouched on the bank of the lake, straining every nerve for some sound of J. (It was so dark I could no longer see.) The howling of the wolves, so near and loud and triumphant and continuous, unnerved me completely. The dogs, by this time thoroughly frightened by my fright, crouched beside me. When I wasn't listening, I know I was praying. It was nine-thirty. At ten I would start out through the big swamps toward the river and the wolves. And then, way down the lake, came a faint creak. It stopped. I had only imagined it. It came again, clear and unmistakable, the creak of oars. It was J. He was safe.

When, tired, hungry, and exalted, J. reached the bank he found, to his consternation, two frantic dogs and his wife, that weak and silly creature, drowned in tears, sobbing incoherently!

This was the story he recounted: He had hurried down the lake and out through the outlet into the river. It was tough work poling up against the current and trying to do it quietly. By the time he got up, there wasn't a sound of the wolves, but there were dozens of wolf tracks, newly made, along the shore and sand bar. The river was thick with kokanee. Some were dead. The run must have started early in August when we were on the Ominecas. J. waited an hour or so by a bank under thick willows. And then a black bear, with its cub, came from bushes on the opposite shore forty feet away. For a few minutes they caught kokanees in shallow water, catching them up in their mouths and swallowing them at a gulp.

The light was very bad. When J. tested it, it didn't look as though he could get a thing, but he was going to take some feet with the movie, anyhow, when suddenly he saw a big gray-black wolf standing in the middle of the river. How he got there J. didn't know. ("He just appeared, that's all!") He looked twice the size of Wahoo and must have weighed a hundred and twenty pounds. The wolf and the bears stared at each other for a minute, then they turned away and began to hunt fish "as unconcerned as you please." After a bit the wolf saw the boat about thirty feet away. He stood like a statue ("Gad, what a sight!") and then he loped slowly — he didn't seem to hurry — and smoothly and gracefully off across the river and disappeared in the willows.

A wolf, J. says, is mighty different from a coyote. He's three times the size, his head is broader, his ears much shorter; except for the wild wonderful expression of the eyes, one could almost take him for a great Husky dog.

Daylight was going fast by then, but J. could see the willows shaking in places. There was something moving behind them. Then they were still and the bears had gone too — just melted off — and there wasn't a sound anywhere. And right then wolves began to sing in the willows just opposite. There must have been ten or twelve of them judging from the noise and different voices. They didn't move around, just kept still and sang. Each outburst was started by one wolf, who had the lowest and most dirgelike note J. ever heard.

He said, "Don't think I ever was so thrilled by anything in my life. I tell you my hair stood right up straight! Don't believe anyone ever heard what I heard — that close."

And he had parked the boat just below the opening of a game trail! It was covered up with hanging willows and he'd never seen the trail at all. It was almost dark when there was a crash above, and there was a grizzly and its cub just about to climb down on him. Apparently they had no idea that J. was there — perhaps his scent was carried away under the bank. He fired just over their heads ("You could see the flash — must have singed 'em") and they were scared stiff and backed off in a hurry. If they'd gone one foot farther they wouldn't have been able to turn back and would have been down right on top of him.

"Jumping Joseph!" J. said. "Was I scared! And I thought that all this would have scared off the wolves, but blest if they didn't start singing again right away, softly at first, and then after a bit that sad-voiced one (must have been the one that scared you — it sure had the most hair-raising notes *I* ever heard) set 'em off and they were at it as loud as ever. Must have

Timber
Wolf

known I was there all along and weren't a bit scared of me. Can't understand it! If you were scared hearing 'em a mile away, you ought to have been right beside 'em. I tell you it was all I could do to keep my nerve up. Never thought of moving or starting home till about half an hour later, though I'd meant to get down before it got pitch-dark. Don't believe anyone on earth has heard what I did. If you'd *only* been there —"

For days after this we explored up and down the river, and found signs of wolves and bears and coyotes and lesser animals everywhere. They were one and all making the most of the kokanee run and enjoying a regular fish banquet. Around sundown, and soon after dawn, we often listened to short songs and calls of the wolves. Sometimes near by, sometimes far off. The loud horse bells and the barking of the dogs did not seem to scare them in the least. But we never heard the high fierce hunting chorus typical of late winter and early spring. In summer, when food is so much more easily obtained, the wolves seldom need to join forces in order to hunt.

Intent on getting pictures, J. twice more tried the same spot up the river, but never saw a wolf. At last he fixed on our favorite fishing pool a half mile down the river from Tetana. Numerous tracks on the wide gravel and sand bars by the pool indicated that this was frequented by the wolves; and a deep still back water, bordered on one side by willows, would, we thought, make an excellent parking place for the boat.

So, nearly every morning for the past weeks, J. has gotten up before 3 A.M. and, loaded with cameras, guns, and a thermos of coffee, has floated off in the cold dark night in order to be well established by daybreak. He has always stuck it out until late morning, sometimes noon or afternoon, when he returns almost too tired to be able to tumble into bed. I've spent hours trying to straighten out the cramps which, after he's been sitting still for six or ten hours at a stretch, have attacked him in every limb.

But his perseverance has been amply rewarded for at least half the time he has *seen wolves face to face!* He has taken hundreds of feet of moving pictures, some of which we can only pray may be good. The wolves have appeared nearly always in the early morning when light has been poor and the river full of mist. The weather too, though it has not actually rained, has been overcast rather than bright. The early mornings have been cold with the thermometer down to 18 and 15 degrees.

J. has proved that here in this region, during certain seasons fish form the wolves' chief food. Indian reports confirm this, for they have told us that wolves not only spend some time getting fish in the rivers when the runs are on, but also come around the large lakes when dead bodies of the big sockeyes are beginning to line the shores.

I have just been out of luck, for the few occasions when I've gone with J. have been the very times when the wolves did not appear. Being cramped up in the tiny boat with J. was bad, not only because it's dangerous going down and up river, but where there is just room enough for one person to stretch his legs in order to avoid serious cramps, two can hardly move at all. And, though we've considered it, my going alone has seemed a bit too risky and foolhardy. I'm not strong enough to manage the boat safely on the river; and going by boat is the only way to reach the parking spot where one can get a clear view of the sand bar which the wolves frequent. So I have just had to be content with hearing them — and I've heard plenty!

We seem to be surrounded by wolves who have for the time being taken up their abode in the Tetana territory. Though the real song choruses are in the evenings and early mornings, at almost any time of the day or night we can hear howls and yawns from young and old. When I walk with Rex and Wahoo, I am certain that sometimes wolves walk with us. There is a slight stirring of bushes and when I go to look at the spot a little hesitantly and fearfully, but quite unable to resist, there is moss springing slowly up from the depression made by a heavy foot, or there are big fresh droppings, or a sprinkle on a log not yet dried. And there is a very strong smell, not a dog smell! Rex and Wahoo must see the wolves for they often come back to me all ruffled and bristling, just as though they'd encountered another dog. I wonder what they all think of each other?

During the past few weeks J. has seen, from his river parking place, sixteen wolves at a distance of fifteen to seventy-five feet. The very first morning when he had sat shivering for two hours after dawn, a spot in the pool about thirty feet off, which had been still and empty, suddenly held a gray wolf. He was standing knee-deep with a flapping little kokanee in his mouth. How he got there J. didn't know because he supposed his own eyes had been glued to the pool every minute. The boat moved a trifle and the wolf saw it instantly. For a second he was motionless, then he lowered his head eight inches and the hairs on his shoulders rose stiffly. In another second, before J. even had time to start the camera, he had loped away.

For three more mornings J. saw nothing, and then on the fourth, a large yellowish wolf appeared on the gravel bar. It moved to the water's edge without a sound, gliding along with the stiff-legged, yet lithe, catlike gait which J. now knows to be characteristic of wolves. It pounced on a little kokanee and then, at the slight sound of the camera, stopped dead. The head lowered and the ruff stood up straight. J. instantly stopped the camera, the wolf relaxed a little; a single movement of a cramped finger and he was off!

On other mornings three more wolves came, but the light was definitely too weak for pictures. They all appeared silently and were, as usual, well out into the open before J. was even aware of their presence. They vanished as silently, stepping always over the small stones of the gravel bar as though they walked on broken glass.

From the Omineca Mountains J. brought home the fatty linings of several goat stomachs. These had not been touched except with sterilized rubber gloves. One morning, as he drifted by, he dropped three pieces on the gravel bar. At four-fifteen a wolf appeared. With head low, moving from side to side, it looked at the meat from a distance. Then it backed carefully away into the willows and vanished. Sometime afterward a low howl came from bushes behind the boat and J. was sure that he was being watched. When the sun was well up crows came and took all the bait.

The next morning at six, with a cold clammy mist lying over the water, a large coal-black bitch appeared. She was thin and very hungry. J. had the impression that she was quite old and without young. She paused to sprinkle on the sand and then, moving leisurely up the gravel bar, she stopped several times to catch a kokanee struggling in the shallows. Without apparently having scented a fresh piece of goat stomach, put there that morning, she came on it suddenly and ate it without hesitation. After which she went to the river again and caught three more kokanee in rapid succession. A few minutes later she vanished, but returned in fifteen minutes or so, examined the place where the bait had been, and once more entered the river. At that moment a number of wolves, possibly a family gathering, began a song near by. There were voices of young pups — high quavery notes — striving to compete with the louder, more mellow ones of the elders. On hearing them the black wolf waded across a little rapid to within twenty feet of J., leapt up the bank which was only three feet high at that point, and sat down in tall grass. Just a vague outline of her body showed; and she began to sing.

In low, vibrating dirge she bewailed her loneliness. She was alone in the world, she sang, her mate dead, her children grown and scattered. No more happy family gatherings for her. She sat there for nearly an hour, sometimes quiet, sometimes singing mournfully. Then she jumped down into the water and, approaching to within fifteen feet of the boat, submerged her head to the shoulders to catch a fish.

A moment later she heard the camera going and, for several minutes, she and J. stared at each other. Her wonderful golden eyes were wide and unblinking. These, with the white and gray whiskers of her muzzle, were the only touches of color in all her coal-black body. Finally she turned slowly, forded the river to the gravel bar, stood where the bait had been and once more, with those wonderful unfathomable eyes of hers, looked long at J., who, with hands shaking from cold and excitement, was trying to expose as much film as possible.

By August 20th only a few live kokanee were left in the river. The run this year occurred earlier than usual, possibly owing to the exceptionally early flood season. The dead fish seemed to have been mostly picked up, and only one or two here and there still struggled in shallow pools. Some days went by without J.'s seeing any wolves, though we heard them occasionally. Bears crashed around in search of berries. We saw an otter in the river below the lake, and two coyotes. Also large numbers of muskrats.

Then again, for several days in succession, J. watched some wolf pups. One was a young male, well-fed and strong, about the size and shape of a full-grown Norwegian elkhound. His belly bulged. He moved slowly but gracefully, and with an air of abandon just like a cat. Approaching within thirty feet of the camera, he saw the boat and stopped, leapt back a dozen yards, and then sat down to watch. After a few minutes he came on again, head lowered, ears pricked forward. He sat down again and peered this way and that, head low, then high, staring at the boat with greatest interest. He was cute enough to hug. J. said "Hello!" and he bounced in the air. For a while he played hide-and-seek with J., in and out of the willows, once interrupting the game for a good long scratch. Then he vanished in the bushes and began to circle the boat. Three times his head peeked out at different places.

Several days later J. saw twice what he was sure was the same pup. On the last occasion he was amused and almost chagrined at the little wolf's complete disregard of his presence. The young chap fished and amused himself happily until a call, which must have been from home, came from way down the river, and off he ran into the forest.

One day, farther down the river, J. also watched another wolf pup who was much thinner and more timorous than the cute little fat one.

Ever since we began to be aware of the constant presence

of wolves and bears, we've kept the horses tied up at night on the east grassy marsh of Tetana. In the daytime we now let them take turns wandering loose, making sure that Lassie is always headed in the direction of the river, so that if she has any notions of going off to Takla she will first have to pass near the cabin. Besides we can always hear her bell and keep track of her. If she gets out of earshot we ring Baldy's bell, and Wahoo of course begins to howl; this never fails to bring her on the run. The same thing holds true of Baldy.

Even this loud ringing of big bells, plus Wahoo's voice, does not scare the wolves. Instead it is quite apt to start them off on a mighty and thrilling chorus, exactly as a big company of Husky dogs gives voice at the evening ringing of the mission bell in a little arctic settlement.

J. and I have pooled our ideas about these wild comrades of ours. We have come to the conclusion that the wolves are well aware of our presence and habits, and like us! They even allow their young to be near us. With their remarkable gift of understanding, they have apparently come to realize that there is nothing to fear from us, that we like them, that we are interested in their welfare. Not only do we hear and see them south down the river a mile away, but we hear them from the west toward the log jam, from the north around the meadow, from the east toward Trail Lake. Though they have been constantly around us for several weeks, they have shown no sign of harming us, our dogs, or our horses. It is hard to say whether they would attack the dogs or horses if they were very hungry and unable to obtain other game. We have never heard authentic cases of horses in this country being attacked by wolves, though the Indians declare that occasionally some of their dogs have been injured or killed by them.

It is rather wonderful that the most intelligent of all our wild companions has reached this basis of tolerance toward us. It seems a fitting fulfillment of our greatest desires. And it makes our coming departure the more sad and unfortunate. That we should have to leave just when we seem to be approaching the goal of our ambitions; just when our wilderness comrades are

beginning to understand that the Tetana area can be a place
where man and beast may live side by side, unhampered one by
the other, respecting one another's rights and habits; and realize
that there is room for us all so long as we are fair and just and
keep the laws of the wild.

September 2

Most of the goat which we brought back from the mountains
had maggots in it, so that we were forced to part with it in
short order. We are badly in need of meat again. I therefore
go out with the .22 almost every day, locate grouse, and bring
them home. Franklin's are easier to bag than the ruffed; apparently they're stupider for they don't take fright and fly off as
quickly. The dogs, who startle them up, are a great assistance.
I can usually down one from almost any angle in some of these
tallest, thickest trees. But satisfying as this is, I still can't imagine killing something even as stupid as a grouse for mere
sport.

Today I nearly collected J.! I had spotted a large flock of
Franklin's grouse in the tall poplars behind the cabin and
rushed out and began firing right and left. Out of a flock of ten
I got seven with eight shots, and was just gathering them up,
smirking a bit over some unusually good shooting on the wing,
when I heard angry shouts and J., red and panting, appeared
suddenly. He had gone for firewood in a quite different direction. Returning on the trail which passes through the poplars,
he had been greeted by a fusillade of shots and had had to run
for his life. He was somewhat mollified when he saw the grouse,
though he said that it was a nice thing for a man to be peppered
with shots by his wife just as he was approaching home.

I am, I suppose, the only white woman in the world who,
having been on an expedition into big game country, has returned without "getting her bear." *And I am proud of it!* For
why should I wish to take life from my comrades of the wilds
just for the sake of a trophy? If ever I have to kill something
big for food or in self-defense, I will; and I think I could do it.
But if these beautiful creatures are to be killed for food or

science, I prefer, every time, that it should not have to be by my hand.

Some time ago we sent word to Charlie, by one of the boys who came down from Bunshaw, that we would give up all thought of another Blue Lake trip and go down with him in his big dugout by river to Takla about September 7th. Two of the boys are to take the horses down the trail, camping with us each night at a previously agreed meeting place along the river. Just in case there may be any last-minute difficulties about Charlie and sons taking us out as agreed (some of them might be "sick" or otherwise discommoded), J. asked Sapolio to come down a few days before we start to receive the keys of the cabin, which we are leaving in his care, and to get various farewell gifts of food and clothing. So, if Charlie should fail us, we won't be left without help and can still hike out with the horses.

Russ has recently made two trips to Bear Lake. On his return from the first one, he scared us nearly out of our wits by circling so low over Tetana that we thought he would have to land. And then we were sure that something terrible had happened because, for the first time in three years, he dropped things in the lake. J. rushed out to them in the boat and called back to me. One was a note in a closed tin can to say that Russ was making another trip to Bear Lake, had heard we were going out, and if we could be at Bunshaw on such-and-such a date he could take us through to the Fort. The other was a duplicate of the first, but four fresh peaches were floating about along with it. One peach was fairly well disintegrated, but three were still in approximately their original shapes. We ate the peaches almost before we read the notes.

Flying would be the easy way to get out, but we could not, in any case, leave the horses to be taken down by the Indians. We intend to hand them over ourselves to the proper caretakers, and make special arrangements for their future welfare.

CHAPTER XVIII

Keep Safe, Tetana

Tetana   *September 5*

Sapolio, Charlie, William, and the two boys arrived several days ago. Charlie has been repairing leaks in his big dugout. Half the payment for the coming trip down the river will be given to Charlie in food supplies for his family. We have a store of good provisions on hand. J. made a list of weights and prices and Charlie, since he needs the food, seems glad to be paid in this manner. It will also save him the long extra haul up from Takla. The boys have taken the things up to Bunshaw, where they will be left for the autumn. The remainder of the payment Charlie will receive in cash when we reach Takla. We made them all liberal presents — old clothes and shoes, bedding, and various odds and ends. When William has helped escort the horses and our belongings safely to Takla, he is to receive our pet lightweight tent in payment. Sapolio has also been given many presents, the keys of the doors, and a small sum in advance for keeping an eye on the cabin and cleaning snow off the roof.

We've tried to make it clear to all of them that if the United States becomes involved in war, J. may be called, and that we shall not be able to return to Tetana as soon as we should like — perhaps not for years. But that we will return someday, and that they are not to give up expecting us, ever, unless they know we are dead! That they are to guard our cabin as if it were their own, and watch over Tetana so that the fine trees will not be burned or cut. That, since we have made Tetana a sanctuary for wildlife, birds and animals and plants must not be harmed. My heart fails me because I know that if we stay away for any length of time, this last proviso will not be kept.

Of all people whom we've known, J. and I have decided that we envy these Indians most. For they are free as very few left on this earth are free. They can be independent in matters of material wealth, for the country in which they live supplies their needs if they choose to make it do so. They need have little, or no, contact with the white man. If they desire possessions obtained in the white man's stores, they can hunt and trap in exchange for them. They can have as good a cabin and as fine a place to live in as we have. The materials and the setting are all there. They can have a healthy and sufficiently varied diet throughout the year if they have the enterprise to obtain it.

The hours and days, the months and years, are each man's to do with as he wills, make of what he desires. And what a country they have to live in! What beauty to look upon! What change of seasons to make life interesting! What new scenes on every side to visit if they grow tired of the old! Deep sheltered valleys for hard cruel winter; big lakes where winds sweep off the heat and insects of summer; great mountains, with new climate and scenery and wildlife, to explore.

All this for those who have the intelligence, character, and experience to work for it, and plan for it, and use it.

One afternoon the men went down the Driftwood in Charlie's canoe to try it out and observe the condition of the river. J., standing in the middle, was fishing, casting his spoon and a big three-barbed hook into a deep pool. On one cast, just as the flashing silver spoon was in mid-air, young Mac, sitting in the bottom, started up and caught the hook fairly in his cheek. One barb went clean through. Charlie, with a big knife, would have cut it out, but J. persuaded him to get Mac back to our cabin, let him clip the forked end of the barb off with his wire clippers, and pull the hook through without mutilating the cheek. When they reached the cabin we gave Mac, silent and self-contained as ever, a stiff dose of brandy, and J. set to work. The hook was especially strong and it took agonizing minutes before he could cut through the barb and break it off without tearing the skin. During all this Mac never moved a muscle. At last the hook was slid out and J. bade Charlie suck the wound. He then poured on S.T. 37, put a dressing over it, and we prayed that it would heal without difficulties.

The profound faith which these people have in the white man's power of healing is rather touching and, I think, a little sad. I had always supposed that these Indians, at least, would be self-sufficient in their knowledge and use of herbs for medicines, but the majority of them have been all too quick to learn the power of modern science. They depend on it too completely, for now, when some emergency case arises which is too far off to receive attention from a trained medical man, most of them appear to be helpless.

Charlie informs me that "the little medicine — the one he jump in water," which I gave him in the summer completely cured his rheumatism and is the best medicine he ever had. Once, when he was here in July, complaining woefully of pains in the back, I gave him four Alka-Seltzer tablets to take home, illustrating first the method of dosage by dropping one in a cup of water. Charlie downed it at a gulp and trotted happily off, bearing the other pills to be taken later. These simple remedies, and cathartics, which they seem always to be in need of, are the only supplies in our large well-stocked medical kit which have ever been used.

Charlie has given us a grizzly skin! It is not a very good fur, but it is a rare and beautiful color, a sort of pale gold or cream. The bear has a history. It was a female, very old, and had been hunted and shot at many times. Once it killed a man. This and its golden fur had marked it down, and it was Charlie, this past year, who apparently at last fired the fatal shot which ended its career. Now an Indian law, according to Charlie, decrees that when a bear has killed a man its skin cannot be sold. So we are the happy recipients. Charlie brought us the skull and had skinned the bear with care, leaving the feet and claws intact, just as we like it. He told us also that Indians say when a bear has killed a man its liver is white. Probably in such cases the whiteness is due to fibrous tumors or cirrhosis.

This summer when J. was at Takla, Mr. Aiken showed him a large grizzly skin which was solid black. It had been killed by

Indians along the east shore of Takla Lake. And in 1939 a Bear
Lake Indian family reported a female grizzly with two cubs seen
at close range; all three were black. Cases of melanism in this
country appear to be fairly common. The most notable ex-
amples are the black gray-headed chipmunks found on a rocky
mountain side sixty miles north of Bear Lake. The Bear Lake
Indians report that all chipmunks in that area are perfectly
black. Alec Bob brought us the skull and skin of one which
was identified by the Museum.

We have never been able to discover a single case in this
country of an unprovoked grizzly attacking a man. But that the
grizzly is dangerous does seem to be borne out by the facts.
Unlike the other animals, they are exceptionally bold and un-
afraid of man. They will not always give way to man and
have often been known to dispute a trail with him.

September 6

We leave Tetana tomorrow. This year I have a foreboding
that it may be long before we shall be here again. I know that
more terrible war is to come, and that J. will be a part of it, by
very virtue of his past experiences, his adventuring forefathers,
and his courage (for he is, so far, the bravest person I know —
never yet have I seen him shrink from hardship).

Once we vowed that if a war ever came again, we would stay
in the Shangri-la of our wilderness. But I think now that if we
would possess the freedom of that wilderness, or make it possible
for others to find it too, we must pay the price for what we wish
to hold. We can't just keep on attending to our own business no
matter how worthy and important that business seems, protected by the bulwark of our creeds and philosophies, and leave
the burden to someone else.

It seems that few places on the earth today may be free of
the evil works of man unless other men fight and agonize to
make them so. The rumble of Alaskan bombers flying high
over this valley during the summer has made this clear to me.
There is the constant rumor of a great Alaskan highway for
military purposes, which we pray will keep far from this re-

gion. And yet, when I look at the mountains, great with a strength and changelessness that men have not, and remember the mighty snows, the floods and avalanches, I believe that, after all, the lessons of a wilderness and the forces of Nature may keep man in his rightful place, teach him in the end those things which he needs to know, remain themselves steadfast and scarred only a little by the most terrible of his deeds.

These things, which J. and I have seen, must be with us in the days to come.

Bulkley House   *September 11*

We left Tetana on the seventh. Charlie, William, J. and I, and our dogs and provisions, started down-river in the big thirty-five-foot dugout; Mac and Alec, with the loaded horses, followed the trail. Before we rounded the point on Tetana's east shore and struck the outlet, I turned for one last, last look.

Old Charlie, paddling stern, said soberly: "You think you see Tetana last time now, Missus. I think you like him here. You know how to do here same like Indian. By gosh, too bad. Mebbe I die before you come again — "

When we flashed out into the river and the current bore down on us, I tried to let my mind go with the river; leave past things behind and search eagerly for new ones ahead. Happily nothing is more conducive to this line of philosophy than a trip in a dugout canoe on a rapid winding river. During our three-day journey down the miles of narrow waterway to Takla Lake (an eighty miles as opposed to the thirty by land), I scarcely had time, in the sheer joy and excitement of wondering what we should see around each new bend, to think sadly of what we were leaving behind.

J. has wanted to cap my experiences of this country by a trip down the river, which he claimed was a special delight. And no wonder! In Charlie's dugout, with three strong men paddling and poling, I have had, for once, not a thing to do but sit still and look on. During the first day we made good time for, at low water, the river is narrow and swift in its upper reaches. We struck a few shallows where we were obliged to unload, and several big log jams, the worst of which had to be tunneled through and caused two hours' delay. Charlie and William, standing above their waists in water so swift that more than once it took their feet from under them, chopped and sawed a passageway through the solid wall of big logs. For the first two days their clothes were constantly dripping wet, since they were in and out of the canoe every mile or so. They had as much disregard for getting wet as a dog has!

During most of the first part of the second day we headed toward the snow peaks of the Frypans. Autumn had begun to paint willows and poplars and shrubs all along the banks with pink and yellow, and touch with white and scarlet the berries of red-osier dogwood and bunchberry. Dozens of rusty blackbirds were breaking the long autumn migration southward to rest and feed along the muddy banks. Where side streams, fresh from the mountain snows, dashed out into the river, we paused to cast a line or two, and nearly always were rewarded by swift strikes from huge nine- and ten-pound Dollies. Once, beyond a long bend of the river, a great creek of milky blue hurled itself over boulders straight into the river.

"That one, he come part from Blue Lake," shouted Charlie above the noise of many waters; "straight from that canyon he come down. Jack, you try the fish here. Beeg ones here, by God — "

So J. cast and had a strike that bent his rod double and almost pulled him out of the canoe.

Charlie shrieked with triumphant glee, "What I tell you, Jack, what I tell you!"

J., with gleaming eyes and bulging arm muscles, played and played a giant trout. Since he was fearful of breaking both the line and the rod, it took half an hour before, with Charlie's help and the net, the slim steel handle of which promptly bent, he landed the fish on the gravel bar. It was a Dolly weighing fifteen pounds ten ounces, and it broke our previous record of fourteen pounds.

Though for the most part we traveled in complete silence, guns and cameras ready, expecting hourly to see a bear (for this is the time when bears should be out berrying on the riverbanks), we never saw one, nor did we see game of any other kind. Late on the third day, not far above Bulkley House, William, who was traveling ahead on the horse trail, killed a black bear at a point near the river. But we missed seeing it.

In the early morning of the third day, we passed through the last and most dangerous rapids of the trip. The river, nearing its end, had broadened out and now carried a considerable volume of water. It was fed here by several large creeks, and there were three stretches of bad rapids, each of which was several hundred yards long. When we started down these, it was impossible for Charlie to give adequate directions to J. and William paddling and poling in the middle and the bow. Well as Charlie knew the rapids he could not anticipate how their courses might have changed in a few months' time, or what new dangerous rocks might have been tossed up near the surface. Even as the canoe bounded down he had to plot the course we took and shout frantic directions to the others. When we came within a fraction of an inch of being smashed against a rock, he cursed and yelled; when we had successfully nego-tiated a bad stretch he laughed and cackled with glee.

It was vastly entertaining, though not especially reassuring, to have Charlie shout, just before we entered a tossing, foam-ing swirl of water: —

"By gosh, I dunno. Bad place now. Mebbe we neber make him. Mebbe canoe he smash in pieces just like matchbox. Then we throw him away on the bank and we walk ourself — Wil-liam!" — and here, as we neared the rapid, would follow a series of unintelligible shouts in his own language. When Charlie gets excited he always reverts to the Indian tongue.

But we got through them all, and then began the long, long weary miles around endless bends of still deep water. The Driftwood Mountains were visible no longer, the Frypans had removed themselves far to the west. Somehow the mountains seemed to have done the traveling. The country had flattened out. There were no more little hills and high rocky banks; willow swamps were more extensive. The river passed through miles and miles of them. Charlie would point out an isolated clump of big spruce — three tall ones, beautifully shaped, two dead ones, one bent one, and one leaning out over the river.

"See that tree, Missus? We go now long way, you think we leave him behind. We paddle, paddle, paddle. We work hard long time. We think we get near Takla pretty soon now. Then we see tree again. Same tree. By gosh, river he come right back again!"

And it was as Charlie had said. We traveled a whole hour under the hot sun, no longer shaded from us by high banks and hills. The men paddled on and on; I paddled; the dogs, who had been so still and good, scared perhaps by the rapid rush of fast water, now grew restless and shifted about in the bottom, which was several inches deep in dirty bilge. We went miles. And there just across a narrow spit of land was the same clump of trees again, three tall ones, two dead ones, one bent one, and the one leaning out over the river! Heavens! At this rate we should never get to Takla.

Once we spotted a huge horned owl, high up on a tree in a thick stretch of forest. Through the glasses we could see his fierce golden eyes blinking in the sunlight. We needed a horned owl for our collection. So, because this one, beautiful creature, had changed his usual owl habit by appearing plainly in broad daylight, he must be sacrificed to science. J.'s big shotgun was up, there was one clean swift shot, and the owl plummeted like a rock down into a thicket on the bank.

In the late afternoon they said we were only six or seven miles from Bulkley House. In a spot where the horse trail followed close to the river we joined the boys and the horses and the Indian dogs. After we had negotiated the last rapid, William had gone ashore to hunt game along the trail, while young Mac had taken his place in the canoe. We were pleased to note that the wound on Mac's cheek had healed well, leaving only a little mark. Each night William helped Mac and Alec attend to the horses. Lassie and Baldy seemed to be in good shape and well cared for. We ourselves had overseen their pasturing every night, and J. had packed them each morning.

But we were not so sure that the possessions in our duffels and pack sacks *had* been well cared for! Judging from their damp and much-wrinkled appearance, it looked as though some of our best down quilts and clothes might have been slept in. And J. strongly suspected designs on his best-loved game rifle, loaned to William for hunting and much coveted by the Indians, who had tried to bargain for it on numerous occasions. The gun had a strange habit of disappearing. J. was certain that it would be left behind on the last morning. So that morning J. wasted, according to Charlie, much valuable time by seeing the boys on their way and examining the camp and trail after they left. Nothing was said to anyone, but for a while relations were a bit strained all round, though on the surface much courtesy and jolly talk prevailed.

Yesterday when we got within five miles of Takla, J. decided to walk the rest of the way with Wahoo, leaving Rex and me in the canoe with old Charlie and Mac. The river now passed through miles of flat open marsh, which bordered the north end of the lake. Here Canada geese by the thousands were gathered to feed before they went south to their winter resorts. As we approached they rose in every direction in clouds of white and gray, outlined against the wild purple-green mountains that lie on the northwest of Takla. Their honking deafened us, the clamor of their wings, and their whirling bodies, as thick as snowflakes, dizzied us. There were also countless flocks of wild ducks — pintails and mallards and mergansers and teal. The earth and sky and the mountains and the waters were filled with birds of every size and shape, from the great geese to the tiny green-winged teal.

J. had instructed Charlie to use his shotgun on the geese and bring some down if he could, for we were all hungry and coveted a meal of goose. But the geese were very wary. Time and again hundreds upon thousands rose from the near marshes and broad river just beyond range of the gun. Without success Mac tried to stalk them across the marshes. Finally a small flock, startled out of the willows around a bend, flew low just over us and Charlie fired. He hit one, which came down to the water, but it was not much hurt because it started swimming rapidly off, calling pitifully all the while to its comrades. And in the manner of wild geese, who are known to be wonderfully faithful to their lifelong mates, the flock wheeled and came back to answer the fallen one. Charlie fired again but, to my great joy, missed, and we concentrated on getting the wounded one. Charlie and Mac took turns trying to hit it with the .22 but missed each time.

Because I can't bear to have anything wounded get away to suffer, I took the .22 and began firing. After seven shots, which I was ashamed to count, I finally hit and killed it instantly. (It was the first time I had ever tried to hit anything that was moving as rapidly as that goose, which was alternately swimming and diving and skimming the surface with great speed!)

Soon after this we negotiated in high wind and rough water the two miles across the north end of Takla and saw J. and Wahoo waiting on the beach. Wahoo, I think, was afraid that Rex and I had been left behind, for as our canoe approached within hailing distance he rushed with roars of joy out into the big waves and started swimming toward us.

Last night we all dined on the goose, and I have certainly never tasted anything more delicious. William has gone on with the horses to the Landing and is to send a boat up for us as soon as possible. Just as he was leaving he fired a last parting shot.

"Hey Jack! You got the big gun? You watch him. Mebbe he lose himself yet!"

Takla Landing   *September 16*

Four days ago we came once more to the Landing. We have our camp on the shore a little above the spot where we stayed on our very first appearance in this land, just four years ago. Mr. and Mrs. Gavin, recently arrived from the Arctic and temporarily in charge of this post, have been just as hospitable as the H. B. C. people always are. They actually appreciate our two big dogs as much as the dogs deserve to be appreciated, and give them the run of their house whenever we go there. We've been winding up affairs, and are waiting for the first opportunity to go out by plane or freight boat. Lassie is to be handed over again to Johnny French, who, now that she has been tamed and gentled, seems glad to have her. Baldy is to be sent by boat to the Fort where we trust he will be handled with the greatest of care. If he were anything less large than a horse, I should insist on taking him with us. J. says, thank God he *is* a horse and that I can't put him in a baggage car.

Soon after we got here, three prospectors from somewhere north arrived. After a half year's prospecting they too are going out to civilization for a time. In the late afternoon they came silently out of the forest, down the long beach of the lake above our camp, three men in battered clothes, a drooping, woefully thin mare, and a small colt, moving slowly and wearily and steadily, as people do who have walked great distances. Later, as they sat resting in front of the little shack where they are putting up temporarily, we were introduced to them. They all rose, lifted their tattered hats, and looked at us with grave, steady eyes.

I liked their quiet poise better than I've often liked the assured bows of polished members of polite society. These prospectors who live far off and work independently of the mines are in keeping with the majority of white men whom I've seen in the North. Literate or illiterate, rich or poor, comely or ugly, they are nearly always real men. For, by virtue of their own behavior in great hardships, they have attained true manhood. Prospectors in this country, contrary to pictures which one acquires from literature of the murderous men of the gold rush, are in general fine and worth-while friends. They acquire their wealth, more worthily than many a big businessman, by digging it with hard and honest toil from the ground. We have been told that the average prospector in this region makes several thousand a year — enough to enable him to live well when he goes outside for a few months, and sufficient to store up for a rainy day.

And so that everything should be just as usual, J. and Charlie

had a last fight! They had far hotter words than ordinary over
the price of this final trip. Their loud talk occurred in the
store before a group of spectators. I thought this an unwise
procedure on J.'s part. He should have conducted the paying-
off in private; but then, as I wasn't there, I don't know the circumstances. It seems that Charlie conveniently and completely
forgot, or failed to understand, that half the price of the trip
had been already paid in food supplies at Tetana; when he received the other half (only a half!) in cash, he spoke loud and
angry words, and accused J. of all manner of things. J., equally
angered, took the opportunity to tell Charlie a few of the
grievances that have been accumulating in his mind for about
three years. But it was all smoothed over finally and Charlie
departed with his cash. That night, report had it that instead
of buying meals for himself and the hungry boys and acquiring
the badly needed food to take home to his family, he spent it
in home-brew and gambling at the Chinaman's. At the last,
however, before they started back, J. treated them all to a big
meal at the restaurant.

On the way down, the Indian dogs, whom the boys had
brought along to carry home the large food supplies that their
father was to have purchased with his cash, ran into a porcupine. They were badly stuck with quills. William sorrowfully
said that they might die, but he made no effort as far as we
knew to free them of the quills, or otherwise keep them from
dying. For several days the dogs remained, apparently without
food or water, tied by ropes or wires about three feet long to
the fence by the Hudson's Bay Post. Several times I threw them
scraps, and finally J. located the boys and insisted that they
let the dogs loose to drink in the lake. I can comprehend and
excuse many reprehensible traits, but this utter indifference
to the welfare of an animal is the one characteristic that I cannot forgive.

Charlie and the boys departed unexpectedly when they had
a chance for a lift by boat up to Bulkley House, taking with
them Simon and his latest wife. Simon is apparently returning
to Bear Lake. They did not come to say good-bye to us, pos-

sibly because of J.'s and Charlie's rather recent todo. But when the old motorboat passed the shore where our camp is, Charlie arose, waved his hat and both arms wildly, and shouted good-byes till they were out of sight. We waved and called good-bye with equal warmth. After all, though we have all in times past been angered one at the other, we are fond of one another, for we have seen and done great things together.

In a few days we shall leave here on the last lap of our journey to the outside world. Whenever it is clear enough to see to the north end of Takla, I look toward the Frypans and Driftwood Mountains, now so remote and far-off, keeping watch over Tetana and our beloved wilderness, forever steadfast and serene, undisturbed by the comings and goings and distresses of mere man.

Keep safe, Tetana, until we come again.

APPENDIX

Lists of Plants and Animals Found in the Driftwood Region[1]

PLANTS

FERNS AND LYCOPODIUMS

Botrychium virginianum (L.) Sw. Rattlesnake Fern.
Botrychium silaifolium Presl. Grape Fern.
Botrychium lanceolatum var. *angustisegmentum* Pease and Moore. Grape Fern.
Cryptogramma acrostichoides R. Br. Parsley Fern.
Phegopteris Dryopteris (L.) Fee. Oak Fern.
Asplenium Filix-femina (L.) Bernh. Lady Fern.
Aspidium spinulosum Sw. var. *dilatatum* (Hoffm.). Spinulose Fern.
Polystichum lonchitis (L.) Roth. Holly Fern.
Cystopteris fragilis (L.) Bernh. Bladder Fern.
Equisetum arvensis L. Horsetail.
Equisetum sylvaticum L. Horsetail.
Equisetum palustre L. Horsetail.
Equisetum fluviatile L. Horsetail.
Lycopodium obscurum L. var. *dendroideum* D. C. Eaton. Club Moss.
Lycopodium Selago L. Club Moss.
Lycopodium annotinum L. Club Moss.
Lycopodium complanatum L. Club Moss.
Lycopodium sitchense Rupr. Club Moss.
Lycopodium alpinum L. Club Moss.

[1] Occasional Papers of the British Columbia Provincial Museum, No. 4, May 1943, "Some Accounts of the Flora and Fauna of the Driftwood Valley Region of North Central British Columbia," by John F. and Theodora C. Stanwell-Fletcher, and "Naturalists in the Wilds of British Columbia" by John F. and Theodora C. Stanwell-Fletcher. *Scientific Monthly,* January, February, March, 1940.
The publishers have used Webster's Dictionary as authority for all English names, in order to standardize usage throughout the book.

FLOWERING PLANTS

Juniperus communis L. var. *montana* Ait. Juniper.

Pinus contorta Dougl. var. *Murrayana* (Balf.) Engelm. Lodge Pole Pine.

Abies lasiocarpa (Hook.) Nutt. Alpine Fir or Balsam.

Picea mariana (Mill.) B.S.P. Black Spruce.

Picea canadensis (Mill.) B.S.P. White Spruce.

Potamogeton filiformis Pers. Pondweed.

Triglochin maritima L. Arrow Grass.

Hierochloe odorata (L.) Wahl. Grass.

Phleum alpinum L. Grass.

Trisetum spicatum (L.) Richter. Grass.

Glyceria pauciflora Presl. Grass.

Poa nemoralis L. Grass.

Poa pratensis L. Grass.

Poa paucispicula Scribn. & Merr. Grass.

Bromus carinatus H. & A. Grass.

Bromus ciliatus L. Grass.

Festuca altaica Ledeb. Grass.

Agropyron repens (L.) Beauv. Grass.

Carex Crawfordii Fernald. Sedge.

Carex Preslii Stend. Sedge.

Carex Hindsii Clark. Sedge.

Carex anthoxanthea Presl. Sedge.

Carex canescens L. Sedge.

Carex festivella Mackenzie. Sedge.

Carex brunnescens Poir. Sedge.

Carex aquatilis Wahl. Sedge.

Carex Kelloggii Boott. Sedge.

Carex pyrenaica Wahl. Sedge.

Carex pauciflora Lightf. Sedge.

Carex limosa L. Sedge.

Carex disperma Dewey. Sedge.

Carex rostrata Stokes. Sedge.

Eriophorum Chamissonis Mey. Cotton Grass.

Eriophorum alpinum L. Cotton Grass.

Eriophorum angustifolium Roth. Cotton Grass.

Luzula Piperi (Cov.) M. E. Jones. Wood Rush.

Luzula Wahlenbergii Rupr. Wood Rush.

Juncus Drummondii Meyer. Rush.

Juncus Mertensianus Bong. Rush.

Clintonia uniflora Kunth. Queen's Cup or Clintonia.

Smilacina racemosa L. False Solomon's-seal.

Smilacina stellata (L.) Desf. False Solomon's-seal.

Disporum trachycarpum B. & H. Fairy Bells.

Streptopus amplexifolius DC. Twisted Stalk.

Veratrum viride Ait. False Hellebore.

Zygadenus elegans Pursh. Zygadene.

Lloydia serotina Reich. Lloydia.

Fritillaria kamtschatcensia Ker. Fritillary.

Corallorhiza innata R. Br. Coral Root.

Calypso bulbosa (L.) Oakes. Calypso.

Habenaria obtusata Richards. Rein Orchid.

Habenaria elegans Lindl. Rein Orchid.

Habenaria leptoceratitis Rydb. Rein Orchid.

Listera nephrophylla Rydb. Twayblade.

Peramium decipiens (Hook.) Ames. Rattlesnake Plantain.

Salix lasiandra Benth. Willow.

Salix arctica Pall. Willow.

Salix Bebbiana Sarg. Willow.

Salix Scouleriana Hook. Willow.

Salix subcoerulea Piper. Willow.

Salix glaucops Anders. Willow.

Salix Barclayi rotundifolia Anders. Willow.

Salix pedicellaris hypoglauca Fernald. Willow.

Salix myrtillifolia Anders. Willow.

Populus tremuloides Michx. Aspen Poplar.

Populus balsamifera L. Balm of Gilead or Balsam Poplar.

Betula glandulosa Michx. Dwarf Birch.

Betula papyrifera Marsh. Paper Birch.

Alnus rubra Bong. Alder.

Urtica Lyallii Wats. Western Nettle.

Commandra livida Richards. Bastard Toad-Flax.

Oxyria digyna (L.) Camptdera. Mountain Sorrel.

Rumex acetosa L. Garden Sorrel.

Polygonum Douglasii Greene. Knotweed.

Polygonum viviparum L. Knotweed.

Polygonum amphibium L. Knotweed.

Sagina saginoides L. Brit. Pearlwort.

Arenaria lateriflora L. Sandwort.

Cerastium alpinum L. Mouse Ear Chickweed.

Stellaria strictiflora Rydb. Chickweed.

Stellaria laeta Rich. Chickweed.

Silene acaulis L. Moss Campion.

Anemone Richardsonii Hook. Anemone.

Anemone multifida Poir. Wind-Flower.

Thalictrum occidentale Gray. Meadow Rue.

Ranunculus lapponicus L. Buttercup.

Ranunculus aquatilis L. Water Buttercup.

Ranunculus circinatus Sibth. Buttercup.

Ranunculus Purshii Richards. Buttercup.

Ranunculus flammula var. *reptans* Mey. Buttercup.

Ranunculus abortivus L. Buttercup.

Ranunculus Eschscholtzii Schlecht. Buttercup.

Ranunculus occidentalis Nutt. Western Buttercup.

Ranunculus Bongardi Greene. Buttercup.

Ranunculus Macounii Brit. Buttercup.

Caltha leptosepala DC. Mountain Marigold.

Aquilegia formosa Fischer. Columbine.

Actaea arguta Nutt. Baneberry.

Delphinium Brownii Rydb. Larkspur or Delphinium.

Aconitum columbianum Nutt. Monkshood.

Thalspi arvense L. Penny Cress.

Radicula nasturtium-aquaticum (L.) Water Cress.

Radicula palustris (L.) Moench. Marsh Cress.

Draba Andina (Nutt.) A. Nels. Whitlow Grass.

Draba Fladnizensis Wulf. Whitlow Grass.

Draba nivalis Lilj. Whitlow Grass.

Arabis lyrata L. var. *occidentalis* Wats. Cress.

Arabis lyrata var. *kamtschatica* Fisch. Cress.

Arabis Drummondii Gray. Cress.

Arabis alpina L. Cress.

Arabis Nuttallii Rob. Cress.

Cardamine bellidifolia L. Alpine Cress.

Cardamine kamtschatica (Regel) Schultz. Bitter Cress.

Barbarea orthoceras Ledeb. Winter Cress.

Drosera rotundifolia L. Round-leaved Sundew.

Drosera anglica Huds. Long-leaved Sundew.

Sedum divergens Wats. Stonecrop.

Rhodiola integrifolium (Raf.) Nels. Stonecrop or Western Rose-root.

Ribes triste Pall. Red Currant.

Ribes glandulosum Grauer. Skunk Currant.

Ribes Hudsonianum Richards. Black Currant.

Ribes oxyacanthoides L. Smooth Gooseberry.

Parnassia fimbriata Banks. Grass of Parnassus.

Mitella nuda L. Mitrewort.

Tellima grandiflora Dougl. Fringe-Cup.

Tiarella trifoliata L. False Mitrewort.

Heuchera glabra Willd. Alum Root.

Leptarrhena amplexifolia (Sternb.) Ser. Pear-Leaf.

Saxifraga tricuspidata Rottb. Saxifrage.

Saxifraga tolmiei T. & G. Saxifrage.

Saxifraga delicatula Rydb. Saxifrage.

Saxifraga rivularis L. Alpine Brook Saxifrage.

Saxifraga Bongardi (Presl.) Pursh. Saxifrage.

Saxifraga nivalis L. Alpine Saxifrage.

Saxifraga Lyallii Engler. Saxifrage.

Rubus parviflorus Nutt. Thimbleberry.

Rubus Chamaemorus L. Cloudberry.

Rubus pubescens Raf. Dwarf Red Blackberry.

Rubus pedatus Smith. Trailing Raspberry.

Rubus acaulis Michx. Raspberry.

Fragaria chiloensis (L.) Duch. Strawberry.

Rosa acicularis Lindl. Wild Rose.

Sanguisorba sitchensis Meyer. Burnet.

Spiraea pectinata T. & G. Spiraea.

Spiraea Douglasii Hook. Hardhack.

Potentilla diversifolia Lehm. Cinquefoil.

Potentilla palustris (L.) Scop. Cinquefoil.

Potentilla nivea L. Cinquefoil.

Potentilla dissecta Pursh. Cinquefoil.

Geum rivale L. Purple Avens.

Pyrus sitchensis (Roem.) Piper. Mountain Ash.

Amelanchier Florida Lindl. Saskatoon.

Lupinus nootkatensis Don. Lupine.

Astragalus alpinus L. Milk Vetch.

Geranium erianthum DC. Northern Geranium.

Geranium Richardsonii F. &. M. White Geranium.

Empetrum nigrum L. Crowberry.
Acer glabrum Torr. Rocky Mountain Maple.
Viola renifolia Gray var. *Brainerdii* Fernald. Kidney-leaved Violet.
Viola palustris L. Swamp Violet.
Viola orbiculata Geyer. Yellow Violet.
Viola adunca Smith. Violet.
Viola canadensis L. Canada Violet.
Shepherdia canadensis Nutt. Soopolallie.
Hippuris vulgaris L. Bottle Brush.
Epilobium angustifolium L. Willow Herb or Fireweed.
Epilobium latifolium L. Willow Herb.
Epilobium adenocaulon Haus. Willow Herb.
Epilobium alpinum L. Alpine Willow Herb.
Osmorrhiza Leibergii C. &. R. Sweet Cicely.
Heracleum lanatum Michx. Cow Parsnip.
Angelica genuflexa Nutt. Angelica.
Aralia nudicaulis L. Sarsaparilla.
Fatsia horrida (Sm.) B. & H. Devil's-club.
Cornus canadensis L. Bunchberry.
Cornus unalaschkense (Ledeb.) Rydb. Bunchberry.
Cornus pubescens Nutt. Western Dogwood.
Cornus stolonifera Michx. Red-osier Dogwood.
Chiogenes hispidula (L.) T. & G. Snowberry.
Vaccinium membranaceum Dougl. Mountain Bilberry.
Vaccinium caespitosum Michx. Dwarf Bilberry.
Pyrola secunda L. One-sided Wintergreen or Pyrola.
Pyrola minor L. Wintergreen or Pyrola.
Pyrola chlorantha Swartz. Wintergreen or Pyrola.
Pyrola asarifolia Michx. var. *uliginosa* T. &. G. Wintergreen.
Moneses uniflora (L.) Gray. One-Flowered Pyrola.
Chimaphila umbellata (L.) Nutt. Pipsissewa.
Ledum groenlandicum Oeder. Labrador Tea.
Arctostaphylos uva-ursi Spreng. Bearberry.
Cassiope Mertensiana Don. Moss Heather.
Andromeda polifolia L. Wild Rosemary.
Phyllodoce empetriformis Don. False Heather.
Phyllodoce glanduliflorus Hook. False Heather.
Kalmia polifolia Wang. American Laurel.
Menziesia ferruginea Smith. False Azalea.
Loiseleuria procumbens Desv. Alpine Azalea.

Oxycoccus microcarpus Turz. Cranberry.

Rhododendron albiflorum Hook. Rhododendron.

Hypopites Hypopites (L.) Small. Pinesap.

Trientalis latifolia Hook. Star Flower.

Trientalis arctica Fishch. Arctic Star Flower.

Gentiana acuta Michx. Northern Gentian.

Gentiana propinqua Rich. Four-Parted Gentian.

Gentiana glauca Pall. Glaucous Gentian.

Menyanthes trifoliata L. Buckbean.

Apocynum androsaemifolium L. Dogbane.

Gilia gracilis Hook. Gilia.

Polemonium occidentale Greene. Greek Valerian.

Polemonium humile R. & S. Greek Valerian.

Lappula floribunda (Lehm.) Greene. False Forget-Me-Not.

Myosotis alpestris Schmidt. Alpine Forget-Me-Not.

Mertensia paniculata Don. Tall Lungwort.

Mentha canadensis L. Canada Mint.

Veronica alpina L. Alpine Speedwell.

Veronica serpyllifolia L. Speedwell.

Veronica americana Schwein. Brooklime.

Mimulus Langsdorfii Don. Monkey Flower.

Castilleja angustifolia Nutt. var. *Bradburyi* Fernald. Indian Paintbrush.

Castilleja miniata Dougl. Indian Paintbrush.

Pedicularis scopulorum Gray. Lousewort.

Pedicularis Euphrasioides Steph. Lousewort.

Pedicularis bracteosa Benth. Lousewort.

Galium boreale L. Bedstraw.

Galium trifidum L. Bedstraw.

Linnaea borealis L. var. *Americana* (Forbes) Rehder. Twinflower.

Lonicera involucrata (Richards) Banks. Honeysuckle.

Symphoricarpos racemosa Michx. Wax Berry or Snowberry.

Sambucus racemosa Hook. Red-fruited Elder.

Viburnum pauciflorum Pyl. Squashberry.

Valeriana septentrionalis Rydb. Valerian.

Valeriana sitchensis Bong. Valerian.

Campanula lasiocarpa Cham. Northern Bluebell.

Erigeron acris L. var. *Draebachiensis* Blytt. Fleabane.

Erigeron aureus Greene. Fleabane.

Erigeron uniflorus L. Fleabane.

Erigeron salsuginosus Gray. Fleabane.
Solidago corymbosa Nutt. Goldenrod.
Solidago ciliosa Greene. Goldenrod.
Achillea millefolium L. Yarrow.
Artemisia longipedunculata Rud. Sagebrush.
Petasites frigida (L.) Fries. Coltsfoot.
Arnica cordifolia Hook. Arnica.
Arnica latifolia Bong. Arnica.
Arnica alpina (L.) Olm. Arnica.
Arnica amplexicaulis Nutt. Arnica.
Senecio discoideus (Hook.) Brit. Groundsel.
Senecio triangularis Hook. Groundsel.
Senecio exaltatus Nutt. Groundsel.
Senecio pauciflorus Rydb. Groundsel.
Antennaria chlorantha Greene. Everlasting.
Antennaria Howellii Greene. Everlasting.
Antennaria racemosa Hook. Everlasting.
Antennaria rosea Greene. Pink-Flowered Everlasting.
Antennaria monocephala DC. Everlasting.
Anaphalis margaritacea (L.) Benth and Hook. Pearly Everlasting.
Circium edulis Greene. Thistle.
Taraxacum officinale Weber. Dandelion.
Taraxacum rupestre Greene. Dandelion.
Agoseris aurantiaca (Hook.) Greene. False Dandelion.
Hieracium albiflorum Hook. Hawkweed.
Hieracium gracile Hook. Hawkweed.

FISH

Acipenser transmontanus Richardson. Pacific Sturgeon.
Salmo gairdneri Richardson. Steelhead Trout.
Salmo gairdneri kamloops Jordan. Kamloops Trout.
Cristivomer namaycush (Walbaum). Lake Trout.
Oncorhynchus nerka (Walbaum). Sockeye Salmon.
Oncorhynchus nerka kennerlyi (Suckley). Kokanee.
Salvelinus malma spectabilis (Girard). Dolly Varden Char or Dolly
   Varden Trout.
Coregonus clupeaformis (Mitchill). Eastern Whitefish.
Prosopium williamsoni (Girard). Rocky Mountain Whitefish.
Catostomus macrocheilus Girard. Large-scaled Sucker.

Catostomus catostomus (Forster). Small-scaled Sucker.
Richardsonius balteatus (Richardson). Shiner.
Lota maculosa (Le Sueur). Ling.

AMPHIBIANS

Ambystoma macrodactylum Baird. Long-toed Salamander.
Bufo boreas boreas Baird and Girard. Northwestern Toad.
Rana pretiosa Baird and Girard. Western Spotted Frog.
Rana cantabrigensis Baird. Northern Wood Frog.

BIRDS

Gavia immer (Brunnich). Common Loon.
Gavia arctica pacifica (Lawrence). Pacific Loon.
Colymbus grisegena holboelli (Reinhardt). Holboell's Grebe.
Colymbus auritus Linnaeus. Horned Grebe.
Phalacrocorax auritus ssp. White-crested Cormorant.
Botaurus lentiginosus (Montagu). American Bittern.
Cygnus columbianus (Ord). Whistling Swan.
Cygnus buccinator Richardson. Trumpeter Swan.
Branta canadensis canadensis (Linnaeus). Common Canada Goose.
Chen hyperborea hyperborea (Pallas). Snow Goose.
Anas platyrhynchos platyrhynchos Linnaeus. Common Mallard.
Chaulelasmus streperus (Linnaeus). Gadwall.
Mareca americana (Gmelin). Baldpate.
Dafila acuta tzitzihoa (Vieillot). American Pintail.
Nettion carolinense (Gmelin). Green-winged Teal.
Querquedula discors (Linnaeus). Blue-winged Teal.
Spatula clypeata (Linnaeus). Shoveler.
Nyroca americana (Eyton). Redhead.
Nyroca collaris (Donovan). Ring-necked Duck.
Nyroca marila (Linnaeus). Greater Scaup Duck.
Nyroca affinis (Eyton). Lesser Scaup Duck.
Glaucionetta clangula americana (Bonaparte). American Golden-eye.
Glaucionetta islandica (Gmelin). Barrow's Goldeneye.
Charitonetta albeola (Linnaeus). Buffle-head.
Clangula hyemalis (Linnaeus). Oldsquaw.
Histrionicus histrionicus pacificus Brooks. Western Harlequin Duck.

Melanitta deglandi (Bonaparte) . White-winged Scoter.

Erismatura jamaicensis rubida (Wilson) . Ruddy Duck.

Lophodytes cucullatus (Linnaeus) . Hooded Merganser.

Mergus merganser americanus Cassin. American Merganser.

Astur atricapillus ssp. Western Goshawk.

Accipiter velox velox (Wilson) . Sharp-shinned Hawk.

Accipiter cooperi (Bonaparte) . Cooper's Hawk.

Buteo borealis ssp. Western Red-tailed Hawk.

Aquila chrysaetos canadensis (Linnaeus) . Golden Eagle.

Haliaeetus leucocephalus alascanus Townsend. Northern Bald Eagle.

Circus hudsonius (Linnaeus) . Marsh Hawk.

Pandion haliaeetus carolinensis (Gmelin) . Osprey.

Falco rusticolus ssp. Gyrfalcon.

Falco peregrinus anatum Bonaparte. Duck Hawk.

Falco columbarius bendirei Linnaeus. Western Pigeon Hawk.

Falco sparverius sparverius Linnaeus. Eastern Sparrow Hawk.

Dendragapus obscurus flemingi Taverner. Dusky Grouse.

Canachites franklini (Douglas) . Franklin's Grouse.

Bonasa umbellus umbelloides (Douglas) . Gray Ruffed Grouse.

Lagopus leucurus leucurus (Richardson) . Northern White-tailed Ptarmigan.

Oxyechus vociferus vociferus (Linnaeus) . Killdeer.

Squatarola squatarola (Linnaeus) . Black-bellied Plover.

Capella delicata (Ord) . Wilson's Snipe.

Actitis macularia (Linnaeus) . Spotted Sandpiper.

Totanus melanoleucus (Gmelin) . Greater Yellowlegs.

Pisobia bairdi (Coues) . Baird's Sandpiper.

Pisobia minutilla (Vieillot) . Least Sandpiper.

Lobipes lobatus (Linnaeus) . Northern Phalarope.

Larus argentatus smithsonianus Coues. Herring Gull.

Larus philadelphia (Ord) . Bonaparte's Gull.

Zenaida macroura marginella (Woodhouse) . Mourning Dove.

Bubo virginianus lagophonus (Oberholser) . Great Horned Owl.

Glaucidium gnoma californicum Sclater. Pygmy Owl.

Scotiaptex nebulosa nebulosa (Forster) . Great Gray Owl.

Cryptoglaux funerea richardsoni (Bonaparte) . Richardson's Owl.

Chordeiles minor minor (Forster) . Pacific Nighthawk.

Selasphorus rufus (Gmelin) . Rufous Hummingbird.

Megaceryle alcyon caurina (Grinnell) . Western Belted Kingfisher.

Colaptes auratus luteus Bangs. Yellow-shafted Flicker.

Colaptes cafer cafer (Gmelin) . Red-shafted Flicker.

Asyndesmus lewis Grey. Lewis's Woodpecker.

Sphyrapicus varius ruber (Gmelin) . Northern Red-breasted Sapsucker.

Dryobates villosus septentrionalis (Nuttall) . Northern Hairy Woodpecker.

Picoides arcticus (Swainson) . Arctic Three-toed Woodpecker.

Picoides tridactylus fasciatus Baird. Alaska Three-toed Woodpecker.

Sayornis saya saya (Bonaparte) . Say's Phoebe.

Empidonax hammondi (Zantus) . Hammond's Flycatcher.

Myiochanes richardsoni richardsoni (Swainson) . Western Wood Pewee.

Tachycineta thalassina lepida Mearns. Violet-green Swallow.

Iridoprocne bicolor (Vieillot) . Tree Swallow.

Stelgidopteryx ruficollis serripennis (Audubon) . Rough-winged Swallow.

Petrochelidon albifrons albifrons (Rafinesque) . Northern Cliff Swallow.

Perisoreus canadensis canadensis (Linnaeus) . Canada Jay.

Cyanocitta stelleri annectens (Baird) . Black-headed Jay.

Pica pica hudsonia (Sabine) . Magpie.

Corvus corax principalis Ridgway. Northern Raven.

Corvus brachyrhynchos hesperis Ridgway. Western Crow.

Penthestes atricapillus septentrionalis (Harris) . Long-tailed Chickadee.

Penthestes gambeli grinnelli Van Rossem. Grinnell's Chickadee.

Penthestes hudsonicus columbianus (Rhoads) . Columbian Chickadee.

Sitta canadensis Linnaeus. Red-breasted Nuthatch.

Certhia familiaris ssp. Rocky Mountain Creeper.

Cinclus mexicanus unicolor Bonaparte. Dipper or Water Ouzel.

Nannus hiemalis pacificus (Baird) . Western Winter Wren.

Turdus migratorius migratorius Linnaeus. Eastern Robin.

Ixoerus naevius ssp. Varied Thrush.

Hylocichla guttata ssp. Hermit Thrush.

Hylocichla ustulata swainsoni (Tschudi) . Olive-backed Thrush.

Hylocichla minima aliciae (Baird) . Gray-cheeked Thrush.

Sialia currucoides (Bechstein) . Mountain Bluebird.

Myadestes townsendi (Aubudon). Townsend's Solitaire.

Regulus satrapa olivaceus Baird. Western Golden-crowned Kinglet.

Corthylio calendula calendula (Linnaeus). Eastern Ruby-crowned
Kinglet.

Anthus spinoletta rubescens (Tunstall). American Pipit.

Bombycilla cedrorum Vieillot. Cedar Waxwing.

Lanius borealis invictus Grinnell. Northwestern Shrike.

Vireo gilvus swainsoni Baird. Western Warbling Vireo.

Vermivora peregrina (Wilson). Tennessee Warbler.

Vermivora celata celata (Say). Orange-crowned Warbler.

Dendroica aestiva rubiginosa (Pallas). Alaska Yellow Warbler.

Dendroica magnolia (Wilson). Magnolia Warbler.

Dendroica coronata (Linnaeus). Myrtle Warbler.

Dendroica auduboni auduboni (Townsend). Audubon's Warbler.

Dendroica townsendi (Townsend). Townsend's Warbler.

Dendroica castanea (Wilson). Bay-breasted Warbler.

Dendroica striata (Forster). Black-poll Warbler.

Seiurus noveboracensis noveboracensis (Gmelin). Northern Water-
Thrush.

Oporornis tolmiei (Townsend). Macgillivray's Warbler.

Geothylpis trichas occidentalis Brewster. Western Yellow-throat.

Wilsonia pusilla pileolata (Pallas). Northern Pileolated Warbler.

Setophaga ruticilla (Linnaeus). American Redstart.

Agelaius phoeniceus ssp. Red-winged Blackbird.

Euphagus carolinus (Muller). Rusty Blackbird.

Euphagus cyanocephalus (Wagler). Brewer's Blackbird.

Hesperiphona vespertina brooksi Grinnell. Western Evening
Grosbeak.

Carpodacus purpureus purpureus (Gmelin). Eastern Purple Finch.

Pinicola enucleator flammula Homeyer. Kodiak Pine Grosbeak.

Acanthis hornemanni exilipes (Coues). Hoary Redpoll.

Acanthis linaria linaria (Linnaeus). Common Redpoll.

Spinus pinus pinus (Wilson). Northern Pine Siskin.

Loxia curvirostra bendirei Ridgway. Bendire's Crossbill.

Passerculus sandwichensis alaudinus Bonaparte. Savannah Sparrow.

Junco hyemalis cismontanus Dwight. Slate-colored Junco.

Junco oreganus montanus Ridgway. Montana Junco.

Spizella arborea ochracea Brewster. Western Tree Sparrow.

Spizella passerina passerina (Bechstein). Western Chipping Sparrow.

Zonotrichia leucophrys gambeli (Nuttall). Gambel's Sparrow.

Zonotrichia coronata (Pallas). Golden-crowned Sparrow.

Passerella iliaca altivagans Riley. Alberta Fox Sparrow.

Melospiza lincolni lincolni (Aubudon). Lincoln's Sparrow.

Melospiza melodia morphna Oberholser. Rusty Song Sparrow.

Calcarius lapponicus alascensis Ridgway. Alaska Longspur.

Plectrophenax nivalis nivalis (Linnaeus). Eastern Snow Bunting.

MAMMALS

Sorex cinereus cinereus Kerr. Masked Shrew.

Sorex obscurus obscurus Merriam. Dusky Shrew.

Myotis lucifugus alascensis Miller. Alaskan Little Brown Bat.

Euarctos americanus ssp. Black Bear.

Ursus tahltanicus Merriam. Tahltan Grizzly Bear.

Martes americana actuosa (Osgood). Alaskan Marten.

Martes pennanti columbiana Goldman. Columbian Fisher.

Mustela cicognanii richardsonii Bonaparte. Richardson Weasel.

Mustela rixosa rixosa (Bangs). Least Weasel.

Mustela vison energumenos (Bangs). Pacific Mink.

Gulo luscus (Linnaeus). Wolverine.

Lutra canadensis evexa Goldman. Otter.

Mephitis hudsonica (Richardson). Northern Skunk.

Vulpes fulva abietorum Merriam. British Columbia Red Fox.

Canis latrans incolatus Hall. Northern Brush Wolf or Coyote.

Canis lupus columbianus Goldman. British Columbia Timber Wolf.

Lynx canadensis canadensis Kerr. Canada Lynx.

Felis oregonensis ssp. Cougar.

Marmota monax petrensis Howell. British Columbia Woodchuck.

Marmota caligata oxytona Hollister. Robson Hoary Marmot.

Eutamias minimus caniceps Osgood. Gray-headed Chipmunk.

Sciurus hudsonicus columbiensis Howell. Columbian Red Squirrel.

Glaucomys sabrinus alpinus (Richardson). Richardson Flying Squirrel.

Castor canadensis sagittatus Benson. Beaver.

Peromyscus maniculatus borealis Mearns. Boreal White-footed Mouse.

Neotoma cinerea saxamans (Osgood). Osgood Wood Rat.

Synaptomys borealis dalli (Merriam). Dall Lemming Mouse.

Lemmus trimucronatus helvolus (Richardson). Tawny Lemming.

Phenacomys intermedius intermedius Merriam. Interior Phenacomys.

Clethrionomys gapperi saturatus Rhoads. British Columbia Redbacked Mouse.

Microtus pennsylvanicus drummondi (Audubon and Bachman). Drummond Meadow Mouse.

Ondatra zibethica spatulata (Osgood). Alberta Muskrat.

Zapus hudsonius hudsonius (Zimmerman). Hudson Bay Jumping Mouse.

Zapus princeps saltator Allen. Alaskan Jumping Mouse.

Erethizon epixanthum nigrescens Allen. Dusky Porcupine.

Lepus americanus pallidus Cowan. Chilcotin Varying Hare or Snowshoe·Rabbit.

Odocoileus hemionus hemionus (Rafinesque). Rocky Mountain Mule Deer.

Alces americanus ssp. Moose.

Rangifer montanus Seton-Thompson. Mountain Caribou.

Oreamnos americanus columbiae Hollister. Columbian Mountain Goat.

Ovis dalli stonei Allen. Sheep.

Acknowledgment

The author wishes to make grateful acknowledgment to Dr. Ian McTaggart Cowan, Professor of Zoology, University of British Columbia, for his reading of the manuscript and his most helpful comments and suggestions.